The New Testament

An Introduction to its Literature and History

J. GRESHAM MACHEN

The New Testament

An Introduction to its Literature and History

Edited by
W. John Cook

The Banner of Truth Trust

THE BANNER OF TRUTH TRUST
3 Murrayfield Road, Edinburgh EH12 6EL
P.O. Box 621, Carlisle, Pennsylvania 17013, U.S.A.

© The Banner of Truth Trust
First published 1976
Reprinted 1981
ISBN 0 85151 240 2

Printed in Great Britain by
R. MacLehose & Co. Ltd
Printers to the University of Glasgow

Preface

This introduction to the New Testament contains two sets of related material written by Dr. J. Gresham Machen, the first a course of studies covering the New Testament in the *Student's Text Book*, and the second an augmented parallel course in the *Teacher's Manual*. These were periodicals published by the Presbyterian Board of Publication and Sabbath School Work, Philadelphia, sixty years ago. It is a singular oversight on the part of publishers, and perhaps a reflection on the 20th-Century Church, that this material has been obtainable for so long and that it has never appeared before in book form. The original title of Machen's course was *The Literature and History of New Testament Times*.

Machen's two distinct courses are here blended together into a harmonious whole. For this, and other necessary editorial work, we are indebted to the Rev. W. John Cook, B.A., B.D., Lecturer in New Testament at South Wales Bible College, Barry. Gratitude is also due to Professor John H. Skilton of Westminster Theological Seminary, U.S.A., who called our attention to the value of Machen's work and made its publication possible by the provision of copies of the original periodicals.

That these pages remain as fresh and convincing as when they were written is a testimony to the soundness of Machen's principles, the accuracy of his scholarship, and the skill of his presentation. We believe that his work possesses a permanence rare in this type of historical and literary introduction.

THE PUBLISHERS

January 1976

Contents

Introduction   *page* 9

THE HISTORICAL BACKGROUND OF CHRISTIANITY

1. The New Testament   13
2. The Roman Background of Christianity   20
3. The Greek Background of Christianity   27
4. The Jewish Background of Christianity: 1. Palestinian
   Judaism   33
5. The Jewish Background of Christianity: 2. The Judaism of
   the Dispersion   39
6. The Messiah   44

THE EARLY HISTORY OF CHRISTIANITY

7. The Book of The Acts   51
8. The Cross and the Resurrection as the Foundation of Apostolic
   Preaching   57
9. The Beginnings of the Christian Church   63
10. The First Persecution   69
11. The First Gentile Converts   74
12. The Conversion of Paul   78
13. The Church at Antioch   84

CHRISTIANITY ESTABLISHED AMONG THE GENTILES

14. The Gospel to the Gentiles   91
15. The Council at Jerusalem   97
16. The Gospel Carried into Europe   103

THE PRINCIPLES AND PRACTICE OF THE GOSPEL

17. Encouragement for New Converts   115
18. The Conflict with the Judaizers   122
19. Problems of a Gentile Church   131
20. The Apostle and his Ministry   138
21. The Gospel of Salvation   147
22. Paul's Journey to Rome   154
23. The Supremacy of Christ   159
24. The Church of Christ   167
25. Christ and his Followers   173
26. Training New Leaders   180

THE PRESENTATION AND DEFENCE OF CHRISTIANITY

27. A Presentation of Jesus to Jewish Christians   191
28. A Graphic Sketch of the Life of Jesus   198
29. A Greek Historian's Account of Jesus   205
30. The Testimony of the Beloved Disciple   215
31. The Jesus of the Gospels   226
32. A Document of the Jerusalem Church   233
33. Jesus the Fulfilment of the Old Testament   242
34. Christian Fortitude   249
35. The Christian's Attitude towards Error and Immorality 256
36. The Life of the Children of God   264
37. The Messages of the Living Christ   270
38. A Vision of the Final Triumph   280
39. Review   285

THE APOSTOLIC CHURCH AND THE CHURCH OF TODAY

40. The Church and the World   293
41. The Christian Message   305
42. The Word and the Sacraments   311
43. Prayer   319

44. The Congregation   330
45. The Relief of the Needy   338
46. Organizing for Service   347
47. A Mission for the World   354
48. The Christian Ideal of Personal Morality   359
49. Christianity and Human Relationships   366
50. The Christian Use of the Intellect   373
51. The Christian Hope and the Present Possession   379
52. Retrospect: the First Christian Century   385

Introduction

This book is primarily historical. It should be studied like a historical course in school. In the study of history the first step is to learn the facts. No amount of topical study, no amount of reflection on the principles of the history, will result in anything better than a mental jumble, unless the memory has first retained the framework of fact.

Biblical history is not different in this respect from any other history. The Bible, after all, is a record of events; the gospel is good news about something that has happened. That something is simply the saving work of the Lord Jesus Christ—his life and death and resurrection—which was explained and applied by the apostles whom he commissioned. Apostolic history, which we shall here study, is different from secular history; for the apostles were in possession of a divine authority which is valid still for the Church of today. The sacredness of the history, however, does not prevent it from being history; and if it is history, it should be studied by the best historical method which can be attained. Modern Christians often seem to suppose that piety is somehow opposed to thinking, that hard study should be reserved for secular schools, that the reader of the Bible may afford to be neglectful of the facts. Such an attitude is dishonouring to the divine revelation. Christianity is not wild speculation or bottomless mysticism. It reaches, indeed, to the highest heavens, but its foundation is laid upon sober fact.

The purpose of the present book is to ground Christian piety more firmly in historical knowledge. Knowledge cannot be acquired without labour. That labour, however, need not be drudgery. On the contrary, it is lack of study which has made the Bible for some people a dull book. If the study here outlined be undertaken with earnestness, it will reveal the wonderful richness and variety of the Bible story, it will do away with the sense of unreality which sometimes oppresses the piecemeal reader, it will show that the extension of the gospel was a real movement in a real world, and finally it will strengthen the conviction that that historical movement was no mere product of human effort, interesting

9

merely to the scholar, but an entrance into human life of the divine power, working permanently for the salvation of men. Historical study is absolutely necessary for a stalwart Christianity. It is necessary, however, not as an end in itself, but as a means to an end. Rightly pursued, the study of ancient Christianity will lead every one of us first to the feet of the living Lord, then to a simple confession of him and an active membership in his Church.

The Historical Background
of Christianity

1 : THE NEW TESTAMENT

Study material: Jer. 31: 31–34; Heb. ch. 8; II Cor. ch. 3;
I Cor. 11: 23–26; John 20: 30, 31; II Tim. 3: 14–17;
II Peter 1: 19–21; 3: 14–18

The Jews and the Bible

The Bible was in existence before the New Testament was written. It was not yet complete, but it was reverenced, as the Bible is reverenced by devout men today. At the time of Jesus the Bible was what we now call the Old Testament. Upon the Old Testament the Jews based the whole of their life. It was to them the sum and substance of education, and the supreme judge in every controversy.

Jesus and the Bible

With this Jewish reverence for the Old Testament Jesus was in full sympathy. He blamed the scribes for interpreting the Scriptures badly, not for regarding them as divine. Jesus himself used the Old Testament just as much as the Pharisees did—only he used it better. With it he confounded the tempter; to it he appealed in controversy; its prophecies he regarded as a decisive testimony to himself. And in the hour of agony on the cross its words came naturally to his dying lips.

The Early Church and the Bible

The same attitude towards the Old Testament appears everywhere in the early Church. 'It is written' was to the New Testament writers always the decisive argument. The very first Christian preaching was full of the Old Testament. By the Scriptures the coming of the Spirit was explained, Acts 2.17–21; by them the message of the resurrection was confirmed, Acts 2.25–28; 13.33–37, and the meaning of the cross unfolded, I Cor. 15.3. From the very beginning Christianity was a religion with a Book.

The New Testament

The New Testament writers, therefore, did not make the Bible; all

13

that they did was to add to the Bible which was already there. But what right had they to add to it? Where is the necessary authority to be found?

It is to be found, ultimately, in Jesus. Jesus laid claim to an authority fully equal to that of the Old Testament writers, and his claim was supported both by his miracles and by the whole nature of his Person. Whatever Jesus said was indubitably true; whatever he commanded must implicitly be obeyed.

But Jesus wrote nothing; none of the New Testament books, not even those that deal with his own words and deeds, come to us directly from him. If the books are to be regarded as authoritative, their authority must apparently be sought elsewhere. What other authority was manifested in the primitive Church in addition to the authority of Jesus?

The answer to this question is plain. The authority of Jesus in the primitive Church was continued by the authority of his apostles. The authority of the apostles appears in their own claim, as it becomes evident particularly in the epistles of Paul. It also appears in the reverence with which they were regarded not only by their contemporaries but also by all subsequent generations. The authority of the apostles differs, however, from that of Jesus in that it was not due to any inherent virtue in the persons of those who possessed it; the apostles were but men, in need of forgiveness like the rest of mankind. Whence, then, was their authority derived? The answer is plain. It was derived from the commission that they had received from Jesus himself. As the Father had sent him into the world, so Jesus sent them into the world, John 17.18; his Spirit would guide them into all truth, John 16.13. Clement of Rome was entirely correct when, writing at about A.D. 95 to the church at Corinth, he said: 'The Apostles received the gospel for us from the Lord Jesus Christ; Jesus Christ was sent forth from God. So then Christ is from God, and the apostles are from Christ.' (I Clement, 42, translated by Lightfoot.)

It was in virtue of this authority that the apostles added to the Bible of their time those books which are comprised in the New Testament. So the Church has maintained from the very beginning; the decisive test for determining whether a book was to be regarded as authoritative was found by the early Church in the genuineness of its 'apostolicity'. Only those books were received by the Church which were written by apostles, or at least—as was the case with the writings of Mark and Luke—were given to the Church under apostolic sanction. The Church did not create the authority of the New Testament books; it only recognized the authority which those books possessed in themselves from the beginning. The apostles had not presumptuously usurped the stupendous function of adding to the Bible; they had received it by virtue of their comprehensive commission from Jesus, and they fulfilled it by the inspiration of the Holy Spirit whom Jesus had promised.

To the writings of these men we owe our Christian life today. Jesus himself, as has already been observed, wrote nothing; even the record of his words and deeds comes to us only on the authority of his apostles. Indeed there were many things which in the very nature of the case could not be said until after the resurrection. Jesus came not merely, and not even primarily, to reveal the nature of God; he came rather to accomplish a work of salvation. Until that work was accomplished the meaning of it could not be fully explained; the full explanation could be given only after the work was done. The proclamation and explanation of the completed work of Christ constituted the apostolic gospel; that gospel, as preserved for us in the New Testament, is still the foundation of the Church.

The Origin and the Meaning of the Name 'New Testament'

The English word 'testament' comes from a Latin word. The equivalent Greek word is hard to translate. As used in the Greek Bible it may mean either 'covenant' or 'testament'. Usually it should probably be translated 'covenant'.

The phrase 'new covenant' occurs about five times in the New Testament. In none of these passages does the phrase refer to the 'New Testament' in our sense. It designates a new relationship into which men have been received with God. The old covenant was made, through the mediatorship of Moses, with the Hebrew nation; the new covenant, hinted at in prophecy, Jer. 31.31, and instituted by the Lord Jesus, I Cor. 11.25, was made with all those, of every tribe and tongue and people and nation, who should through faith accept the salvation offered by Christ. Those who believe become, like Israel of old, members of the community of God's chosen people, and enter into the warmth and joy of the divine communion. The names 'old and new covenants', then, were applied first to these two special relationships into which God entered with men. Afterwards the names were applied to the books

15

in which the conditions of those relationships were set forth. Perhaps it would have been better if we had started to say 'New Covenant' where we now say 'New Testament'. At any rate, the idea alluded to in the name is the inspiring idea, realized in Christ, of an alliance with God. The New Testament is the divine treaty by the terms of which God has received us rebels and enemies into peace with himself.

The Purpose of the Bible

The Bible is the Word of God—that is the chief thing to know about it. We cannot ourselves find out God. He reveals himself, it is true, in his works. 'The invisible things of him since the creation of the world are clearly seen, being perceived through the things that are made, even his everlasting power and divinity.' (Rom. 1.20.) But we need to know a good deal more than his 'everlasting power and divinity'. We are sinners, and we need to know his goodness and the means he has taken to save us. That is the subject of the Bible. The Bible reveals to us the way of salvation. The way is hinted at in the Old Testament; and in the New Testament, in the life and death and resurrection of Jesus Christ, it is made gloriously plain. We could not have discovered it for ourselves. 'For who among men knoweth the things of a man, save the spirit of the man, which is in him? even so the things of God none knoweth, save the Spirit of God.' (I Cor. 2.11.) If we are to know God, God must tell us. He has told us in the Bible.

The Method of the Bible

He has told us, however, in his own way. We might have expected the Bible to be simply a systematic textbook in religion—a compendium of information that would serve the same purpose for religion as our ordinary textbooks serve for other branches of knowledge. Instead of that the Bible is a whole library. It is composed of many books, written by many different authors and under many different circumstances. Even those parts of it, such as the epistles of Paul, which are regarded as most doctrinal, most theoretical in character, are deeply rooted in circumstances now long past. The Epistle to the Galatians, for example, is not a treatise on Christian liberty, but a passionate appeal written in view of imminent danger. The books of the Bible have a message to everyone, but that message is given in varied form. God is speaking in the Bible, but he has chosen to speak by means of men.

In this book we shall study the special circumstances under which a number of the Biblical books were written. We shall ask who the human authors were, when they wrote and why. We shall study the New Testament as a record of events long past. The study will do us harm rather than good if it keeps us from applying the Bible to ourselves. There is no reason, however, why it should have any such effect. On the contrary, if we study aright, the Bible will become to us more and more a living Book. We shall come to see that God's way, after all, is best. In the wonderful richness and variety of the Bible, due to the varying experience of its human writers, we shall see the bountiful hand of the divine Author of the whole.

The Four Divisions of the New Testament

[1] THE GOSPELS

Christianity is based upon historical facts. Attempts, it is true, are often made to separate it from history. But they are bound to result in failure. Give up history, and you can retain some things. But you can never retain a gospel. For 'gospel' means 'good news', and 'good news' means tidings, information derived from the witness of others. In other words, it means history. The question whether religion can be independent of history is really just the old question whether we need a gospel. The gospel is news that something has happened—something that puts a different face upon life. What that something is is told us in Matthew, Mark, Luke and John. It is the life and death and resurrection of Jesus Christ.

[2] THE BOOK OF THE ACTS

The Book of The Acts is a history of the extension of Christianity from Jerusalem out into the Gentile world. It represents that extension as guided by the Spirit of God, and thus exhibits the divine warrant for the acceptance of us Gentiles, and for the development of the Christian Church. It provides the outline of apostolic history without which we could not understand the other New Testament books, especially the epistles of Paul. It illustrates to the full what has been said above about the value of the historical form in which the Bible teaching is presented. By reading this vivid narrative we obtain an impression of the power of the Holy Spirit which no systematic treatise could give.

[3] THE EPISTLES

The Epistles of the New Testament are not just literature put in an epistolary form, but real letters. It is true that the addresses of some of them are very broad, for example, those of James and of I Peter; and that some of them contain no specific address at all, for example, Hebrews and I John. But the great majority of them, at least, were written under very special circumstances and intended to be read first by very definite people.

The chief letter-writer of the New Testament was the apostle Paul. To a certain extent he used the forms of letter-writing of his time, just as everyone today begins a letter with 'Dear Sir'. From 1897 onwards a great number of Greek private letters, dating from about the time of Paul, has been discovered in Egypt, where they have been preserved by the dry climate. It is interesting to compare them with the letters of Paul. There are some striking similarities in language, for both these letter-writers and Paul used the natural language of daily life rather than the extremely artificial language of the literature of that period. To a certain extent, also, Paul used the same epistolary forms. The differences, however, are even more instructive than the resemblances. It is true, the Pauline epistles are not literary treatises, but real letters. But on the other hand they are not ordinary private letters intended to be read and thrown away, like the letters that have been discovered in Egypt. Most of them were intended to be read originally in churches. It is natural, then, that they should have been written in a loftier style than is to be found in mere business communications and the like. And if Paul uses the epistolary forms of his time he uses them in an entirely new way. Even the mere openings of the epistles are made the vehicle of Christian truth. 'Grace to you and peace from God our Father and the Lord Jesus Christ'—there is nothing like that in contemporary letter-writing. The openings of the Pauline epistles form an interesting study. They are varied with wonderful skill to suit the varied character and subject matter of the letters that follow. Paul is never merely formal.

The letters of Paul differ widely among themselves. The Epistle to the Romans is almost a systematic exposition of the plan of salvation. Philemon is concerned with a little personal matter between Paul and one of his converts. But even where Paul is most theological he is personal, and even where he is most personal, he is faithful to his theology. Theology in him is never separate from experience, and experience never separate from theology. Even petty problems he settles always in the light of eternal principles. Hence his letters, though the specific circumstances that gave rise to them are past and gone, will never be antiquated.

[4] THE APOCALYPSE

The Christian life is a life of hope. Inwardly we are free, but our freedom is not yet fully realized. We are in danger of losing our hope in the trials or in the mere humdrum of life. To keep it alive, the Apocalypse opens a glorious vision of the future. The vision is presented in symbolical language. It is not intended to help in any calculation of the times and seasons. But it shows us the Lamb upon the throne—and that is enough.

Christianity and the Bible

Christianity is a religion of a Book. That is sometimes regarded as a reproach. The reproach would be justified if the Bible were an ordinary book. But the Bible is not an ordinary book. It is a message from God. To submit too exclusively to an ordinary book might be slavish. But when God speaks, who can refuse to hear? Obedience to him is perfect freedom. Christianity is the religion of a Book. But what a Book! Not a dead thing, but a transforming power. A Book that has entered like iron into the fibre of men's souls. A Book that has been transmuted gloriously, through the ages, in never-ending variety, into life. A Book that has given us God. No enslaving code. But the very charter of human freedom.

TOPICS FOR STUDY

1. What are the meanings of the words 'covenant' and 'testament'? What do these words usually refer to in the New Testament? Compare the Authorized and the Revised versions.

2. Collect the passages where the phrase 'new testament' or 'new covenant' occurs in the New Testament. What does the phrase mean in these passages? Where is the 'old covenant' mentioned? What does this term mean?

3. Compare the new covenant with the old covenant.

4. What are some of the expressions used in the New Testament to designate the Bible? Which is the most common?

5. How did the term 'New Testament' come to be used in its present sense?

6. Cite a number of passages to show (a) how Jesus, and (b) how Paul, used the Old Testament (two topics).

2 : THE ROMAN BACKGROUND OF CHRISTIANITY

Study material: Mark 12: 13–17; Rom. 13: 1–7;
John 18: 28 to 19: 16; Acts 18: 12–17; 22: 23–29

Christianity is a gift of God. It came into the world from outside. But it came at a definite point in the world's history, and it cannot be fully understood without a study of the conditions that prevailed among its first adherents. These conditions, as well as Christianity itself, were the work of God. The manner of his working was different in the two cases. The historical conditions under which Christianity arose are works of providence; Christianity itself is a new creation. But both are works of God. Both should be studied with reverence.

Christianity originated under the Roman Empire. If the early history of Christianity is to be understood, the empire must be studied. It will be the subject of our study in this chapter.

Roman History up to the Establishment of the Empire

By the middle of the first century before Christ, the city of Rome, originally an insignificant Italian town, had become mistress of a realm that extended all around the Mediterranean Sea. Since the expulsion of the kings, which took place at a very early time, Rome had been a republic. But in 48 B.C., after a civil war, Julius Cæsar acquired the supreme power. After his assassination there were more civil wars, until, in 31 B.C., Octavius became sole ruler. In 27 B.C. the permanent form of his authority was fixed, and his name Augustus was assumed. That date is regarded as marking the beginning of the Roman Empire. The forms of the old republic were preserved; the ancient Senate, particularly, retained important functions. But the republican forms were little more than a pretence and the Senate was subservient. The real power was concentrated in the hands of Augustus; and under his successors, though very gradually, more and more even of the form of royalty was assumed.

Advantages of the Imperial Government

In Rome itself, the establishment of the empire was galling to a certain party which clung to the ancient institutions; but in the provinces it was hailed with acclamations of unfeigned joy. Augustus was welcomed as the saviour of society. And rightly.

In the first place, after many years of ruinous civil war, the empire at last brought permanent peace. The 'Roman peace', embracing the civilized world, was the prime requisite for a healthy development of commerce and general well-being.

In the second place, the empire secured a great improvement in the administration of the provincial governments. Under the republic, the governors of the provinces, unchecked by any strong central authority, had used their brief terms of office simply to amass private wealth. Against their rapacity the subject populations had been almost without redress. But now the governors were held in check by a central authority which had in view not the mere wealth of individuals but rather the good of the whole empire. The emperor's ear was, sometimes at least, open to just complaints. Roman rule began to be used to some extent for the advantage of the governed. The worst abuses of the tax system were removed. Order was established out of chaos.

Augustus himself was an able and prudent ruler. Some of his successors were very monsters of iniquity. But even the worst emperors were dangerous rather to their immediate associates or to the people of Rome itself than to the empire at large. On the whole, despite a good deal of oppression and injustice, the reign of Roman law, judged by ancient standards, was a beneficent thing.

Under the lasting peace that began with the reign of Augustus there was a healthy development of commerce. The causes of final collapse were already at work, but during the period which we shall study the commercial development was at its height.

Both for purposes of commerce, and also for civil and military administration, nothing is more important than safe and easy communication. Under the Roman Empire a remarkable system of roads rendered land travel probably easier than it has been up to modern times. Brigands on land and pirates on the sea were held in check. Travel became a common thing. A merchant of Hierapolis in Phrygia is declared to have made the voyage to Italy no less than seventy-two times.

Of course, the ease of travel must not be exaggerated. It did not compare with modern conditions. Perils of rivers, perils of robbers, perils in the wilderness, perils in the sea, were not lacking. (II Cor. 11.26.) It is difficult for us to form any adequate conception of the hardships of a missionary life like that of Paul— especially since, except for men of means, the land journeys would have to be made on foot. Nevertheless the value of the Roman system of communication remains. Even with it, the early Christian mission was difficult; without it, it would have been impossible.

Roman Administration under the Empire

The general advantages of the Roman imperial government have been considered above. It will next be advisable to consider one or two features a little more in detail. Much of what follows can be illustrated from the New Testament, for the acquaintance of New Testament writers, especially of Luke, with Roman administration is not only accurate but also minute. Readers are encouraged to seek New Testament illustrations for themselves.

[1] THE PROVINCES

The provinces of the empire are to be distinguished from the territories of subject kings or princes. The latter were quite subservient to Rome, but were given more independence of administration. A good example of such a subject king, theoretically an ally, but in reality a vassal, was Herod the Great, who ruled over all Palestine till 4 B.C.

The provinces themselves were divided into two great classes— imperial provinces and senatorial provinces.

The imperial provinces were under the immediate control of the emperor. They were governed by 'legates', who had no regular term of office, but served at the emperor's pleasure. The imperial provinces were those in which, on account of unsettled conditions, or for the defence of the empire, large bodies of troops had to be maintained. Thus, by keeping the appointment of the legates exclusively in his own hands, the emperor retained the direct control of the all-important power of the army. A good example of an imperial province is the great province of Syria, with capital at Antioch. Palestine was more or less under the supervision of the Syrian legate.

Districts different from the great imperial provinces, but, like them, under the immediate control of the emperor, were governed by 'procurators'. Judea, from A.D. 6 to A.D. 41, and from A.D. 44 on, is an example.

The senatorial provinces were governed by 'proconsuls', chosen by lot from among the members of the Senate. The proconsuls served for only one year. Even over these provinces and their governors the emperor retained the fullest supervisory authority. The senatorial provinces comprised the central and more settled portions of the empire, where large standing armies would not be needed. Examples are Achaia, with capital at Corinth, and Cyprus with capital at Paphos. Proconsuls of both of these provinces are mentioned in the New Testament by name.

[2] LOCAL GOVERNMENT

The Romans did not attempt to introduce perfect uniformity throughout the empire. The original Greek unit of political life was the city, and Greek cities were scattered over the east before the Roman conquest. With regard to local affairs, many of the cities retained a certain amount of independence. It is interesting to observe the local peculiarities of the cities described in The Acts.

In addition to the Greek cities, many of which were more or less 'free' in local affairs, many 'Roman colonies' had been established here and there throughout the empire. The original colonists were often veterans of the Roman armies. Of course the populations soon came to be mixed, but Roman traditions were cultivated in the colonies more than elsewhere. A number of the cities of The Acts were colonies, and one, Philippi, is expressly declared to be such. Acts 16.12. In that city the Roman character of the magistrates appears clearly from Luke's narrative. There were 'prætors' and 'lictors'.

[3] ROMAN CITIZENSHIP

Before New Testament times Roman citizenship had been extended to all Italy. Italy, therefore, was not a province or group of provinces, but was regarded as a part of Rome. Outside of Italy Roman citizenship was a valuable special privilege. It raised a man above the mass of the provincial population. Some of the advantages of it appear clearly in the New Testament narrative. Because Paul was a Roman citizen he was legally exempt from the most degrading forms of punishment, and had a right to appeal to the court of the emperor. Roman citizenship was sometimes acquired by money, but Paul inherited it from his father.

The Empire and Christianity

Everything that has been said about the benefits of Roman rule has an obvious bearing upon the early history of Christianity. Christianity was a world religion; the Roman Empire laid the world open before it. Barriers of race and of nationality were obliterated. Travel was easy. Peace was permanent. Everything was favourable for a world-wide mission. Christianity did not miss the opportunity.

Of course if the Roman Government had at the start been actively hostile to Christianity, the advantages of Roman rule would have been nullified. But such was not the case. In the course of time the irreconcilable conflict between Christianity and the religion of the Roman state—especially between Christianity and the worship of the emperor—became apparent, and a bitter struggle was the result. But then it was too late for Christianity to be crushed out. In the beginning, the Roman policy was protective, or at any rate indifferent, rather than hostile. There were several reasons for this favourable policy.

In the first place, polytheism is naturally tolerant. Roman religion was, indeed, closely connected with patriotism, and disloyalty to the imperial gods was regarded as disloyalty to the empire itself. But, on the other hand, the various subject peoples were not molested in their own worship. The various religions of the empire were not mutually exclusive, and a man could with perfect consistency worship the gods of Syria or of Egypt and at the same time be a fervent worshipper of the gods of Rome.

It is true, Christianity was not satisfied with such a position. The God of the Christians could not be worshipped along with others. He claimed an exclusive service. Christianity, therefore, required privileges with which other religions could consistently dispense. But here the early Church was protected by its connection with Judaism.

In the first century the Jews were scattered abroad all over the empire, and had secured unique privileges. They constituted not only a religion, but also a nation, and as a nation, in accordance with the policy of Rome in dealing with her subject populations, their peculiarities were respected. They were, indeed, despised as peculiar. Their refusal to unite with the worship of other peoples caused them to be regarded as enemies of the human race. But so stubborn were their prejudices that it would have been difficult to coerce them, and Rome avoided such difficulties when she could.

At the beginning, Christianity appeared to be little more than a Jewish sect, and as a Jewish sect it enjoyed the privileges of Judaism. Thus, when in the very earliest period Christianity was attacked by the Jews, the Roman authorities were often inclined to regard the conflict as a quarrel within Judaism of which it was not necessary for them to take cognizance. At the beginning, Rome actually appears as the protector of Christianity against the Jews.

The conflict was bound to break out sooner or later. Christianity could never be satisfied with being tolerated as an obscure and inoffensive sect. It came forward with a world-wide appeal. It could not be satisfied so long as the Roman gods continued to be worshipped at all. Ultimately there was bound to be a war to the death. But at first Rome was not aware of the seriousness of her danger. Her persecution of the Church, therefore—for even at an early time there was persecution—was desultory. When Rome finally resolved to fight the Church, it was too late. Christianity was then ready to ascend the throne of the Cæsars.

The Plan of God

These things did not come by chance. It was not by chance that Jesus was born in the golden age of the Roman Empire, when the whole of the civilized world—the world which was to determine the whole subsequent course of history—was for the first time unified, so that a movement started in an obscure corner could spread like wildfire to the centre and from the centre to all the extremities. God is the ruler of history. His times are well chosen. The Roman Empire was an instrument in his hand. And so are the nations of the modern world.

TOPICS FOR STUDY

1. The Roman officials who are mentioned in the New Testament.
2. The vassal kings or rulers who are mentioned in the New Testament.
3. What, according to the New Testament, were the charges that were made before Roman officials against Jesus and the early Christians?
4. Who made the charges, and why?

5. What was the attitude of the officials towards the charges, and towards the prisoners?

6. What Roman officials, military or civil, were favourably affected by Christianity?

7. Persecutions in the early Church.

3 : THE GREEK BACKGROUND OF CHRISTIANITY

Study material: Acts 21: 37–40; I Cor. 1: 18 to 2: 16;
ch. 8; 10: 14–33; Acts 14: 8–18; 17: 16–34; ch. 19

In the first century, the Roman Empire was Greek as much as it was Roman. This chapter, therefore, is very closely connected with the previous chapter.

The Greek Language

In the fourth century before Christ, Philip of Macedon conquered Greece. His son, Alexander the Great, through a series of astonishing campaigns, became master of an empire that extended from Greece to the borders of India. When Alexander died, in 323 B.C., his empire fell to pieces. It was divided into a number of independent kingdoms, including Syria and Egypt. The kings of Syria, whose capital was Antioch, were called the Seleucids; the kings of Egypt, whose capital was Alexandria, were the Ptolemies. Both of these kingdoms, by the middle of the first century before Christ, had been conquered by Rome.

Alexander did not succeed in founding a permanent empire, but he accomplished what was far more important. He extended Greek culture and the Greek language over the entire eastern world of his time. His conquest was one of the most important events in all history.

When Macedon under Philip emerged from its obscurity, it had adopted the dominant culture of the age—the culture of Greece. The Greek language had been divided into a number of dialects. But gradually the Attic dialect, the dialect of Athens, had become dominant. Through the commercial, political and literary supremacy of Athens it had been spread abroad. And now, finally, it was adopted by the Macedonian Empire. The military triumph of Alexander became an intellectual triumph of Athens.

The Attic dialect had to pay a price for this enormous extension of its influence. It lost much of its original character. Formerly it

27

had been the language of a small district with tenacious literary traditions. Now it became a world language, a common medium of communication between men of various tongues. Naturally it was very seriously modified. The process had been going on even before Alexander's time. The Attic dialect had been stripping off its peculiarities in the extension of its influence. But the conquest of Alexander brought the process in some sort to a conclusion. The Greek world language which was written and spoken from about 300 B.C. to about A.D. 500 was different from any of the dialects that preceded it. It was based upon Attic, but it was not Attic. It requires a separate name. The name which is usually applied to it is 'the Koine', that is, 'the common [language]'.

The kingdoms into which Alexander's empire was divided after his death were Greek kingdoms. In them Greek was at least the dominant language of the courts and of the large cities. Thus the results of Alexander's conquest were conserved.

As a result of this remarkable extension of Greek influence, the Romans, when they conquered the east, found the Greek language dominant. They did not try to uproot it. To have done so would have been contrary to the Roman policy of toleration. And what is more, the Romans themselves were highly susceptible to Greek influences. They had come into contact with Greek culture in southern Italy and in Greece itself. They had felt the superiority of Greek literature. Roman life had been profoundly influenced by Greece. No wonder, then, that when the Romans became masters of a Greek-speaking world, the Greek language continued to be the language of trade, the language of international intercourse, the ordinary language of the cities, and along with Latin, the language of government administration. The language of the Roman Empire was Greek perhaps more than it was Latin.

In the first century, then, Greek had become a world language. It had been originally the language of Greece and of the western coast of Asia Minor. Now it was spoken throughout the known world. In Asia Minor it was dominant. Though other languages continued to be used—the Lycaonian language, for example, is mentioned in The Acts—Greek was the language of educated men, and was perhaps understood by almost everyone. In Syria Greek was the dominant language of the cities, the original languages being used in the country districts. Going farther to the east from Antioch, one would have heard less and less Greek, but it was probably used by merchants, even where no considerable portion of the population was acquainted with it. The conditions in Palestine will be studied in the next chapter. In Egypt, Greek was the language of the capital, Alexandria, and of many other towns, though the native dialects continued to be used by the mass of the people. A great many ancient Greek documents have been discovered in Egypt since the last decade of the nineteenth century. Even in the western part of the empire, Greek was used along with Latin. Paul's Greek Epistle to the Romans shows that there was a large Greek-speaking population in Rome itself. The earliest Christian literature in Rome and in southern Gaul (France) was Greek. Greek was really a universal language. Other languages continued to be used alongside of it, but Greek was a common medium of intercourse.

The Roman Empire, then, was a unit not only politically but also linguistically. The Greek language kept pace with Roman law. This remarkable uniformity of language is of obvious importance for the early history of Christianity. Without it, the Christian mission would have encountered serious difficulties. With every extension of the field new languages would have had to be learned. As it was, the Roman world formed in some sort one community. A religion which arose in one part could spread rapidly to the whole.

Greek Religion and Greek Philosophy

The unifying influence of Greece upon the Roman Empire was felt not only in language, but also in religion and philosophy. Non-Greek religions continued to be practised, but even they were often Hellenized—transformed under the influence of the Greek spirit.

From the time of Homer on, the religion of Greece had been a kind of artistic polytheism. The gods were conceived of as living in a lofty region of light and gladness. They had passions like men, they engaged in strife and deceit. But even when they were evil, they were beautiful. Greek religion, in its characteristic form, was aesthetic rather than moral; it was based upon the sense of beauty rather than upon the conscience. Its characteristics appear most clearly in the beautiful images of the gods—those unequalled masterpieces which are the wonder and delight of the civilized world. Beauty of form, but no satisfaction for the deepest needs of the soul!

There are, indeed, elements in Greek religion which go deeper than the mythology of the Olympian gods. The 'mysteries' of

Eleusis, for example, even at an early period sought to bring men into vital connection with some divine mysterious power. Especially during the first centuries of the Christian era a number of other 'mysteries' were introduced from eastern religions. By engaging in certain mysterious rites, like forms of initiation, men were thought to be lifted above the limitations of human nature into a higher life. The prevalence of such mysteries is interesting, for it indicates a widespread desire, very vague and imperfect, it is true, for liberation from the present evil world. But that which is offered in answer to this craving is sometimes disgusting and always unsatisfying. Especially during the second century there was a triumphal march of various mystery religions even into the western part of the empire. The movement indicates the religious need of the time. But the mysteries all passed away. Christianity remained. For Christianity accomplished what the mysteries could merely attempt. Christianity alone could really offer men freedom from the world and communion with the eternal God.

The rise of the mystery religions itself shows the religious insufficiency of the gods of Olympus. If the gods of Homer had been sufficient, the mysteries would not have been introduced. But the gods were also subjected to direct criticism at the hands of poets and of philosophers.

The poets of the fifth century before Christ and later had begun to be keenly aware of the moral imperfections of the Homeric mythology. The misdeeds of Zeus might naturally be taken as sanctioning immorality among men. Consequently there was a tendency among the poets to interpret the ancient stories in such a way that their immoral implications would be avoided. In emphasizing the primacy of Zeus as a moral governor of gods and men, the poets sometimes moved in the direction of a monotheistic conception.

The criticism of the ancient religion, however, was more definite and pronounced in the teachings of the philosophers. Philosophy was dissatisfied with polytheism. It sought some one common principle which should explain the facts of the world. That principle was not usually conceived clearly as a personal God, yet the philosophic movement at least opened the way for monotheism. Philosophy was willing to maintain the old system as a civic institution, even where personal belief was gone. But although it did not always seek to combat the old religion, it subordinated it.

In the later period, embracing the first century after Christ, certain forms of Greek philosophy concerned themselves especially with the preaching of morals. The Stoics and the Cynics, for example, carried on an active propaganda through wandering preachers. The Stoics held up the ideal of the wise man who should be independent of the passions and desires, and base his life altogether upon inward strength. In some respects it was a high ideal. But Christianity made effective in plain men and women what to the Stoics was but an ideal to be attained at best by a few. And Christianity accomplished more. Its moral ideal is vastly richer than that of Stoicism—richer by so much as Jesus is more than Seneca, its greatest exponent (died A.D. 65).

Greek Culture and Christianity

Some things in Greek thinking afforded positive preparation for the gospel. Paul himself in his speech at Athens appealed to the religious aspirations of his pagan hearers, and to such vague approach to monotheism as was to be found in the Greek poets.

But another side should not be forgotten. From the beginning Christianity was a religion with a Book. And that Book was not Greek. On the contrary it was intensely un-Grecian. The Old Testament is intolerant of heathen ideas. It is deeply rooted in the life of the chosen people. How could a Hebrew book be used in the Greek world?

The difficulty might have been serious. But in the providence of God it had been overcome. The Old Testament was a Hebrew book, but before the Christian era it had been translated into Greek. From the beginning Christianity was provided with a Greek Bible. It is always difficult to make a new translation of the Bible. Every missionary knows that. The introduction of a new translation takes time. It was fortunate, then, that a Greek-speaking Church had a Greek Bible, the Septuagint, ready to hand (see Chapter 5).

The Greek world was desperately in need of the gospel. Despite the aspirations of the poets and the preaching of the moralists, the world was lost in sin. The terrible picture which Paul draws of the heathen world in the first chapter of Romans is confirmed again and again in every one of its details by the descriptions in pagan writers. The world was lost in sin. But God saved it—through the gospel.

When the gospel came, it was listened to. God had shaped the course of history to prepare for it. For the first time the whole world was open. Roman law and Greek culture had made of the

B

world one great community. In such an age, the banner of the cross, wherever raised, would soon be seen by all.

TOPICS FOR STUDY

1. What languages are mentioned in the New Testament? In what languages is the Old Testament written? How did the New Testament come to be written in Greek?

2. What can be learned from the New Testament—(a) about the religion and (b) about the philosophy of the Greek world (two topics)?

3. Find in the New Testament a number of examples of heathen superstition.

4. Find a number of examples of early Christian preaching to Gentiles.

5. What problems came up in the early Church with regard to the Christian's attitude toward idolatry? What is Paul's solution of those problems?

6. In what respects was the Greco-Roman world like the world of today? What are some of the differences?

4 : THE JEWISH BACKGROUND OF CHRISTIANITY

1. Palestinian Judaism

Study material: Matt. 5: 17–48; 15: 1–20; 22: 15–46;
Luke 1: 5–10; 2: 22–52; 4: 16–21; John 18: 12–14, 19–24, 28–40;
19: 20; Acts 22: 30 to 23: 11

The Jewish background of Christianity is far more important than the Roman background and the Greek background which have been studied in the last two chapters. These have to do with the environment of Christianity, but Judaism is connected with the very essence of Christianity itself. Christianity was not an entirely new religion. It was rooted in the divine revelation already given to the chosen people. Even those things which were most distinctive of Christianity had been foreshadowed in Old Testament prophecy. Salvation was of the Jews.

In order, however, to understand the circumstances under which Christianity arose, the study of the Old Testament, though most important of all, is not sufficient. It will also be necessary to examine the actual condition of the Jewish people at the time of Christ.

Government

At the time of Christ and of the earliest apostolic preaching, Judea was governed by Roman procurators. But in internal affairs a large measure of power was left to the Jews themselves. These affairs were conducted by a council called the Sanhedrin, of which the presidency was held by the high priest. The high priest served practically at the procurator's pleasure. The Sanhedrin was composed of 'chief priests', that is, members of the aristocratic families from which the actually officiating high priest could be chosen, 'scribes', that is, men learned in the Mosaic law and in the oral interpretations of it, and 'elders'. The Sanhedrin was not only an administrative assembly, but also a court.

Parties

There were two chief parties among the Jews—the Pharisees and the Sadducees.

The Sadducees were the wealthy aristocracy. From their ranks the high priests were chosen. They occupied the positions of worldly authority. As men of wealth and high position they were content with the existing order of things. They were supporters of the Roman government, and hospitable to Greek culture. They accepted the Mosaic law, but favoured the laxer interpretation of it, rejecting the traditions of the scribes.

The Pharisees, on the other hand, were strict in their interpretation of the Mosaic law, and bitterly hostile to foreign influences. To them belonged most of the 'scribes', or professional interpreters of the law. In order to ensure the keeping of the law the scribes had put about it a 'fence' of oral tradition, which in the guise of interpretation really imposed new legislation of the most oppressive kind. To keep the Sabbath or to observe the distinction between ceremonial cleanness and uncleanness according to the requirements of the scribes was an art which required the minutest attention to endless details.

In addition to the practical difference between the two parties there were also doctrinal differences, several of which are mentioned in the New Testament. The Sadducees rejected the doctrine of the resurrection, Matt. 22.23, and did not believe in the existence of angels or spirits, Acts 23.8.

Both Pharisees and Sadducees were represented in the Sanhedrin. The Sadducees occupied the positions of highest authority. The Pharisees, however, had more real power, for the Pharisees had the people on their side. The Sadducees were a worldly aristocracy, out of touch with the springs of their people's life.

Language

Some centuries before Christ, Hebrew had ceased to be the ordinary language of Palestine. As the language of the Old Testament it continued to be studied. Old Testament passages in Hebrew were read in the synagogue. Hebrew was used also to some extent as the language of learned discussion. But for all ordinary purposes its place had been taken by Aramaic, a language of the Semitic family closely related to Hebrew. At the time of Christ Aramaic was the spoken language of the Palestinian Jews. Even in the synagogues, the Old Testament passages, after having been read in Hebrew, were translated orally into the language which the people could understand.

But, since the time of Alexander the Great, another language had made its way into Palestine along with Aramaic. This was the Greek. As we have already seen, the kingdoms into which Alexander's empire was divided were Greek kingdoms. Two of them, Syria and Egypt, bore rule alternately over Palestine. With the Greek government came Greek culture and the Greek language. Then, under Antiochus Epiphanes—he died in 163 B.C.—there was a mighty reaction. Thereafter religion, at least, was kept altogether free from Greek influences.

In other spheres, however, under the Maccabean leaders and still more under the Romans, Greek culture effected an entrance. At the time of Christ there were typical Greek cities not only to the east of the Jordan in Decapolis, where magnificent ruins even today attest the ancient Greco-Roman civilization, and not only along the coast of the Mediterranean, but even within the confines of Palestine proper. With some truth Palestine in the first century may be called a bilingual country. Greek and Aramaic were both in use.

Aramaic was the language of the mass of the people. Many, no doubt, could speak no other language. But if a man desired to make his way in the world in any public capacity or in trade he would be obliged to learn the cosmopolitan language of the time. No doubt very many could speak both languages.

Jesus and his apostles belonged to those circles which were least affected by the encroachments of Greek civilization. The whole atmosphere of the Gospels is as un-Greek as could be imagined. As is proved by the presence of Aramaic words even in our Greek Gospels, Aramaic was undoubtedly the language in which the gospel was originally proclaimed. Aramaic was the language of Jesus' boyhood home, and Aramaic was the language of his intercourse with the disciples and of his public preaching.

It is perfectly possible, however, that even Jesus may have used Greek upon rare occasions, for example in conversation with Pilate, the Roman procurator. His disciples, after the resurrection, found themselves at the head of a Greek-speaking community. The early Church in Jerusalem was composed not only of 'Hebrews', but also of 'Grecians', or Hellenists, Acts 6.1. The Hellenists were Greek-speaking Jews of the dispersion who were sojourning more or less permanently in the holy city. The apostles seem to have entered upon their new functions without difficulty. Some knowledge of Greek, no doubt, all of them brought with them from their Galilean homes, and their knowledge would be increased through practice. It is not surprising then that several of the original apostles and two of the brothers of Jesus were the authors of Greek books of the New Testament.

Religious Life

The religious life of the Palestinian Jews found expression in two institutions; in the first place in the temple, and in the second place in the synagogue.

At the time of Christ, the temple of Zerubbabel had recently been rebuilt magnificently by Herod the Great. The temple services were continued in the form prescribed in the Old Testament. The worldliness of the officiating priests did not affect the zeal of the pious Israelites. Not all of the Jewish people was composed of worldly Sadducees and hypocritical Pharisees. There were also simple folk who were waiting for the consolation of Israel. They are introduced to us in the first two chapters of Luke. In them the piety of the Old Testament, with its poetry too, found glorious expression. And not all the priests were worldly, not all were Sadducees. There were not wanting among the priestly order devout men like Zacharias, the father of John the Baptist. At any rate, whatever was the private character of the priests, the elaborate service and offerings went on unchanged. The Old Testament types and symbols, with their promise of what was to come, continued until the great fulfilment appeared. And then, soon after, they disappeared in the final catastrophe. In A.D. 70, by the torch of the Roman soldiers, the temple and its services disappeared for ever. But what need of shadows when the reality itself had come?

The other great religious institution of the Jews was the synagogue. The synagogue provided worship and especially instruction. Through the synagogue, religion touched all classes of the people. Sacrifice was conducted at Jerusalem alone. Synagogues were scattered throughout the length and breadth of the land. If we could have attended a synagogue service we should have felt surprisingly at home. The essential features were very much the same as in our Protestant churches today. The utmost simplicity prevailed. There was a simple form of prayer, there was reading of a Biblical passage from the Pentateuch and one from the prophets, there was an explanatory discourse, and there was a benediction. The informality and democracy of the synagogue service is very striking. There was a 'ruler of the synagogue', but his function was merely to provide in general for the orderly conduct of the service.

No doubt the trained experts in the law, the scribes, were most often heard, but anyone who had the necessary qualifications might speak. Jesus was not a trained rabbi. He spoke as one having authority, and not as the scribes. Yet no one objected to his speaking in the synagogues. 'Teaching in their synagogues' had a large place in his public ministry.

The Jewish synagogue has had a profound influence upon the course of subsequent history. The temple has passed away. But the synagogue remains. No need for the blood of bulls and goats now that the one great Sacrifice has been offered! But the need of religious instruction is permanent. From the Jewish synagogue has sprung the congregation of the Christian Church.

Education in Palestine at the time of Christ was almost exclusively religious. For young and old the Old Testament was practically the sum and substance of learning. It may be called a narrow training. But it was not so narrow as it seems. The Old Testament is a world in itself. Other things must not be neglected. But if you had to confine yourself to one book, the Bible would not be a bad book to choose!

What the Church owes to Palestinian Judaism

In some ways Christianity was a protest against the Judaism of the first century. Judaism under the scribes had become a system of external rules.

But the other elements in Judaism must not be ignored. Even the legalism of the Jews was but the perversion of a great truth. The Jews were not wrong in exalting the law of God. The trouble was merely that they were satisfied with a very imperfect sort of obedience. By multiplying commandments they disguised the fact that their fulfilment even of the greatest commandments was imperfect. Had their consciences been alive to the weightier matters of the law, they would have known that they were sinners, and would have welcomed the Saviour.

The Judaism of the first century was in some ways perverted. An external legalism had dulled the sense of sin, and hindered communion with the living God. But at least the Jewish nation had preserved, though in earthen vessels, the precious deposit of truth. The Jews were different from all other peoples. In that nation God had spoken, and still his word was heard.

TOPICS FOR STUDY

1. Describe the government of Judea at the time of the origin of the Church, citing New Testament passages. What were the powers of the high priest, of the Sanhedrin, and of the procurators? How is the Sanhedrin designated in the New Testament?

2. Describe (a) the Pharisees and (b) the Sadducees on the basis of New Testament passages. What other Jewish parties are mentioned in the New Testament?

3. Describe a synagogue service on the basis of New Testament passages. Compare the synagogue (a) with the temple and (b) with a modern church.

4. What was the attitude of the Jewish parties toward Christianity? Mention various reasons for the opposition.

5. Describe and estimate the Jewish treatment of the law.

6. Outline the history of Palestine from the conclusion of Old Testament history to the destruction of Jerusalem.

5 : THE JEWISH BACKGROUND OF CHRISTIANITY
2. The Judaism of the Dispersion

Study material: Acts 2: 5–13; 13: 13–52; 18: 1–17; 28: 16–28

When a foreign missionary enters a new city, the first difficulty which confronts him is the difficulty of getting an audience. In the Gentile mission of the early Church this particular difficulty had been overcome. In practically every city of the Greco-Roman world, the Christian missionaries found an audience ready for them. The audience was provided by the synagogue of the Jews. Why and how it was provided will become clear in the course of the present chapter.

Causes and Extent of the Dispersion

In the first century, the Jews were scattered all over the civilized world, as they are today. The causes of this dispersion were manifold. In the first place, many Jews, at various times, were taken away by force. Other causes, however, were equally potent. Sometimes wars and famine at home made a foreign residence seem desirable. In the early part of the sixth century before Christ, for example, a company of fugitives went into Egypt, taking with them Jeremiah the prophet, who had protested against their flight, Jer. 42.7–22; ch. 43. The Seleucid kings of Syria encouraged Jewish colonies in the cities of Asia Minor. Often, no doubt, emigration was induced simply by the ordinary advantages of commerce. The process was hastened by the ease of travel in the Greco-Roman world.

At any rate, whatever the causes of the dispersion, it had in the first century become very extensive. Of all foreign countries Syria, according to the Jewish historian Josephus, had the largest Jewish population. The Jews were particularly numerous in Antioch, the capital. In Egypt, the Jewish population goes back at least to the sixth century before Christ. That fact is attested by the passage which has already been cited from Jeremiah. It is also attested by some very interesting original documents which were discovered at Elephantine, in southern Egypt, some six hundred miles from the mouth of the Nile, in 1904–08. These documents show that there was a Jewish community at Elephantine at least as early as 525 B.C. In Alexandria, capital of Egypt, and second city of the Roman Empire, the Jews in the first century were predominant in two of the five city districts. Jews had been in the city from the time of its founding by Alexander the Great. In Rome, the Jewish colony was of later origin, but was certainly important. The attempts which were made by Tiberius and by Claudius, Acts 18.2, to expel the Jews from Rome were found to be quite impracticable.

Life in the Jewish Communities

The legal status of the Jewish communities was widely different in different cities. In Alexandria, the Jews were organized politically in a district of their own. Elsewhere their status was more like that of ordinary religious bodies. But everywhere they seem to have possessed a certain independence of administration. They were also granted certain special privileges, especially the privilege of exemption from military service. Military service under the empire was abhorrent to the Jews because it involved, for example, violation of the Sabbath. Often the Jews possessed the citizenship of the cities in which they lived, and sometimes the citizenship of Rome. Paul, for example, was both a Roman citizen and a citizen of Tarsus.

Ordinarily the Jews of the dispersion used the Greek language, which prevailed throughout the cities of the empire. Aramaic was also in use among those who had only recently left Palestine, but usually, no doubt, the second or third generation would depend altogether upon the language of the new home. With the Greek language came a certain amount of Greek culture. New habits of thought were often acquired, which made the Jews of the dispersion different from the Jews of Palestine. Philo, for example, the great first-century Jewish writer of Alexandria, possessed a wide acquaintance with Greek philosophy, and based his own philosophical system upon it.

Yet the Jews of the dispersion were usually loyal to the religion of their fathers. They continued to observe the law of Moses, even in the face of bitter opposition. So steadfast was their devotion to the law that the Gentile authorities gave up trying to coerce them. The Jews of the dispersion submitted themselves sometimes to the ruling of the Sanhedrin. They sent regular contributions to the temple, and often attended the great feasts at Jerusalem.

This union of the Greek language with Hebrew religion gave rise to the 'Septuagint' translation of the Old Testament. The Jews of Alexandria in Egypt were loyal to the Hebrew scriptures, yet they came to be unable to read them. The need of a translation became imperative. The translation was made by various men at various times. The Pentateuch was translated first, in the third century before Christ. Before the time of Christ the translation of the whole of the Old Testament had been completed. This translation became the Bible of Greek-speaking Jews not only in Alexandria, but throughout the world. Moreover it became the Bible of the Greek-speaking Christian Church, including the writers of the New Testament.

The religious life of the Jews of the dispersion found expression in the synagogues. Graphic descriptions of synagogue services are given in the book of The Acts. The language of the synagogues was Greek, and the Old Testament was read in the Septuagint translation. But the procedure seems to have been very much the same as in the synagogues of Palestine. There was, for example, the same remarkable liberality about listening to visiting teachers. Paul made repeated use of this opportunity. The synagogue provided him with an audience wherever he went.

The Proselytes

The audiences in the synagogues consisted not only of Jews but also of Gentiles. That fact is of enormous importance. In a Jewish synagogue of the present day will be found Jews and only Jews. The reason is that Judaism, for many centuries, has ceased to seek converts. But in the first century the case was entirely different. In the first century, Judaism was a missionary religion, and a missionary religion of the most active kind.

The Gentiles who attended the synagogues fall into two classes. In the first place there were those who had united themselves fully and definitely with the people of Israel. These were the 'proselytes' in the strict sense. No doubt many such converts had been made, but in the first century they were becoming less numerous. In all probability most of those Gentiles who attended the synagogues belonged to the second class, which consisted of those who had not become full Jews, but were simply more or less interested in Judaism and had accepted some of its teachings.

THE NEW TESTAMENT

Gentile converts of this second class are called in the book of The Acts 'devout' men, or men who 'feared God' ('God-worshippers' or 'God-fearers'). Various elements in the Jewish faith would be attractive to earnest Gentiles of the first century—for example the conception of the one God and the lofty morality of Judaism. Of the ceremonial law, certain requirements, such as the Sabbath and the abstention from swine's flesh, could also readily be accepted. The more burdensome requirements were often kept in abeyance.

So when the Christian missionaries spoke in the synagogues of the Greco-Roman world, they spoke not only to Jews but also to Gentiles. Judaism was, therefore, helpful to the Gentile mission. It provided a Gentile audience, and not only a Gentile audience, but a picked audience. For those Gentiles who were assembled in the synagogues were just the Gentiles who would be most receptive to the Christian gospel. They already had the presuppositions of the gospel. They had the one God and the expectation of a future life and the desire for holiness and the Old Testament Scriptures. Contrast Paul's difficulties before the superstitious mob at Lystra with the large measure of assent that he could count on in dealing with the 'God-worshippers', and you gain some conception of the debt which Christianity owes to the synagogues of the dispersion.

The Service of the Dispersion to Christianity

The dispersion of the Jews helped Christianity in four ways. In the first place, many of the early Christian missionaries were themselves men of the dispersion, and as such they possessed just that training—just that union of Jewish religion with Greek language and customs—which was needful for their Gentile work. The unnamed men of Cyprus and Cyrene who founded the first Gentile church, Acts 11.20, were Jews of the dispersion. So was the apostle Paul. In the second place, the dispersion provided legal protection. It is true, the Jews themselves were usually hostile. But their hostility was more than offset by the advantage of their status under Roman law. Christianity was at first regarded as a Jewish sect. As such it shared the privileges of Judaism. In the third place, the dispersion, through its synagogues, provided an audience for the Christian missionaries. In the fourth place, in the Septuagint it provided a Greek Bible.

The dispersion of the Jews, with Roman law and the Greek language, was part of a threefold preparation for the gospel. God's plans were sure. At last his time had come.

TOPICS FOR STUDY

1. Trace the extent of the dispersion on the basis of New Testament passages.

2. Comment on Acts 18.12–17 in the light of what you know about the dispersion.

3. Which of the early Christian missionaries were Jews of the dispersion?

4. Describe a synagogue service of the dispersion on the basis of New Testament passages. Compare it with a Palestinian service.

5. Collect New Testament evidence for the connection of the Jews of the dispersion with the mother country.

6. Collect the passages where Gentiles are mentioned who attended the synagogues. What was their attitude toward Christianity?

6: THE MESSIAH

Study material: Gen. 12: 1–3; 17: 1–8; 49: 8–12; II Sam. 7: 1–17;
Psalms 2, 16, 110; Isa. 9: 1–7; ch. 11; 52: 13 to 53: 12; ch. 55; ch. 61;
Dan. ch. 7; Joel 2: 28–32; Zech. 8: 1–8; Luke 4: 16–21; Acts 2: 14–36

As has been shown in the last two chapters, the pre-suppositions
of the gospel were established in the Judaism of the first century.
The Jews were familiar with the living God, with the coming
judgment, with a high moral ideal, and with the authoritative
Scriptures. These ideas had been imparted also to the many
Gentiles who attended the synagogue services. In the synagogues
of the Jews the Christian missionaries could take a good deal for
granted. They did not have to begin at the very beginning. The
gospel had been prepared for by the people of Israel.

Israel had established the presuppositions of the gospel. But
she had done more. She had proclaimed the very gospel itself. She
had proclaimed it, it is true, not plainly and definitely, but only as
a glorious hope. She had proclaimed it in the promise.

The promise, though it proceeded from Israel, was not produced by Israel. It was the gift of God. It had made of Israel a
nation apart from all others, a covenant people. It had been given
to Abraham. It had been unfolded through the subsequent history.
In times of sin and trouble it had been obscured, but never obliterated. The outstanding feature of Old Testament history is the precious promise of God. That promise is the subject of this chapter.

The Promise

The promise had been given at the very beginning, when the need
of it arose. The need of it was caused by sin. When sin came, then
came also God's promise of its overcoming. When, after the first
transgression, Adam shrank in shame and fear from the face of
God, Gen. 3.8, the hope of man was gone. In the place of communion, there was hopeless guilt. There was no hope in man. But
there was hope in God. God's mercy is all-powerful. God is more
powerful than sin.

God did not condone sin. 'All mankind, by their fall, lost communion with God, (and) are under his wrath and curse.' (Westminster Shorter Catechism, 19.) But with the curse, at the very beginning, came a promise of mercy. Sin was not to conquer. The woman's seed was to bruise the serpent's head, Gen. 3.15. That was the promise. That was the beginning of the gospel. The rest of the Bible is the unfolding of that hope. The promise was vague at first; but the fulfilment was sure. The conquest of sin was slow; but at last the Saviour came.

The promise was repeated to Abraham, and so much more definitely as to mark a new beginning. The words at the fall were preliminary. The promise may rather be dated from Abraham. It is dated so by Paul.

The promise to Abraham included material blessings. But material blessings in the Old Testament are associated closely with the blessing of communion with God. The land of Canaan was to Abraham's descendants a symbol of the divine favour. The deeper elements of the promise, however, are not implicit merely, but also explicit. Abraham was promised the land of Canaan. But he was promised more than that. 'I will establish my covenant between me and thee and thy seed after thee throughout their generations for an everlasting covenant, to be a God unto thee and to thy seed after thee.' Gen. 17.7. 'In thee shall all the families of the earth be blessed.' Gen. 12.3. More than the land of Canaan was promised. God was promised. God was the heritage of Abraham's seed. And that relationship between God and the seed of Abraham was to be a blessing to the world.

There is the promise which runs all through the subsequent history—God the possession of Israel, and through Israel of the world. The fulfilment of the promise was progressive. It began in Israel. It will continue to the end of the world. The promise is fulfilled in a process. But the culmination of the process is Christ.

The Unfolding of the Promise

From the time of Abraham on, the principle of divine choice appears in the fulfilment of the promise. Abraham had a number of children; but Isaac was chosen. Isaac had two sons; but Jacob was chosen. Jacob had twelve sons; but Judah was chosen, Gen. 49.10. Finally, out of all the families of Judah, the family of David was chosen. 'Thy throne', said the prophet Nathan to David, 'shall be established for ever'. II Sam. 7.16.

The promise to David is unfolded in the Psalms and prophecies of the Old Testament. It was fulfilled first of all in the succession of Davidic kings, and in the prosperity which they brought to Israel. That, however, was but a small part of the fulfilment. The greater King was still to come. In the prophecies about the house of David, expressions are used which transcend the limits of humanity. The prophets are speaking sometimes about Israel, sometimes about the reigning kings of David's line. But it is not the actual Israel which they have in view, or an actual sovereign. The actual Israel was rebellious, the actual kings were sinful. The prophets see a loftier vision. It is an ideal Israel and an ideal king of whom they speak. And the ideal Israel is Christ. Christ is not only the fulfilment of the prophecies, but he is the culmination of a progressive hope.

The prophetic ideal is first of all a king. 'I have set my king upon my holy hill of Zion.' Psa. 2.6. As king he is the 'anointed one'. The actual kings of Israel were anointed. Saul is repeatedly called 'the Lord's anointed'. The Hebrew word for 'anointed' is 'Messiah'; the Greek word for Messiah is 'Christ'. 'Christ' means, then, first of all, the ideal king of Israel.

The ideal king stands in a peculiar relation to Jehovah. 'Jehovah said unto me, Thou art my son; this day have I begotten thee.' Psa. 2.7. He is to be under Jehovah's care. 'Thou wilt not leave my soul to Sheol; neither wilt thou suffer thy holy one to see corruption.' Psa. 16.10. But he is not only under Jehovah's care. He is himself more than man. 'His name shall be called Wonderful, Counsellor, Mighty God, Everlasting Father, Prince of Peace.' Isa. 9.6. These are mysterious words—but they are plain in the fulfilment.

The king is to be a mighty ruler—a mighty ruler because he is God's son, Psa. 2.8, 9. But the dominion is to be a righteous dominion, Isa. 11.3, 4. Not merely power, but also peace is the mark of the promised kingdom, vs. 6–9. The blessing, moreover, is not for Israel alone, but for the world, v. 10. And what will the nations find? The greatest of all blessings! They will find the knowledge of God.

But the ideal is not only a king. It is also a suffering servant. That element appears in the latter part of Isaiah. 'The servant of Jehovah' in that prophecy is thought by many to be a collective name for the Israelitish nation. That is by no means certain. But even then it is an ideal Israel which is meant, and that ideal finds its full realization in Christ. The suffering of the servant was not for his own sins. It was a suffering for the sins of others. 'Surely he hath borne our griefs, and carried our sorrows.' Isa. 53.4. 'The Lord hath laid on him the iniquity of us all.' Isa. 53.6. This element of the promise was not fully understood. It was too wonderful, too divine. But it was gloriously fulfilled. It was fulfilled on the cross. And then a child could understand.

The Fulfilment of the Promise

We have outlined the promise. The promise was not a product of human meditation. It was a revelation of God. To Israel it meant life and hope. It was a present possession, as well as a promise. What good is it to us?

In the first place, it is a proof of the gospel. The ancient promise was marvellously fulfilled. It was fulfilled in Christ, it was fulfilled in the Spirit, and it was fulfilled in the gospel. The fulfilment extended even to details. Such fulfilments are pointed out by the New Testament writers. They were used as arguments in the synagogues of the Jews. They are not to be despised. Greater, however, than fulfilment of details is the fulfilment of the whole. The promise is a wonderful thing. That ideal—a nation set apart to be a blessing for the world, a righteous king, a suffering servant, a divine Saviour—there is nothing like that in history. But it was no idle dream. In Jesus Christ it became a glorious reality. Through the promise, Christianity is saved from isolation. Christ is seen to be the culmination of a divine purpose. The ages were laid at his feet. We, too, then, must bow.

In the second place, the history of the promise is an inspiration to faith. The promise was made to Abraham. How was it received? It was received by faith. 'Abraham believed God, and it was reckoned unto him for righteousness.' Gal. 3.6; Gen. 15.6. Not by doing something, but simply by receiving—so he obtained the promise. And so we receive the fulfilment. The principle is ever the same. God the Author of blessing—God and only God.

The promise is still in force. The fulfilment is not yet over. Still we live by hope. True, we have the Saviour. But now we see him not. Glory is still to come. We wait for the consummation. But we wait in faith. God's word has never failed. Patriarch and psalmist and prophet—these all lived by promise. And the promise was fulfilled. In God's good time the Messiah came. We, too, live by promise. We wait for the day of his appearing. We wait in trial and perplexity and labour and sorrow. But God has begun. Shall he not finish?

TOPICS FOR STUDY

1. Collect the promises that were made to Abraham, and tell the substance of them.

2. What does the New Testament say about these passages?

3. Where are the other Old Testament passages of the study material referred to (a) in The Acts and (b) in the rest of the New Testament (five or six topics)?

The Early History of Christianity

7 : THE BOOK OF THE ACTS

Study material: Luke 1 : 1–4; Acts ch. 1; 16: 1–21; 20: 1 to 21: 17; 27: 1 to 28: 16; Col. 4: 10–14; Philem. 24; II Tim. 4: 11

A considerable part of this book is concerned with the history of the early Church as it is outlined in The Acts. Before we study the contents of The Acts in detail, it will be well to make some general inquiries about those contents as a whole. These inquiries will occupy this chapter.

Authorship

The author of The Acts is not named in the book, but according to an early tradition his name was Luke. Luke was also the author of the Third Gospel. The two books are dedicated to the same man, and in Acts 1.1 there is a definite reference to the author's earlier work. There is also between Luke and The Acts a marked similarity of style and method.

Who was this Luke, who wrote the two books? Very little is known about his life. He was a Gentile, not a Jew, for in Col. 4.10, 11, 14, Paul distinguishes Luke from the Jews who were with him. Luke was a physician, and a friend of Paul ('the beloved physician', v. 14), and his co-worker, Philem. 24. He was with Paul during Paul's first Roman imprisonment, Col. 4.14; Philem. 24, and also during the last imprisonment when all others had gone, II Tim. 4.11.

This much can be learned from the three references in the Pauline epistles. The only other certain biographical information about Luke is to be derived from the book of The Acts itself and from the prologue of the Third Gospel. From the prologue of the Gospel it appears that Luke was not with Jesus during his earthly ministry, but received the reports of others. From the occasional use of the first person plural in The Acts, it appears that Luke accompanied Paul on certain of his missionary journeys. What these journeys were is easy to determine. It is necessary only to single out the so-called 'we-sections', of the book, the sections where the author says 'we' instead of 'they'. By this method, it can be determined that Luke joined Paul at Troas on the second missionary journey and travelled with him as far as Philippi. There he escaped the imprisonment to which Paul and Silas were subjected. When Paul travelled from Philippi to Thessalonica and Greece, Luke was not with him. Apparently he remained at Philippi, for he was there the next time he appears, some years later, at the close of the third missionary journey. From Philippi he travelled then with Paul to Jerusalem. Finally, after Paul's two years' imprisonment at Jerusalem and Cæsarea, Luke accompanied him on his journey to Rome. On this journey, the famous shipwreck occurred. Acts 16.10–18; 20.5 to 21.17; 27.1 to 28.16.

These biographical details, scanty though they are, are sufficient to show that Luke had abundant opportunity for collecting the information necessary for his book. His close association with Paul of course acquainted him thoroughly with the Gentile mission. His presence in Palestine, as well as his association with Palestinian Christians—for example with Silas on the second missionary journey—gave him abundant materials for the history of the Jerusalem Church. Probably he remained in Palestine during Paul's two-year imprisonment under Felix and Festus (probably A.D. 58–60), for at the beginning of that period he arrived in Palestine with Paul, and at the close of it he was still ready at hand to sail with Paul to Rome. In Palestine he must have come into close contact with the chief actors in the early history of the Church. Luke had, therefore, singular opportunities for collecting the materials for his book.

Date

There is a good deal to be said for putting the date of The Acts at about A.D. 63. That would explain best of all the apparently abrupt ending of the book. The outcome of Paul's trial could not be narrated if it had not yet occurred. Other explanations, however, have been suggested. The matter is not quite certain. The book may have been written at some later date within the lifetime of a contemporary of Paul—say about A.D. 80.

Literary Characteristics

The author of The Acts was well acquainted with the Old Testament. He was able to catch the spirit of the primitive Palestinian church. His books exhibit the influence of the Semitic languages. But he was also capable of a Greek style which would have passed muster in the schools of rhetoric. Luke 1.1-4, for example, is a typical Greek sentence. Evidently Luke could move with ease in the larger Greek world of his time. His references to political and social conditions are extraordinarily exact. His narrative is never lacking in local colour. He knows the proper titles of the local officials, and the peculiar quality of the local superstitions. His account of the shipwreck is a mine of information about the sea-faring of antiquity. Evidently he was a keen observer, and a true traveller of a cosmopolitan age. His narrative is characterized by a certain delightful urbanity—an urbanity, however, which is deepened and ennobled by profound convictions.

Plan

What is the scope and plan of the book of The Acts? What is the real subject of the book? The title 'Acts of the Apostles' does not go back to the original author. It is not part of the book itself. It does not belong to the Bible. It was added later for purposes of convenience. This title is not inconvenient. But if interpreted strictly it may become misleading. Biography of the apostles is certainly not the subject of the work. Most of the apostles are barely mentioned. Two only—Peter and Paul—appear with any prominence, and even with regard to them there is no attempt at complete biography.

It is rather tantalizing that Luke himself was apparently on the point of formulating the subject of his book, but then went on to something else. At the beginning of The Acts, Luke describes his 'former treatise' apparently in order to contrast with it the second work. But the second member of the contrast is omitted. Nevertheless the subject of the book can be determined from the book itself. The eighth verse of the first chapter is the key, 'Ye shall receive power, when the Holy Spirit is come upon you: and ye shall be my witnesses both in Jerusalem, and in all Judea and Samaria, and unto the uttermost part of the earth'. The spread of the gospel by the power of the Holy Spirit, acting through the apostles, from Jerusalem into the Gentile world—that is the subject of the book.

The book might be divided in various ways. A twofold division, for example, is possible. The former part centres in Jerusalem and in the work of Peter; the latter part, in the Gentile mission and

Paul. But it would be rather hard to draw the line between the two. Perhaps, therefore, a threefold division is better—(a) the Church in Jerusalem, ch. 1.1 to 8.3; (b) the transition, ch. 8.4 to 12.25; (c) the Gentile mission, ch. 13.1 to 28.31. A perfect division is impossible, for the parts overlap. The book forms one great connected narrative. Sometimes two threads of narrative—for example Antioch and Jerusalem—are kept going alternately.

The author of The Acts is concerned with the extensive rather than with the intensive progress of the Church—with the winning of new converts rather than with questions of principle or morals or policy. This observation must not, indeed, be pressed too far. For example, Luke is very well aware of the difficulties of principle which stood in the way of the Gentile mission. He gives a detailed account of the gradual settlement of these difficulties. Acts 10.1 to 11.26; 15.1–35; 16.3; 21.17–26. He is no mere chronicler of external happenings, but a genuine historian with a comprehension of underlying principles. It remains true, however, that what is in the forefront of interest in The Acts is the extension of the Church, not its internal affairs. The Acts must be supplemented, therefore, by such sources as the Pauline epistles. For the inner life of a typical congregation, one can turn, for example, to the First Epistle to the Corinthians. Read that epistle carefully and you receive a new appreciation of the labours of the early missionaries. With the winning of converts the labour was not done. Christianity had to conquer not only all men, but also the whole of man. Heathenism and sin died hard even within the Church. The conflict was within as well as without. The Acts, however, is concerned with the external conflict.

The book of The Acts, then, gives for the most part only one side of the life of the early Church. That limitation is an advantage rather than a disadvantage. It is conducive to unity. There are other sources for the study of the details of church life. It is well that one book at least confines itself chiefly to a broad, sweeping view of the extension of the kingdom.

Fortunately, however, the author did not confine himself to a mere summary, a mere catalogue of new churches. He diversifies his book, here and there, with detailed narratives. The journeys of the 'we-sections', for example, where Luke himself was present, are narrated with circumstantial minuteness. Especially vivid is the account of the shipwreck on the journey to Rome. But this wealth of detail is not confined to the 'we-sections'. The scene at

Ephesus, for example, Acts 19.23–41, is a marvel of lifelike description.

These vivid incidents have sometimes been felt to mar the formal symmetry of the book. What place for the details of a shipwreck of the exact itinerary of the missionaries in a brief history of the Church? In reality, however, the incidents form not the least valuable part of the book. What was the actual daily life of the missionaries? What did Paul look like in a time of danger? Unless these questions are answered, our view of early Christian history is comparatively dim and distant. We need pictures as well as summaries. Luke has provided both.

Importance of The Acts

The importance of The Acts for the modern Christian may perhaps be summed up under three headings:

In the first place, The Acts provides the historical framework without which much of the New Testament could not be understood. Without The Acts the epistles of Paul, for example, would be hanging in the air. The work of Luke enables us to assign them their place in a connected account of Paul's life.

In the second place, The Acts exhibits the divine warrant for the Gentile mission, and hence for our presence in the Church. It is true, we are not dependent upon The Acts alone. The Pauline epistles show how the fundamental principles of the gospel involve freedom from the Jewish law. But it is a vast help to have the same thing taught in two entirely different ways. Paul teaches it chiefly by argument, by deduction from the principles of the faith; the book of The Acts teaches it by a concrete narrative of the divine guidance.

In the third place, the book of The Acts exhibits the divine beginnings, not only of the Gentile mission, but of the Church itself. The account of Jesus' earthly ministry, if alone, would be insufficient. It would tell us how men could be disciples of Jesus when he was on earth. But the conditions of our discipleship are very different. The life of the Church as we know it began with the resurrection. The Acts tells us how it began. It was from the first a divinely ordered life. In such a life we may safely join.

The real actor in the book of The Acts is the Holy Spirit. Read the book all together, or read it in great stretches, and you obtain an irresistible impression of the Spirit's power. Jews and Gentiles, rulers and kings, the sea and its tempests—all are powerless before the march of the gospel. Joyous, abundant, irresistible power—that is the keynote of the book. The triumphant progress of the Church of God!

TOPICS FOR STUDY

1. How do you know that The Acts was written by some companion of Paul?
2. How do you know that it was written by Luke?
3. Make a full outline of the journeys which Luke made with Paul.
4. Make a list of the Palestinian Christians with whom Luke came into contact.
5. Outline the history of Peter as narrated in The Acts.
6. Make an outline of the first twelve chapters of The Acts.

8: THE CROSS AND THE RESURRECTION AS THE FOUNDATION OF APOSTOLIC PREACHING

Study material: Luke 23: 50 to 24: 53; Acts 1: 1–14; 2: 14–42;
I Cor. 15: 1–8; II Cor. 5: 11–21; Rom. 3: 21–31; 6: 1–23

The Resurrection

In the early part of the first century, Jesus of Nazareth began in Palestine a remarkable career of preaching and of healing. At first he attained a considerable degree of popularity, but soon his popularity began to wane. There were 'hard' sayings in his teaching. By his attitude toward tradition he came into irreconcilable conflict with the religious leaders. Finally he was convicted on a trumped-up charge, and executed.

During his life he had gathered about him a band of disciples, but they had given him but little assistance in his work. Evidently they were men of a lower stamp. They had failed to understand the lofty teaching of their Master. What little power they had was derived from their intercourse with Jesus. When he was taken from them, their power was all gone. His shameful death plunged them into utter dejection.

Jesus had started a promising movement. But it seemed to have died with him. It had been too exclusively dependent upon the Founder. It was incapable of surviving him. Never was a movement more hopelessly dead. Nothing was left but disappointment. 'We hoped that it was he who should redeem Israel.' Luke 24.21. We hoped—but now our hope is gone.

Then, however, the surprising thing happened. It is the most surprising thing in history. Those poor, disappointed men, the same who had quarrelled childishly about the great places in the coming kingdom, who had fled like cowards in the hour of their Master's need, those same men, within a few days, in Jerusalem, the very scene of their failure, instituted a missionary campaign the like of which the world has never seen. During the lifetime of Jesus those men had been weak and cowardly. They had not succeeded in winning any great number of people to their Master's cause. When he was arrested they had left him and fled. Then, however, shortly after his shameful death, they stood suddenly with indomitable boldness before the rulers of the Jews. 'We must obey God rather than men.' Acts 5.29. What had brought about the change? What was it which within a few days had changed a humble band of mourners into the spiritual conquerors of the world?

History is here facing a puzzling question. But the answer has been given. It has been given by the New Testament. The mourning of the apostles was changed into triumphant joy by one thing and one thing only—by the resurrection of Jesus from the dead. On the third day after Jesus had been crucified, some women had found his tomb empty. He himself had appeared to Peter and to many others, at different times. They had touched him; with him they had eaten and drunk. Finally he had ascended, in visible form, into heaven. But he had not left his disciples alone. Through his Spirit he continued to work in them—and far more powerfully than before. By his resurrection and ascension he had been freed from limitations of time and space. What he himself in his earthly ministry had not accomplished was accomplished by his disciples. Not, however, in their own strength. They themselves were infinitely weaker than their Master. Even when he had been with them they had accomplished little. After his death they had been utterly helpless. Their new activity was due solely to the power of the risen Lord.

The Christian Church, then, is founded upon the resurrection of Christ from the dead. If the resurrection be denied, then the origin of the Church becomes an insoluble problem. The Church itself is a witness to the resurrection. Not merely isolated passages, but the whole of the New Testament, bears testimony.

Paul himself was a direct witness of the resurrection. He saw the risen Lord, I Cor. 9.1; 15.8. In I Cor. 15.1–8, however, he does not content himself with his own witness, but reproduces the testimony of others in an extended list. That testimony had come to Paul by ordinary word of mouth. 'I delivered unto you first of all,' says Paul, 'that which also I received.' In what follows there is a list of the appearances of the risen Christ. 'He appeared to Cephas; then to the twelve; then he appeared to above five hundred brethren at once, of whom the greater part remain until now, but some are fallen asleep; then he appeared to James; then to all the apostles; and last of all, as to the child untimely born, he appeared to me also.' Evidently these appearances are not conceived of merely as 'visions', but as events in the external world. The mention of the burial, v. 4, is a plain hint that what Peter and the rest saw was the body of Jesus raised from the tomb.

That view of the matter is amply confirmed in the Gospels and in the book of The Acts. In the Gospels, we are told that the tomb was found empty on the morning of the third day after the crucifixion. It was found empty by some women and by Peter and John. Since the tomb was empty, the body which appeared to the disciples had some connection with the body which had been taken down from the cross. Furthermore, the Gospels and The Acts make the bodily character of the appearances abundantly plain. Jesus did not merely appear to the disciples at a distance. He walked with them on the road to Emmaus. He broke bread with them. He came into the very midst of them when they were assembled in a room. Thomas could even touch his hands and his side. These are merely examples. Clearly the testimony of the disciples is testimony not to mere spiritual experiences, but to the bodily presence of the Lord. It may be admitted that the body was a glorified body. After his resurrection Jesus was freed from the limitations of his earthly life. Nevertheless, he was not merely a 'spirit'. Luke 24.39. There was some real, though mysterious, connection between the glorified body and the body that had been laid in the tomb. The New Testament attests not only the immortality of Jesus, but his resurrection.

If Jesus was raised from the dead, then his lofty claims were established. If the resurrection is a fact, then Jesus of Nazareth was no mere man—but God and man, God come in the flesh.

The Church is founded not upon the memory of a dead teacher, but upon the presence of a living Lord. The message, 'He is risen' —that is the very heart of the gospel.

The Death

Only one other fact is worthy to stand beside the resurrection. That fact is of a different kind. It seems at first sight not a fact of glory, but a fact of shame. It is the fact of Jesus' death.

The cross was to the Jews a stumbling block, to the Greeks foolishness. No wonder! The Christians were worshipping a miserable convict! A poor weak man, who could not even save himself from the executioner! Certainly the Jews were expecting no Messiah like that. They were expecting a victorious king, or a heavenly judge. No wonder they found the cross a stumbling block!

In the face of Jewish opposition to the crucified Messiah, the attitude of the Church was not merely apologetic. It *was* apologetic, but it was something more. It is true, the Christians set the resurrection over against the cross. 'Jesus is Messiah,' they said, 'although he was crucified; for he has been vindicated by the resurrection. After humiliation came exaltation. You must believe, despite the cross, on account of the resurrection.' That was an effective apology. He who has been raised from the dead must have been approved by God, no matter what could be said against him. The resurrection was an adequate apology for the cross. But the Christians were not satisfied with an apology. The cross was not treated merely as a difficulty to be explained away; it was put into the very centre of the gospel.

Evidently the death of the Messiah must serve some divine purpose. Pontius Pilate and the rulers of the Jews were not frustrating God's purpose, but were, unknowingly, instruments in his hand. Jesus was delivered up 'by the determinate counsel and foreknowledge of God'. The murderers could do only whatsoever God's hand and God's counsel foreordained to come to pass, Acts 2.23; 4.28. The whole divine plan had been foreshadowed in prophecy—not only the resurrection, but also the death of the Lord. 'The things which God foreshowed by the mouth of all the prophets, that his Christ should suffer, he thus fulfilled.' Acts 3.18.

The Lord's death, then, served some divine purpose. What that purpose was is explained most fully by Paul and in the Epistle to the Hebrews. But the essence of the explanation was known to the Church from the beginning. Paul did not originate it. It belonged to what Paul had received. 'For I delivered unto you first of all,' he says, 'that which also I received: that Christ died for our sins according to the scriptures.' I Cor. 15.3.

'Christ died for our sins'—there is the purpose of the cross. We are sinners. As sinners we are transgressors of the law of God. As transgressors we are under God's wrath and curse. 'The soul that sinneth, it shall die.' Ezek. 18.4. What shall we do? Shall we take comfort in the thought of God? God is righteous, and the thought of him to the penitent sinner is a source of terror, not of joy. If we could only wipe out the past! If we could only forget out past sins and know that God has forgotten! But there is no hope. Conscience will not let us rest. Sometimes we may drown its threatenings. But if we do, our last state is worse than the first, for then we have darkened the very light that is in us. And at any time the old fear may return. It is useless to gloss over our sin.

In ourselves there is no hope. But Christ has saved us. He has saved us by his death. His death was no mere martyrdom to a holy cause. It was no mere inspiring example of self-sacrifice. It was a death on our behalf. In his hour of agony Christ took upon himself the punishment of our sins. It is as though we ourselves had died. And if we have died, the law has no more claim upon us.

Its penalty has been exacted; its terror is gone. The death of Christ is an act of God's grace by which we are given a fresh start, assured of the favour of God. God, though holy, has received us sinners into living fellowship. He has received us, not because he is complacent toward sin, but because through the gift of his Son, he himself has paid its dreadful penalty.

The death of Christ, in the modern Church, is often subordinated. Exclusive emphasis is laid upon the holy example and teaching of the Galilean prophet. The modern theologians would be right if there were no such thing as sin. If there were no such thing as guilt, and if there were no such thing as a dreadful enslaving power of evil, then a noble ideal might be sufficient. But to talk about an ideal to a man under the thraldom of sin is a cruel mockery.

Sin may indeed be glossed over. Let us make the best of our condition, we are told, let us do the best we can, let us simply trust in the all-conquering love of God. Dangerous advice! By it a certain superficial joy of life may be induced. But the joy rests upon an insecure foundation. It is dangerous to be happy on the brink of the abyss. Permanent joy can come only when sin has been faced honestly, and destroyed. It is destroyed by the death and resurrection of our Lord Jesus Christ.

It is true that God is loving. He has manifested his love, however, better than by complacency toward sin. He has manifested it by the gracious gift of a Saviour.

Faith

How shall we appropriate the benefits of Christ's death? The answer of the New Testament is plain. Not by doing anything, but simply by receiving. In other words, simply by faith. 'Believe on the Lord Jesus, and thou shalt be saved'—that means, 'Instead of trying to save yourself, let Christ save you'. Salvation is a free gift of God in Christ Jesus our Lord.

Faith is not itself a meritorious act. It is not a way of earning salvation. It is a way of receiving a gift. But though faith is not itself a work it results in work. Faith works itself out through love, Gal. 5.6, and love means the fulfilling of the whole moral law. Faith in Christ is the beginning of a long conflict with sin. But it is a victorious conflict—victorious through the power of the risen Christ.

TOPICS FOR STUDY

1. What did Jesus say during his earthly ministry about his death and the significance of it?

2. What predictions did he make about his resurrection? How were these predictions received by the disciples?

3. What does the book of The Acts tell us about the meaning of Jesus' death?

4. Why were the disciples so utterly discouraged after Jesus' death?

5. Give a list of those who saw Jesus after his resurrection.

6. Outline the teaching which was given by the risen Christ.

7. What is the importance to us of the resurrection of Christ?

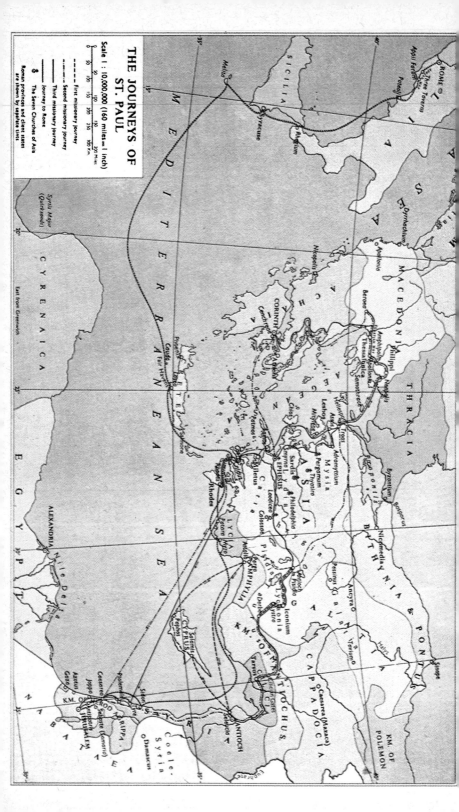

THE JOURNEYS OF
ST. PAUL.

Scale 1 : 10,000,000 (160 miles = 1 inch)

Scale markers:	50	100	150	200	250	300 Km.
	50	100	150	200 Miles		

- - - - - First missionary journey
- · - · - Second missionary journey
· · · · · · · Third missionary journey
————— Journey to Rome

☩ The Seven Churches of Asia

Roman provinces and client states
are shown by separate tints

Syrtis Major
(Quicksand)

East from Greenwich

9: THE BEGINNINGS OF THE CHRISTIAN CHURCH

Study material: Acts 1: 1 to 5: 16

Waiting for Power

During forty days after the resurrection Jesus continued to appear to his disciples. The manner of his intercourse with them was not entirely different from that which had prevailed during his earthly ministry. There was indeed an element of mystery and of un-expectedness in his appearances. Evidently he was no longer a denizen of the earth. Nevertheless he communicated with them through the avenue of the senses. He taught them by word of mouth. Conceivably, he might have continued thus to be the visible leader of his Church. But as a matter of fact his plans were different—different and more glorious.

The teaching of the risen Lord was merely preparatory to what was to follow. The disciples did not at first understand. 'Lord,' they said, 'dost thou at this time restore the kingdom to Israel?' Acts 1.6. Such was not the Lord's will. The disciples were given instructions for their future work: 'Go ye therefore, and make disciples of all the nations, baptizing them into the name of the Father and of the Son and of the Holy Spirit.' Matt. 28.19. They were given instructions, but in the accomplishment of the instructions, they were told to wait. Jesus was not to lead his Church in bodily presence. He was to lead it in a more effective and more glorious way. He was to lead it through the Holy Spirit. He charged the disciples not to depart from Jerusalem, but to wait for the promise of the Father. 'Ye shall receive power, when the Holy Spirit is come upon you: and ye shall be my witnesses both in Jerusalem, and in all Judæa and Samaria, and unto the uttermost part of the earth.' Acts 1.8.

After the Lord was taken up into heaven, there was a brief period of waiting. The place of the traitor Judas was filled, but nothing else seems to have been done. No signs of power as yet! Just a little

c

company of plain men and women, meeting for prayer in an upper room! But that upper room contained the hope of the world. In that room the Christian Church received its baptism of power.

The Coming of the Spirit

At the feast of Pentecost, which was celebrated fifty days after the passover, the promise of Jesus was fulfilled. The little band of disciples was assembled. Of themselves they were not a formidable body. But now God's time had come. There was a mysterious sound as of rushing wind. A tongue of fire descended upon every one of the company. These things were signs of the Spirit's presence. Another sign was the miraculous gift of tongues. The disciples began to speak in other languages. They were understood by the Jews who had assembled at the feast from all parts of the known world. This gift was not intended to be useful in missionary work. There is no evidence that the early Christians were by a miracle spared the labour of learning languages. At first, indeed, no such miracle was needed, on account of the wide extension of Greek. The gift of tongues was not a practical help in missionary work. In the form in which it appeared at Pentecost it was a temporary thing.

The gift of tongues, as it was exercised on the day of Pentecost, is not altogether an isolated phenomenon. It appears also elsewhere in The Acts, Acts 10.46; 19.6, though it may be doubted whether in all three cases it assumed exactly the same form. In the First Epistle to the Corinthians, Paul discusses the gift at considerable length, I Cor. ch. 14. It is interesting to compare that passage with the passage in the second chapter of The Acts.

There are a number of resemblances between the two. Both Paul and Luke represent the gift of tongues as a supernatural thing, a special endowment from the Spirit of God. Both Paul and Luke, furthermore, represent the gift as an ecstatic, temporary expression of spiritual exultation rather than as a faculty intended to be practically useful in the work of the Church. On the other hand, there are such marked differences between the two accounts as to make it evident that the gift, as it was manifested at Pentecost, was very considerably different from that which was exercised in the church at Corinth.

On the day of Pentecost the outsiders who heard the sound of the rushing wind or of the speaking with tongues came together to learn of this strange thing. That gave Peter his opportunity for the first sermon of the Christian Church. It was a very simple sermon and a very powerful one: 'This strange event is nothing less than the fulfilment of Joel's prophecy. Jesus, approved by miracles, raised from the dead in accordance with the Scriptures, has poured forth his Spirit. Jesus whom you crucified is Lord and Christ.' The sermon was effective. Three thousand were converted and baptized. All of those who were converted received the Holy Spirit, Acts 2.38. The Spirit belongs not to a special class within the Church. He is the possession of every Christian.

With the conversion of the three thousand the Church had begun its career of conquest. The poor, disheartened disciples had become the instruments of victorious mercy. The humiliation of Christ was over. All power, at last, was given to him. And he was using his power for the salvation of men.

The Life of the Church

The new Christian community did not at first regard itself as distinct from Judaism. The disciples continued in diligent observance of the temple worship. Though in reality Christianity was from the beginning a new dispensation, it appeared to the careless observer to be nothing more than a Jewish sect. Even the disciples themselves were unaware of any break with their ancestral religion.

From the beginning, however, the disciples of Jesus were conscious of the bond that united them with one another and separated them from all others. Their unity found expression in various ways.

In the first place, the authority of the apostles, which was derived from Jesus himself, led to a community in belief.

In the second place, 'the breaking of bread' symbolized the benefits received from the crucified Lord. Every meal that the disciples ate together was a reminder of the fellowship of Jesus with his disciples. One form of meal was peculiarly sacred. At the last supper of which Jesus partook before his crucifixion he had given bread and wine to the little company of apostles. The broken bread and the wine poured out were symbols of his death. He had commanded that the simple ceremony be continued. The Lord's Supper was from the beginning, along with baptism, a sacrament of the Christian Church. Both had been instituted definitely by Christ.

A third bond of union among the disciples was prayer. That

requires no explanation. Then as now, prayer was the very life of the Church.

The fourth form in which unity was expressed was a community of worldly goods. 'And all that believed were together, and had all things common; and they sold their possessions and goods, and parted them to all, according as any man had need.' Acts 2.44, 45. At first sight it might seem to have been a socialistic plan. It might seem as though private property were altogether given up. But the contributions to the common cause, then, were purely voluntary. 'Not one of them said that aught of the things which he possessed was his own; but they had all things common'—Acts 4.32—that means simply that the Christians regarded their private possessions as held in trust for God, so that no brother who was in need could call in vain. Not compulsory socialism, but a generous stewardship was the ideal of the early Church. It is an ideal which must ever be maintained.

The Incident of Ananias and Sapphira

The Acts warns us, however, that a certain man, Ananias, and Sapphira his wife, after they had sold their possession kept back part of the price. In itself that was not necessarily wrong. Their sin was the sin of deception. They pretended to have given all, though they had really given only a part. A more destructive sin could scarcely have been imagined. They had lied unto the Holy Spirit. Such conduct would bring contempt upon the Church. Ananias and Sapphira discovered that God cannot be trifled with. And the judgment wrought upon them inspired fear in all who heard.

It is well that this incident has been recorded. It prevents a one-sided impression of the Church's life. The power that animated the Church was beneficent. But it was also terrible and mysterious and holy. In the presence of it there was joy. But that joy was akin to fear. 'It is a fearful thing to fall into the hands of the living God.' Heb. 10.31. The lesson is of permanent value. The Spirit of God must be received with joy. But not with a common joy. Not with the joy of familiarity. But rather with the wondering, trembling joy of adoration.

The Speeches in The Acts

The speeches in The Acts are apparently either verbatim reports of what was actually said, or else summaries based upon trustworthy tradition. If they had been composed freely by the historian himself their characteristic differences and their perfect adaptation to different occasions would be difficult to explain.

The speeches of Peter and of the earliest disciples, in particular, are very different from those of Paul. They contain a number of features which occur either not at all or only rarely in the rest of the New Testament. The designation of Jesus as 'the Servant', for example, a designation taken from the latter part of Isaiah, is characteristic of these speeches. Another characteristic designation of Jesus is 'Prince' or 'Prince of life'. Acts 3.15; 5.31. In general, the representation of Jesus in the early chapters of The Acts is just what might have been expected under the circumstances. At the beginning of the Church's life, everything is simple and easy of comprehension even by outsiders. The apostles represented Jesus first as a man approved of God by the miracles which he had wrought. To have delivered up such a man to death was itself a grievous sin. But that was not all. This Jesus who was crucified had been raised from the dead; and both in his death and in his resurrection he had fulfilled the Messianic predictions of the ancient prophets. He was then nothing less than the Christ. Now, too, his period of humiliation was over. He had been given the full powers of Lordship. From him had come the wonder-working Spirit. It will be observed that these speeches, though they begin with what is simplest and easiest of acceptance by an outsider, really contain, at least in germ, the full doctrine of the divine Christ.

Favour and Opposition

The disciples enjoyed the favour of the people. What is more surprising, even the Pharisees seem at first not to have been actively hostile. The reasons for their indifference will be discussed in the next chapter.

The earliest opposition came not from the Pharisees but from the Sadducees; it was induced not by fanatic zeal, but by worldly wisdom. The Sadducees were friends of the existing order of things. They were opposed to disturbances of all sorts. They were opposed to the preaching of the resurrection, not merely because it was contrary to their scepticism, but because it was connected with a Messianic movement, and a Messianic movement against which they had already adopted violent measures. They were sore troubled, not merely because the apostles proclaimed the resurrection from the dead, but because they 'proclaimed in Jesus the resurrection from the dead'. Acts 4.2.

The event which aroused the first opposition was a notable miracle wrought by Peter and John. A beggar, lame from birth, well known to all multitudes who went in at the 'Beautiful Gate' of the temple, was suddenly healed. He was healed in the name of that same Jesus who had been delivered up to death by the rulers only a few weeks before. It was a dangerous name to boast of before the chief priests. But the apostles did not hesitate. 'In none other,' they said, 'is there salvation: for neither is there any other name under heaven, that is given among men, wherein we must be saved.' Acts 4.12. A bold utterance! It has a far wider reference than that which first occasioned it. It gives the ground of Christianity's exclusive claim. Faith in Christ is not merely a way of salvation. It is the only way.

TOPICS FOR STUDY

1. Give a complete summary in your own words of Acts 1.1 to 5.16.

2. Find on a map the countries mentioned in Acts 2.7–11.

3. Compare the gift of tongues as it is described in the second chapter of The Acts with the account in I Cor. 14. Is the same gift described in the two passages? Where else in the New Testament is the gift of tongues mentioned?

4. What can be learned from the study material about prayer and the answer to it?

5. Give summaries in your own words of the speeches of Peter contained in the study material.

6. What members of the early Jerusalem church are mentioned by name?

10: THE FIRST PERSECUTION

Study material: Acts 5: 17 to 8: 13

Persecution by the Sadducees

It was observed in the last chapter that the earliest opposition to the Church came not from the Pharisees but from the Sadducees. At first this opposition was held in check by the favour which the disciples enjoyed among the people. When Peter and John had been arrested after the healing of the lame man, the rulers had been able to do nothing more than warn them not to speak any more in the name of Jesus—and the warning had been boldly and frankly rejected. 'We cannot but speak the things which we saw and heard.' Acts 4.20.

After the second arrest of the apostles, the rulers ventured to proceed to actual punishment, but even then extreme measures were avoided. The second arrest, like the first, was due to jealousy on account of the popularity of the new sect. The apostles were imprisoned by the Sadducean rulers, but were miraculously released, and used their freedom in order to teach in the temple, in defiance of all prohibitions. The officers then brought them before the Sanhedrin—as quietly as possible, since any show of violence would have been dangerous on account of the enthusiastic popular favour which the offenders enjoyed.

Incensed by the boldness of the apostles, who replied to all official rebukes by the unanswerable words, 'We must obey God rather than men', the rulers were considering how they might inflict the death penalty, when they were hindered by the counsel of Gamaliel the Pharisee.

Gamaliel was one of the most famous of the rabbis. He was the same as the 'Gamaliel the elder', who is a well-known figure in Jewish tradition. In the New Testament he appears elsewhere as the teacher of the youthful Paul, Acts 22.3. Though there is no evidence that Gamaliel was at all friendly to the disciples, his counsel shows at least that he was not, like the Sadducees, bitterly incensed against them. 'Let this movement alone', he said. 'If it is of men, it will come to nothing anyway. If it is of God, opposition to it is useless.' The advice of Gamaliel prevented extreme measures; the rulers contented themselves with the punishment of scourging. That punishment was altogether without effect. The apostles simply rejoiced 'that they were counted worthy to suffer dishonour for the Name', and continued their preaching of Jesus as the Christ.

Up to this point, the Pharisees, though not friendly, had been indifferent. Certainly their favour was not obtained by any unworthy spirit of compromise on the part of the Church. The apostles did not hesitate to lay the blame of Jesus' death exactly where it belonged. The Church, however, seemed at first sight to be far less radical than Jesus. Jesus had opposed the Pharisaic interpretation of the law. He had opposed the purely mechanical observance of the sabbath. He had exhibited the secondary character of the distinction between ceremonial cleanness and uncleanness. These were the things that had aroused the hostility of the Pharisees. Against the apostolic Church, there seemed to be no such ground of complaint. The disciples after Pentecost continued in diligent observance of the temple services. They seemed to be devout Jews even in the Pharisaic sense. Of course, the Pharisees were mistaken. The Church was really from the beginning something entirely new. Sooner or later a conflict was inevitable. A new seed had been implanted in the midst of Judaism. It was destined to grow into a tree. But for a time it was concealed in the mother soil.

The earliest opposition, then, came not from the Pharisees, but from the Sadducees. Such opposition was not very effective. It is true, the Sadducees occupied the positions of highest authority. But they were opposed by the people. The very things that aroused the jealousy of the Sadducees evoked the enthusiasm of the populace. The Sadducees opposed innovations; the people, galled by the Roman yoke, welcomed them. The Sadducees were made jealous by the miracles of healing; the people received them with gratitude. The Sadducees, then, were seriously hampered. In arresting the apostles, the officers were actually in danger of being stoned. Official jealousy was powerless against popular favour.

A really dangerous persecution could arise only through a revulsion of popular feeling. Such a change could never be wrought by the Sadducees. The Sadducees were a worldly aristocracy, out of sympathy with patriotic ideals. The real leaders were the Pharisees. Though officially inferior, they had the ear of the people. If their indifference should be changed to active opposition, then the peace of the Church would be over.

Persecution by the Pharisees

This change actually occurred. The centre of opposition shifted from the Sadducees to the Pharisees. A serious persecution was the result. The Church was no longer protected by popular favour. Opposition from the Pharisees meant opposition from the people Popularity gave place to fanatical resentment.

The change was occasioned by the activity of Stephen. Stephen had come into prominence through a simple matter of internal administration. That matter is of considerable independent interest.

The Jerusalem church was composed of two classes of members. There were 'Hebrews' and there were 'Hellenists'. The 'Hebrews' were Palestinian Jews who used the Aramaic language; the 'Hellenists', or Grecian 'Jews', were Jews returned from the dispersion, who used Greek. In the distribution of charity the Hellenists felt that they were not fairly treated. Their widows were being neglected in the daily ministration. The difficulty might have been settled by the existing leaders of the Church, the apostles. But since the apostles were fully occupied with preaching and teaching, a division of labour seemed advisable. Special officers were set over the administration of charity. For this office, as well as for the office of preacher, the possession of the Holy Spirit was a necessary qualification, Acts 6.5. Of the seven men who were chosen, two at least, Stephen and Philip, exercised spiritual as well as temporal functions. One of these has the glory of being the first Christian martyr.

Stephen seems clearly to have been a Jew of the dispersion. Like all the others of the seven, his name was Greek, and—what is more significant—his activity apparently lay in those synagogues in Jerusalem which were frequented by Jews of Rome and Cyrene and Alexandria and Cilicia and Asia. These Jews, being unable to withstand him in debate, instigated against him a significant charge. 'This man,' the witnesses said, 'ceaseth not to speak words against this holy place, and the law: for we have heard him say, that this Jesus of Nazareth shall destroy this place, and shall change the customs which Moses delivered unto us.' That was a very serious charge. It was like one of the charges that had brought Jesus to the cross. It was far more dangerous than the jealousy of the Sadducees. It could inflame the entire nation. 'Stephen is speaking against the law'—no charge was better suited to change the favour of the people into hatred. The Jews were devoted to the law. It was to them the sign of Israel's privilege. An enemy of the law was an enemy of the nation—and an enemy, too, of God. When the disciples were accused of blaspheming the Mosaic law, there seems to have been a revulsion of popular feeling. Before, the jealousy of a ruling class had been held in check by the favour of the people; now, the passions of the mob were let loose. Woe betide the man who aroused the ire of the Jewish populace! Even the Romans were cautious about facing that storm.

The witness against Stephen was a false witness, Acts 6.13, but like many false witnesses it contained an element of truth. It was false in so far as it represented Stephen as an advocate of violent measures against the temple and the law, but it was correct in representing Christianity as a new dispensation, which would eventually destroy the particularism of the Jews. At first, the revolutionary character of the new movement was unknown. But in the teaching of Stephen it perhaps came more to the surface.

In defending himself, Stephen gave a summary of Hebrew history. At first sight, that summary might seem to have little bearing upon the specific charges that had been made. But the history which Stephen recited was a history of Israel. 'You are destroying the divine privileges of Israel'—that was the charge. 'No,' said Stephen, 'history shows that the true privileges of Israel are the promises of divine deliverance. To them law and temple are subordinate. From Abraham on there was a promise of deliverance from Egypt. After that deliverance another deliverance was promised. It is the one which was wrought by Jesus. Moses, God's instrument in the first deliverance, was rejected by his contemporaries. Jesus, the greater Deliverer, was rejected by you. We disciples of Jesus are the true Israelites, for we, unlike you, honour the promises of God.'

The bold defence of Stephen aroused the Pharisaic opponents to fury. They rushed upon him and dragged him out of the city and stoned him. It was a piece of lynch justice. The council before whom Stephen had stood was indeed the Sanhedrin, the legal assembly. But the Sanhedrin could not legally inflict the death penalty without the consent of the Roman procurator. This time the restriction was disregarded. The forms of the Mosaic law were to some extent preserved, the witnesses performed their allotted function of casting the first stones, the punishment was the legal punishment for blasphemy—but the legal forms were at best a mere cloak for rash and ungovernable fury. The fury of the persecutors was in contrast to the bearing of the martyr. 'Lord,' he said, 'lay not this sin to their charge.' Stephen was a true disciple of the Lord Jesus.

The Result of the Persecution

The death of Stephen was not a disaster. It was an instrument in the extension of the gospel. It gave rise, indeed, to a fierce persecution. But persecution did not destroy, it merely scattered, the disciples. 'They were all scattered abroad throughout the regions of Judæa and Samaria, except the apostles.' It is dangerous to scatter the disciples of Jesus! Those who were scattered became triumphant missionaries. In trying to remove the Church from Jerusalem the Pharisees had given the Church to the world.

TOPICS FOR STUDY

1. Outline the history of the persecution up to and including the stoning of Stephen.

2. Compare the trial and death of Stephen with the trial and death of Jesus.

3. What is known about Gamaliel?

4. Were the seven men named in Acts 6.5 'deacons'? What is known about these men?

5. Find on a map the places mentioned in Acts 6.9.

6. Show how Stephen's speech answered the charge.

11: THE FIRST GENTILE CONVERTS

Study material: Acts 8: 4–40; 9: 31 to 11: 18

A severe persecution raged in Jerusalem after the death of Stephen. Prominent among the enemies of the Church was a young rabbi, Saul of Tarsus. The persecution drove great numbers of the disciples away from Jerusalem. The apostles remained, but the other leaders were scattered. Their scattering, however, resulted in the extension of the gospel. 'They therefore that were scattered abroad went about preaching the word.' Acts 8.4. One of them went to Samaria.

The Gospel in Samaria

The Samaritans cannot be called Gentiles; they were rather schismatic Jews. They rejected a large part of the Old Testament. They did not worship in Jerusalem, and indeed would not have been permitted to do so. They were despised by orthodox Jews. In race, they were the product of a mixture. On the other hand, there was much that united them with Judaism. They accepted the Pentateuch, and awaited a Messiah, John 4.25.

Jesus himself had made converts among the Samaritans. The extension of the gospel to Samaria, therefore, was not revolutionary. It was only a preparation for the more widespread work that was to come.

The first Christian preacher in Samaria was Philip. He is to be distinguished from the apostle of the same name. In Acts 21.8 he is called 'Philip the evangelist'. He was one of the seven men who had been appointed to assist in the distribution of charity.

The work in Samaria was begun at the capital, 'the city of Samaria'. The people of Samaria received the preaching of Philip with gladness. The success of the work was due in considerable measure to the miracles that were wrought. Miracles were regularly an accompaniment of the early extension of the gospel. The power that worked in the Church was subject to no ordinary limitations. It was nothing less than the power of God.

At Samaria the Christian mission came into contact with a very interesting and very widespread feature of ancient life—the practice of magic. Simon, a sorcerer, had acquired considerable influence in the city. Apparently he had represented himself as an incarnation of the divine power. Now, however, the people saw that a greater and more genuine power was in the midst of them. They deserted Simon for Philip. Even Simon himself was convinced.

The conversions wrought by the preaching of Philip were genuine conversions. They were sealed by the sacrament of baptism. But one thing was lacking. The Holy Spirit had not been given. That does not mean that the Spirit of God had not been operative in Samaria. He had attended the preaching of Philip and had created faith in the hearts of the hearers. It is rather the special, miraculous manifestation of the Spirit's presence that seems to be meant. That manifestation was connected especially with the apostles. It was not till Peter and John came down from Jerusalem that the Samaritans 'received the Holy Spirit'. In that way the unity of the Church was preserved. The apostles were in possession of a divine authority.

After Simon had witnessed the giving of the Spirit, he revealed the falsity of his faith. He thought that the power of bestowing the Spirit could be obtained by money. In other words, he thought that Christianity was just a form of magic. It was a woeful error. Magic seeks to gain control of supernatural powers by external means; Christianity demands purity of heart. Magic tries to bend the gods to human desires; Christianity bows before the gracious, mysterious will of God.

The Conversion of the Ethiopian

After the successful work in Samaria, Philip was sent upon a strange errand. He was told to go to the desert road that leads from Jerusalem to Gaza. It was an unlikely place for missionary service. But the true evangelist is not his own master.

On that road he met a solitary traveller, an Ethiopian official, who had gone to Jerusalem to worship. The connection of the Ethiopian with Israel is not perfectly clear. Possibly he was a 'God-worshipper'—a Gentile who was interested in Judaism without becoming a full member of the people of Israel. When Philip, by command of the Spirit, joined himself to the chariot, the Ethiopian was reading the fifty-third chapter of Isaiah, doubtless in the Septuagint translation. Without the fulfilment, that was a puzzling passage. But it was explained by the cross. The Scriptures, interpreted by a true evangelist, led the Ethiopian to Christ.

The Conversion of Cornelius

After narrating the conversion of the Ethiopian, Luke inserts the story of a greater conversion—the conversion of Paul. That story will be studied in the next chapter.

After the conversion of Paul, the Church had peace, Acts 9.31. Perhaps the fury of the persecution had simply run its course, or perhaps the removal of an arch-persecutor was the turning point. At any rate, the period of quiet that ensued resulted in the building up of the Church. At this time there were disciples in Galilee, in Samaria, and in other regions, as well as in Judæa.

So far, however, the gospel had been preached only to Jews. The Samaritans were half-Jews. The exact relation of the Ethiopian treasurer to Judaism cannot be determined with certainty. At any rate, even if he is to be called a Gentile pure and simple, his immediate withdrawal kept in abeyance the question of his relation to the Church. The question of the reception of Gentile converts had not yet been settled. It was settled by the case of Cornelius.

Cornelius was a Roman officer, a centurion. He was a 'God-worshipper' of a particularly devout kind. But that did not make him a Jew. He was not a proselyte. He had not united himself with the people of Israel. Against intercourse with him, Jewish scruples would be in full force. Cornelius was a Gentile. If he should be received into the Church, then Gentile Christianity would have been begun.

This important step was actually taken. It was taken, under immediate divine guidance, by Peter.

As an introduction to the story of Cornelius, Luke inserts two incidents in the work which Peter carried on in the coast country of Syria. The apostles had endured the first storm of persecution in Jerusalem. But afterwards, during the period of peace, they devoted themselves more and more to missionary journeys. On one of these journeys, Peter healed a palsied man in Lydda and raised a woman from the dead in Joppa. From Joppa he was called to even more important service.

The reception of Cornelius and his friends at Cæsarea was an important event. Gentiles were received into the Church without being required to become Jews. This step gave rise to anxious questionings in Jerusalem.

In defence, Peter appealed simply to the manifest authorization which he had received from God. That authorization had appeared first of all in the visions which Peter and Cornelius had received, with other direct manifestations of the divine will, and also more particularly in the bestowal of the Spirit. If the Spirit was given to uncircumcised Gentiles, then circumcision was no longer necessary to membership in the Church. In the narrative about Cornelius, there is a remarkable heaping up of supernatural guidance. Vision is added to vision, revelation to revelation. The reason is plain. A decisive step was being taken. If taken by human initiative, it was open to criticism. The separateness of Israel from other nations was a divine ordinance. Since it had been instituted by God, it could be abrogated only by him. True, Jesus had said, 'Make disciples of all the nations'. Matt. 28.19. But the how and the when had been left undecided. Were the Gentiles to become Jews in order to become Christians, and was the Gentile mission to begin at once? Those were grave questions. They could not be decided without divine guidance. That guidance was given in the case of Cornelius.

Peter's defence was readily accepted by the church at Jerusalem. 'And when they heard these things, they held their peace, and glorified God, saying, Then to the Gentiles also hath God granted repentance unto life.' The active opposition to the Gentile mission did not arise until later. But how could that opposition arise at all? Since God had spoken so clearly, who could deny to the Gentiles a free entrance into the Church?

TOPICS FOR STUDY

1. Outline the steps in the extension of the gospel up to and including the conversion of Cornelius.

2. Collect all the information that you can find about (a) Philip the Evangelist, (b) Simon Magus, (c) Cornelius.

3. Give an account of Samaria (the city and also the country) and the Samaritans.

4. Collect the references to the Samaritans which occur in the Gospels.

5. Discuss the importance of the Cornelius incident.

6. Find the following places and countries on a map, and give information about some of them:—Ethiopia, Gaza, Azotus, Cæsarea, Lydda, Joppa, Sharon.

12 : THE CONVERSION OF PAUL

Study material: Acts 9: 1–19; 22: 1–16; 26: 1–18

The last two chapters have shown how the gospel began to be preached outside of Jerusalem—first in Judea and then in Samaria. Here and there even Gentiles had been won. A beginning of missions had been made. But it was only a beginning. The Gentile mission was still without a leader. Chapter nine of The Acts shows how the leader was provided. The leader was the apostle Paul.

At Tarsus

Paul was born in Tarsus, capital of Cilicia. Tarsus was 'no mean city', Acts 21.39. Aside from its very considerable commercial importance, it is to be placed, along with Alexandria and Athens, among the great university cities of the Roman Empire. The prevailing language of the city was Greek, the world language of that day.

The parents of Paul are not mentioned by name in the New Testament, but a number of things are known about them. The father of Paul was a Roman citizen, for Paul was not only a Roman but a Roman born, Acts 22.28. As a Roman citizen Paul probably had his name 'Paul', from the beginning. He also had a Jewish name, 'Saul'. Such double naming of Jews was not uncommon. The book of The Acts uses the Roman name for the part of Paul's life which was spent outside of a Jewish environment. The possession of Roman citizenship indicates for the family of Paul an estimable social position in the life of Tarsus. Certainly the family was not uncomfortably poor, for Paul's father was able to send him to Jerusalem to be educated.

Paul's family thus belonged rather to the well-to-do class of the population of Tarsus. It could not have been altogether unaffected by the surrounding civilization. The Greek language, at least, was doubtless known to Paul from boyhood. He did not have to learn it when he grew up. It was not to him a foreign language.

But the Greek influence upon Paul's boyhood, important though it was, was far less important than another influence. Paul was a citizen of Tarsus and of the Roman Empire; but he was also a Jew, and a child of a Jewish home. That is the most important fact of all. It was the Jewish influence that really moulded his life. His father was not only a Jew, but a loyal Jew, who could trace his descent back to the ancient tribe of Benjamin, Rom. 11.1; Phil. 3.5. In religion, the family belonged to the strictest sect of Judaism. Paul was a Pharisee, a son of Pharisees, Acts 23.6. Even in language the genuine Jewish traditions were preserved. No doubt many of the Jewish inhabitants of Tarsus could speak only Greek, but in the boyhood home of Paul, Aramaic, the language of Palestine, was also spoken, Phil. 3.5; II Cor. 11.22. Without doubt, also, Paul could read the Old Testament, which was fundamental in all his work, in the original Hebrew as well as in the Greek translation. The double language—Semitic and Greek—is typical of the double preparation for his work. His gospel, on the one hand, sprang from Judaism. It was the fulfilment of the Jewish hope. It was supported by the Old Testament. But the Jewish gospel was to be proclaimed among the Gentiles; and Paul was acquainted not only with the gospel which he proclaimed, but also with the people to whom he proclaimed it.

At Jerusalem

In his early youth he was sent to Jerusalem to complete his education. At Jerusalem he attended what we should call the theological seminary of Judaism. For he was destined to become a religious teacher, a rabbi. His principal teacher is mentioned by name, Gamaliel, the leading rabbi of his time. The date of Paul's going to Jerusalem cannot be fixed with accuracy. Certainly, however, it was before the crucifixion of Jesus, and a few years after the crucifixion he was still in Jerusalem at the time of the death of Stephen, Acts 7.58; 8.1. Possibly then he may have seen Jesus before Jesus' death. But it is hardly probable that he did. He says nothing plainly about it in any of his letters.

Paul was an apt pupil of Gamaliel. He advanced in the Jews' religion beyond many of his own age among his countrymen, 'being more exceedingly zealous for the traditions' of his fathers, Gal. 1.14. His zeal displayed itself especially in the persecution of

79

the Christian Church, Phil. 3.6. Various reasons may be suggested for Paul's opposition to the Church.

In the first place, Jesus was not the kind of Messiah that Paul was looking for. Paul expected a Messiah who should be a glorious king upon the throne of David. Instead of that, the Messiah of the Christians was a miserable criminal; a poor, weak man, at least, who could not even save himself from the executioner. The form of his death was singularly shameful. If that was the only kind of Messiah there was, then the hope of Israel was dead! The belief of the Christians seemed to be horrible blasphemy against the precious promises of God.

In the second place, Paul opposed the Christians because he was devoted to the law. In that he was a genuine Pharisee, Phil. 3.5. Pharisaism was essentially a law religion. Fulfil the law of God, said the Pharisees, and you will be saved. In itself, that principle was perfectly correct. But the trouble was that the Pharisees were satisfied with a very imperfect sort of fulfilment of the law. They went on the principle that the more separate commandments you fulfil, the more surely you will win salvation. So they multiplied the commandments even far beyond the Old Testament. But they did not see clearly enough that all their obedience, even to the weightiest commandments, was hopelessly imperfect. They sought to enter into an account with God. They sought to earn their salvation. They did not see that in view of human sinfulness, salvation, if it comes at all, can come only by the free gift of God. Pharisaism was a law religion. Christianity—and Paul was keen enough to see it—was entirely different. Though the Christians continued to observe the Mosaic law, they were really depending for their salvation, not upon their obedience, but solely upon their faith in the crucified Saviour. If the Christians were right, then the Pharisees' law-righteousness was wrong, and the Jews, with their law, were not much better off than sinners of the Gentiles; the exclusive position of Israel was destroyed.

Before Paul was converted, he was not gradually coming nearer to Christianity. If anything, he was moving farther off. It is true, we must not suppose that he was altogether satisfied with his condition. He was no hypocrite. He was earnestly striving after righteousness. And probably he was dissatisfied, in his heart of hearts, with the measure of righteousness that he had attained. But the more he became dissatisfied, the greater would become his devotion to the law and the more earnest his opposition to the

Christians. If his obedience was not perfect enough, it must be made more perfect just by rooting out the blasphemous sect. The persecution of the Christians seemed to be a meritorious work, which would earn for Paul the favour of God.

In persecuting the Christians Paul thought he was doing God service. He 'did it ignorantly in unbelief'. I Tim. 1.13. That, however, was no adequate excuse. The persecution of the Church was deadly sin. Paul himself came to regard it as such, I Cor. 15.9; I Tim. 1.15. And Paul was perfectly right. Not only his persecution of the Church but also his whole Pharisaic life was sinful. It was better than most lives are, but still it was sin. It was an effort to buy heaven by the imperfect righteousness of man. A futile effort! The power of sin was too strong. Even if Paul wanted to do good, evil was present with him. His whole inner life was impure. His soul was really in rebellion against God. In other words, he was just like the rest of men—a guilty sinner under God's wrath and curse.

The Conversion

And yet he attained salvation. It came in the strangest way. He was at the height of his persecuting zeal. He was making havoc of the Church of God, Gal. 1.13. He had consented to the death of the first Christian martyr, Acts 7.58; 8.1; 22.20; 26.10. He was breathing threatening and slaughter, Acts 9.1. Not satisfied with the destruction that he had wrought in Jerusalem, he obtained authority from the Sanhedrin to extend the persecution to Damascus. And then, suddenly, when it was least expected, the wonderful thing happened. Paul was nearing Damascus with his companions. It was midday. Suddenly a light more intense than the light of the sun shone around him. His companions saw the light. But Paul saw more than they. He saw the Lord Jesus Christ, I Cor. 9.1; 15.8; Acts 9.17, 27; 22.14; 26.16. He became a witness to the resurrection. His companions heard a voice; but Paul alone understood what was said, Acts 9.7; 22.9. It was the voice of the Lord calling him to be a servant and an apostle. It was useless to resist. Jesus had broken every barrier down. 'It is hard for thee to kick against the goad.' Acts 26.14. The crucified Teacher whom Paul had despised was really risen from the dead, the Lord of glory, the true Messiah of Israel. The shameful death on the cross was really the divine sacrifice for the sins of men. All of Paul's life crumbled away beneath him. In miserable blindness he groped his

way into Damascus, a poor, wretched, broken-spirited man! All
his zeal had been nothing but rebellion against the King of Israel.
Yet Jesus had appeared to him, not to put him to shame, but to
save him. The poor, bewildered, broken-spirited rabbi became the
most influential man in the history of the world!

The Meaning of the Conversion

Paul's conversion shows that Christianity is a supernatural thing.
Up to the conversion Paul's life had been a natural development,
but the conversion itself was a sudden blaze of glory. It is very
much the same with all of us. True, the form of Christ's appearing
is very diverse. We do not see him with the bodily eye. We do not,
like Paul, become witnesses to the resurrection. Many of us do not
know when first we saw him. It is a great mistake to demand of
every man that he shall be able, like Paul, to give day and hour of
his conversion. Many men, it is true, still have such a definite
experience. It is not pathological. It may result in glorious
Christian lives. But it is not universal, and it should not be induced
by tactless methods. The children of Christian homes often seem
to grow up into the love of Christ. When they decide to unite
themselves definitely with the Church, the decision need not
necessarily come with anguish of soul. It may simply be the
culmination of a God-encircled childhood, a recognition of what
God has already done rather than the acquisition of something
new.

In any case, however, Christian experience is not just a continuance of the old life, but the entrance of something from outside.
Many men are content with this world. Like the youthful Jew of
Tarsus, they are content with doing what other men do. But Chris-
tianity is contact with the unseen and eternal. Its beginning
in the soul cannot be predicted and cannot be explained. Paul was
a persecutor of Christ's followers. We, too, are sinners. But Christ
met Paul on the way to Damascus, and he meets us, too, today.
We cannot explain why he should receive us. We do not deserve it.
But he does receive us, and then he gives us work to do. Paul, the
Christian, was still able to use all the preparation of his years at
Tarsus and all of his Jewish training. But after Christ appeared to
him he used them not for earth but for heaven. Christ will treat
us as he treated Paul. Whatever our walk in life, be it exalted or be
it humble, Christ can make it worth while. After the vision came
the apostleship. There is a big work for all of us, if only Christ be

our leader. The true Christian life, no matter how humble, is never commonplace. It brings, first, the joy of peace with God, and second, the joy of work that is worth while.

TOPICS FOR STUDY

1. Compare the three accounts of the conversion.

2. Collect all the passages (a) in The Acts and (b) in the Pauline epistles which refer (a) to Paul's life at Tarsus and (b) to his pre-Christian life at Jerusalem. (Four topics.)

3. Was Paul told at the very time of the conversion that he was to be an apostle to the Gentiles?

4. Give an account of Paul's life for three years after the conversion, using The Acts, Galatians, and II Corinthians.

5. What other prominent conversions are mentioned in the New Testament?

6. Give an account of one or more important conversions outside of the Bible.

13: THE CHURCH AT ANTIOCH

Study material: Acts 9: 19–30; 22: 17–21; Gal. 1: 15–24;
II Cor. 11: 30–33; Acts 11: 19 to 12: 25

The events which followed the conversion of Paul are narrated not
only in The Acts but also by Paul himself in the Epistle to the
Galatians. Paul, however, is not intending to give a complete
narrative; the details which he mentions are not those which were
most important in themselves, but those which would establish
most clearly the independence of his apostleship. Both accounts
are partial: they should, therefore, be permitted to supplement
each other.

Arabia and Damascus

After the conversion, Paul says, he went away into Arabia. This
journey is not mentioned in The Acts, and it is difficult to determine where it should be inserted in Luke's narrative. It might be
put, for example, either at Acts 9.19—after the baptism and before
the 'certain days' which Paul spent with the disciples in Damascus
—or else during the 'many days' of Acts 9.23. The journey need
not necessarily have been very extensive; for the name 'Arabia'
was used in a broad sense to include even the country in the
immediate vicinity of Damascus. How long Paul remained in
Arabia is uncertain. It must have been less than three years, Gal.
1.18. As to what Paul did in Arabia, two opinions have been held.
Some suppose that he meditated on the deeper meaning of his
recent experience, and developed the principles of his gospel;
others, that he engaged in missionary work. Even if the latter view
is correct, the former should not be excluded. Labour, in the life
of Paul, was always accompanied by thought.

In Damascus, Paul preached in the synagogues. The essence of
his preaching was simple: 'Jesus is the Christ.' From that proposition, the gospel would follow. Naturally the sudden transformation
of a bitter persecutor into a fervent disciple occasioned surprise.

Among the unconverted Jews it soon occasioned opposition also. The Jews watched the gates of the city in order to prevent Paul from escaping; but he was lowered through the wall in a basket and escaped their hands. This striking incident is narrated not only in The Acts, but also by Paul himself in II Cor. 11.32, 33. Paul's account, however, mentions the ethnarch of Aretas the king as the one who guarded the city. Probably, as so often in the early history of Christianity, the Jews were the instigators of the persecution; and probably in this case the ethnarch employed them in the actual work of watching the gates. Aretas was monarch of an Arabian kingdom. The exact nature of his authority in Damascus is not quite clear.

First Visit of Paul to Jerusalem

Escaping in this way from Damascus, Paul went to Jerusalem. Paul says that three years had elapsed since the conversion, Gal. 1.18.

In Jerusalem, when Paul tried to unite himself with the disciples, they were afraid of him; and the intervention of Barnabas was necessary in order to bring him to the apostles. It may seem rather strange that the disciples were still afraid of Paul so long after his conversion. The distrust entertained by the disciples may perhaps indicate that the stay in Arabia occupied a considerable part of the three years; for in Arabia Paul's Christian life would be less within the notice of the Jerusalem Christians than in Damascus. However, the attitude of the disciples is in any case not altogether unnatural. Personally, they had known Paul only as a persecutor; their knowledge of his conversion came by hearsay. Feeling in such cases is stronger than reason: the Christians could not at first overcome an instinctive shrinking from him who had been their arch-enemy.

According to Galatians, the only leaders of the Jerusalem church whom Paul saw at this time were Peter and James. This James was the brother of the Lord, not one of the two men of the same name among the Twelve. When Luke says that Paul was brought to 'the apostles', he is either using the word 'apostles' in a broad sense to include James—compare Acts 14.4, 14—or else he means the apostles as they were represented by that one of their number who was present. Apparently the other apostles were out of the city. The period of missionary journeys had begun.

In Jerusalem Paul engaged in preaching; but apparently only two weeks had elapsed, Gal. 1.18, before opposition from the

Greek-speaking Jews led the disciples to send Paul away to a place of safety. Paul himself seems at first to have been unwilling to comply with the wishes of his friends. Jerusalem had been the scene of his persecution of the Church, and he was anxious to repair the mischief that he had wrought there. But in a vision Jesus himself commanded him to go, Acts 9.29, 30; 22.17–21. Paul himself says merely that he went into the regions of Syria and of Cilicia; Luke tells us that he went to the capital of Cilicia, to Tarsus, his original home. At Tarsus he appears some years later, when he was summoned to Antioch, Acts 11.25. During the interval he engaged in missionary work, Gal. 1.23, not improbably in work for Gentiles; but so far as any definite information is concerned, this period of Paul's life is for us a blank. After all, our knowledge of this great man is fragmentary. A good portrait, however, can be drawn by a master in a few strokes. So it is with the portrait of Paul. We know only a little about him; but what we know is sufficient to reveal with astonishing vividness both the characteristics of his work and the deepest springs of his tremendous religious experience. Paul, as revealed by himself in his letters and by Luke in The Acts, is one of the living figures on the stage of history.

Antioch

Antioch on the Orontes was founded by Seleucus Nicator, the first monarch of the Seleucid dynasty, and under his successors it remained the capital of the Syrian kingdom. When that kingdom was conquered by the Romans, the political importance of Antioch did not suffer. Antioch became under the Romans not only the capital of the province Syria but also the residence of the emperors and high officials when they were in the east. It may be regarded as a sort of eastern capital of the empire.

The political importance of Antioch was no greater than its commercial importance. Situated near the north eastern corner of the Mediterranean Sea, where the Mediterranean coast is nearer to the Euphrates than at any other point, where the Orontes valley provided easy communication with the east and the Syrian gates with the west, with a magnificent artificial harbour at Seleucia, about twenty miles distant, Antioch naturally became the great meeting point for the trade of east and west. It is not surprising that Antioch was the third city of the empire—after Rome and Alexandria.

A Missionary Church

In Paul, God provided a leader for the Gentile mission; in Antioch, a centre for the leader's work. Already individual Gentiles had been converted, but at Antioch there was a Gentile Christian community. The Gentile work at Antioch was begun, not by any of the great men of early Christian history, but by certain unnamed Jews of Cyprus and Cyrene. After all, the expansion of Christianity was the work, not of any one man, however great, nor of any one group of men, but of the Spirit of God, who employed various instruments in the accomplishment of his purpose.

At first those who had been scattered abroad by the persecution which followed upon the death of Stephen, preached only to Jews; but some of them, men of Cyprus and Cyrene, when they came to Antioch took the important step of preaching also to the Gentiles (the word 'Greeks' here means simply 'Gentiles'). Acts 11.20. The interest of the Jerusalem church being aroused, Barnabas was sent to Antioch to investigate. The choice of Barnabas was wise. As Luke says, 'he was a good man, and full of the Holy Spirit and of faith'. Barnabas recognized joyfully the grace of God which had been bestowed upon the Gentiles at Antioch, and after encouraging the church went to Tarsus to look for Paul. Apparently Paul was known already as one whose special mission was to the Gentiles. In bringing Paul to Antioch, Barnabas rendered a notable service to the Christian cause; for it was Paul who was to be the real leader in the Gentile mission. The part which Barnabas plays in early Christian history is singularly attractive. At first, as the older man, he seems to have taken precedence of Paul, but when he was outstripped by his younger associate he displayed no sign of jealousy. On two occasions, indeed, he rendered notable assistance to the converted persecutor—once at Jerusalem, when he introduced him to the apostles, and again at Antioch when he brought him into the centre of the Gentile mission. Evidently Barnabas was one of the first to recognize the greatness of the apostle to the Gentiles.

At Antioch, the disciples were for the first time called 'Christians'. This name was evidently applied not by the Christians themselves (for in the New Testament the name is used scarcely at all), and not by the Jews (for of course they would not designate by the name of the Messiah those whom they regarded as disciples of a false Messiah), but by the Gentile population. The coining of the name is exceedingly significant. At first, Christianity had been regarded as a Jewish sect, without interest for outsiders; but at Antioch it became so distinct from Judaism that a special name was required. Even the Gentiles at last became aware that a new movement had been begun.

The Second Visit of Paul to Jerusalem

The new Christian community at Antioch soon found an opportunity of expressing its devotion to the mother church; for after Agabus prophesied a famine, the Antioch Christians sent assistance to their Jerusalem brethren, Barnabas and Paul being chosen as bearers of the gift. This journey to Jerusalem is not mentioned by Paul in Galatians; for he is there concerned only with his relations to the original apostles, and apparently at this time all of the apostles were out of the city. They might well have been driven out by the persecution which was carried on at about this time by Herod Agrippa I, Acts 12.1–4. In that persecution James the son of Zebedee lost his life, and Peter escaped only by a miracle, which is narrated in The Acts in a remarkably lifelike manner, Acts 12.5–19. The death of Herod Agrippa I occurred in A.D. 44.

TOPICS FOR STUDY

1. Outline the life of Paul from his conversion to his entrance upon the work at Antioch, using both The Acts and the Pauline epistles.

2. Tell all that is known about the life of Barnabas up to the time of Acts 12.25.

3. Outline the extension of the gospel up to the time of Acts 12.25.

4. What information is given in the New Testament about collections for the benefit of the church at Jerusalem?

5. Give some account of Antioch. How was it fitted to be the seat of a missionary church?

6. What terms are used to express the idea 'Christians' in The Acts and in the rest of the New Testament?

Christianity Established Among the Gentiles

14: THE GOSPEL TO THE GENTILES

Study material: Acts, chs. 13, 14

The preparations for the Gentile mission were at last complete. There was a missionary church and there was a great missionary. At last the work could begin. .

It began, however, not by human initiative, but by direct command of God. The command came in unmistakable fashion. Of the five prophets and teachers in Antioch, two were chosen for the new enterprise. While the five were engaged in religious services, the Holy Spirit said, 'Separate me Barnabas and Saul for the work whereunto I have called them'. Probably the command was given through the mouth of one of the prophets; whether it was to be executed simply by the prophets and teachers or by the congregation at large is not clear. At any rate, Barnabas and Saul were sent away with fasting and prayer and the laying on of hands. This act was a consecration, not to the apostleship—for Paul had been made apostle before, without human mediation, by Christ himself—but merely to a special work.

Cyprus

At first the missionaries turned to the island of Cyprus. For various reasons that was a natural choice. Barnabas was a native of Cyprus, Acts 4.36, and so were some of the early preachers at Antioch, Acts 11.20. Proximity, furthermore, may have been a determining factor. Cyprus is said to be actually visible on a clear day from the bay outside of the harbour of Seleucia itself.

A short sail from Seleucia, then, brought the missionaries to Salamis, on the east coast of the island. Here 'they proclaimed the word of God in the synagogues of the Jews'. It was the natural course of procedure, and the course which was ordinarily followed throughout all the missionary journeys. Even if the ultimate mission was to the Gentiles, the synagogues afforded a starting point, and an audience composed of Gentiles as well as Jews. Apparently the Jews were especially numerous in Salamis, for synagogues (in the plural) are mentioned.

In connection with the work in Salamis, a helper of the missionaries is mentioned for the first time. Evidently he was making the journey in an altogether subordinate capacity. This was John Mark, a cousin of Barnabas, Col. 4.10, a member of the Jerusalem church, Acts 12.12, whom Barnabas and Paul had taken back with them from Jerusalem to Antioch after their delivery of the contribution made in view of the famine.

Proconsul and Sorcerer

Passing through the island from Salamis, the missionary party came to Paphos, the capital. Here two interesting characters were encountered. One was a certain Bar-Jesus, or Elymas, a sorcerer, or 'Wise-man'. The other was no less a person than the proconsul, Sergius Paulus.

Luke is demonstrably correct in representing the ruler of Cyprus as a proconsul. Previously the island had been governed as an imperial province, but at this time it was senatorial. A proconsul Paulus is actually mentioned in an inscription that can be dated to the year A.D. 55. That a sorcerer should have been in the train of a high Roman official, apparently with some influence over him, may seem surprising, but it is quite in accord with the facts of ancient life. It was a day of religious propaganda. The proconsul was a seeker after God. Before Paul arrived he was somewhat interested, apparently, in oriental magic; now he gave himself to a higher faith.

When the Jewish sorcerer is first mentioned he is called Bar-Jesus—that is, 'son of Jesus', Jesus being a common Jewish name. Then, a little below, the same man is called 'Elymas the sorcerer', and the explanation is added, 'for so is his name by interpretation'. Apparently the new name Elymas is introduced without explanation, and then the Greek word for 'sorcerer' is introduced as a translation of that. The word Elymas is variously derived from an Arabic word meaning 'wise'. or an Aramaic word meaning 'strong'. In either case the Greek word, 'magos', for which our English Bible has 'sorcerer', is a fair equivalent. That Greek word is the word that appears also in Matt. 2.1, 7, 16, where the English Bible has 'Wise-men'; and words derived from the same root are used to describe Simon of Samaria in Acts 8.9, 11. The word could designate men of different character. Some 'magi' might be regarded as students of natural science; in others, superstition and charlatanism were dominant.

In connection with this incident, Luke begins to use the name Paul instead of Saul, and from now on Paul takes precedence of Barnabas. The missionaries have now emerged into the larger world of the time, and in that world the apostle to the Gentiles, with his Roman name and Roman citizenship—and also with his divine commission—was supreme.

Perga

From Paphos, the missionaries sailed to Perga in Pamphylia, on the southern coast of Asia Minor. Before they proceeded into the interior, John Mark left them and returned to Jerusalem. Apparently some blame was to be attached to his departure, for at the beginning of the next journey Paul was unwilling to take him along, Acts 15.37, 38.

Pisidian Antioch

From Perga, Paul and Barnabas travelled northward through the Taurus mountains until they reached Pisidian Antioch, on the central plateau of Asia Minor. The report which Luke gives of Paul's speech at Antioch affords us our only extended sample of Paul's missionary preaching to Jews and 'God-fearers'. The speech is divided into three parts, each marked off by words of address. The first division, vs. 16–25, exhibits the coming of Jesus as the culmination of Israelitish history; the second, vs. 26–37, presents the fundamental gospel facts about Jesus and supports them by prophecy; the third, vs. 38–41, extends the offer of salvation by faith, with a solemn warning against neglect of the message.

It has been thought surprising that this speech contains so little of the Pauline doctrine which is prominent in the epistles. A more futile objection could scarcely be imagined. The letters were addressed to Christians; the speech was addressed to unconverted Jews and adherents of Judaism. Naturally the speech ends where the letters begin. Paul was not a man to talk to all men in exactly the same way. He adapted his methods to the requirements of his hearers, I Cor. 9.19–22. Paul was a man of principle, but he was also a man of tact. Beginning with things that were admitted, he went on to what was in dispute. Even in dealing with the heathen he sought common ground, Acts 17.22–31; and far more so in dealing with Jews. The speech at Pisidian Antioch is just what could be expected. It contains the Pauline doctrine of justification —not, however, at the beginning, where it would have been unintelligible, but exactly where it belonged, at the end. The thought that the law was insufficient, vs. 38, 39, was to the Jews in the highest degree paradoxical. To have put such a thought at the beginning would have been absurd. It could come only as the climax of the speech. Luke has here supplemented in a most valuable way the information provided by the epistles. The epistles show how Paul dealt with Christians; Luke has here exhibited his preaching to Jews.

When the Jews became jealous, Paul and Barnabas turned definitely to the Gentiles. That does not mean that Gentiles had not already been offered the gospel, or that they would never have received it except for the unbelief of the Jews. Gentile preaching was intended, on this journey, from the beginning. What the words mean is that, as far as Antioch was concerned, the missionaries now relinquished the Jewish part of their work. They had preached to Gentiles formerly; now, on account of the opposition of the Jews, they began to preach exclusively to Gentiles. The Jews had lost their opportunity.

The work at Antioch continued long enough to spread the gospel throughout the surrounding region. Finally, however, the Jews succeeded in driving the missionaries out. They did so by influencing the civil authorities. As in many cities of the Roman world, Jewish influence had made itself felt, so far as the higher classes were concerned, especially among the women; and perhaps we are to understand that it was these 'devout women of honourable estate' who induced the hostile attitude among their husbands, 'the chief men of the city'.

Iconium and Lystra

At Iconium the course of events was very much the same as at Pisidian Antioch. At Lystra, on the contrary, a unique incident occurred. Astonished at the instantaneous healing of a man who had been lame from birth, the crowds were about to pay divine honours to the missionaries. It may seem rather strange that Paul and Barnabas should have been identified with great gods of Olympus rather than with lesser divinities or spirits, but who can place a limit upon the superstition of an uncultured people of the ancient world? The identification may have been rendered easier by the legend of Philemon and Baucis, which has been preserved for us by Ovid, the Latin poet. According to that legend, Zeus and Hermes appeared, once upon a time, in human form in Phrygia, the same general region in which Lystra was situated. Zeus and Hermes are the gods with whom Barnabas and Paul were identified; the A.V. and R.V. simply substitute for these Greek names the names of the corresponding Roman deities. The temple of Zeus-before-the-city and the preparations for sacrifices are described in a most lifelike way, in full accord with what is known of ancient religion. We find ourselves here in a somewhat different atmosphere from that which prevails in most of the scenes described in The Acts. It is a pagan atmosphere, and an atmosphere of ruder superstition than that which prevailed in the great cities. The 'speech of Lycaonia', v. 11, is an especially characteristic touch. Apparently the all-pervading Greek was understood at Lystra even by the populace; but in the excitement of their superstition they fell very naturally into their native language.

At this point, Luke has preserved a valuable example—less extended, it is true, than that in Acts 17.22–31—of Paul's preaching to pure Gentiles. It should be compared with the speech to Jews and 'God-fearers' at Pisidian Antioch. In both cases, Paul started with what his hearers could understand. But in the case of the superstitious mob he had to begin with the very rudiments.

The Return

The enthusiasm of the mob, discouraged by the missionaries, was soon transformed by the Jews of Antioch and Iconium into hatred, and Paul actually endured stoning, and narrowly escaped death. To this narrow escape he refers in II Cor. 11.25—'Once was I stoned.' After a ministry in Derbe, which, like Lystra, was a city of Lycaonia, Antioch and Iconium being cities of Phrygia, the missionaries, instead of proceeding direct to Syrian Antioch by the Cilician and Syrian gates, retraced their steps through Asia Minor in order to confirm the disciples in the faith. In every city they chose elders to conduct the affairs of the churches. Paul and Barnabas were no mere thoughtless enthusiasts. They were wise missionaries. At the very beginning the need of organization was recognized.

When the missionaries returned to Antioch, there was rejoicing in the church. And no wonder! A notable beginning had been made. Greater things would surely follow. The west had been opened to the gospel. Evidently Christianity was no mere Jewish sect, but a world-wide movement.

TOPICS FOR STUDY

1. What Roman provinces and what smaller districts were traversed on the first missionary journey?

2. Give some account of the following places, mentioning all the inhabitants of them who appear in the New Testament, and outlining the New Testament history of their churches:—(a) Pisidian Antioch, (b) Iconium, (c) Lystra, (d) Derbe, (e) Cyprus (about four topics).

3. Summarize Paul's speech at Pisidian Antioch in your own words. Compare with it other speeches of Paul.

15: THE COUNCIL AT JERUSALEM

Study material: Acts 15: 1–35; Gal. ch. 2

The first missionary journey had extended the gospel into the centre of Asia Minor. Evidently the Church was in possession of a conquering power. Notable victories had been won. Of themselves, however, such victories could not be permanent. The geographical extension of the kingdom would have to be accompanied by an examination of principles. The reception of the Gentiles needed to be justified at the bar of reason.

The Issue

After the return of Paul and Barnabas from Asia Minor, the Gentile mission was subjected to serious criticism. This criticism should not be misunderstood. It was not directed against the Gentile mission as such: no one, either Jew or Christian, had any objection to the winning of Gentiles for the true faith; even the Pharisees compassed sea and land to make one proselyte. Not the reception of the Gentiles as such was objected to, but the terms on which they had been received. They had been received on condition of faith alone; the critics desired to impose upon them also the keeping of the Mosaic law. Would the Gentiles have to become Jews if they were to become Christians? That was the real question at issue.

The Objection

The question was raised by certain Jewish Christians who had gone down from Jerusalem to Antioch. These men were 'Judaizers'; they belonged to an extreme legalistic party in the Jerusalem church. In spirit they were Jews rather than Christians.

Undoubtedly the motives of the Judaizers were partly of a very unworthy character. Nevertheless a very plausible argument could be constructed for their position. It was by no means perfectly clear from the start that Christianity was independent of Judaism, and it was by no means clear that the keeping of the Jewish law had become unnecessary. Jesus himself had preached only to Jews, and Jesus had kept the law. The apostles also were diligent in their attendance upon the temple services. Jesus had, indeed, commanded the winning of Gentile converts, Matt. 28.19, 20. But that did not settle the question of the terms upon which the Gentiles were to be received. Christianity was founded upon Judaism; Jesus himself was the Jewish Messiah. The Jewish law, as everyone admitted, was given by God himself. By what right, therefore, was it limited? Must not the Jewish law be applied to all disciples of the Jewish Messiah? And was not the law necessary to Christian discipline? Would not the abrogation of it leave the door wide open to immorality?

The Answer

These were weighty arguments. Modern church leaders might have responded simply by an appeal to the practical necessities of the case; but fortunately the apostles were not the men to sacrifice principle to practical necessity. The arguments of the Judaizers were overcome both by an appeal to the immediate guidance of God, and also by an examination of the basic principles of the gospel. The law was indeed of divine institution, but the purpose of its institution was temporary. It was a schoolmaster unto Christ. By making the will of God clear and definite, the law exhibited the sinfulness of men. It made men hopeless, just in order that they might receive salvation not by their own works but simply by the free gift of God. The law could not indeed simply be abrogated. It pronounced a curse upon transgressors. That curse must be fulfilled. But it had been fulfilled on the cross. By his death, Christ had paid the penalty of our transgressions. The law, furthermore, in its moral aspect, was in one sense of permanent validity. God would never tolerate sin. But how should the law be kept? Not by obedience, through man's efforts, to a set of external commandments, but by a mighty inward impulse—the power of the Holy Spirit in the heart. The Christian, therefore, is saved from the law, first because Christ has paid the law's penalty for him, and second because the Spirit enables him to do all that the law commands.

The Council

In order to put an end to the discussion which was carried on by the Judaizers at Antioch against Paul and Barnabas, the two missionaries went up to Jerusalem, accompanied by certain other persons, to obtain some pronouncement from the original apostles. The Judaizers had appealed to the original apostles—let them now be refuted out of the mouths of their own champions! Paul might have hesitated to go, since his going at first sight might give the impression that he was subordinate to his brother apostles; but a revelation from God removed all doubt, Gal. 2.1, 2.

As to what happened in Jerusalem, Paul in the Epistle to the Galatians is interested in his personal relations to the original apostles and their recognition of his independent apostleship; while Luke is interested rather in the public action which was taken by the apostles and the Jerusalem church. From this difference of purpose comes the difference in the details that are narrated. Here again, as everywhere else, The Acts is clearly independent of the Pauline epistles.

The result of Paul's meeting with the original apostles was that they gave him the right hand of fellowship. They said to Paul: 'Your apostleship is quite independent of ours. We have absolutely nothing to add to you. You do not need our endorsement. God has already approved your work. You and Barnabas are missionaries to the Gentiles just as we are missionaries to the Jews. Only we hope that in one respect at least you will work for Jews as well as for Gentiles—we hope that you will remember the poor of the Jerusalem church.'

Evidently the Judaizers were repudiated by the original apostles. That is implied even in Galatians. In The Acts it is explicit. According to The Acts, after speeches by Peter and by James, the leaders of the Jerusalem church promulgated a formal decree in which the Judaizers were repudiated, the work of Paul and Barnabas approved, and the freedom of the Gentiles from the law clearly recognized. According to the decree, it is true, the Gentile Christians were to observe four rules, of which three were apparently ceremonial rather than moral in character. But these prohibitions were not imposed upon the Gentile Christians as though a part of the Jewish law were necessary to salvation. The prohibitions were rather intended simply to help solve the practical problem of mixed communities where Jews and Gentiles were united in the same church. It was not intended—even Paul did not demand it—that Jewish Christians should give up the keeping of the law. But how could they keep the law in churches where there were

Gentiles? The very association with the Gentiles would be a violation of the law. The four prohibitions of the apostolic decree were intended to remove at least a part of the difficulty. Out of love for their Jewish Christian brethren, and also in order to win non-Christian Jews to the faith, the Gentile Christians in these mixed communities were to refrain from those elements of Gentile custom which would be most abhorrent to the Jewish mind.

It will be observed that the decree was not addressed to Gentile Christians generally, but only to those in Antioch and Syria and Cilicia. The churches in these regions were closely connected with the mother church at Jerusalem. Paul entered into no obligation whatsoever to impose the decree upon the Gentile churches generally. Apparently he chose to do so in some of the churches of southern Galatia, Acts 16.4; but it is evident from the epistles that the decree was of limited range.

The Acts and Galatians

This section is based upon the assumption that Gal. 2.1–10 is an account of the same visit of Paul to Jerusalem as the visit which is described in Acts 15.1–29. That assumption is not universally accepted. Some scholars identify the event of Gal. 2.1–10, not with the Apostolic Council of Acts 15.1–29, but with the 'famine visit' of Acts 11.30; 12.25. Indeed, some maintain that the Epistle to the Galatians not only contains no account of the Apostolic Council, but was actually written before the Council was held—say at Antioch, soon after the first missionary journey. Of course this early dating of Galatians can be adopted only in connection with what is known as the 'South Galatian theory'; for according to the 'North Galatian theory' the churches addressed in the epistle were not founded until after the Council, namely at the time of Acts 16.6.

Undoubtedly the identification of Gal. 2.1–10 with Acts 11.30; 12.25, avoids some difficulties. If Gal. 2.1–10 be identified with Acts 15.1–29, then Paul in Galatians has passed over the famine visit without mention. Furthermore there are considerable differences between Gal. 2.1–10 and Acts 15.1–29. For example, if Paul is referring to the Apostolic Council, why has he not mentioned the apostolic decree of Acts 15.23–29? These difficulties, however, are not insuperable, and there are counter difficulties against the identification of Gal. 2.1–10 with the famine visit.

One such difficulty is connected with chronology. Paul says that his first visit to Jerusalem took place three years after his conversion, Gal. 1.18, and—according to the most natural interpretation of Gal. 2.1—that the visit of Gal. 2.1–10 took place fourteen years after the first visit. The conversion then occurred seventeen years before the time of Gal. 2.1–10. But if Gal. 2.1–10 describes the famine visit, then the time of Gal. 2.1–10 could not have been after about A.D. 46. Counting back seventeen years from A.D. 46 we should get A.D. 29 as the date of the conversion, which is, of course, too early.

This reasoning, it must be admitted, is not quite conclusive. The ancients had an inclusive method of reckoning time. According to this method three years after 1914 would be 1916. Hence, fourteen plus three might be only what we should call about fifteen years, instead of seventeen. Furthermore, Paul may mean in Gal. 2.1 that his conference with the apostles took place fourteen years after the conversion rather than fourteen years after the first visit.

The identification of Gal. 2.1–10 with the famine visit is not impossible. But, on the whole, the usual view, which identifies the event of Gal. 2.1–10 with the meeting at the time of the Apostolic Council of Acts 15.1–29, must be regarded as more probable. The Apostolic Council probably took place roughly at about A.D. 49. The conversion of Paul then should probably be put at about A.D. 32–34.

Peter at Antioch

That the Jerusalem decree did not obviate all practical difficulties became only too evident at Antioch a short time after the Council. The church at Antioch was mixed. It contained both Jews and Gentiles. In order to hold fellowship with their Gentile brethren the Jews relinquished the strictness of their legal observance. They even entered into table companionship with the Gentiles— which was impossible on a strict interpretation of the law even when the Gentiles observed the four prohibitions of the apostolic decree. When Peter came to Antioch he fell in with the general custom. He ate with the Gentiles. After a time, however, certain men came to Antioch from James, the head of the Jerusalem church. Why they came, or whether they had any real commission from James, we do not know. They are not directly blamed by Paul. At any rate, their coming had an unfortunate effect upon Peter. He was afraid of what they would say, and therefore withdrew from his intimacy with the Gentile Christians. For this he was taken to task by Paul. The disagreement, however, was a disagreement of practice, not principle. What Paul said to Peter in effect was this: 'You and I are perfectly agreed about salvation by faith alone, and about freedom from the law. Why, then, do you belie your principles by your vacillating conduct?' The very incident, therefore, that shows disagreement in practice is the clearest evidence of agreement in principle. In principle Paul was in essential agreement with Peter. That is a fact of enormous importance. In all probability Peter soon admitted his practical error. At any rate the Pauline epistles, as well as other evidence, show clearly that there was no permanent disagreement between Peter and Paul.

TOPICS FOR STUDY

1. Outline the life of Paul up to and including the Apostolic Council.
2. Outline the development of Gentile Christianity to the same point.
3. What was decided at the Apostolic Council? What was left to be decided?
4. Identify the leaders of the Jerusalem church who are mentioned in connection with the Apostolic Council.
5. What is known about the relations between Paul and Peter after their meeting at Antioch?
6. Why does Paul not mention the apostolic decree in Gal. 2.1–10? What is the meaning of Acts 15.21?

16: THE GOSPEL CARRIED INTO EUROPE

Study material: Acts 15:36 to 18:17

After the Judaistic opposition had been silenced, for the moment at least, by the Council at Jerusalem, the Gentile mission could proceed. The first intention was to revisit the churches which had already been founded, but by divine guidance the sphere of the mission was greatly extended.

Separation of Paul and Barnabas

Barnabas desired to take along his cousin John Mark again, but Paul was dissatisfied with the previous withdrawal of Mark at Perga. Accordingly, the two missionaries separated. Barnabas went to Cyprus, his original home; while Paul revisited the churches in Asia Minor. Evidently Barnabas had overcome the weakness which he had displayed in withdrawing from the Gentiles at Antioch, Gal. 2.13; for otherwise no further ground of separation from Paul would have been required. It is barely possible, however, that that previous weakness may have contributed to Paul's dissatisfaction. At any rate, the disagreement was not fundamental. Paul speaks of Barnabas afterwards with respect.

Paul chose as his companion Silas, a member of the Jerusalem church, who had been one of the delegates selected to bring the apostolic decree to Antioch. Apparently Silas had to be summoned expressly from Jerusalem, for he had returned thither after the delivery of the decree, Acts 15.33. Again the missionaries, when they started out, were entrusted to the grace of the Lord, v. 40.

Asia Minor

This time, the cities of central Asia Minor were reached by the direct land route through the Syrian and Cilician gates. At Lystra, there was an addition to the party in the person of Timothy. Timothy was of mixed parentage. His father was a Gentile, but his mother was a Jewish woman, whose name, Eunice, is mentioned by Paul in II Tim. 1.5.

Titus and Timothy

At Lystra, Paul had Timothy circumcised, Acts 16.3. This action has been considered strange in view of the attitude which Paul had previously assumed. At Jerusalem, only a short time before, he had absolutely refused to permit the circumcision of Titus. Evidently, too, he had regarded the matter as of fundamental importance. Had Titus been circumcised, the freedom of the Gentile Christians would have been seriously endangered.

The different policy which Paul adopted in the case of Timothy, as compared with his policy about Titus, is amply explained by the wide differences in the situation.

In the first place, when Titus was at Jerusalem, the matter of Gentile freedom was in dispute, whereas when Timothy was circumcised the question had already been settled by a formal pronouncement of the Jerusalem church. After Paul had won the victory of principle, he could afford to make concessions where no principle was involved. Timothy was recognized as a full member of the Church even before his circumcision. Circumcision was merely intended to make him a more efficient helper in work among the Jews.

In the second place—and this is even more important—Timothy was a half-Jew. It is perhaps doubtful whether Paul under any circumstances would have authorized the circumcision of a pure Gentile like Titus. But Timothy's mother was Jewish. It must always be borne in mind that Paul did not demand the relinquishment of the law on the part of Jews; and Timothy's parentage gave him at least the right of regarding himself as a Jew. If he had chosen to follow his Gentile father, the Jews could have regarded him as a renegade. His usefulness in the synagogues would have been lost. Obviously the circumcision of such a man involved nothing more than the maintenance of ancestral custom on the part of Jews. Where no principle was involved, Paul was the most concessive of men. See especially I Cor. 9.19–23. The final relinquishment of the law on the part of Jews was rightly left to the future guidance of God.

The Route Through Asia Minor

The difficulty of tracing the route of the missionaries beyond

Lystra is due largely to the difficulty of Acts 16.6. A literal translation of the decisive words in that verse would be either 'the
Phrygian and Galatian country' or 'Phrygia and the Galatian
country'. According to the advocates of the 'South Galatian
theory', 'the Galatian country' here refers not to Galatia proper
but to the southern part of the Roman province Galatia. 'The
Phrygian and Galatian country' then perhaps means 'The Phrygo-
Galatic country', or 'that part of Phrygia which is in the Roman
province Galatia'. The reference then is to Iconium, Pisidian
Antioch and the surrounding country—after the missionaries had
passed through the Lycaonian part of the province Galatia (Derbe
and Lystra) they traversed the Phrygian part of the province. The
chief objection to all such interpretations is found in the latter part
of the verse: 'having been forbidden of the Holy Spirit to speak
the word in Asia.' It looks as though the reason why they passed
through 'the Phrygian and Galatian country' was that they were
forbidden to preach in Asia. But South Galatia was directly on the
way to Asia. The impossibility of preaching in Asia could therefore
hardly have been the reason for passing through south Galatia.

Apparently, therefore, the disputed phrase refers rather to some
region which is not on the way to Asia. This requirement is satisfied if Galatia proper is meant—the country in the northern part
of the Roman province Galatia. When they got to Pisidian Antioch,
it would have been natural for them to proceed into the western
part of Asia Minor, into 'Asia'. That they were forbidden to do.
Hence they turned north, and went through Phrygia into Galatia
proper. When they got to the border country between Mysia and
Galatia proper, they tried to continue their journey north into
Bithynia, but were prevented by the Spirit. Then they turned
west, and passing through Mysia without preaching arrived at last
at the coast, at Troas.

Nothing is said here about preaching in Galatia proper. But in
Acts 18.23, in connection with the third missionary journey, it is
said that when Paul passed through 'the Galatian country and
Phrygia' he established the disciples. There could not have been
disciples in the 'Galatian country', unless there had been preaching
there on the previous journey. On the 'North Galatian' theory,
therefore, the founding of the Galatian churches to which the
epistle is directed is to be placed at Acts 16.6, and the second visit
to them, which seems to be presupposed by the Epistle, is to be
put at Acts 18.23. If it seems strange that Luke does not mention

the founding of these churches, the hurried character of this section of the narrative must be borne in mind. Furthermore, the Epistle seems to imply that the founding of the churches was rather incidental than an original purpose of the journey; for in Gal. 4.13 Paul says that it was because of an infirmity of the flesh that he preached the gospel in Galatia the former time. Apparently he had been hurrying through the country without stopping, but being detained by illness used his enforced leisure to preach to the inhabitants. It is not impossible to understand how Luke came to omit mention of such incidental preaching. On the second missionary journey attention is concentrated on Macedonia and Greece.

Nowhere else perhaps is the guidance of the Holy Spirit more strongly emphasized than in the brief summary of this journey through Asia Minor. Again and again the plans of the missionaries were countermanded by the divine will. The very form of the narrative seems to point to some greater movement that is to come. In vs. 9, 10 the mystery is explained. The gospel was to invade the west! Hence the strange, hurried, zigzag movement through Asia Minor. Hence the abrupt style of the narrative. The whole narrative is leading up to the decisive movement across the Ægean Sea.

At Troas the three missionaries were joined by Luke, the author of The Acts; for at this point the use of the 'we' begins. On the way to Greece proper, Macedonia was traversed. The two principal churches which were founded in Macedonia were the churches at Philippi and at Thessalonica.

Philippi

The work at Philippi was conducted under unusual conditions. Apparently the Jews in the city were not numerous; there was a place of prayer near the city, but it is not clear whether this was a regular synagogue.

The departure of the missionaries from Philippi was hastened by the expulsion of a demon from a slave girl. Usually it was Jewish jealousy that gave rise to persecutions; here, as afterwards at Ephesus, it was Gentile greed. The magistrates who imprisoned Paul and Silas are accurately designated by Luke by the Greek word for 'prætors' or 'duumviri'; and lictors also appear in the narrative, v. 35 (R.V. margin). Philippi was a Roman colony, with Roman magistrates. At Philippi Paul was subjected to one of the three beatings with rods which he mentions in II Cor. 11.25.

Beating with rods was a Roman punishment, whereas the 'forty stripes save one', which Paul received five times, was Jewish. Roman citizens were exempt from scourging, and though it is easy to understand why Paul may have thought it wise not to appeal to his Roman citizenship against the authorities of his own nation, it is not so clear why he did not insist on his rights before the Roman magistrates. Perhaps he desired to avoid the delay which would have been caused by such an appeal with the trial which might have followed. It may also sometimes have been difficult to gain a hearing for the plea. On the morning after his arrest Paul insisted for himself and Silas on what practically amounted to a public apology from the prætors. The ground for such action was probably not merely a justifiable pride, but rather the interests of the Christians at Philippi. It was important that the founders of the church should be regarded as something more than strolling preachers. Respect for the missionaries would be reflected upon the converts.

The church which Paul left behind at Philippi stood in a peculiarly cordial relation to him, as appears from the letter which he addressed to it. From Philippi Paul was able to accept material assistance without opening himself to any of the suspicions which hampered him elsewhere, Phil. 4.15,16. The most interesting thing of all at Philippi was the incident of the earthquake and the subsequent conversion of the jailer. This incident is narrated in the most graphic and lifelike way. Luke himself was not present, for apparently both he and Timothy had escaped imprisonment, but of course he had every opportunity of listening to those who were immediately concerned.

Thessalonica

At Thessalonica, events took a more usual course. There was the customary preaching in the synagogue, attended by the customary success among the 'God-fearers', but followed by the customary jealousy and opposition of the Jews. This time Paul and Silas and Timothy, through the care of the converts, escaped imprisonment. A certain Jason, in whose house the missionaries apparently had been staying, was required to give security to keep the peace. The narrative in The Acts need not necessarily be interpreted to mean that the departure from Thessalonica took place immediately after the three weeks mentioned in Acts 17.2. Though that interpretation is possible, it is also possible that the three sabbaths or three weeks in the synagogue were followed by a period of labour under independent conditions.

Athens

After labouring in Berœa, where the course of events was somewhat similar to that in Thessalonica, Paul arrived at last at Athens. Here he found himself in the very centre of Greek culture. Although the political importance of Athens had long ago been lost, and although even in the field of literature and art and learning Alexandria had become a successful rival, still Athens retained as a university city a position, if not of absolute pre-eminence, at least of very great prominence. The golden age was over, but even the memory of it was full of splendour.

In Athens Paul preached as usual in the synagogue to Jews and 'God-fearers'; but he also adopted another and more unusual method—he simply took his stand without introduction in the market place, and spoke to those who chanced to pass by. This method was characteristically Greek; it reminds us of the days of Socrates.

In the market place, Paul encountered certain of the Epicurean and Stoic philosophers. Both of these schools of philosophy had originated almost three hundred years before Christ, and both were prominent in the New Testament period. In their tenets they were very different. The Stoics were pantheists. They conceived of the world as a sort of great living being of which God is the soul. The world does not exist apart from God and God does not exist apart from the world. Such pantheism is far removed from the Christian belief in the living God, Maker of heaven and earth; but as against polytheism, pantheism and theism have something in common. Paul in his speech was able to start from this common ground. In ethics the Stoics were perhaps nearer to Christianity than in metaphysics. The highest good they conceived to be a life that is led in accordance with reason—that reason which is the determining principle of the world. The passions must be conquered, pleasure is worthless, the wise man is independent of external conditions. Such an ethic worked itself out in practice in many admirable virtues—in some conception of the universal brotherhood of mankind, in charity, in heroic self-denial. But it lacked the warmth and glow of Christian love, and it lacked the living God.

The Epicureans were materialists. The world, for them, was a vast mechanism. They believed in the gods, but conceived of them as altogether without influence upon human affairs. Indeed, the deliverance of man from the fear of the gods was one of the purposes of the Epicurean philosophy. The Epicureans were interested chiefly in ethics. Pleasure, according to them, is the highest good. It need not be the pleasure of the senses; indeed Epicurus, at least, the founder of the school, insisted upon a calm life undisturbed by violent passions. Nevertheless it will readily be seen how little such a philosophy had in common with Christianity.

The conditions under which Paul made his speech cannot be determined with certainty. The difficulty arises from the ambiguity of 'Areopagus'. 'Areopagus' means 'Mars' hill'. But the term was also applied to the court which held at least some of its meetings on the hill. Which meaning is intended here? Did Paul speak before the court, or did he speak on Mars' hill merely to those who were interested? On the whole, it is improbable at any rate that he was subjected to a formal trial.

The speech of Paul at Athens is one of the three important speeches of Paul, exclusive of his speeches in defence of himself at Jerusalem and at Cæsarea, which have been recorded in The Acts. These speeches are well chosen. One of them is a speech to Jews, Acts 13.16–41; one a speech to Gentiles, Acts 17.22–31; and the third a speech to Christians, Acts 20.18–35. Together they afford a very good idea of Paul's method as a missionary and as a pastor. As is to be expected, they differ strikingly from one another. Paul was large enough to comprehend the wonderful richness of Christian truth. His gospel was always the same, but he was able to adapt the presentation of it to the character of his hearers.

At Athens, an altar inscribed TO AN UNKNOWN GOD provided a starting point. The existence of such an altar is not at all surprising, although only altars to 'unknown gods' (plural instead of singular) are attested elsewhere. Perhaps the inscription on this altar indicated simply that the builder of the altar did not know to which of the numberless gods he should offer thanks for a benefit that he had received, or to which he should address a prayer to ward off calamity. Under a polytheistic religion, where every department of life had its own god, it was sometimes difficult to pick out the right god to pray to for any particular purpose. Such an altar was at any rate an expression of ignorance, and that ignorance served as a starting point for Paul. 'You are afraid that you have neglected the proper god in this case', says Paul in effect. 'Yes, indeed, you have. You have neglected a very important god indeed, you have neglected the one true God, who made the world and all things therein.'

In what follows, Paul appeals to the truth contained in Stoic pantheism. His words are of peculiar interest at the present day, when pantheism is rampant even within the Church. There is a great truth in pantheism. It emphasizes the immanence of God. But the truth of pantheism is contained also in theism. The theist, as well as the pantheist, believes that God is not far from every one of us, and that in him we live and move and have our being. The theist, as well as the pantheist, can say, 'Closer is he than breathing, nearer than hands and feet'. The theist accepts all the truth of pantheism, but avoids the error. God is present in the world—not one sparrow 'shall fall on the ground without your Father'—but he is not limited to the world. He is not just another name for the totality of things, but an awful, mysterious, holy, free and sovereign Person. He is present in the world, but also Master of the world.

Corinth

If the work at Athens could show only small results, the work at Corinth was gloriously successful. Corinth was not a university city, but a centre of commerce. Situated on an isthmus, it was a meeting place for the trade between east and west. Here, amid the seething population of a great commercial city, in the face of all the hideous immorality of the ancient world, was planted a flourishing church.

At Corinth Paul met two interesting persons, who were destined to play an important part in the subsequent history. They were Aquila, a Jew of Pontus, and Priscilla his wife. The edict of Claudius, by which they had been driven from Rome, is mentioned by the Roman historian Suetonius. The words of Suetonius— though he himself did not understand the matter—are usually thought to indicate that the reason why Claudius expelled the Jews was that tumults had arisen through disputes between the Christians and the other Jews. If so, Aquila and Priscilla may have been Christians before they left Rome. It is possible, however, that they were converted by Paul.

At any rate the reason why Paul lived with them was that both he and Aquila practised the same trade, the trade of tent-making. It may seem rather surprising that Paul should have known how to work with his hands; for, as we have seen, his family was evidently well-to-do. But, by a salutary Jewish custom, a rabbi was expected always to learn a trade. Tent-making was part of Paul's rabbinical preparation; and now it stood him in good stead. His reasons for not accepting support from the Corinthian Christians are set forth in I Cor. ch. 9; II Cor. 11.7–15. Corinth was not the only place where he laboured with his hands. He had done the same thing, for example, at Thessalonica, I Thess. 2.9; II Thess. 3.7–9; Phil. 4.16. Compare I Cor. 4.12.

The work in Corinth proceeded on the lines that were made natural by the situation. At first there was preaching in the synagogue; and then, on account of opposition, the specifically Jewish work was given up. This time the house of Titus (or Titius) Justus, a 'God-fearer', provided the necessary centre of operations. From the year and a half and more which Paul spent in Corinth Luke has narrated scarcely anything except what happened near the beginning and near the end. Fortunately Paul's two epistles fill out the picture.

At the expiration of eighteen months, the opposition of the Jews culminated in an accusation of Paul before the Roman magistrate. The result of the accusation has already been studied in connection with the Roman and with the Jewish background of Christianity. The judge before whom the case was brought was Gallio, proconsul of Achaia. Achaia was at this time a senatorial province of which Corinth was the capital. Gallio is well known to secular history. He was a brother of Seneca, the famous Stoic writer. By an inscription discovered at Delphi, the date of Gallio's proconsulate has been determined. The inscription shows that Gallio was proconsul in A.D. 52, and since proconsuls held office for only one year, the date of Paul's stay in Corinth is fixed with considerable accuracy. Since it has been very difficult to date events in apostolic history, the Gallio inscription is of great value. By counting forward and backward from A.D. 52, something like a chronology of the apostolic age can be constructed.

TOPICS FOR STUDY

1. Trace the route of Paul and Silas on the map.

2. Summarize all that can be learned (a) about Silas and (b) about Timothy, from The Acts and from the Pauline epistles (two topics).

3. Compare Paul's speech at Athens (a) with the speech at Lystra and (b) with the speech at Pisidian Antioch.

4. By using all the information which Luke expressly gives, and by estimating periods of time which he leaves indefinite, determine approximately the date of some important events in apostolic history from the

conversion of Paul to his imprisonment in Jerusalem, using the pro-consulate of Gallio as a fixed point.

5. What is known about the Crispus who is mentioned in Acts 18.8? Is anything else known about Sosthenes except what is told in Acts 18.17? Who beat Sosthenes and why did they do it?

The Principles and Practice of the Gospel

17: ENCOURAGEMENT FOR NEW CONVERTS

Study material: The First and Second Epistles to the Thessalonians

In the history of early Christianity the really surprising thing is not so much that Gentile churches were founded as that, after they were founded, they endured. The materials of which they were composed were woefully faulty. They were surrounded with heathenism and immorality. They were subjected to persecutions. How could the tide of heathenism be kept out?

The Christian missionaries were carrying the war into the enemies' country. After every new conquest, annoying guerilla warfare was set up behind them. Heathenism and immorality, in a thousand forms, were always pressing in upon the territory that had been won. The early converts were often made of very feeble clay. They had only begun to understand the principles of the Christian life. When Paul had left them, when they were thrown upon their own resources, would they not simply drift back to their old ways?

This question must always have filled Paul with anxiety. In facing it he needed all his faith in the power of God. Anxiety must have been particularly intense when, as so often, Paul was driven out of a new church before his work in it was done. With what eagerness, after such a forcible departure, must Paul have awaited the first news of the youthful church!

In First Thessalonians we discover just how Paul felt when the first news arrived. First Thessalonians is the only one of the Pauline Epistles which was written at just such a time. Hence its peculiar interest.

Occasion of First Thessalonians

The situation in which the Epistle was written is very simple. Paul had been driven out of Thessalonica by persecution. From Thessalonica he had gone to Berœa. Thither also the hatred of the

Jews had pursued him. From Beroea he had gone to Athens. At Athens his preaching had produced only meagre results. But it was not only his immediate work that troubled him. He was thinking also about the Thessalonian church which he had left behind. Some missionaries would not have worried. They would simply have done their duty and not cared much about the result. But Paul was not that kind of man. He put his very heart and soul into his work. When he founded a new church he bestowed upon it the very depths of his affection. So it was at Thessalonica. He had laboured hard to save those men and women from spiritual death. Would his labour be all in vain?

Certainly the church at Thessalonica gave reason for anxiety. It was composed chiefly of Gentiles, I Thess. 1.9. These Gentiles had been leading the degraded life of the ancient world. The very idea of the one God had been new to them. They had never been accustomed to associate morality at all with religion. It is hard for us to realize the contrast between the old life of these converts and the new. All of their thinking and all of their habits were suffused with superstition and idolatry. How could they possibly be prevented from sinking back to the lower plane?

Some of them, it is true, had been prepared by Judaism. Some had been 'God-fearers' before they became Christians. The value of the synagogue as a preparation for Christianity was undoubtedly enormous. At Thessalonica, however, many of the converts, if not the majority of them, came into the Church fresh from heathenism. Persecutions, moreover, as well as the allurements of the old life, were a source of grave danger. Was Christian conviction rooted deep enough to stand the heat of the day?

The presence of Timothy was, indeed, a safeguard. Timothy had been sent back to them from Athens. But Timothy was not Paul; and there had been an interval when even Timothy had not been with them. After the founding of the church the Thessalonian Christians had been left, for a time at least, to their own devices. The period of Paul's presence with them was almost certainly brief. Moreover, it was interrupted in a way that might well have seemed disheartening. There had been little time for the Thessalonian Christians to become firmly grounded in the Christian life.

Paul had every reason, then, to await the report of Timothy with anxiety. At last, however, at Corinth, Timothy arrived, and the news he brought was good. Paul did not delay his answer. At once, in First Thessalonians, he gave expression to his joy. It is a fine, warm, simple letter, full of encouragement not only to the Thessalonian Christians but to all generations of the Christian Church.

Contents of First Thessalonians

The first three chapters are devoted to an unstudied expression of Paul's feelings since he had left Thessalonica and to an outpouring of thanksgiving for the good news which he had just received. Apparently Paul had feared that the character of his work at Thessalonica had been misrepresented. Such misrepresentation perhaps came from the Jews. In refutation of it, it was sufficient to call to mind the unselfishness and sincerity of his conduct. He had not even accepted material assistance from the Thessalonian Christians, but had laboured with his hands. Surely he could not be accused of greed. There had been no flattery and deceit about his message. On the contrary he had proclaimed to them in all humility the pure gospel of God. Apparently Paul was afraid also lest his sudden departure and his failure to return might be interpreted to indicate coldness toward them. He takes pains, therefore, to say how earnestly he had longed to see them. Finally, he says, let them not be discouraged by their persecutions. He himself had told them that afflictions were to come.

If the first three chapters are concerned primarily with the past, the last two are concerned with the future. Naturally the Thessalonian church, though making satisfactory progress, was by no means perfect. Much remained to be done.

In the first place, there was constant danger of impurity and of covetousness. In the second place, a tendency to idleness had made itself felt on the part of some. Perhaps this tendency was connected with the expectation of the immediate coming of Christ. If the end of the present age of the world was immediately at hand, why be diligent in business? At any rate, in the third place, the Thessalonians needed to be reassured with regard to the manner of Christ's coming. Apparently they had expected all Christians to live until Christ should appear. They had therefore been puzzled and disheartened by the deaths that had occurred. Paul had to explain that if he and some of the Christians should be alive at the coming of Christ, they would have no advantage over those who had died; for the dead would be raised up to meet the Lord. The time of Christ's coming is uncertain. But the true Christian need not be caught unprepared.

Finally, in a series of brief commands the Christians are urged to live a quiet, sober, and yet fervent life. The last two chapters of the Epistle, though earnest, are not severe. There were faults; but evidently the life of the church was fundamentally sound. The marvel had been accomplished. A Christian church had been established in the midst of the heathen world. Paul knew to whom thanks were due. They were due to God. Christianity was not the work of men. The converts were weak and ignorant. Paul could not be everywhere at once. But the Spirit of God was caring everywhere for his Church.

Second Thessalonians

Second Thessalonians was written undoubtedly very soon after First Thessalonians, and also at Corinth. The same two men are associated with Paul in the address; the condition of the Thessalonian church has not materially altered; and finally, the two Epistles themselves are strikingly similar. Since the writing of First Thessalonians Paul had heard that what he had said in that letter had not quite accomplished all that he had desired. Indeed some things had apparently been misunderstood. Some of the moral defects also had become more acute. Accordingly Paul wrote the second letter as a sort of supplement to the first. Perhaps, before writing, he even read over again his rough draft of the former letter. At any rate, since his teaching was being misunderstood, it was natural for him to recall to his mind exactly what he had already said. That explains the similarity between the two Epistles. In Second Thessalonians, parts of First Thessalonians are reiterated, with explanations and additions.

The chief addition is the instruction about the second coming of Christ which is contained in II Thess. 2.1–12. Apparently some people in Thessalonica had misinterpreted Paul's teaching, as though he meant that the day of Christ was already present, II Thess. 2.2 (R.V.). In reply, Paul calls attention to certain elements in the oral teaching which he had given at the beginning. Christ will not come until 'the lawless one' has been revealed. At present there is something which restrains that supreme manifestation of evil.

This passage is exceedingly difficult. Many different interpretations have been proposed. The restraining force to which Paul refers—that which holds lawlessness in check—has often been thought to be the Roman Empire. The manifestation of 'the lawless one' is for us as for the Thessalonian Christians still in the future, and only the future can bring a complete interpretation.

The Second Coming of Christ

Undoubtedly the second advent, with the events which are immediately to precede it, occupies a central position in the Thessalonian Epistles. Evidently the expectation of Christ's coming was a fundamental part of Paul's belief, and had a fundamental place in his preaching. 'Ye turned unto God from idols, to serve a living and true God, and to wait for his Son from heaven'—these words show clearly how the hope of Christ's appearing was instilled in the converts from the very beginning, I Thess. 1.9, 10. To serve the living God and to wait for his Son—that is the sum and substance of the Christian life. All through the Epistles the thought of the Parousia—the 'presence' or 'coming'—of Christ appears as a master motive. I Thess. 2.19; 3.13; 4.13 to 5.11, 23, 24; II Thess. 1.5 to 2.12.

This emphasis upon the second coming of Christ is explained if Paul expected Christ to come in the near future. The imminence of the Parousia for Paul appears to be indicated by I Thess. 4.15: 'For this we say unto you by the word of the Lord, that we that are alive, that are left unto the coming of the Lord, shall in no wise precede them that are fallen asleep.' This verse is often thought to indicate that Paul confidently expected before his death to witness the coming of the Lord. Apparently he classes himself with those who 'are left unto the coming of the Lord' as over against those who will suffer death. In the later epistles, it is further said, Paul held a very different view. From Second Corinthians on, he faced ever more definitely the thought of death, II Cor. 5.1, 8; Phil. 1.20–26. A comparison of I Cor. 15.51 with II Cor. 5.1, 8 is thought to indicate that the deadly peril which Paul incurred between the writing of the two Corinthian Epistles, II Cor. 1.8, 9, had weakened his expectation of living until Christ should come. After he had once despaired of life, he could hardly expect with such perfect confidence to escape the experience of death. The possibility of death was too strong to be left completely out of sight.

Plausible as such a view is, it can be held only with certain reservations.

In the first place, we must not exaggerate the nearness of the Parousia according to Paul, even in the earliest period; for in II Thess. 2.1–12 the Thessalonians are reminded of certain events that must occur before Christ would come. The expression of the former Epistle, I Thess. 5.2, that the day of the Lord would come as a thief in the night, was to be taken as a warning to unbelievers to repent while there was yet time, not as a ground for neglecting ordinary provision for the future. In Second Thessalonians Paul finds it necessary to calm the overstrained expectations of the Thessalonian Christians.

Furthermore, it is not only in the earlier epistles that expressions occur which seem to suggest that the Parousia is near: Rom. 13.11; Phil. 4.5. And then it is evident from II Cor. 11.23–29 and from I Cor. 15.30–32 that Paul had undergone dangers before the one mentioned in II Cor. 1.8, 9, so that there is no reason to suppose that that one event caused any sudden change in his expectations.

Lastly, in I Cor. 6.14 Paul says that 'God both raised the Lord, and will raise up us through his power'. If that refers to the literal resurrection, then here Paul classes himself among those who are to die; for if he lived to the Parousia, then there would be no need for him to be raised up.

It is therefore very doubtful whether we can put any very definite change in the apostle's expectations as to his living or dying between First Corinthians and Second Corinthians. A gradual development in his feeling about the matter there no doubt was. During the early part of his life his mind dwelt less upon the prospect of death than it did after perils of all kinds had made that prospect more and more imminent. But at no time did the apostle regard the privilege of living until the Parousia as a certainty to be put at all in the same category with the Christian hope itself. Especially the passage in First Thessalonians can be rightly interpreted only in the light of the historical occasion for it. Until certain members of the church had died, the Thessalonian Christians had never faced the possibility of dying before the second coming of Christ. Hence they were troubled. Would the brethren who had fallen asleep miss the benefits of Christ's kingdom? Paul writes to reassure them. He does not contradict their hope of living till the coming of Christ, for God had not revealed to him that that hope would not be realized. But he tells them that, supposing that hope to be justified, even then they will have no advantage over their dead brethren. He classes himself with those who were still alive and might therefore live till Christ should come, as over against those who were already dead and could not therefore live till Christ should come.

Certain passages in the epistles of Paul, which are not confined to any one period of his life, seem to show that at any rate he did not exclude the very real possibility that Christ might come in the near future. But such an expectation of the early coming of Christ was just as far removed as possible from the expectations of fanatical chiliasts. It did not lead Paul to forget that the times and the seasons are entirely in the hand of God. It had no appreciable effect upon his ethics, except to make it more intense, more fully governed by the thought of the judgment seat of Christ. It did not prevent him from laying far-reaching plans, it did not prevent his developing a great philosophy of future history in Romans, chapters 9 to 11. How far he was from falling into the error he combated in Second Thessalonians! Despite his view of the temporary character of the things that are seen, how sane and healthy was his way of dealing with practical problems! He did his duty, and left the details of the future to God. Hence it is hard to discover what Paul thought as to how soon Christ would come—naturally so, for Paul did not try to discover it himself.

TOPICS FOR STUDY

1. Give a complete summary (a) of First Thessalonians and (b) of Second Thessalonians (two topics).
2. Supply Biblical references in support of what is said in the chapter.
3. Trace the movements of Silas and Timothy from the time when Paul left Thessalonica up to the writing of the first Epistle.
4. Summarize the teaching of the Thessalonian Epistles about the second coming of Christ and related events.
5. Supplement Luke's narrative of the founding of the church at Thessalonica by the information to be collected from the Thessalonian Epistles.

18: THE CONFLICT WITH THE JUDAIZERS

Study material: Acts 18: 18 to 19: 40; The Epistle to the Galatians

After having been brought before the judgment seat of Gallio, Paul remained many days in Corinth. His work was not suddenly interrupted as at Thessalonica and at many other places. The proconsul Gallio proved to be less susceptible to Jewish influence than lesser magistrates had been.

Instead of returning by the land route through Macedonia, Paul went direct by sea to Ephesus. At Ephesus, Aquila and Priscilla, who had accompanied Paul so far, were left behind. Paul contented himself, this time, with only a very brief stay, and after a sea voyage landed at Cæsarea on the coast of Palestine. After landing, 'he went up and saluted the church'. What church is meant here—the church at Cæsarea or the great church at Jerusalem? The latter view is more probable. Since Cæsarea was ordinarily used as the seaport for Jerusalem, the name Jerusalem did not have to be mentioned. Probably, then, we have here Paul's fourth visit to Jerusalem after his conversion.

After spending some time in Antioch, Paul went through the Galatian country and Phrygia, thus beginning the third missionary journey. These were the same regions that had been visited on the second journey, Acts 16.6; but this time they were taken in the reverse order. Probably Galatia proper is meant, rather than some other part of the Roman province Galatia. After passing through the high central portion of Asia Minor, Paul came at last to the coastal plain, to Ephesus, Acts 19.1.

In Ephesus, Paul was able to preach somewhat longer than usual in the synagogue; but finally, after three months, he was driven out, as in so many other cities, and engaged for over two years in a purely Gentile work. A few of the incidents of this Ephesian residence are narrated by Luke, and narrated with characteristic vividness and accuracy. The school of Tyrannus, the Jewish exorcists, the books of magic, Demetrius the silversmith, the craftsmen, the great temple of Diana, the assembly in the theatre, the Asiarchs, the town clerk—these are all described in a way that betokens the genuine historian, dependent upon first-hand information. There is scarcely any more absorbing piece of narrative, even in The Acts.

The Date of Galatians and the Location of the Churches

At some time during the three-year stay of Paul at Ephesus, and probably during the earlier rather than the later part of that period, the Epistle to the Galatians seems to have been written. This dating is dependent upon the correctness of the 'North Galatian theory', which places 'the churches of Galatia' to which the Epistle is addressed in the northern part of the Roman province Galatia, and supposes that the churches had been founded on the journey described in Acts 16.6, and revisited at the time of Acts 18.23. Another widely prevalent theory—the 'South Galatian theory'—identifies 'the churches of Galatia' with the congregations at Pisidian Antioch, Iconium, Lystra and Derbe, in the southern part of the Roman province Galatia. Since these congregations were formed on the first missionary journey, the South Galatian theory admits of an earlier dating of the Epistle than is possible on the North Galatian theory. It is very difficult to decide between the North Galatian and the South Galatian theories. Weighty arguments have been adduced on both sides. Provisionally, the North Galatian view has been adopted in the arrangement of this book.

Fortunately, the interpretation of the Epistle is very largely independent of 'the Galatian question'. Wherever the churches addressed in the Epistle are to be placed, at any rate the situation that prevailed in those churches—the situation that gave rise to the Epistle—can be reconstructed pretty clearly on the basis of the Epistle itself, without reference to the narrative in The Acts.

The Situation Presupposed by the Epistle

'The churches of Galatia' to which Paul writes had been founded by Paul himself, Gal. 1.8; 4.12–20. Their membership was composed chiefly of Gentiles; for it was just to prevent the Galatian Christians from becoming Jews that the Epistle was written. At Paul's first visit to the churches he had been ill, indeed his illness seems actually to have been the cause of his preaching to them.

This illness was a temptation to them to reject his message, for physical weakness was in that day regarded with loathing rather than with sympathy, as a visitation of the divine wrath. Yet the Galatians had overcome the temptation nobly; they had received Paul 'as an angel of God, even as Christ Jesus'. Gal. 4.14.

Paul's preaching in Galatia no doubt included all the fundamental elements of the gospel. Jesus Christ crucified, he says, was openly set forth before their eyes as on a great placard or picture. The eager faith of the Galatians was followed by the bestowal of the Spirit, who manifested himself not only in a holier life, but also in miraculous powers. Evidently the Spirit became the possession of all who believed, Gal. 3.1–5.

Probably Paul had visited the churches a second time before the Epistle was written, Gal. 4.13; and it was probably at this second visit that he took occasion to warn them against false teaching, Gal. 1.9. The danger, however, seems not to have been imminent at that time. The early part of the churches' life was altogether satisfactory. 'Ye were running well', says Paul, Gal. 5.7.

A short time before the Epistle was written, however, certain Jewish false teachers had entered into the churches from the outside. These men throughout the letter are sharply distinguished from the Galatian Christians themselves, whom despite their faults Paul addresses as 'brethren'. The false teachers were 'Judaizers', and seem to have been very much like the Judaizers who are described in Acts 15.1, 5, 24. They insisted on observance of the Mosaic law, in addition to faith in Christ, as necessary to salvation. The Gentiles, they said, must unite themselves with the chosen people; they must become Jews if they were to become Christians.

In order to gain a hearing for this new teaching, the Judaizers were obliged to undermine the authority of Paul. Paul, they said, had received his apostleship only through the mediatorship of those who had known Jesus on earth and had been commissioned directly by him. If an apostle, therefore, he was at best only an apostle of the second rank. His authority was certainly not equal to that of Peter and the rest. Furthermore he was not even consistent. He adapted his message to the likes and dislikes of men. On occasion he could even advocate what he now opposed, Gal. 1.10; 5.11.

The activity of the Judaizers had been surprisingly successful. The Galatian Christians had already begun to waver in their devotion to Paul, Gal. 4.15, 16; and already they had begun to give heed to the claims of the law. Already they were observing Jewish fasts and feasts, v. 10. The decisive step, it is true, had not yet been taken. They had not yet united themselves definitely with the people of Israel. But they were in grave danger. If they were to be saved for the gospel, there was no time to lose.

Naturally the Epistle to the Galatians is a polemic from beginning to end—and a powerful, sharp polemic, too. It has just one purpose—to prevent the Galatian Christians from yielding to the demands of the Judaizers.

The Address. Gal. 1.1–5

The addresses of the Pauline epistles are never merely formal. Paul does not wait for the beginning of the letter proper in order to say what he has in mind. Even the epistolary forms are suffused with the deepest religious feeling.

The opening of the present letter is anticipatory of what is to follow. Dividing the opening into three parts—the nominative (name and title of the writer), the dative (name of those to whom the letter is addressed), and the greeting—it will be observed that every one of these parts has its peculiarity as compared with the other Pauline epistles.

The peculiarity of the nominative is the remarkable addition beginning with 'not from men', which is a summary of the first great division of the Epistle, Paul's defence against the personal attack of his opponents. Since the Epistle to the Galatians is polemic from beginning to end, it is not surprising that the very first word after the bare name and title of the author is 'not'. Paul cannot mention his title 'apostle'—in the addresses of First and Second Thessalonians he had not thought it necessary to mention it at all—without thinking of the way in which in Galatia it was misrepresented. 'My apostleship,' he says, 'came not only from Christ, but directly from Christ.'

The peculiarity of the dative is its brevity—not 'beloved of God, called to be saints', or the like, but just the bare and formal 'to the churches of Galatia'. The situation was not one which called for pleasant words!

The greeting is the least varied part in the addresses of the Pauline epistles. The long addition to the greeting in Galatians is absolutely unique. It is a summary of the second and central main division of the epistle, Paul's defence of his gospel. 'Christ has died to free you. The Judaizers in bringing you into bondage are

making of none effect the grace of Christ, manifested on the cross.'
That is the very core of the letter. In all of the Pauline epistles
there is scarcely a passage more characteristic of the man than the
first five verses of Galatians. An ordinary writer would have been
merely formal in the address. Not so Paul!

The exultant supernaturalism of the address should be noticed.
This supernaturalism appears, in the first place, in the sphere of
external history—'God the Father, who raised him from the dead.'
Pauline Christianity is based upon the miracle of the resurrection.
Supernaturalism appears also, however, in the sphere of Christian
experience—'who gave himself for our sins, that he might deliver
us out of this present evil world.' Christianity is no mere easy
development of the old life, no mere improvement of the life, but
a new life in a new world. In both spheres, supernaturalism is
being denied in the modern Church. Pauline Christianity is very
different from what is going under the name of Christianity today.

Finally, this passage will serve to exhibit Paul's lofty view of the
person of Christ. 'Neither through man,' says Paul, 'but through
Jesus Christ.' Jesus Christ is here distinguished sharply from men
and placed clearly on the side of God. What is more, even the
Judaizers evidently accepted fundamentally the same view. Paul
said, 'Not by man, but by Jesus Christ'; the Judaizers said, 'Not
by Jesus Christ, but by man.' But if so, then the Judaizers, no less
than Paul, distinguished Jesus sharply from ordinary humanity.
About other things there was debate, but about the person of Christ
Paul appears in harmony even with his opponents. Evidently the
original apostles had given the Judaizers on this point no slightest
excuse for differing from Paul. The heavenly Christ of Paul was
also the Christ of those who had walked and talked with Jesus of
Nazareth. They had seen Jesus subject to all the petty limitations
of human life. Yet they thought him divine! Could they have been
deceived?

The Purpose of the Epistle. Gal. 1.6–10

The thanksgiving for the Christian state of the readers, which
appears in practically every other of the Pauline epistles, is here
conspicuous by its absence. Here it would have been a mockery.
The Galatians were on the point of giving up the gospel. There
was just a hope of saving them. The letter was written in a desperate crisis. Pray God it might not be too late! No time here for
words of thanks!

In vs. 6–10, Paul simply states the purpose of the letter in a few uncompromising words: 'You are falling away from the gospel and I am writing to stop you.'

Paul's Defence of His Apostolic Authority.
Gal. 1.11 to 2.21

After stating, Gal. 1.11, 12, the thesis that is to be proved in this section, Paul defends his independent apostolic authority by three main arguments.

In the first place, vs. 13–24, he was already launched upon his work as apostle to the Gentiles before he had even come into any effective contact with the original apostles. Before his conversion, he had been an active persecutor. His conversion was wrought, not, like an ordinary conversion, through human agency, but by an immediate act of Christ. After his conversion it was three years before he saw any of the apostles. Then he saw only Peter (and James) and that not long enough to become, as his opponents said, a disciple.

In the second place, Gal. 2.1–10, when he finally did hold a conference with the original apostles, they themselves, the very authorities to whom the Judaizers appealed, recognized that his authority was quite independent of theirs, and, like theirs, of directly divine origin.

In the third place, Gal. 2.11–21, so independent was his authority that on one occasion he could even rebuke the chief of the original apostles himself. What Paul said at that time to Peter happened to be exactly what he wanted to say, in the Epistle, to the Galatians. This section, therefore, forms a transition to the second main division of the Epistle. It has sometimes been thought surprising that Paul does not say how Peter took his rebuke. The conclusion has even been drawn that if Peter had acknowledged his error Paul would have been sure to say so. Such reasoning ignores the character of this section. In reporting the substance of what he said to Peter, Paul has laid bare the very depths of his own life. To return, after such a passage, to the incident at Antioch would have been pedantic and unnecessary. Long before the end of the second chapter Paul has forgotten all about Peter, all about Antioch, and all about the whole of his past history. He is thinking only of the grace of Christ, and how some men are trampling it under foot. O foolish Galatians, to desert so great a salvation!

E

Paul's Defence of His Gospel. Gal. 3.1 to 5.12

Salvation cannot be earned by human effort, but must be received simply as a free gift. Christ has died to save us from the curse of the law: to submit again to the yoke of bondage is disloyalty to him—that is the great thesis that Paul sets out to prove.

He proves it first by an argument from experience, Gal. 3.1–5. You received the Holy Spirit, in palpable manifestation, before you ever saw the Judaizers, before you ever thought of keeping the Mosaic law. You received the Spirit by faith alone. How then can you now think that the law is necessary? Surely there can be nothing higher than the Spirit.

In the second place, there is an argument from Scripture. Not those who depend upon the works of the law, but those who believe, have the benefit of the covenant made with Abraham, vs. 6–22.

In the third place, by the use of various figures, Paul contrasts the former bondage with the present freedom, Gal. 3.23 to 4.7. The life under the law was a period of restraint like that of childhood, preliminary to faith in Christ. The law was intended to produce the consciousness of sin, in order that the resultant hopelessness might lead men to accept the Saviour, vs. 23–25. But now all Christians alike, both Jews and Gentiles, are sons of God in Christ, and therefore heirs of the promise made to Abraham, vs. 26–29. Being sons of God, with all the glorious freedom of sonship, with the Spirit crying, 'Abba, Father', in the heart, how can we think of returning to the miserable bondage of an external and legalistic religion? Gal. 4.1–11.

In the fourth place, Paul turns away from argument to make a personal appeal, vs. 12–20. What has become of your devotion to me? Surely I have not become your enemy just because I tell you the truth. The Judaizers are estranging you from me. Listen to me, my spiritual children, even though I can speak to you only through the cold medium of a letter!

In the fifth place, Paul, in his perplexity, bethinks himself of one more argument. It is an argument that would appeal especially to those who were impressed by the Judaizers' method of using the Old Testament, but it also has permanent validity. The fundamental principle, says Paul, for which I am arguing, the principle of grace, can be illustrated from the story of Ishmael and Isaac. Ishmael had every prospect of being the heir to Abraham. It seemed impossible for the aged Abraham to have another son.

Nature was on Ishmael's side. But nature was overruled. So it is today. As far as nature is concerned, the Jews are the heirs of Abraham—they have all the outward marks of sonship. But God has willed otherwise. He has chosen to give the inheritance to the heirs according to promise. The principle of the divine choice, operative on a small scale in the acceptance of Isaac, is operative now on a large scale in the acceptance of the Gentile church.

Finally, Paul concludes the central section of the Epistle by emphasizing the gravity of the crisis, Gal. 5.1–12. Do not be deceived. Circumcision, as the Judaizers advocate it, is no innocent thing; it means the acceptance of a law-religion. You must choose either the law or grace; you cannot have both.

The Results of Paul's Gospel. Gal. 5.13 to 6.10

In this third main division of the Epistle Paul exhibits the practical working of faith. Paul's gospel is more powerful than the teaching of the Judaizers. Try to keep the law in your own strength and you will fail, for the flesh is too strong. But the Spirit is stronger than the flesh, and the Spirit is received by faith.

Conclusion. Gal. 6.11–18

This concluding section, if not the whole Epistle, was written with Paul's own hand, v. 11. In his other letters Paul dictated everything but a brief closing salutation.

In the closing section, Paul lays the alternative once more before his readers. The Judaizers have worldly aims, they boast of worldly advantages; but the true Christian boasts of nothing but the cross. Christianity, as here portrayed, is not the gentle, easy-going doctrine that is being mistaken for it today. It is no light thing to say, 'The world hath been crucified unto me, and I unto the world.' But the result is a new creature!

Permanent Value of Galatians

The Judaizers are dead and gone, but not the issue that they raised. Faith or works—that is as much as ever a living issue. 'Salvation by character' is just a modern form of Judaizing, and a modern form of bondage to the law. Christ crucified needs still to be held up before our eyes; and still we need to receive by faith the gracious, life-giving power of his Spirit. Paul in Galatians was fighting the age-long battle of the Christian Church. 'Just as I am, without one plea but that thy blood was shed for me'—these words would never have been written if the Judaizers had won.

TOPICS FOR STUDY

1. Summarize in your own words (a) Gal. chs. 1 and 2; (b) ch. 3.1 to 5.12; (c) ch. 5.13 to 6.18 (three topics).

2. Where were 'the churches of Galatia' to which the Epistle to the Galatians was addressed? Discuss the two possible views.

3. Compare the address of the Epistle to the Galatians, Gal. 1.1–5, with the addresses of the other Pauline epistles, and show how the peculiarities of this address are connected with the peculiarities of the whole Epistle.

4. Give a full account of the Judaizers, using both The Acts and Galatians.

5. What does Paul mean in Galatians by 'the law'? What is the importance for us of his teaching about the law? Compare Rom. 2.14–16.

19: PROBLEMS OF A GENTILE CHURCH

Study material: The First Epistle to the Corinthians

The First Epistle to the Corinthians affords more information than any other New Testament book about the internal affairs of an apostolic church. The Book of The Acts is interested rather in the geographical extension of Christianity than in the details of congregational life. Most of the epistles of Paul are concerned too exclusively with individual problems to offer any general survey of the churches to which they are addressed. The Epistle to the Galatians, for example, is directed altogether against the Judaizers: in view of the one imminent danger, Paul had no time to concern himself with other matters. The Second Epistle to the Corinthians is very largely personal: it is devoted to a defence of the apostle and of his ministry. The Thessalonian Epistles are more general in character, but they were addressed to an infant church, whose life had not yet become complex enough to be typical. First Corinthians alone presents the practical problems of an early church in the fulness of their puzzling variety.

Value of the Epistle
Such an Epistle is of the highest value. Its value, in the first place, is historical. After all, history is something more than a succession of a few great events. The great events are interspersed with periods of almost imperceptible development; the great actions are prepared for by long, level years of humdrum daily life. So it is with the early Church. Christianity can never be understood if attention is confined exclusively to the great men or the exciting crises. Christian life after all has its dreary valleys as well as its heights of vision. It was all very well for the humble tradesmen or the downtrodden slaves of Corinth to listen to the glorious message of the one holy and merciful God and the new, free brotherhood of his children. But after the first flush of joy, the stern facts of life came

pressing in again with double force. It was all very well to turn from idols to serve the living and true God. But the whole life of that day was suffused with idolatry. How could the Christian avoid contamination? Where should he draw the line? The enthusiasm of the early Church could not deliver men from the petty problems of human life; and in many respects these problems were even far more perplexing then than they are today. How ought Christian faith to work out in practice?—that was a difficult question for the Corinthian Christians to answer. Only by understanding these practical difficulties can we sympathize with the Church's failures—and only so can we appreciate, too, the full wonder of her final triumph.

The value of such an Epistle as First Corinthians is, however, practical as well as historical. First Corinthians deals with certain concrete problems of an ancient church. Those problems are not our problems. Conceivably they might have been discussed in a way which for us would be at best of purely historical interest. But as a matter of fact they were discussed by Paul, and Paul had the remarkable faculty of viewing even petty problems in the light of eternal principles. Here is the remarkable thing about First Corinthians—every question that is discussed in it is tested by the fire of evangelical truth. Hence the permanent value of the Epistle. How to apply the lofty principles of the gospel to the routine of daily life is the fundamental problem of Christian conduct. That problem cannot be solved for any man in detail, for the details of life are of endless variety; but the method of solution has been set forth in First Corinthians.

Occasion of the Epistle

The history of Paul's relations to the Corinthian church up to the writing of the Epistle is not difficult to reconstruct. The church was founded on the second missionary journey, Acts 18.1–18. It was composed, chiefly at any rate, of Gentiles, I Cor. 12.2; and chiefly, though not exclusively, of men of humble position—no doubt including many slaves, I Cor. 1.26–29. Paul does not appear to have visited the church more than once before he wrote the Epistle. He had, however, written to the Corinthians a letter earlier than First Corinthians, a letter which has been lost. In this lost letter, he had cautioned the Corinthians against holding Christian fellowship with persons of impure life. First Corinthians was written from Ephesus, I Cor. 16.8, during the three-year period described in Acts 19.1 to 20.1. It was certainly not written during the first visit of Paul to Ephesus at the conclusion of the second journey, Acts 18.19–21, for in the Epistle Paul holds in prospect a journey, not to Jerusalem or Antioch, but to Corinth. Apparently it was written in the spring of the year: Paul intends to remain in Ephesus up to Pentecost, I Cor. 16.8. Before writing the Epistle Paul had dispatched Timothy to Corinth; yet apparently he expects the Epistle to arrive before Timothy, I Cor. 4.17; 16.10. He seems, indeed, not to be quite certain whether Timothy will arrive at all. The conditions of the problem are all satisfied if Timothy was sent, not to Corinth direct, but first of all to other churches. It is not impossible, therefore, to identify the mission of Timothy which is mentioned in the Epistle with the mission of Acts 19.22. Perhaps Timothy was sent first to Macedonia, with the commission to proceed afterwards to Corinth; while the Epistle was dispatched by the direct sea route.

The information which gave rise to the Epistle was derived from several sources. In the first place, the Corinthians had written Paul a letter in which they had asked his opinion about a number of practical questions. This letter is actually mentioned in I Cor. 7.1 —'Concerning the things whereof ye wrote'—and no doubt Paul is answering questions contained in it in the sections that follow. Several of them begin with a formula similar to that in v. 1— 'concerning virgins', v. 25, 'concerning things sacrificed to idols', ch. 8.1, 'concerning spiritual gifts', ch. 12.1. A large part of First Corinthians, then, is written in direct answer to a letter of the Corinthian church. The letter had probably been brought to Paul by Stephanas, Fortunatus and Achaicus, who had recently come to Ephesus from Corinth, ch. 16.17, and these men may have supplemented the letter by word of mouth. At any rate, additional information of a very important kind had been brought by the people of Chloe, ch. 1.11, who were perhaps slaves in the household of a rich woman. The active intercourse between Paul and the Corinthian church is not surprising. Ephesus and Corinth were both important commercial cities, and the voyage between them was not long or difficult.

Contents of First Corinthians

After the address of the Epistle (where a certain Sosthenes is associated with Paul), ch. 1.1–3, and the customary thanksgiving for the Christian state of the readers, vs. 4–9, Paul discusses first the party spirit which has become prevalent at Corinth, ch. 1.10 to 4.21. Information about it had been brought by the people of Chloe.

In opposing the party spirit, Paul emphasizes the simplicity of the gospel as against the wisdom of men. The formation of the parties, then, had probably been due to intellectual pride. The Corinthian Christians seem to have been 'sermon-tasters'; they regarded themselves as connoisseurs of good preaching. Discussing the question as to which was the best of the Christian workers that they had known, they had come to pay more attention to the form of preaching than to its content. In reply, Paul seeks to bring them back to the simplicity of the gospel. It makes no difference, he says, whether the form of preaching is more or less in accordance with human tastes—the main thing is the message itself. Not all Christians, indeed, are alike in knowledge. There is such a thing as a Christian wisdom. But the Corinthians had mistaken the way in which it could be attained. They thought it could be attained only by intellectual effort. They despised simple-minded men and reached out toward a more profound knowledge. Here, Paul tells them, they are wrong. This higher wisdom is not to be attained by pride of intellect. It is to be attained only by humble reliance upon the Spirit, by submission to him in purity of life. 'If you would be truly wise, if you would get beyond the childhood stage of Christian life, if you would be taught the deep mysteries of the faith— then stop your quarrelling!' Such teaching must have seemed very surprising to men of Greek education.

In the next two chapters, chs. 5, 6, Paul rebukes certain moral faults of the Corinthians. Immorality and worldliness had not been excluded altogether from the church. Information about these matters, as about the party spirit, had perhaps been brought by the people of Chloe.

Then, beginning with the seventh chapter, Paul takes up one by one the questions which had been asked in the letter of the Corinthian church—about marriage, ch. 7.1–24, about virgins, vs. 25–40, about things offered to idols, ch. 8.1 to 11.1, about spiritual gifts, chs. 12 to 14, about the resurrection, ch. 15. It is doubtful whether any question had been asked about the proper conduct of religious services and in particular of the Lord's Supper. These subjects are discussed in ch. 11.2–34.

Finally, ch. 16, Paul gives directions about the collection for the Jerusalem church, announces his plan for a journey to Corinth, and deals with certain personal details.

More Detailed Consideration of two Matters

[1] THE PARTIES

Paul mentions four parties that had been formed in the Corinthian church—a Paul-party, an Apollos-party, a Cephas-party and a Christ-party. These parties do not seem to have been separated from one another by any serious doctrinal differences, and it is impossible to determine their characteristics in detail. In the section where the party spirit is discussed, Paul blames the Corinthians for intellectual pride. This fault has often been connected with the Apollos-party. Apollos was an Alexandrian, and probably had an Alexandrian Greek training. He might therefore have unconsciously evoked among some members of the Corinthian church an excessive admiration for his more pretentious style of preaching, which might have caused them to despise the simpler manner of Paul. Even this much, however, is little more than surmise. At any rate, Apollos should not be blamed for the faults of those who misused his name. He is praised unstintedly by Paul, who was even desirous that he should return at once to Corinth, I Cor. 16.12. Paul blames the Paul-party just as much as any of the other three.

The Peter-party was composed of admirers of Peter, who had either come to Corinth from the scene of Peter's labours elsewhere, or simply had known of Peter by hearsay. It is unlikely that Peter himself had been in Corinth, for if he had Paul would probably have let the fact appear in First or Second Corinthians. The Christ-party is rather puzzling. A comparison with the false teachers who are combated in Second Corinthians has led some scholars to suppose that it was a Judaizing party, which emphasized a personal acquaintance with the earthly Jesus as a necessary qualification of apostleship. In that case, however, Paul would probably have singled out the Christ-party for special attack. More probably these were simply men who, in proud opposition to the adherents of Paul, of Apollos and of Cephas, emphasized their own independence of any leader other than Christ. Of course, the watchword, 'I am of Christ', if used in a better spirit, would have been altogether praiseworthy, and indeed Paul desires all the parties to unite in it, I Cor. 3.21–23.

Perhaps it is a mistake to attribute to these parties anything like stability. On the whole, the passage gives the impression that it is not the individual parties that Paul is condemning, but the party spirit. That party spirit was manifested by watchwords like those which are enumerated in I Cor. 1.12, but that that enumeration was meant to be complete, does not appear. The whole effort to determine the characteristics of the individual parties—an effort which has absorbed the attention of many scholars—should perhaps be abandoned.

Paul's treatment of the party spirit exhibits his greatness not only as an administrator, but also as a writer. The subject was certainly not inspiring; yet under Paul's touch it becomes luminous with heavenly glory. The contrast of human wisdom with the message of the cross, I Cor. 1.18–31, where a splendid rhythm of language matches the sublimity of the thought, the wonderful description of the freedom and power of the man who possesses the Spirit of God, the grand climax of the third chapter, 'For all things are yours; whether Paul, or Apollos, or Cephas, or the world, or life, or death, or things present, or things to come; all are yours; and ye are Christ's; and Christ is God's'—these are among the passages that can never be forgotten.

[2] THINGS SACRIFICED TO IDOLS

The question of meats offered to idols, which Paul discusses in I Cor. 8.1 to 11.1, was exceedingly intricate. To it Paul applies several great principles. In the first place, there is the principle of Christian freedom. The Christian has been delivered from enslaving superstitions. Idols have no power; they cannot impart any harmful character to the good things which God has provided for the sustenance of man. In the second place, however, there is the principle of loyalty. The fact that idols are nothing does not render idol-worship morally indifferent. On the contrary, idolatry is always sinful. If the eating of certain kinds of food under certain conditions involves participation in idolatry then it is disloyalty to the one true God. The joint operation of the two principles of freedom and of loyalty seems to lead in Paul's mind to the following practical conclusion:—The Christian may eat the meat that has been offered to idols if it is simply put on sale in the market place or set before him at an ordinary meal; but he must not take part with the heathen in specifically religious feasts. The whole question, however, is further viewed in the light of a third principle—the principle of Christian love. Even things that are in themselves innocent must be given up if a brother by them is led into conduct which for him is sin. Christ has died for that weaker brother; surely the Christian, then, may not destroy him. Thus love, even more than loyalty, limits freedom—but it is a blessed limitation. The principles here applied by Paul to the question of the Corinthian Christians will solve many a problem of the modern Church.

TOPICS FOR STUDY

1. Construct an outline of First Corinthians.
2. Summarize fully in your own words (a) the first four chapters; (b) ch. 8 : 1 to 11 : 1; (c) chs. 12 to 14 (three topics).
3. Collect the biographical information about Paul which is contained in First Corinthians.
4. Give as full an account as possible of Apollos.
5. What error is Paul refuting in the fifteenth chapter? Give a summary of this chapter.

20: THE APOSTLE AND HIS MINISTRY

Study material: Acts 20: 1–3; The Second Epistle to the Corinthians

A comparison between the two Epistles to the Corinthians reveals some very important differences. First Corinthians is concerned chiefly with the congregation; Second Corinthians with the apostle himself. First Corinthians is for the most part rather calm in tone; Second Corinthians is instinct with mingled joy and bitterness. Second Corinthians is the most personal of all the greater epistles of Paul. In this letter the apostle has laid open before us the very innermost secrets of his soul.

In doing so, he has made the Church his debtor. The inner life of Paul, as it is revealed in Second Corinthians, is an inspiration for Christians of all ages. It has an especial lesson for the Church of today. The modern Church is inclined to cherish experience apart from theology; in Second Corinthians the two are inextricably intertwined. Here is the real value of this remarkable self-revelation. In Second Corinthians Paul has taught us that dogma is the guide of life. The theology of the fifth chapter of Second Corinthians is no cold and formal thing, but the very lifeblood of the Church.

The Occasion of the Epistle

INTERVAL AFTER FIRST CORINTHIANS

The history of Paul's relations to the Corinthians could easily be traced up to the time of First Corinthians; but the subsequent period is full of obscurity. At first sight the reader may be tempted to place the writing of the second letter only a short time after the first. In I Cor. 16.5, 6, Paul announces a plan of journeying to Corinth by way of Macedonia. At the time of Second Corinthians just such a plan was actually being carried out. Paul was writing from Macedonia on his way to Corinth. In II Cor. 1.15, 16, it is true, another plan is mentioned as having been entertained pre-

viously—Paul had intended to sail to Corinth direct, then go to
Macedonia, and finally return to Corinth. But the announcement
of this plan could easily be put before the writing of First Corinthians. The course of events would then be as follows: Originally
Paul had intended to sail to Corinth direct and then return thither
again after a visit to Macedonia. This plan had in some way become
known to the Corinthians. A change, however, was announced in
First Corinthians. In First Corinthians Paul declared that he would
go to Corinth only by way of Macedonia. The change of plan had
given rise to criticism. Paul had been accused of fickleness.
Accordingly he defends himself in II Cor. 1.17–24.

This reconstruction is tempting, but it must certainly be given
up. The true course of events was not so simple. There are clear
indications in Second Corinthians that a considerable period had
elapsed since the writing of the first Epistle. During the interval a
number of important events had taken place, and the whole situation had become different. The journey plan which was being
carried out at the time of Second Corinthians was probably formed
later than the similar plan of I Cor. 16.5.

THE SECOND VISIT

In the first place, before the writing of Second Corinthians, Paul
had visited Corinth a second time. He practically says as much in
II Cor. 12.14; 13.1, 2, and the visit 'with sorrow' which he mentions in ch. 2.1 can hardly be identified with the successful visit
which was made when the church was founded. This second visit
cannot be put before the writing of First Corinthians, for if it had
taken place then it would almost certainly have been mentioned
and discussed in First Corinthians instead of in Second Corinthians. It took place then in the period between the two Epistles.

THE SECOND LOST LETTER

In the second place, between the two canonical Epistles, Paul had
written another letter to the Corinthian church. a letter which has
been lost. This letter is referred to in II Cor. 2.4; 7.8–12; for the
expressions which are used in these passages do not apply to First
Corinthians. First Corinthians was certainly not written 'out of
much affliction and anguish of heart' or 'with many tears', and it
was not so severe that Paul could almost come to regret that he
had written it. Still less can the first lost letter be meant—the letter
which was written before First Corinthians—for evidently the

sorrowful letter was the last that had been written before Second Corinthians; it was the letter whose effect at the time of Second Corinthians had just become known. Paul wrote, then, at least four letters to the Corinthian church: first, a lost letter; second, our First Corinthians; third, a second lost letter; fourth, our Second Corinthians.

THE COURSE OF EVENTS

The course of events between the writing of our two Epistles was somewhat as follows: Timothy, who had been sent before the writing of First Corinthians, I Cor. 4.17; 16.10, or some other messenger, returned to Paul, and reported that the condition of the church had become worse rather than better. Paul then went to Corinth from Ephesus. This visit is not mentioned in The Acts, but the omission is not particularly surprising. Corinth was within easy reach of Ephesus; a flying trip there and back need not have meant any continued interruption of Paul's Ephesian work. Luke mentions, after all, only a few incidents from the long period of the Ephesian residence. At Corinth, on this flying visit, Paul met with a bitter experience. He had demanded the punishment of an offender; but that punishment had been refused, and he had been obliged to return to Ephesus without accomplishing his purpose, II Cor. 2.1, 5; 7.11, 12. Paul's failure in this matter had aroused the scorn of his opponents. 'His letters,' they said, 'are weighty and strong; but his bodily presence is weak, and his speech of no account.' II Cor. 10.10. After the discouraging return to Ephesus, Paul had made one supreme effort to win the Corinthians back to their allegiance. He had written them a sharp letter in anguish of heart and with many tears; and he had sent Titus to re-inforce the letter. What would be the effect? It must have been an anxious time for Paul. He had spent years in founding the Corinthian church. Apparently it had been the most successful work of his life. He had put his very soul into it. Yet it seemed to be all in vain. The church was in open rebellion. Immorality was freely tolerated. False apostles were being allowed to lead. To all this maddening anxiety was added a terrible personal danger. In Asia, a short time before the Epistle was written, Paul had despaired of his life. Having escaped by the mercy of God, he had gone to Troas, eager for news from Corinth. But Titus had not returned. Paul could stand it no longer. He went on into Macedonia. And there, at last, Titus met him—and brought good news!

The Corinthians had been made repentant by Paul's letter. They were ready to punish the offender. The old devotion was restored.

Second Corinthians

At that joyful moment, Paul wrote Second Corinthians. It is a wonderful letter. In it, with a sort of trembling joy, Paul lives over again all the anguish of his terrible suspense, in order to pour forth the more abundant thanks. A great man is here revealed. Paul was not one of those passionless creatures who can simply take things as they come. For such men it is easy to trust God, but Paul was one who had to fight for his faith. He fought—and he won. He won, no matter whether God sent success or failure. After every gloomy valley he pushed his way upward by God's grace to the clear heights, whither he has led the successive generations of the Christian Church.

ADDRESS AND THANKSGIVING. II COR. I.I–II

In First Corinthians the obscure Sosthenes is found to be associated with Paul in the address of the Epistle; in Second Corinthians it is Timothy, one of the best-known of the helpers of Paul. Even if that mission of Timothy to Corinth which is mentioned in First Corinthians had resulted in failure, Timothy's usefulness in the church was not permanently affected.

After the address, comes, as is usual in the Pauline epistles, an expression of thanksgiving to God. This time, however, it is not thanksgiving for the Christian state of the readers, but thanksgiving for Paul's own escape from danger. The absence of thanksgiving for the readers does not mean here, as in the case of Galatians, that there was nothing to be thankful for in the church that is being addressed, for the whole first section of the letter is suffused with a spirit of thankfulness for the Corinthians' return to their true allegiance; it means rather simply that the thought of the deadly personal danger, and of the remarkable escape, were for the moment in the forefront of Paul's thought. Even that personal matter, however, was used by Paul to fortify his readers against similar trials, and especially to strengthen still further the bonds of sympathy which had at last been restored between him and them.

THE APOSTLE AND THE MINISTRY OF RECONCILIATION.
II COR. I.12 TO 7.16

Immediately after the thanksgiving for his escape from death, Paul begins the defence of his ministry. After the suspense of the previous days, he feels the need of reviewing the methods and motives of his labour among the Corinthians, in order that the last vestige of suspicion may be removed. This he does in an unrestrained, informal sort of way, which reveals the deepest secrets of his heart, and culminates here and there in grand expositions of the very essence of the gospel.

First, in just a passing word, ch. 1.13, 14, he defends his letters against that charge of obscurity or concealment which is hinted at elsewhere in the Epistle. Compare ch. 4.1–4; 11.6.

Next, he defends himself against the charge of fickleness in his journey plans. At some time, probably during or after the unsuccessful visit alluded to in ch. 2.1, Paul had formed the plan of returning to Corinth by the direct route. This plan he had not carried out, and his abandonment of it apparently confirmed the impression of weakness which had been left by the unsuccessful visit. 'He is very bold in letters,' said his opponents, 'but when he is here he is weak, and now he is afraid to return.' It was a petty criticism, and a lesser man might have answered it in a petty way. But Paul was able to lift the whole discussion to a loftier plane. His answer to the criticism was very simple—the reason why he had not returned to Corinth at once was that he did not want to return again in grief and in severity; for the sake of the Corinthians themselves he wanted to give them time to repent, before the final and fatal issue should be raised. Characteristically, however, Paul does not content himself with this simple answer; indeed he does not even begin with it. A specific explanation of the change in his plans would have refuted the criticism immediately under consideration, but Paul felt the need of doing far more than that. What he desired to do was to make not only this criticism, but all similar criticisms, impossible. This he does by the fine reference to the positive character of his gospel. 'You say that I am uncertain in my plans, that I say "yes" and "no" in one breath. Well, the gospel that I preached, at any rate, was no such uncertain thing as that. My gospel was a great "Yes" to all the promises of God.' Such a method of refutation lifts the reader far above all petty criticisms to the great things of Paul's gospel.

Yet this reference to great principles is no mere excuse to avoid the simple question at issue. On the contrary, Paul is perfectly frank about the reason why he had not gone to Corinth as he had intended. It was out of love to the Corinthian church, and this had also prompted the writing of a severe letter. Here, ch. 2.5–11, Paul refers to the offender whose case had been made a test at the time of the recent painful visit. This offender was probably different from the incestuous person who is so sternly dealt with in I Cor. 5.1–5. His offence is thought by many to have been some personal insult to Paul, II Cor. 2.5, but this is not quite certain. At any rate, whatever his original offence, Paul's demand for his punishment had become a test of the loyalty of the church. At first the demand had been refused, but now the majority of the congregation has agreed and the man himself is deeply repentant, so that Paul is only afraid lest severity may go too far. It is hardly worth while saying that the character of Paul was entirely free from vindictiveness. When the discipline of the Church would permit it, Paul was the first to propose counsels of mercy.

The reference to the epistles of commendation which had been used by Paul's opponents in Corinth, ch. 3.1, has been made the basis of far-reaching conclusions about the whole history of the apostolic age. From whom could the opponents have received their letters of introduction? Only, it is said, from Palestine, and probably from the original apostles. This conclusion is hasty, to say the least. It should be noticed that not only letters to the Corinthian church but also letters from the church are apparently in mind, v. 1. If, then, the Corinthian church had been asked to supply these false teachers with letters of commendation, perhaps the other churches that had supplied them with letters were no nearer to Jerusalem than Corinth was.

The mention of these letters of commendation introduces one of the grandest passages in the New Testament. 'I,' says Paul, by way of transition, 'do not need any letters of commendation. My work is sufficient commendation. What I have accomplished in the hearts of men is an epistle written by the Spirit of God.' Then follows the magnificent exposition of the ministry of the new covenant. That ministry is first contrasted with the old dispensation, perhaps with reference to an excessive valuation, by the opponents, of a continued Judaism in the Church. The old covenant was glorious, but how much more glorious is the new! The old was a ministry of condemnation, but the new is a ministry of justification. The old was a ministry of an external law, the new is a ministry of the life-giving power of the Spirit of God. There is no reason any longer for concealment. The Spirit brings freedom and openness and light.

This treasure is held indeed in earthen vessels. The recent danger that Paul has passed through, as well as the overpowering hardships of his life, make him painfully conscious of human weakness. But that weakness is blessed which in all the fuller glory reveals the all-conquering power of God. The Christian need never despair, for by the eye of faith he can detect those unseen things which are eternal. The present body may be dissolved, but the resurrection body will be ready. Indeed, even if the Christian is separated for a time altogether from the body by death, he need not fear. To be absent from the body is to be present with the Lord.

The climax of the whole glorious passage is the brief exposition of the ministry of reconciliation which begins with ch. 5.11. Here we are introduced to the secret of the remarkable life which is revealed in Second Corinthians and in the other epistles of Paul. Reconciliation with God through the death of Christ in our behalf and in our stead, consequent freedom from sin and from the world, a new glorious life under the favour of God—these are the things that Paul experienced in his own life, these are the things that he preached to others, regardless of all hardship and criticism, and these are the things, now and always, which contain the real springs of the Church's power.

After an uncompromising warning against impurity and worldliness, delivered from the lofty vantage ground that has just been reached, the apostle gives expression once more to the joy that he has received from the good news which Titus brought him; and then proceeds to an entirely different matter.

THE COLLECTION. II COR. CHAPTERS 8, 9

Two whole chapters of the Epistle are devoted to the collection for the Jerusalem church. The history of this matter, so far as it can be traced, is briefly as follows: At the time of the Jerusalem council, the pillars of the Jerusalem church had requested Paul to remember the Jerusalem poor. At the time when First Corinthians was written, Paul had already started a collection for this purpose in the churches of Galatia, and in First Corinthians he asks the Corinthians to take part, I Cor. 16.1–4. In Second Corinthians he announces that the churches of Macedonia have contributed bountifully, II Cor. 8.1–5, and urges the continuance of the collection in Corinth. Finally, in the Epistle to the Romans, which was written from Corinth only a short time after Second Corinthians, he mentions the collection in Macedonia and Achaia, announces his intention of journeying to Jerusalem with the gifts, and asks the Roman Christians to pray that the ministration may be acceptable to the Jerusalem church, Rom. 15.25–27, 31, 32.

With his customary foresight, Paul made careful provision for the administration of the gifts, in order to avoid all possible misunderstanding or suspicion. For example, the churches are to choose delegates to carry their bounty to Jerusalem, I Cor. 16.3. Possibly the delegates are to be identified with the persons who are named in Acts 20.4. Luke does not mention the collection, but it is alluded to in Acts 24.17.

Paul's treatment of the collection in II Cor. chs. 8, 9, was not only adapted to accomplish its immediate purpose, but also has been of high value to the Christian Church. These chapters have assured to the right use of wealth a place of real dignity among the forms of Christian service.

THE OPPONENTS. II COR. CHAPTERS 10 TO 13

The striking change of tone at ch. 10.1 is amply explained by the change of subject. In the first part of the Epistle, Paul has been thinking of the return of the majority of the congregation to their allegiance; now he turns to deal with the false teachers who have been causing all the trouble. It is still necessary to meet their attacks and remove every vestige of influence which they may still have retained over the church. Their attack upon Paul was of a peculiarly mean and unworthy character; the indignation which Paul displays in these chapters was fully justified.

The opponents were certainly Jews, and prided themselves on the fact, ch. 11.22. But it does not appear with certainty that they were Judaizers. If they were intending to come forward with any demand of circumcision or of observance of the Mosaic law, such demand was still kept in the background. Indeed, there is no indication that the doctrine that they preached was different in important respects from that of Paul. In particular, there is no indication that they advocated a different view about Jesus. One verse, ch. 11.4, has, indeed, been regarded as such an indication, but only by an exceedingly doubtful interpretation. Probably the other Jesus whom the opponents preached existed only in their own claim. They said merely, 'Paul has kept something back', v. 6, margin; ch. 4.3; 'we alone can give you adequate information; we alone can proclaim the true Jesus, the true Spirit and the true gospel.' In reality, however, they had nothing new to offer. Paul had made the whole gospel known.

It is further not even quite clear that the opponents laid stress upon a personal acquaintance with the earthly Jesus, and so played the original apostles off against Paul. The expression 'chiefest apostles', ch. 11.5, is clearly nothing more than an ironical designation of the false teachers themselves. It is true, the false teachers claimed to belong in a special sense to Christ, ch. 10.7, and to be in a special sense 'ministers of Christ', ch. 11.23. But it is not at all clear—despite ch. 5.16—that the connection which they claimed to have with Christ was that of personal acquaintance, either directly or through their authorities, with the earthly Jesus. Finally, these false teachers cannot with any certainty be connected with the Christ-party of First Corinthians.

The chief value of the last four chapters of the Epistle is the wealth of autobiographical material which they contain. Against the insidious personal attacks of the opponents, Paul was obliged to speak of certain personal matters about which he might otherwise have been silent. Had he been silent, the Church would have been the loser. To know the inner life of the apostle Paul is to know Christ; for Paul was in Christ and Christ was in Paul. What could compensate us for the loss of II Cor. 12.7–10? Through these words the bodily weakness of Paul has forever been made profitable for the strength of the Church.

TOPICS FOR STUDY

1. Construct an outline of Second Corinthians.
2. Summarize in your own words each of the three main divisions of the Epistle (three topics).
3. Outline the history of the collection in the Corinthian church and in the churches of Macedonia.
4. Discuss Paul's opponents in Corinth, and compare them with the Judaizers in Galatia.
5. Collect the biographical information about Paul which is contained in II Cor. chs. 10 to 13.

21: THE GOSPEL OF SALVATION

Study material: The Epistle to the Romans

The Second Epistle to the Corinthians was written from Macedonia on the journey which is mentioned in Acts 20.1, 2. The Epistle to the Romans was written a short time after, during the three-months' stay in Corinth, v. 3. This dating is established by clear indications in the Epistle itself. At the time when the Epistle was written, Paul had finished his work in the east, Rom. 15.23, but was intending, despite his desire to preach in Spain, to go first to Jerusalem with the gifts of the churches, v. 25. Evidently, then, the Epistle was written a short time before the journey that is narrated in Acts 20.3 to 21.17. It could not have been written, however, during the stormy period just before Second Corinthians, or at any time on a journey; for so long and carefully composed an Epistle requires a certain amount of leisure. It must have been written, therefore, during the three months of the last stay in Corinth; and this conclusion is confirmed by certain minor indications in the sixteenth chapter. The quiet tone in which the letter is written, quite free from the intensity of Second Corinthians, shows what the final result of the Corinthian controversy had been. Paul could not have composed a letter of this sort in Corinth unless the peace of the Corinthian church, and the personal confidence of the Corinthian Christians in the apostle, had been fully restored.

The Church at Rome

No account of the founding of the Roman church is contained in the New Testament. Probably, however, the church was founded at an early time. A well-known passage in Suetonius, the Roman historian, seems to show that there were Christians at Rome at least as early as A.D. 50. The passage reads as follows: 'He (Claudius) expelled the Jews from Rome because under the instigation of Chrestus they were incessantly making tumults.' (Suetonius, Life of Claudius, 25.) Apparently Suetonius thought that 'Chrestus' was the direct instigator of riots in Rome; but since the familiar name 'Chrestus' was often, through a natural error, substituted by early observers of Christianity for the unfamiliar 'Christus', it is probable that the fact lying behind Suetonius' words was a disturbance caused by disputes between Christians and non-Christian Jews of Rome. Suetonius seems to have supposed that the 'Chrestus' whose name was prominent in the record of the disturbance was actually present. The date of this edict of Claudius was probably A.D. 49 or 50. Compare Acts 18.2.

Even without this definite information, however, the early origin of the Roman church could be inferred from the New Testament. The Epistle to the Romans does not look as though it were written to an infant congregation.

The absence of any account of the founding of the church at Rome is only one indication more of the fact which has been observed again and again, that our knowledge of the apostolic age is only fragmentary. There were various ways in which the gospel could easily have been carried to Rome. Roman Jews must often have returned to the feasts at Jerusalem. Some of them were present on the day of Pentecost, Acts 2.10. Between the mother country and the large Jewish colony at Rome there must have been many opportunities of intercourse. In general, one must bear constantly in mind what was said in chapter 2 about the system of communication in the Roman Empire; and Rome was the centre of the system.

Probably the Roman church began among the Jews. But it is also just as probable that it soon spread among the Gentile population, especially among the 'God-fearers'. As soon as it did so, the jealousy of the non-Christian Jews would naturally be aroused, as at so many other places, and, as also happened at those other places, their hostility would find expression in more or less disorderly accusations of the Christians. These disorders may well have given occasion for the edict of Claudius; and the effect of that edict would be to hasten still further the separation of the church from the synagogue.

General considerations, therefore, make it probable that at the time when the Epistle to the Romans was written, the Roman church was composed predominantly of Gentiles. This conclusion is confirmed rather than overthrown by the Epistle itself. Some passages have indeed been urged against it, and the question has been hotly debated; but on the whole the Gentile character of the church, with a Jewish Christian minority, is most probable.

The Purpose of the Epistle

The occasion of the Epistle is to be sought not so much in peculiar conditions within the Roman congregation itself as in the general situation in which Paul found himself and in the general position of Rome as the capital of the world. Paul had passed through years of conflict. He had been obliged to defend his gospel of salvation by faith alone against the insistent opposition of the Judaizers and against the moral laxness of Gentile converts. The conflict had been hard fought. But it had been won. At last there was a breathing space. At last Paul was able to turn his attention to fresh fields of labour. First, however, he felt the need of summing up the results of the previous period. Such a summary forms the principal contents of the Epistle to the Romans.

It must not be supposed, however, that Romans is merely a systematic treatise, addressed to the Roman church only by way of literary device. Like the other epistles of Paul, this is a real letter. By it Paul hoped to accomplish something, not merely in the Church in general, but very specifically in Rome. Paul was intending to preach in the extreme western part of the Empire. For such labour one city only was fitted to be a base of operations. Antioch was too remote; Rome only would meet the need. But the Roman church had not been founded by Paul, and indeed he was personally unknown to the mass of the Roman Christians. If, therefore, Rome was to serve Paul as a base of operations, it was highly desirable that the church should be furnished with a full exposition of Paul's gospel. Such an exposition would provide Paul, on his approaching visit to Rome, with the best possible introduction.

Furthermore, Paul was by no means ignorant of the internal affairs of the Roman church. By his coming visit he hoped to impart to the Roman Christians some spiritual gift, Rom. 1.11, and even in his letter he seeks, though with perfect tactfulness, to correct some of their faults, and to fortify them against specific dangers. These matters, however, are far less prominent than in any of the epistles that have been studied so far. Romans is primarily an exposition of the gospel of God's grace, with special reference to the claims of the law and of the Jewish people, written in view of Paul's approaching visit to Rome.

Contents of the Epistle

The first eight chapters are concerned with an exposition of the gospel. The theme of this section is given in Rom. 1.16, 17. The development of the theme is thoroughly logical.

In the first place, the need of the gospel is established, ch. 1.18 to 3.20. All have transgressed; all are under God's wrath and curse; all are subject to a dreadful power of evil.

After the need has been established, there is a condensed statement of the way of escape, ch. 3.21–31. Sin is not something that can simply be treated as though it had never been. The justice of God demands punishment. But that punishment, through mysterious grace, has been exacted, not from us, but from Christ. The death of Christ was a divine sacrifice for the sins of men. The benefits of it cannot be earned; they must simply be received. In other words, salvation is not by works, but by faith.

Next, the nature of faith is illustrated by the case of Abraham, ch. 4. The analogy is itself a proof. Justification by faith has Scripture warrant.

In the next four chapters the nature and results of justification by faith are set forth. If we have once been 'justified'—'pronounced righteous'—for the sake of Christ, then the fullest salvation will inevitably follow. Christ died for us while we were yet sinners; how much more will he save us now! ch. 5.1–11. Sin and death entered into the world through Adam's transgression; the law served only to make sin more heinous; but life was restored through Christ, vs. 12–21. Faith brings not only pardon of the guilt of sin, but also freedom from the power of sin; the Christian life is a life of holiness, ch. 6. This freedom from sin is also freedom from the law; the law of itself was powerless to check transgression, ch. 7. But the Christian is in possession of a new power, which is sufficient to overcome all the forces of evil—the power of the Spirit of God, ch. 8.1–11. The gift of Christ and of his Spirit means that we are sons of God and have absolutely nothing to fear in the whole universe, ch. 8.12–39.

In chs. 9 to 11 Paul faces the problem of the rejection of Israel. The natural Israel has been rejected, but the true, spiritual Israel, composed of those who believe, has been saved. And who can reason with God? Who can prescribe rules for the Creator? Furthermore, a remnant even of the natural Israel has been saved; and the present unbelief of the mass of the people is part of a divine plan which will culminate in the salvation both of Israel and of the other nations.

In chs. 12 to 16, Paul exhibits some of the practical results of his gospel, urges especially the duty of subjection to the civil power, applies the principle of love, as in First Corinthians, to mooted questions of conscience, announces his plans for a mission in the west, sends special messages to individuals in the Roman church and from individuals in his own company, warns against false teaching, and closes with a doxology.

Two Matters of Special Interest

ADDRESS, THANKSGIVING AND SUBJECT. ROM. I.I–17

The address of the Epistle to the Romans is remarkable for the long addition which is made to the name of the author. Paul was writing to a church which he had never seen. His excuse for writing was to be found only in the gospel with which he had been entrusted. At the very start, therefore, he places his gospel in the foreground. Here, however, it is rather the great presupposition of the gospel which is in mind—Jesus Christ in his double nature. One who has been commissioned to preach to the Gentiles the gospel of such a Christ may certainly address a letter to Rome.

In connection with the customary thanksgiving, Paul mentions his long-cherished desire of visiting the Roman Christians. He desires to impart unto them some spiritual gift—no, he says, rather he desires to receive from them as well as to give. The correction is characteristic of Paul. Some men would have felt no need of making it. As a matter of fact, Paul was fully in a position to impart spiritual gifts. But he was afraid his readers might feel hurt—as though the apostle thought they could make no return for the benefit which the visit would bring them, vs. 11–12. It is an exquisite bit of fine discernment and delicate courtesy. But like all true courtesy, it was based on fact. Paul was really not a man to decline help and comfort from even the humblest of the brethren.

In vs. 16, 17, the theme of the epistle is announced—the gospel the power of God unto salvation, the gospel which reveals a righteousness of God that is received by faith. The meaning of 'a righteousness of God' has been much disputed. Some think that it refers to the righteousness which is an attribute of God. More probably, however, it is to be interpreted in the light of ch. 10.3; Phil. 3.9. It then refers to that right relation of man to God which

God himself produces. There are two ways of receiving a sentence of acquittal from God the Judge. One is by keeping the law of God perfectly. The other is by receiving through faith the righteousness of Christ. The former is impossible because of sin. The latter has been made possible by the gift of Christ. As sinners, we are subject to the punishment of death. But that punishment has been paid for us by Christ. We therefore go free; we can start fresh, with the consciousness of God's favour. We are 'justified'—that is, 'pronounced righteous'—not because we are free from sin, but because by his grace God looks not upon us but upon Christ. We have been pronounced righteous, but not on account of our own works. We possess not our own righteousness but 'a righteousness of God'.

This righteousness of God is received by faith. Faith is not a work, it is simply the willingness to receive. Christ has promised by his death to bring us to God. We may not understand it all, but is Christ to be believed? Study the Gospel picture of him, and you will be convinced that he is.

Justification by faith, then, means being pronounced righteous by God, although we are sinners. It might seem to be a very dangerous doctrine. If we are pronounced righteous whether we are really righteous or not, then may we not go on with impunity in sin? Such reasoning ignores the results of justification. Faith brings more than forgiveness. It brings a new life. In the new life sin has no place. The Christian has broken for ever with his old slavery. Though perfection has not yet been attained in practice, it has been attained in principle, and by the power of the Spirit all sin will finally be removed. The Christian cannot compromise with sin. Salvation is not only from the guilt of sin, but also from the power of it. The sixth chapter of Romans leaves no room for moral laxness.

THE PAULINE PHILOSOPHY OF HISTORY. ROM. CHAPTERS 9 TO 11

Chapters 9 to 11 of this epistle are interesting in a great many ways. They are interesting, for example, in their tremendous conception of the mystery of the divine will. The ninth chapter of Romans is a good corrective for any carelessness in our attitude toward God. After all, God is a mystery. How little we know of his eternal plan! We must ever tremble before him. Yet it is such a God who has invited us, through Christ, to hold communion with himself. There is the true wonder of the gospel—that it brings us into fellowship, not with a God of our own devising, not with one who is a Father and nothing else, but with the awful, holy, mysterious Maker and Ruler of all things. The joy of the believer is the deepest of all joys. It is a joy that is akin to holy fear.

These chapters are also interesting because they attest the attachment of Paul to the Jewish people. Where is there a nobler expression of patriotism than Rom. 9.1–5? Exclusive attention to the polemic passages where Paul is defending the Gentile mission and denying the efficacy of the Mosaic law, has produced in the minds of some scholars a one-sided view of Paul's attitude toward Israel. Paul did not advocate the destruction of the identity of his people. He believed that even the natural Israel had a part to play on the stage of history. These chapters of Romans, together with some other passages in the epistles, such as I Cor. 9.20, confirm what the book of The Acts tells us about Paul's willingness, when no principle was involved, to conform to Jewish custom.

TOPICS FOR STUDY

1. Construct an outline of the Epistle.
2. Summarize in your own words the first eight chapters of the Epistle (about four topics).
3. Where was Illyricum, and when did Paul visit it? Rom. 15.19.
4. Collect information about the persons mentioned in the sixteenth chapter.

Study material: Acts chs. 20 to 28

The Journey to Jerusalem

When Paul was in Corinth on the third missionary journey, Acts
20.3, he had already formed the plan of visiting Rome and the
west. First, however, it was necessary for him to go to Jerusalem
with the offerings from the Gentile churches, Rom. 15.22–33.
From the beginning, he was conscious of the danger of such a visit
to Judea, v. 31, and during the journey itself prophetic voices confirmed his apprehensions; but the path of duty was plain, and he
did not hesitate to walk in it.

On account of haste, Paul did not visit Ephesus, where he might
have been detained, but summoned the elders of the Ephesian
church to meet him at Miletus. The discourse of Paul to the elders
is a fine example of his manner of speaking to Christian leaders.
The speech has preserved for us a precious saying of Jesus which
is not recorded in the Gospels. Acts 20.35.

The Arrival at Jerusalem

Paul was received in the most friendly way by James and the elders
of the Jerusalem church, who glorified God for the success of the
Gentile mission. They told him, however, that the large body of
Jewish Christians—evidently those in Judea are especially meant—
had been informed that he was teaching the Jews of the dispersion
to forsake their ancestral customs. In order to refute this charge,
they suggested that Paul should take part in a vow which was
being carried out according to Jewish custom by four men in
Jerusalem. To this proposal Paul agreed.

The vow in which Paul took part at the request of James was at
least similar to the Nazirite vow described in Num. 6.1–21. Not all
the details of such vows are perfectly clear. Paul himself, on his
own account, had assumed a similar vow on his second missionary

journey, Acts 18.18—unless indeed, as is grammatically possible, the words in that passage refer to Aquila rather than to Paul.

It was not true, as the Christians of Judea had been led to think, that Paul taught the Jewish Christians of the dispersion to forsake the law of Moses, though he was insistent that the Gentile Christians must not adopt that law. It was not even true that he himself, on principle, had given up keeping the law, though the exigencies of his Gentile work required him to do so very often, and though he regarded himself as inwardly free from the law. His willingness to take part in a Jewish vow in Jerusalem is therefore not surprising. His action on this occasion was fully justified by the principles of his conduct as described in I Cor. 9.20, 21. The keeping of the law was not for Paul a means of obtaining salvation. Salvation was a free gift of God, through the death of Christ. But for the present the general relinquishment of the law and abandonment of the distinctive customs of Judaism on the part of Jewish Christians was not required. Paul was willing to leave that question to the future guidance of God.

Imprisonment in Jerusalem and Cæsarea

The non-Christian Jews, however, informed by their countrymen who had returned from the dispersion about the alarming spread of the Christian mission, were thoroughly incensed against Paul; it required only a spark to set their resentment into a blaze. The spark was provided by the false accusation that Paul had taken Gentiles into the inner court of the temple. This offence was punishable with death.

Only the prompt interference of the Roman tribune, with the soldiers who were quartered in the castle of Antonia, northwest of the temple area, prevented Paul from falling a victim to the violence of the mob. As on many other occasions, Paul's double education stood him in good stead. His knowledge of Greek prevented the tribune from confusing him with an Egyptian impostor; his knowledge of Aramaic gained him a better hearing from the crowd. Being permitted to speak from the steps of the castle, he defended himself by a review of his past life. He was, he said, no Gentile, without rights in the temple, but a genuine Jew. He had not started out with a prejudice against the law. On the contrary, after all the advantages of a rabbinical education, he had exhibited his zeal by persecuting the disciples of Jesus. Nothing but an immediate act of God had made him an adherent of the new sect; nothing but a divine revelation had then caused him to cease working for the Jews in Jerusalem. He had become the apostle to the Gentiles not by any disloyalty to Israel, but by command of God—that was the point of his defence.

He was not allowed, however, to finish what he had to say. At the first mention of the Gentiles, carefully prepared for though it had been, the fury of the mob broke forth afresh. Taken then by the soldiers into the castle, he was about to be scourged, in order that he might be forced by torture to tell the truth, when his Roman citizenship saved him. The respect of his captor, gained to some extent by his Greek education, was now greatly heightened. Such a prisoner could not be summarily disposed of.

In order that the charge might be ascertained more definitely, the tribune took his prisoner the next day before the Sanhedrin. Here the disagreement between Pharisees and Sadducees prevented any definite result. Again Paul had to be rescued by the Roman soldiers from the violence of his countrymen. The following night, however, a revelation from the Lord afforded full recompense for the dangers of the day. Despite all opposition, the apostle was to bear his testimony in Rome!

The proposal of another hearing before the Sanhedrin was a mere pretext, in order to give an opportunity for assassination. The hostility of the Jews would stick at nothing in order to destroy the hated apostate. Fortunately a nephew of Paul got wind of the plot, and used his knowledge in the nick of time. Under cover of darkness, the troublesome prisoner was sent down under a strong guard to the procurator at Cæsarea.

The procurator at this time was the notorious Felix, whose misgovernment helped prepare the way for the approaching Jewish war. The first hearing before Felix is narrated at some length. The Jews hired a professional orator to press their charges against Paul; and Paul replied. Felix adjourned the hearing; and although he afterwards listened frequently to Paul, he came to no decision. His attitude toward Paul's message seems to have been due partly to his desire for a bribe, partly to a certain curiosity born of guilty fear, and partly to a desire not to offend the Jews.

During the two years that elapsed until the deposition of Felix, Paul remained a prisoner at Cæsarea. Festus, the successor of Felix, after representations by the authorities at Jerusalem, proposed to Paul that he should go to Jerusalem for trial. Knowing that such a change in the place of trial might be fatal, Paul appealed to the court of the emperor at Rome. As a Roman citizen he had the right to make such an appeal, though apparently unless the importance or difficulty of the case was sufficient, the appeal might have been refused. This time, the appeal was granted.

In order to obtain some more definite accusation, Festus conceived the plan of holding a joint hearing in company with Herod Agrippa II, king of a district comprising what had previously been the tetrarchy of Philip, and Bernice, his notorious sister. Military tribunes and notables of the city of Cæsarea also took part. In his defence before Agrippa, as before the Jewish mob, Paul gave an account of his past life, especially of his conversion, showing how he had been acting under divine guidance, in full loyalty to the Messianic hope which Israel had always cherished. The speech was at any rate not received with indifference. Both Festus and Agrippa were strongly affected by it, though not in exactly the way that might have been desired. Evidently there was something overpowering about the personality of Paul.

So far as the legal charge was concerned, the hearing had an altogether favourable result. The authorities came to the conclusion that Paul had done nothing worthy of death or of bonds. This conclusion was quite in accord with the attitude of the Roman authorities all through the earliest period of the Church. Evidently Christianity was not regarded as politically dangerous. Opposition to it was due, not to Roman concern for law and order, but to Jewish jealousy.

The Journey to Rome

The favourable result of the last hearing could not alter the determination that had already been reached. Paul was sent as a prisoner to Rome. Though a prisoner he was treated with consideration. He was accompanied by Aristarchus and Luke, the latter of whom has preserved a minute account of the eventful journey.

This account is valuable to the student of ancient life, because of the unique wealth of information which it affords with regard to the seafaring of antiquity; it is valuable to the Christian because of the first-hand information which it affords about Paul. Nowhere else in the New Testament is there such a vivid picture of the way Paul looked in a time of danger. One thing is clear in this picture— the power of Paul was the power of his religion. On that ship of Alexandria, with its two hundred and seventy-six persons, with its officers and soldiers and sailors, the true master of the situation was the disciple of Jesus. At first they despised him as a prisoner; but in time of peril they obeyed his commands.

Paul in Rome

Even before he arrived at Rome, Paul was met by a delegation from the Roman Christians. They had received his Epistle a few years before; they had heard of his wonderful labours throughout the eastern world; some of them knew him personally, and now, despite his bonds, they welcomed him with gladness.

Only three days after his arrival, Paul began his efforts to win over the Roman Jews; but although at an appointed time they came to his lodging in great numbers, and although some believed, the majority rejected the gospel. Among the Gentiles, however, Paul was able to labour with success. The comparatively lenient form of his imprisonment permitted him to receive in his own hired dwelling all who desired to come. The promise which the Lord had given him after that discouraging day in the synagogue over two years before had at last been fulfilled. At last the apostle to the Gentiles had arrived at the capital of the Gentile world.

One stage in the history of Christianity was complete. The Church was established from Jerusalem to Rome.

TOPICS FOR STUDY
1. Give an account of each of the persons named in Acts 20.4.
2. Trace the journeys on a map.
3. What was there false about the charge mentioned in Acts 21.21? For your answer, use both The Acts and the Pauline epistles.
4. Explain the nature of the vow mentioned in Acts 21.23–27.
5. Show how the speeches of Paul refuted the charges which were brought against him.
6. Give some account of Felix, Festus and Agrippa.
7. Describe Paul's voyage and shipwreck.

23: THE SUPREMACY OF CHRIST

Study material: The Epistle to the Colossians and the
Epistle to Philemon

Connection between Colossians and Philemon

The Epistle to the Colossians and the Epistle to Philemon were
written at the same time. The same persons—Aristarchus, Mark,
Epaphras, Luke and Demas—appear in both epistles in the company of Paul. Col. 4.10–14; Philem. 23, 24. Only Jesus Justus,
Col. 4.11, who was probably not known personally to Philemon,
Tychicus, the bearer of the Epistle to the Colossians, and Timothy,
the associate with Paul in the address of Colossians, are not mentioned in the Epistle to Philemon. It is true, Aristarchus, in Col.
4.10, is designated as Paul's 'fellow-prisoner', while in Philem. 23
this term is applied to Epaphras. Perhaps, however, it is only
chance that both terms are not applied to both men in both of the
letters. Or else the variation may mean only that the two Epistles
were not written on the same day. Aristarchus and Epaphras and
others may have taken turns in sharing the apostle's imprisonment.
The two letters, at any rate, even if written on different days, were
evidently dispatched at the same time. Onesimus, the bearer of the
Epistle to Philemon, was to accompany Tychicus, who was
apparently the bearer of the Epistle to the Colossians. Col. 4.7, 8.

The Church at Colossæ

The town of Colossæ was not a particularly important place,
being overshadowed by its two neighbours. Laodicea and Hierapolis. These three cities were situated close together in the Lycus
valley, about a hundred miles east of Ephesus. The churches at
Colossæ and at Laodicea, and no doubt also the one at Hierapolis,
had not been founded by Paul himself, Col. 2.1; 4.13. The church
at Colossæ, however, had been founded by Epaphras, who was
one of Paul's fellow labourers, and probably one of his converts,
Col. 1.7. Probably, in preaching at Colossæ, Epaphras had acted

F

directly as an emissary of Paul. Evidently Paul reckoned the churches of Colossæ, Laodicea and Hierapolis distinctly to his own field. The tone which he adopts toward his readers in Colossians is, for example, entirely different from that which appears in Romans. He treats the Colossians practically as his own spiritual children. See especially Col. 1.24 to 2.5.

In all probability the church had been founded during the three years which Paul spent at Ephesus on the third missionary journey. During that period 'all they that dwelt in Asia heard the word of the Lord, both Jews and Greeks'. Acts 19.10. Colossæ was in the province of Asia, in the Phrygian part of it. Even if 'Asia' in the passage in The Acts should be taken in a narrower sense, still the words show at least that the effects of Paul's preaching in Ephesus spread far beyond the limits of the city. It may well have spread to Colossæ, which lay directly on the great road from Ephesus to the east. Probably Epaphras, who was a resident of Colossæ, Col. 4.12, was converted during a visit to Ephesus, and then on his return became the evangelist of his native city.

The church at Colossæ was certainly composed predominantly, if not exclusively, of Gentiles, Col. 1.21, 27; 2.13. Indeed, even Epaphras himself, the founder of the church, was a Gentile; for in Col. 4.10–14 he is distinguished, along with Luke and Demas, from the Jews.

The Date of Colossians and Philemon

The Epistle to the Colossians and that to Philemon were written while Paul was in prison, Col. 4.2, 10, 18; Philem. 1, 9, 23. Yet the conditions of his imprisonment were such as to permit him the companionship of his friends and leisure for correspondence. These conditions were clearly present during the two years of the Roman imprisonment, Acts 28.16, 30, 31. At Cæsarea also, Paul seems to have been treated rather leniently, and some scholars have preferred to date our Epistles during the two years which Paul spent there, Acts 24.27. That dating, however, is far less probable. The Epistles may be confidently assigned to the Roman imprisonment.

Condition of the Colossian Church

At the time when Colossians was written, Epaphras, the founder of the Colossian church, was with Paul. He had given a generally favourable account of the progress of the church. Perhaps other and later news had come from other quarters. Onesimus was another Colossian who was with Paul, Col. 4.9; but it is perhaps unlikely that he possessed any very intimate knowledge of the church, because, as we shall see, he did not become a Christian until after he had left Colossæ.

Not all the news which had been received by Paul from Colossæ was satisfactory. False teaching had become prevalent. The nature of this false teaching is very difficult to determine—many different hypotheses have been proposed with regard to it. One thing is clear—the false teachers insisted upon an ascetic manner of life, Col. 2.20–23. 'Handle not, nor taste, nor touch', was their ordinance. Apparently they forbade the use of animal food and wine, Col. 2.16. There was also an excessive emphasis upon feast and fast days. The speculative side of their teaching, on the other hand, is obscure. It looks, however, as though they had inordinate reverence for angels, and boasted of higher mysteries to which they had attained. Whether the false teachers were Jews or Gentiles is uncertain. Colossians 2.11–15, which points out the freedom of the Christian from the law and the superiority of baptism over the rites of the Old Covenant, might seem to indicate that the Colossians had been imbued with a false notion of the continued validity of Judaism.

The errorists in Colossæ, however, were not Judaizers, as were those of Galatia, for the tone of Paul's refutation is far milder than in that former case. The Colossian Christians were not being led away from the fundamental principles of the gospel; they were merely being troubled with useless speculations, which would distract their attention from what is essential, and with an alleged higher morality, which would destroy the simplicity of the Christian life. The error was indeed serious enough. That is demonstrated by the history of the Church. Excessive reverence for beings lower than God is always dangerous. Probably the Colossian errorists did not directly attack the supremacy of Christ. Neither did those who afterwards introduced saint-worship into the Catholic Church. But in both cases the effect was to rob Christ of his rightful place in Christian devotion.

Paul's Refutation of the Errorists

In refutation, Paul proceeds positively rather than negatively. Instead of filling his letter with invective, he points out the all-sufficiency of what the Colossians have already received, in order to prevent them from seeking anything new. They have already been delivered from the power of darkness, Col. 1.13. They are already in full possession of the mystery, vs. 25–27; ch. 2.2, 3. They are already free from the world, and have a new life in Christ, ch. 2.11–15, 20; 3.1–4. There is therefore no need for a supposed higher, ascetic manner of life, and no need for abstruse specula- tions. No manner of life can be higher than that which is described in Col. 3.1 to 4.2; no mystery can be profounder than the mystery of Christ.

The speculations about angels, in particular, are refuted not so much by direct attack, as by an emphasis upon the supremacy of Christ. If Christ is what he is declared to be in Col. 1.13–23; 2.8–15, then there is no need for a worship of angels. Here lies what is really distinctive of the Epistle to the Colossians. In the previous letters, a lofty view of the person of Christ was always presupposed, but there was no occasion to set it forth in detail. At last the occasion had arrived.

The Christology of Colossians

The Epistle to the Colossians is peculiarly 'Christological'. More fully and more expressly than in any other of his letters Paul here develops his view about the person of Christ. Even here, however, this teaching is incidental; it was simply Paul's way of refuting certain errors that had crept into the Colossian church. Except for those errors Paul would perhaps never have written at length, as he does in Col. 1.14–23, about the relation of Christ to God and to the world. Yet in that case his own views would have been the same, and they would have been just as fundamental to his whole religious life. In the epistles, which are written to Christians, Paul takes many things for granted. Some of the things which are most fundamental appear only incidentally. Just because they were fundamental, just because they were accepted by everyone, they did not need to be discussed at length.

So it is especially with the person of Christ. From the first epistle to the last, Paul presupposes essentially the same view of that great subject. Practically everything that he says in Colossians could have been inferred from scattered hints in the earlier epistles. From the beginning Paul regarded Jesus Christ as a man, who had a real human life and died a real death on the cross. From the beginning, on the other hand, he separated Christ sharply from men and placed him clearly on the side of God. From the beginning, in other words, he attributed to him a double nature—Jesus Christ was always in Paul's thinking both God and man. Finally, the pre-existence of Christ, which is so strongly emphasized in Colossians, is clearly implied in such passages as Gal. 4.4; and his activity in creation appears, according to the best-attested text, in I Cor. 8.6.

Nevertheless, the more systematic exposition in Colossians is of the utmost value. It serves to summarize and explain the scattered implications of the earlier epistles. Christ according to Paul is, in the first place, 'the image of the invisible God'. Col. 1.15. He is the supreme Revealer of God, a Revealer, however, not merely by words but by his own nature. If you want to know what God is, look upon Christ! In the second place, he is 'the firstborn of all creation'. Of itself that phrase might be misconstrued. It might be thought to mean that Christ was the first being that God created. Any such interpretation, however, is clearly excluded by the three following verses. There Paul has himself provided an explanation of his puzzling phrase. 'The firstborn of all creation' means that Christ, himself uncreated, existed before all created things; he was prior to all things, and, as befits an only son, he possesses all things. Indeed he himself was active in the creation of all things, not only the world, and men, but also those angelic powers— 'thrones or dominions or principalities or powers'—upon whom the errorists in Colossæ were inclined to lay too much emphasis. He was the instrument of God the Father in creation. And he was also the end of creation. The world exists not for its own sake, but for the sake of Christ. Especially is he the Head of the Church. His headship is declared by his being the first to rise from the dead into that glorious life into which he will finally bring all his disciples. In a word, the entire 'fulness' of the divine nature dwells in Christ. That word 'fulness' was much misused in the 'Gnostic' speculations of the second century. It is barely possible that the word had already been employed in the incipient Gnosticism of the Colossian errorists. If so, Paul by his repeated use of the word in Colossians and Ephesians, is bringing his readers back to a healthier and simpler and grander conception.

The Person of Christ and the Work of Christ

In Col. 1.20–23, Paul bases upon the preceding exposition of the nature of Christ, a noble description of Christ's work. The work which has been entrusted to Christ is nothing less than that of reconciling the creation unto God. Through sin, an enmity had been set up between God and the work of his hands. That enmity applies primarily of course to the sinful persons themselves. They are under God's wrath and curse. Sin is not a trifle. It cannot simply be treated as though it had never been. If God be righteous, then there is such a thing as a moral order. The wrath of God rests upon the sinner. But by the sacrifice of Christ, that enmity has been wiped out. Christ has paid the awful penalty of sin. Christ has brought the sinner again near to God. The enmity and the following reconciliation concern primarily the men who have sinned. But they also apply to the whole world. The ground has been cursed for man's sake. The end of the reconciliation will be a new heaven and a new earth. The groaning and travailing of the creation will one day have an end. Compare Rom. 8.18–25.

This brief description of the work of Christ in Col. 1.20–22; 2.10–15, can be richly paralleled in the earlier epistles. What now needs to be emphasized is that the Pauline view of Christ's work depends absolutely upon the Pauline view of Christ's person. All through the epistles of Paul the life and death and resurrection are represented as events of a cosmic significance. But they can have such significance only if Christ is the kind of being that is described in the Epistle to the Colossians. The glorious account of salvation, which runs all through the epistles and forms the especial subject of the second group, is unintelligible if Christ were merely an inspired prophet or merely the greatest of created beings. It becomes intelligible only if Christ is 'the image of the invisible God, the firstborn of all creation'. The mysterious Christology of Colossians lies at the very heart of the Christian faith.

The Epistle to Philemon

The Epistle to the Colossians, though addressed to a church that Paul had never visited, is full of warm-hearted affection. Paul could hardly have been cold and formal if he had tried. He was a man of great breadth of sympathy. Hence he was able to enter with the deepest interest into the problems of the Colossian Christians—to rejoice at their faith and love, to lament their faults, and to labour with whole-souled devotion for their spiritual profit.

The simple, unconstrained affection of Paul's nature, however, had freer scope in the delightful little letter to Philemon. Philemon apparently was a convert of Paul himself, Philem. 19. He was not a man with whom Paul had to be on his guard. Paul is perfectly confident that Philemon will fully understand the motives of his action and of his letter.

The letter is addressed to Philemon primarily, but also to Apphia and to Archippus and to the church in Philemon's house. We are here introduced into a Christian household of the apostolic age. Apphia was probably Philemon's wife and Archippus perhaps his son. Evidently Archippus held some sort of office in the Colossian church. 'Say to Archippus,' says Paul in a strangely emphatic way, at the very end of the Epistle to the Colossians, 'Take heed to the ministry which thou hast received in the Lord, that thou fulfil it.' We should like to know what the ministry was which Archippus had received. At any rate, we hope that he fulfilled it. It was a solemn warning which he received—a warning which might well have made him tremble. We also may well take the warning to heart. Our task of imparting Bible truth is no light responsibility. To us also the warning comes, 'Take heed to the ministry which thou hast received in the Lord, that thou fulfil it.'

The letter is addressed not only to Philemon and his family, but also to the 'church' which met in his house. This 'church' was a part of the Colossian congregation. In the early days, when it was difficult to secure meeting places, well-to-do Christians frequently offered the hospitality of their own homes. A certain Nympha or Nymphas—the name varies in the manuscripts—performed this service in Laodicea, Col. 4.15, Aquila and Priscilla in Corinth, I Cor. 16.19, and also Gaius in the same city, Rom. 16.23.

The occasion of the Epistle to Philemon is very simple. Onesimus, a slave of Philemon, had run away from his master, possibly appropriating some of his master's money, Philem. 18. In some way he had come to Rome and had been converted by Paul. Paul would have liked to keep him as a helper. But that was not Paul's way. Instead, he sent the slave back at once to his master. Christianity was to be no excuse for shirking the duties of the various relationships of society as it was then constituted. The freedom of the Christian was an inward freedom. It was fully consistent with the faithful performance of common duty. The letter which Paul gave to Onesimus, asking forgiveness and bespeaking an affectionate welcome for one who was now a brother as well as a servant, is a delightful little letter, simple and affectionate as the occasion required, but by no means belying the great apostle. In the simplest affairs of life, Paul was always both the true gentleman and the unswerving minister of a transcendent gospel.

TOPICS FOR STUDY

1. Summarize Colossians and Philemon in your own words.
2. What does Colossians teach about the nature of Christ? Show how this teaching is presupposed in the earlier epistles (two topics).
3. Summarize the false teaching combated in Colossians.
4. Give some account of Colossæ, Hierapolis, Laodicea, Aristarchus, Mark, Luke, Demas, Archippus, Philemon (about three topics).

24 : THE CHURCH OF CHRIST

Study material: The Epistle to the Ephesians

Date

The Epistle to the Ephesians is closely connected with the Epistle to the Colossians, which was studied in the last chapter. In the first place, both Epistles were written while Paul was a prisoner, Eph. 3.1; 4.1; 6.20; Col. 4.3, 10, 18. In the second place, both were sent by the hand of the same messenger, Tychicus, who is commended in similar terms, Eph. 6.21, 22; Col. 4.7–9. In the third place, the two Epistles are strikingly similar throughout, not only in thought but also in phraseology. These indications are sufficient to prove beyond any reasonable doubt that Ephesians and Colossians were written at the same time. When Tychicus left Rome with the letter to the Colossian church he was also entrusted with the letter which is to be studied in the present chapter.

Destination

The date of the Epistle to the Ephesians can thus be placed with the utmost confidence at some time within the two years which Paul spent in prison at Rome, Acts 28.30, 31. It is by no means so easy to determine who the first readers of the Epistle were. The date is certain, but the destination is somewhat obscure. The Epistle was written by Paul at Rome; but to whom was it written?

This question might seem at first sight to be settled by the words 'at Ephesus' in the first verse. But the trouble is that these words are omitted by our two earliest and best manuscripts, the Codex Vaticanus and the Codex Sinaiticus, supported by some additional evidence. Possibly therefore the words 'at Ephesus' were not written by Paul, but were added by some early copyist. If so, the Epistle itself contains no direct testimony as to its destination; for the heading, 'To the Ephesians', which appears in early manuscripts, is not a part of the Epistle, but was probably added for purposes of convenience, to distinguish this Epistle from others. What remains in favour of the Ephesian destination of the Epistle, if the words 'at Ephesus' be removed, is simply a strong tradition, attested both by the ancient heading and by many early Christian writers.

This tradition is thought by very many scholars to be opposed by the character of the Epistle; Ephesians does not look altogether like what we should have expected a letter to the Ephesians to be. It will be remembered that Paul had spent three years at Ephesus, Acts 20.31, and must therefore have been intimately acquainted with the Ephesian church. A letter to that church would therefore naturally be full of local details, as is the case, for example, with the Epistles to the Corinthians. Yet as a matter of fact there is no other Epistle of Paul in which local details are so completely absent as they are in Ephesians. The Epistle is couched in the most general terms, which would be as suitable to strangers as to intimate friends, and the usual personal greetings are altogether omitted. How could such a letter be addressed to a church with which Paul had been personally acquainted for years?

Such considerations, among others, have led many modern scholars to adopt the text which omits 'at Ephesus' in the first verse, and to reject the tradition of the Ephesian destination. But if the letter was not addressed to the Ephesian Christians, to whom was it addressed? A plausible suggestion might seem to be that it was addressed simply to Gentile Christians in general; and indeed such a suggestion does justice to many of the facts. As has already been observed, the Epistle is quite general in character. But the hypothesis is opposed by Eph. 6.21, 22, where Tychicus is specially commended to the readers; for Tychicus could hardly have been dispatched on a mission to all the Gentile Christians throughout the Empire. On the one hand, then, the Epistle hardly seems to have been addressed exclusively to the church at Ephesus; but on the other hand it also seems not to have been addressed without limitation to Gentile Christians. An intermediate hypothesis, therefore, has won wide acceptance in recent years—an hypothesis which regards the primary destination of the Epistle as broader than Ephesus but narrower than the whole Gentile Christian world. According to this hypothesis the Epistle was sent neither to an individual church nor to the whole body of Gentile churches, but to a definite group among the Gentile churches. The Epistle is thus thought to be a circular letter, addressed to a group of churches, probably in Asia Minor. If this group is thought to include Ephesus, then justice is done both to the general character of the Epistle and to the early Christian tradition in favour of the Ephesian destination. In such a circular letter Paul might very naturally avoid matters of local interest; yet at the same time such a letter could easily become identified in Christian tradition with the principal church among those that were addressed. Even, therefore, if the words 'at Ephesus' were not written by Paul, and even if the letter were not addressed specifically to the Ephesian church, the ancient heading can hardly be called altogether erroneous.

It must be confessed that this question with regard to the address of the Epistle cannot be settled with certainty. Fortunately, it is by no means the most important question. No matter what the first destination may have been, the peculiar character of the Epistle is perfectly plain. Even if the Epistle was addressed to the Ephesian Christians it was certainly addressed to them, not as individuals or even as a congregation, but simply as representatives of Gentile Christianity in general. In Ephesians the special circumstances prevailing among the readers are far less in view than in any other of the Pauline Epistles—far less, even, than in the Epistle to the Romans. Elsewhere, the letters of Paul are intimately concerned with the local conditions in the congregations addressed; whereas here the apostolic vision ranges unhindered over the whole realm of the Church universal.

Occasion

It is altogether natural that such an Epistle should have been written at just the time when Ephesians actually appeared. At the time of the first Roman imprisonment Paul had passed through years of struggle with Judaizing opponents, who would exclude from the Church all Gentiles unwilling to become Jews. At last, however, the battle had been won; at last the right of Gentiles to a position in the Church had been established beyond question. We are sometimes inclined to underestimate the importance of this victory, but we can do so only because long familiarity has obscured the truly astonishing character of the result that was attained. Under the old dispensation, salvation was limited to the chosen people; here at length it was offered to men of every nation and every race. The right of the Gentiles to a place in the kingdom of the Messiah was indeed, as Paul calls it, a mystery—that is, a secret, something that could never have been discovered by human wisdom but was now at length revealed, in accordance with the eternal plan of God. Very naturally, after the conflict was over, after the Judaizers had been refuted and the Pauline gospel heartily approved even by the original apostles to whom the Judaizers falsely appealed, after the power of the Spirit had been manifested in the firm establishment of the Church throughout the whole world—very naturally, after the accomplishment of this mighty work of God, the thanksgiving of the apostle to the Gentiles found expression in an Epistle which is more like an exuberant hymn of praise than like an ordinary letter. The subject of the Epistle to the Ephesians is the universal Church of Christ—its divine origin and its divine purpose.

The Universal Church

The peculiar occasion of the Epistle appears most clearly in Eph. 2.11–22, where the former wretched position of the Gentiles is contrasted with their present blessedness as fellow citizens with the saints and members of the household of God. The old enmity between Jew and Gentile, Paul says, has been for ever done away. But it has been done away not by any mere incorporation of the Gentiles in the nation of Israel, but by the salvation given both to Jew and to Gentile by Jesus Christ. Peace has been established between Jew and Gentile only because both alike have been brought by the atoning death of Christ into peace with God. This new and blessed union, this destruction of the ancient enmity, constitutes the Church of Christ.

The Lord

The Church is never contemplated in the Epistle by itself, but always in connection with the work of him who is both its Founder and its Preserver. Christ is the Head, the Church is his body; Christ is the Husband, the Church is his holy bride. Behind the very existence of the Church stands a work of saving grace which the apostle never tires of celebrating with all the exuberance of language that he can command. In subject as well as in date and in form Ephesians and Colossians are twin Epistles; the presentation of the Church in Ephesians would be incomplete if it did not everywhere presuppose the presentation of the person of Christ which is the chief concern of Colossians. In one passage, particularly, Paul breaks out anew into a celebration of the majesty of the ascended Lord, Eph. 1.20–23. But the thought of this passage as well as of all that is said of Christ in Colossians is presupposed in Ephesians from beginning to end. It is impossible to maintain Paul's doctrine of the majesty and universality of the Church without maintaining also his doctrine of the divine Christ, who was before all things and in whom all things consist.

The Plan of God

In contemplating the Church, however, the vision of the apostle extends even behind the historic work of the Founder; it extends back into the eternal counsel of God. The blessed work of redemption, the choice of those who should be received into the glorious company of the redeemed, the glory of the consummation—all are part of an eternal plan. Human merit is altogether excluded; good works are the result, not the cause, of salvation; the Christian life is the creation of divine grace, Eph. 1.9, 10. God has chosen us in Christ 'before the foundation of the world, that we should be holy and without blemish before him in love: having foreordained us unto adoption as sons through Jesus Christ unto himself, according to the good pleasure of his will'. (vs. 4, 5). And as God is the beginning, so also God is the end; the whole work of redemption is 'to the praise of the glory of his grace'. (v. 6).

The Christian Life

As in the case of the other Pauline Epistles, the 'doctrinal' portion of Ephesians is followed by a 'practical' portion. But the two are inextricably intertwined. The weighty 'therefore' of Eph. 4.1, as of Rom. 12.1, should never be forgotten. It is the calling of which the readers are here exhorted to walk worthy which forms the subject of all that has gone before. Doctrine, in Paul's mind, was absolutely essential to life, as life was the necessary result of doctrine. The lesson needs to be learned. It is useless to try to attain the lofty ideal of conduct in Eph. chs. 4 to 6, without attending to the heavenly vision in chs. 1 to 3; just as on the other hand the vision itself grows faint and disappears unless it is made effective in holy living from day to day.

TOPICS FOR STUDY

1. Construct an outline of Ephesians, and summarize the Epistle in your own words (about three or four topics).

2. Point out the resemblances and the differences that exist between Colossians and Ephesians (several topics).

3. Where else does the figure of speech which is worked out in Eph. 6.10–17 appear in the New Testament?

4. Where in the other Epistles of Paul is the Church represented under the figure of a body? Compare these passages with the corresponding passages in Ephesians.

25: CHRIST AND HIS FOLLOWERS

Study material: The Epistle to the Philippians

After the puzzling question of the destination of Ephesians, it is rather a relief to turn to an Epistle that was written to a well-known church. This is the case with the Epistle to the Philippians. The church at Philippi was the first church which was founded in Macedonia after Paul had crossed over from Troas on the second missionary journey. Of certain events connected with its founding we have in The Acts the vivid account of an eyewitness, Acts 16.11–40. By piecing together the narrative in The Acts, the Epistle to the Philippians, and the scattered notices in others of the Epistles of Paul, it is possible to collect a considerable body of information about the Philippian church.

Paul and the Philippian Church

What stands out prominently in the whole history of the church, and especially in the letter which Paul addressed to it, is the intimacy and mutual confidence which existed between the church and its founder. The high degree of confidence which Paul reposed in the Philippian Christians appears most clearly of all in the fact that he was always ready to accept material assistance from them. In other churches, in order to refute the charge of covetousness, he was obliged to maintain a strict independence; but in Philippi he evidently considered himself quite safe from all such unworthy insinuations. Here, at least, was a case where the gifts could be accepted freely in the spirit in which they were given.

Not only was Paul, with his brother missionaries, entertained hospitably on his first visit to Philippi, but the ministrations of the Philippians followed him after his departure. The first assistance arrived very quickly, while he was still in Thessalonica; and during the brief period of his labour in that city, according to the usual interpretation of Phil. 4.16, the gift was repeated. Then, after he

173

had left Macedonia, assistance was again sent to him, vs. 15, 16. It is probably to this assistance that he refers in II Cor. 11.8, 9. In Corinth, on account of the danger of base accusations, he had been obliged to make himself independent of the local church by labouring with his hands, and what he earned in this way received a welcome supplement from the assistance which came from Macedonia. No doubt 'Macedonia' refers especially to Philippi; for in Thessalonica, for example, he had earned his living as in Corinth, I Thess. 2.9; II Thess. 3.7–9. Paul's refusal to accept material assistance from his churches must not, of course, be misinterpreted. It did not necessarily cast any reflection upon the zeal or upon the devotion of his converts. No doubt the decision of the apostle was determined by a variety of circumstances, I Cor. ch. 9; II Cor. 11.7–15. In Corinth, it was determined not so much, perhaps, by any fault of the local church as by the presence of false teachers from outside. Nevertheless, the fact remains that an exception to Paul's general practice could not have been made in the case of Philippi without a particularly cordial relation to the Philippian church. Paul does not indeed say that in the course of all his missionary labours the Philippians were the only ones who assisted him in a material way, but only that they were the only ones who did so at or immediately after his departure from Macedonia, Phil. 4.15; II Cor. 11.8. The acceptance of such assistance, however, was probably an unusual thing.

Date

At the time when the Epistle to the Philippians was written, Paul was in prison, Phil. 1.7, 13, 14, 17. That this imprisonment was the Roman imprisonment is made perfectly evident not only by general considerations, as in the case of the epistles which have just been studied, but also by the mention of 'Cæsar's household' in ch. 4.22, and perhaps by the reference to the 'prætorian guard' in ch. 1.13. Whether Philippians was written before or after the group consisting of Colossians, Philemon and Ephesians, cannot be determined with certainty. The probability, however, is somewhat in favour of the later date. In Philippians, the trial of Paul is represented as approaching a crisis. Before long he will probably either be executed or set at liberty. The conditions in the Roman church, as they are described in this Epistle, also indicate that the imprisonment of Paul had been protracted. These indications are not, indeed, absolutely conclusive. It is possible that Philippians was written before the other three epistles. Such questions must carefully be distinguished from matters about which real certainty can be attained.

Gifts of the Philippian Church

The situation that gave rise to the Epistle to the Philippians was manifold. The most immediate occasion, perhaps, was the arrival of certain gifts from the Philippian church. After a lapse of years, during which there had been no opportunity, the Philippians had again resumed their ministration to Paul's material needs. Naturally, Paul desired to acknowledge the gift. The letter does not, indeed, contain any exuberant thanks. It was just because Paul knew that the Philippian church would not expect that kind of return that he was so ready to accept from them a gift which he might have refused from others. The gift, after all, was valuable not so much for its own sake, as for what it indicated of affection and devotion in the givers. Paul could have done without the material aid, but he could not easily have done without the knowledge of true progress among his spiritual children. So he puts it in ch. 4.10–20, and he is perfectly sure that his readers will understand what he means. He himself cannot make any adequate return, whether in kind or by way of thanks; it is God who will bestow the true reward.

The gifts of the Philippian church had been transmitted by a certain Epaphroditus. The name 'Epaphroditus' is only a longer form of 'Epaphras'; but since it was a common name, there is no reason whatever for identifying the Philippian, Epaphroditus, with the Epaphras who was the founder of the Colossian church. After leaving Philippi, Epaphroditus had undergone a serious illness, of which in some way the Philippians had heard. He was now exceedingly anxious to return home; and accordingly Paul sent him, no doubt as the bearer of the letter. In the letter, the Philippians are assured that Epaphroditus has faithfully discharged his commission, and that his illness was incurred in the performance of duty.

Affairs at Rome

One principal purpose of the letter was to inform the Philippians of the progress of Paul's own affairs. The Epistle to the Philippians, therefore, supplements in very welcome fashion the scanty information afforded by The Acts about the singularly interesting period which Paul spent as a prisoner in Rome. Of course, the readers knew considerably more than we do to start with, so that some allusions in the Epistle, which to them were perfectly plain, are to us obscure. Apparently, the Philippians had been exceedingly anxious about the turn affairs were taking in Rome; but Paul reassures them. Events which in themselves seemed disquieting have resulted in the furtherance, rather than in the hindrance, of the gospel, ch. 1.12. The very imprisonment itself has not been an unmixed evil, for on account of it Paul has been spoken of in wide circles, and the preaching of the gospel has received a fresh impetus, vs. 13, 14. It is easy to see how Paul's bonds could become 'manifest in Christ throughout the whole prætorian guard'. Although Paul was treated with comparative leniency and permitted to occupy his own hired house, Acts 28.30, yet he was constantly chained to a soldier, vs. 16, 20; Eph. 6.20; and as one soldier relieved another in this duty, the news about the remarkable prisoner would soon become widely known. God had overruled even the worst that Paul's enemies could do against him.

The preaching which was being carried on in Rome was not all actuated by the highest motives. 'Some indeed,' says Paul, 'preach Christ even of envy and strife.' It has been suggested that these blameworthy preachers had regarded Paul as a rival. The rival was now removed by imprisonment, and they made the best use of their opportunity by getting as far ahead of him as they could. The way in which Paul speaks in Col. 4.11 about the Jewish Christians in Rome suggests that these envious preachers mentioned in Philippians belonged to the Jewish part of the Roman church; and the severe words about Jews or Jewish Christians in Phil. 3.2 perhaps point in the same direction. It seems hardly probable, however, that these Roman rivals of Paul came forward with definitely Judaistic teaching, like that which is combated in Galatians, for in that case Paul would hardly have spoken of them as he does in ch. 1.18. More probably, the content of their preaching was not seriously at fault, however faulty were their motives. Without sacrifice of principle Paul was able to speak of them with magnanimity. They had thought, by their rivalry, to add fresh affliction to his bonds; but he was even able to rejoice in what they were doing. By their efforts, Christ was being proclaimed. It was better that he should be proclaimed from unworthy motives than that he should not be proclaimed at all.

With regard to the outcome of his trial, Paul was able to calm the fears of the Philippian Christians. Personally, indeed, he was able to meet the outcome with equal fortitude, no matter what it might be. He had reached the point of Christian heroism where he could say, 'To me to live is Christ, and to die is gain.' (ch. 1.21.) His readers, however, were deeply solicitous, and he was able to reassure them. One judicial hearing had perhaps already been held, with a favourable result, ch. 1.7. Timothy would bring word as soon as there was anything more definite to tell, ch. 2.19–23. Meanwhile Paul was confident that he would finally be released and be restored to his beloved Philippians, ch. 1.25, 26. In the next chapter we shall see that as a matter of fact his expectations were fulfilled, and that he did visit Philippi, or at any rate Macedonia, again.

Finally, Paul desired by his letter to correct certain faults in the Philippian church. Admirably as the church had developed, it was of course not perfect; and with earnestness, though with the utmost delicacy and tenderness, Paul admonishes the Philippian Christians to remove what might mar the splendid Christian life which they had always maintained. Possibly there was danger of the intrusion of Judaizing error. That, however, is doubtful. Philippians 3.2–11 may be directed against Jews rather than Judaizers, or against Jewish Christians in Rome rather than in Philippi. The chief fault of the Philippian church seems to have consisted rather in a certain tendency to disharmony. Two women, in particular, Euodia and Syntyche, both of them formerly true co-labourers with Paul, had disagreed with one another. Apparently a similar tendency had made itself felt generally in the church, ch. 2.1–4. In counteracting it, Paul could do no better than appeal to the example of Christ. By relinquishing the glories of heaven, by becoming man, by submitting to the shameful death on the cross, Christ has held up before all his followers the supreme example of unselfishness and humility. If the Philippian Christians would think of that example, they would speedily do away with contention.

On the whole, the letter leaves an exceedingly favourable impression of the Philippian church. Even the tendency to disharmony had apparently not yet reached very serious lengths. There is in the Epistle nothing of the bitter denunciation of II Cor. chs. 10 to 13, nothing even of the shaming rebuke of I Cor. 1.10 to 4.21. Evidently the disagreements in Philippi were very different from the parties in Corinth. Paul is simply grieved that good, true Christian people should mar the peace of the church by useless quarrels. We may probably have confidence in the result. We may well hope that Euodia and Syntyche yielded readily to the representations of Paul's 'true yokefellow' and the rest.

Two Matters for Extended Comment

THE ADDRESS. PHIL. 1.1, 2

The address of Philippians is remarkable because of the mention of bishops and deacons, which occurs in this way in no other of the Pauline epistles. Possibly, as has been suggested, these officers are here mentioned because they had had a special part in sending the gifts of the church. It is important to observe that there was a plurality of bishops in the Philippian church. At a later time, when the 'bishops' were exalted above the other presbyters, there was only one bishop in every church. In The Acts and in the Pauline epistles, 'bishop' and 'presbyter' appear plainly as nothing more than two names for exactly the same office.

It should be noticed that the title 'apostle', which appears at the beginning of all the other Pauline epistles addressed to churches, except First and Second Thessalonians, the two earliest, is lacking in the address of Philippians. Perhaps in writing to such a devoted church Paul considered it unnecessary to mention his apostleship as he had regularly done in his epistles since the denial of it in Galatia. On account of the peculiar nature of the Philippian church, the Epistle to the Philippians partakes somewhat of the informality and intimacy of such a letter as that to Philemon, where the title is also lacking in the address.

Very naturally Timothy is associated with Paul in the address of the Epistle, for he had been one of Paul's companions in founding the Philippian church. At what time Timothy had come to Rome we do not know. His name appears also in the address of Colossians and of Philemon. Luke, although he had journeyed with Paul to Rome, and was in Rome at the time when Colossians and Philemon were written, Col. 4.14; Philem. 24, was apparently absent at the time of Philippians; for since he, like Timothy, had assisted in founding the Philippian church, and perhaps had even remained in Philippi for years after the departure of the others, he would probably have been associated in the address, or at least would have sent greetings, if he had been at hand.

EXHORTATION TO UNITY. PHIL. 2.1–18

With the utmost earnestness, Paul here appeals to his readers to keep their Christian life free from selfishness and quarrelling. The stupendous 'Christological' passage of the Epistle, vs. 5–11, which has given rise to endless discussion, is introduced merely in an incidental way, in order to strengthen the apostle's exhortation. So it is frequently in the letters of Paul. The apostle was always able to make the profoundest verities of the faith immediately effective in conduct. Theology in Paul was never divorced from practice. The converse of the proposition, however, is also true. If Paul's theology did not exist apart from practice, neither did his practice exist apart from theology. It is the latter proposition which needs to be emphasized today. Modern liberalism has sometimes endeavoured to reproduce Paul's religion apart from his theology; but the effort has resulted in failure.

The example of Christ which Paul holds up before his readers is briefly as follows: Originally Christ not only existed in the form of God—that is, was in full possession of the divine attributes— but also lived in glory, in a way befitting Deity. Instead, however, of keeping hold of this equality with God as though it were a booty which he had seized, he gave it up freely. He divested himself, not indeed of his divine attributes, but of the enjoyment of his divine glory, by becoming man. He who was Lord of all took the position of a servant, like other men. And even more. His obedience extended even to death, and to the shameful death of the cross. But after humiliation came exaltation. God gave to him a name that is above every name. At the name of Jesus every knee shall bow, in earth and in heaven, to the glory of God the Father.

TOPICS FOR STUDY

1. Construct an outline of Philippians.
2. Summarize the Epistle in your own words (two topics).
3. Trace the previous history of the Philippian church.
4. Collect the information afforded by the Epistle about affairs in Rome.
5. Discuss the persons mentioned in the Epistle. Whom else might you have expected to find mentioned?

Study material: The First Epistle to Timothy, the Epistle to Titus, and the Second Epistle to Timothy

First and Second Timothy and Titus were written during a period in the life of Paul which is not covered by the narrative in The Acts. All attempts to fit these Epistles into the period of the first three missionary journeys and the first Roman imprisonment have resulted in failure. They must clearly be assigned to a later period in the life of the apostle.

The Pastoral Epistles not mere Private Letters

These letters are addressed to intimate associates of Paul. It might therefore be expected that they would be even more informal and intimate in character than such epistles as the Epistle to the Philippians and the Epistle to Philemon. This expectation, how-ever, is not realized. As a matter of fact, the Epistles to Timothy and the Epistle to Titus, far from being more informal than the other letters of Paul, are perhaps in some respects the least informal of all. The explanation is simple. These Epistles are not merely private letters. Though addressed to individuals among Paul's friends, they are addressed to them not as individuals, but rather as leaders in the Church. From the first they were intended to be read not by Timothy and Titus alone, but also by the churches over which these men were placed. With some justice they may be called the 'Pastoral Epistles'; in them Timothy and Titus are addressed in their capacity as pastors. The Pastoral Epistles are—if the word be properly understood—'official' communica-tions.

It is true, the personal element is by no means altogether absent from the letters. In Second Timothy it is especially noticeable. The cloak which Paul left at Troas, II Tim. 4.13, cannot be regarded as a matter of public interest. These letters, therefore, are not mere literary compositions put into epistolary form. They served a private as well as a public purpose. The public purpose, however, is dominant. Paul is here addressing his intimate associates; but the form in which he does so is always limited and directed by the thought of a wider circle of readers.

The Pastoral Epistles are very different from the other epistles of Paul. The difference is due partly to a difference of subject and a change in the readers, partly to a change in Paul himself.

The Subject of the Pastoral Epistles

The principal subject of these Epistles is the organization of the Church, both for the preservation of sound teaching and for the conduct of government. The first period in the history of Christianity was over. Christianity had been established in many of the cities of the Empire. The existing churches had grown enormously since the writing of Paul's first epistles. The church at Ephesus, for example, at the time of First Timothy, was no longer a small group of believers with all of whom the apostle could be intimately acquainted. It had grown, no doubt, into a community of very considerable size.

The increase in numbers brought with it certain disadvantages, and certain needs. One disadvantage was the impossibility of intimate personal acquaintance of all members of the church with the apostle. An epistle of Paul intended for the church at Ephesus or for a circle of churches in Asia Minor could no longer be an unrestrained outpouring of affection for intimate friends and disciples. It is no wonder that the Pastoral Epistles are different from the earlier letters. In them Paul is thinking not merely of intimate friends, but of great churches with a complex life.

With the growth of large Christian communities there arose an increasing need for stability of tradition and for organization. At first Christianity was a mighty upheaval. Revelation followed revelation with marvellous rapidity. The full glory of Christian truth seemed to burst upon the world all at once. It was a glorious time—that first entrance of the Church upon her world-wide conquest. It was glorious, but it was also insufficient. Something else was needed if the Church was to retain her power. Conquest had to be followed by defence; production by conservation. It was not God's plan that every new generation should be obliged to rediscover Christianity afresh. The divine method is the method of growth. Not every age need begin at the beginning. Rather must the children stand upon the shoulders of the parents; the second generation must build upon a precious deposit of truth and of experience. Such is the divine law of progress.

The Pastoral Epistles may be regarded as marking the beginning of the second stage in the life of the Church. The age of origination was nearly over; the age of conservation had begun. The Church must now be looked upon as an established institution. Great principles were needed for its guidance, principles which should serve not only for special circumstances, but for all generations.

Fortunately, in entering upon this new stage of her life, the Church was still under apostolic guidance. There is a divine warrant for sound instruction and for orderly government as well as for missionary zeal. The necessity of education and organization was, in fact, recognized from the beginning. The very earliest Christians in Jerusalem attended to the 'teaching' of the apostles; the earliest known churches of Paul were given elders, Acts 2.42; 14.23. The First Epistle to the Corinthians, in particular, points out the necessity of a well-ordered ecclesiastical life. In the Pastoral Epistles, however, these things become more prominent and more explicit.

Development in Paul

In addition to the changing needs of the churches, there is un-doubtedly to be observed in the Pastoral Epistles a change in Paul himself. These Epistles are quieter, more restrained, more deliber-ate than the earlier letters. The change is striking. But it was not altogether abrupt. The tendency which culminates in the Pastorals was observed already in the epistles of the first imprisonment. Even in Colossians, Philemon, Ephesians and Philippians, the passionate outbursts of Galatians and Second Corinthians had given place to a quieter tone. The period of conflict was over. At the time of the Pastorals, the results of the change had become more clearly marked. The life of Paul was approaching its close. It had been a life of tireless activity, of bitter disappointments, of glorious successes. At length the long struggle was nearly over. But what of the future? What would become of the Pauline churches when Paul had died? This question began to occupy an ever larger place in the apostle's thought; with it the Pastoral Epistles are concerned.

Under the circumstances, then, the peculiarities of the Pastoral Epistles, striking though they are, are not altogether surprising. Small groups of Christians, all personally acquainted with the apostle, have given place to great congregations; the Church is ready to settle down as a permanent factor in the world's life. The apostle himself has passed through the period of origination and of conflict into the inward calm of his closing years.

Biographical Information in the Pastoral Epistles

The Pastoral Epistles supply some very valuable biographical information. The outstanding facts are that Paul was set at liberty after his first imprisonment and continued his labours in the east. This information is confirmed and supplemented by the important testimony of Clement of Rome. According to Clement, Paul taught righteousness to the whole world and went 'to the bound of the west'. The expression can hardly mean anything else than that Paul actually carried out his intention of preaching in Spain, Rom. 15.24, 28. The letter of Clement in which the passage occurs was written in the name of the church at Rome to the church at Corinth at about A.D. 95. With regard to the release of Paul from his first Roman imprisonment, then, the Pastorals are confirmed by Clement; with regard to what he did afterwards they are supplemented by him. Putting the two sources of information together, it appears that after regaining his liberty Paul went both to the east and to Spain—probably in the reverse order, though the order is perhaps not absolutely certain.

The release of Paul from his first Roman imprisonment is only what might have been expected in view of such passages as Philem. 22; Phil. 1.25; 2.24. Evidently when the Epistle to the Philippians was written the situation was hopeful. Acquittal had already become probable. The evidence of the Pastoral Epistles and of Clement simply shows that the hopes which Paul held out to his converts were not disappointed.

At the time of Second Timothy, however, the situation was quite different from that which existed in the first captivity. Sentence, indeed, had not already been pronounced; an immediate execution was not in view; Paul might still have need of that cloak which he had left at Troas. But death was at no very great distance. The close of Paul's life, at last, had come, II Tim. 4.6–8. Credible tradition informs us of the issue. At some time before the death of Nero, Paul was beheaded on the road to Ostia near Rome.

The great man's work was over. It had been a wonderful life. Paul has set his mark for ever on the history of the world. Few men, to say the least, have wielded one tenth-part of his influence. To the historian, he is an object of perennial interest. To the Christian, he is more—and the Christian view is right. Paul was not a philosopher, not a reformer, not a statesman. He was an apostle. He had been sent on a mission. His gospel had been given him by Christ. His life is a revelation from God.

The First Epistle to Timothy

At the time when First Timothy was written, Paul had recently made a journey to Macedonia, I Tim. 1.3. Perhaps he had gone thither from Ephesus, though the words do not make that perfectly clear. At any rate, he had directed Timothy to remain in Ephesus, where he hoped to join him before long. In case of delay, however, he writes the Epistle, chs. 3.14, 15; 4.13.

On a previous occasion, perhaps by word of mouth when he had been in Ephesus, he had warned Timothy to put a stop to certain false teaching in the Church, and the warning is now reiterated in the Epistle. The exact nature of this teaching is somewhat difficult to determine. Apparently it had been concerned with the Jewish law, ch. 1.7–11; compare Titus 1.10, 14. Like the false teaching at Colossæ, it seems not to have been directly subversive of the truth of the gospel. At least, however, it diverted attention from the great things of the faith to useless questionings, I Tim. 6.4. The myths and endless genealogies, ch. 1.4, compare 4.7, were perhaps elaborations of the Old Testament history. Whether the ascetic tendency which is combated in ch. 4.3, 8, is connected with this same teaching, is not certain, but it is on the whole perhaps probable.

The first reference to the false teaching, ch. 1.3–10, leads Paul to speak of the norm by which it could be combated, vs. 11–20. That norm was the gospel with which he had been entrusted. The bestowal of the gospel had changed him from a blasphemer and persecutor into an apostle. The gospel had been bestowed purely by the free grace of Christ, and its content was the salvation which Christ offers. A doxology to God, v. 17, is natural whenever that gospel is mentioned. That gospel will overcome all error, and if attended to diligently will prevent disasters like that which has befallen Hymenæus and Alexander.

In the second chapter, Paul insists upon gravity and order in the public worship of the Church. In the prayers which are to be offered, the civil authority is not to be forgotten, even though it be non-Christian. The sympathies of the Christian must be broad. God desires all men to come to a knowledge of the truth.

The highest regular officers of the Church are in the third chapter called 'bishops'. It is abundantly evident, however—especially from Titus 1.5, 7—that 'bishop' is only another name for 'presbyter' or 'elder'. At a later time the term 'bishop' was applied to an officer who had the supreme oversight over a church and to whom the elders were subject. These conditions did not prevail at the time of the Pastoral Epistles. At first sight, indeed, it might seem as though Timothy and Titus themselves were 'bishops' in the later sense of the word. But this is also false. Timothy and Titus do not appear at all as officers of individual congregations. They had oversight over a plurality of churches, and evidently their authority was special and temporary. They did not fill an office which was intended to become permanent in the Church, but were simply special representatives of the apostle. As the apostles had no successors, so no man after the apostolic age had a right to assume the functions of Timothy and Titus.

The fourth chapter calls attention to the revelation of the Holy Spirit, probably through the lips of Christian prophets, that in the future there would appear apostates from the faith. The errorists who are combated in vs. 7–10 are apparently to be regarded as forerunners, still within the Church, of the more open apostasy which is one day to follow.

The institution of the 'widows', which is discussed in the fifth chapter, is to us somewhat obscure. Evidently those who were accounted 'widows', being helpless, were entitled to support by the church. The necessity of sound teaching, with emphasis upon the really fundamental things of the faith, is again insisted upon; and certain false teachers are accused of practising or inculcating piety as a means of worldly gain, ch. 6.3–10. The last warning of the Epistle characteristically concerns vain babblings and oppositions of a so-called knowledge. Probably these errors are connected in some way with those which are combated in the first section of the Epistle. In the final words, 'Grace be with you', the 'you' in the Greek, according to the best attestation, is plural; and in the corresponding passages at the end of Titus and of Second Timothy, it is certainly plural. This may furnish an indication—to be added to more general considerations—that the Pastoral Epistles were intended not merely for those to whom they are formally addressed, but also to the churches under their care.

The Epistle to Titus

The address of the Epistle to Titus is noteworthy for the long addition to the title of the author, which is to be compared with the similar addition in Romans.

At the time when the Epistle was written, Paul had recently been with Titus in Crete. Paul had not laboured on that island before the first Roman imprisonment. His journeys in the east between the two imprisonments therefore involved something more than the revisitation of former fields. The reason why Titus was left behind in Crete was somewhat similar to the reason why Timothy, according to First Timothy, was told to remain in Ephesus. Titus was to give attention to organization, and to the maintenance of sound instruction.

Like Timothy, Titus is given the power of establishing presbyters, and of establishing them not merely in one church but in various churches. The function of the presbyter was that of 'bishop' or 'overseer', Titus 1.5–7. In vs. 9–16, the close connection of organization with sound doctrine becomes particularly apparent. One important function of the presbyters was to counteract the errors which were springing up. The account of the errorists in Crete is perhaps in some respects clearer than that which is given of the related phenomenon in Ephesus. The false teachers were animated by a love of gain, v. 11. Some of them were Jews or proselytes, v. 10. They had a fondness for Jewish fables. Apparently, also, they tried to atone for a lack of real inward purity by an outward asceticism, vs. 15, 16. They were concerned with vain questionings and genealogies and legal disputes. These last are perhaps to be regarded as casuistic discussions like those which play such a large part in Jewish tradition.

The Epistle to Titus is somewhat richer than First Timothy in personal details. After Titus has been relieved in Crete by Artemas or Tychicus, who may soon be sent, he is to join Paul in Nicopolis. Tychicus, it will be remembered, had served as Paul's messenger during the first imprisonment. He was the bearer of Colossians and Ephesians. The Nicopolis where Paul is intending to pass the approaching winter is probably the chief of the many cities of that name, the Nicopolis in Epirus. Zenas, a lawyer otherwise unknown, and the well-known Apollos, who appears so prominently in The Acts and in First Corinthians, are to be furnished in Crete with everything that they need for their further journey.

The Second Epistle to Timothy

The First Epistle to Timothy and the Epistle to Titus are in many respects strikingly similar. A certain strong family resemblance extends also to Second Timothy. Evidently all three of the Pastoral Epistles belong to the same general period of Paul's life, and were intended to subserve similar purposes. Second Timothy, however, as compared with the other two, exhibits some marked peculiarities.

The personal element, in particular, is in this letter much more prominent. Second Timothy contains a wealth of interesting biographical details about Timothy, about Paul, and about a very considerable number of other persons. Some of these last are known only from this Epistle; others have been brought to our attention again and again.

In Second Timothy Paul appears as a prisoner, no doubt at Rome. This time there seems to be little hope of his release. Apparently his imprisonment is not of long standing. Only recently he has been at Corinth and at Miletus, II Tim. 4.20. He speaks in one place of his first defence, v. 16. Some suppose that this is a reminiscence of the trial which had taken place years before, during the first imprisonment. More probably it refers to some preliminary hearing which had only recently been held. Paul is oppressed with a sense of loneliness, even more than during the first imprisonment. There was no one to stand by him at his first hearing. For one reason or another, his intimate associates have been scattered—some of them, no doubt, for good and sufficient reasons, but Demas, at any rate, out of an unworthy love of the world. Luke, fortunately, is still with him; and Timothy, with Mark, is urged to come before the winter, vs. 11, 21. Mark seems to have changed since he turned back from the work at Perga. At the beginning he was rebuked for desertion; but now at the end he is one of the few faithful ones.

It is not quite clear where Timothy was when the letter was addressed to him. The greeting to Priscilla and Aquila might seem to point to Ephesus. They had lived there before; perhaps they returned thither after a residence in Rome, Rom. 16.3. If Timothy was in Ephesus, then Tychicus, who was sent thither, II Tim. 4.12, was probably expected to linger by the way; otherwise his sending would be no news to the reader of the letter. Something is to be said, perhaps, for the view that Timothy was not at Ephesus, but perhaps at Lystra, his original home.

The Second Epistle to Timothy contains warnings against false teaching similar to those which appear in First Timothy and Titus. But the characteristic feature of the letter is to be found in the references to the apostle's own life. Even the warnings and admonitions are brought into relation to these. Paul does not hesitate to point to himself as an example for his beloved followers. He does so, without a touch of vain glory, in the simple consciousness of a divine commission. Second Timothy is a letter of farewell, in which reminiscence and exhortation are characteristically blended. It is a farewell from the apostle, primarily for Timothy, though he is expecting to see Timothy again, but also for all of the Pauline churches. The letter has taken deep hold of every generation in the history of the Church. The fitting end of a life of true service, the calm facing of death, the certainty of heavenly communion with the Lord—these are the things above all others that have been learned from the last of the epistles of Paul.

TOPICS FOR STUDY

1. Construct outlines of the Pastoral Epistles.
2. Summarize the Pastoral Epistles in your own words (three topics).
3. Collect the biographical information to be derived from the Pastoral Epistles (a) about Paul, (b) about Timothy, (c) about other persons (three or four topics).
4. Describe the false teaching which is combated in the Pastoral Epistles.

The Presentation and Defence
of Christianity

27: A PRESENTATION OF JESUS TO JEWISH CHRISTIANS

Study material: The Gospel according to Matthew

In the previous chapters we have studied the early history of the Christian Church. Now we begin a brief study of the basis of that history. Though the Gospels themselves were possibly not produced until after the epistles of Paul, the information that they contain was known from the beginning. At first it was probably handed down simply by word of mouth; then, perhaps, even before the origin of our Gospels, parts of it were put into writing; but however it was preserved one thing is certain—knowledge of the life of Jesus was never absent from the Christian Church.

For the early Christians, the facts about Jesus could be obtained in ways too numerous to mention; eyewitnesses could be questioned, not only in Jerusalem, but also throughout Palestine and even in the Gentile world. For us, however, the sources of detailed information about the life of Christ are limited. They are confined almost exclusively to the New Testament, and in particular to the four Gospels.

The Greek word for 'gospel' means 'good news'. Nowhere in the New Testament, however, is that word applied to a book. There is no reference in the New Testament to a 'Gospel' of Matthew or of Mark or of Luke or of John. In the New Testament the word 'gospel' has a more general reference. It designates the 'good news' which lies at the basis of Christian preaching, however that news may be known. Christianity is based upon 'a piece of information'. The subject of that information is the life and death and resurrection of Jesus Christ. Without Christ we should have been hopeless, but Christ has saved us. Information about what he has done for us, however that information be conveyed, is the gospel.

The Synoptists and John
The four Gospels fall naturally into two divisions. The last Gospel

G

of the four, the Gospel of John, belongs clearly in a division by itself. The first three are so strikingly alike that they are well called the 'Synoptic' Gospels. 'Synoptic' means 'viewed together'; the first three Gospels can easily be arranged in a 'synopsis' or 'harmony', by which the similar passages appear in parallel columns. The reasons for the striking similarity among the Synoptic Gospels and the striking difference of all of them from the Gospel of John will be considered briefly in subsequent chapters.

The Heading 'According to Matthew'

The Gospel of Matthew does not itself declare that it was written by Matthew or by one of the twelve apostles; the title, 'Gospel according to Matthew', or, in a still earlier form, simply 'According to Matthew', is not to be regarded as part of the book itself, but is probably just a convenient heading, intended to distinguish this Gospel from the others. Undoubtedly, however, it is very ancient, and forms a valuable element in the Christian tradition about the authorship of the First Gospel.

The Apostle Matthew

In the four lists of the apostles, Matt. 10.2–4; Mark 3.16–19; Luke 6.13–16; Acts 1.13, Matthew is designated by the bare name, except in his own Gospel, where he appears as 'Matthew the publican'. In Matt. 9.9, his call is narrated. In the parallel passages in Mark and Luke, Mark 2.14; Luke 5.27, 28, the name of the publican who was called is given only as 'Levi'. Without the Gospel of Matthew we should not have been able to identify Levi and Matthew. Evidently the apostle had two names, as was the case with so many others of the persons mentioned in the New Testament. After his call, Matthew made a great feast for Jesus, Luke 5.29; compare Mark 2.15. Matthew himself, alone among the Synoptists, does not even make it perfectly clear that it was he in whose house Jesus sat at meat. The peculiarities of the First Gospel in what is said about Matthew become significant when the authorship is known.

Tradition

AUTHOR

The very early and uniform tradition which connects the apostle

Matthew with the first Gospel should certainly be trusted. It is difficult to see how the tradition could have arisen unless it was based upon fact. Matthew was one of the most obscure of the apostles; if the desire had been to win acceptance for the Gospel by attributing it to some great man of the apostolic age, surely Peter or Philip or James would have been chosen as the supposed author, rather than Matthew.

DATE

According to tradition, the Gospel of Matthew was written first among the four Gospels. This tradition is very widely rejected by modern scholars, who date Mark before Matthew, but it may well be correct. The further tradition that the Gospel was written while Peter and Paul were preaching in Rome dates the Gospel in the sixties of the first century.

PURPOSE

Another element in the tradition is that Matthew was written for Jews. This is almost certainly correct. It is supported decisively by the character of the Gospel itself.

Traditional Purpose Confirmed by the Gospel Itself

JESUS AS THE JEWISH MESSIAH

Evidently one chief purpose of the evangelist is to exhibit Jesus as the Jewish Messiah. This purpose is subserved especially by the very frequent references to Old Testament prophecy. The expression, 'that it might be fulfilled which was spoken by the Lord through the prophet', is characteristic of the Gospel of Matthew. It occurs, with slight variations, no less than four times in the first two chapters, and is frequent also in the rest of the book. The Old Testament citations in the Gospel of Matthew vary from the Septuagint more frequently than those in most of the New Testament, and display acquaintance with the Hebrew original.

OTHER INDICATIONS

The treatment of the Old Testament by Matthew is itself sufficient to show that the Gospel was intended especially for Jews. But other peculiarities point in the same direction. For example, in Matt. 27.62–66; 28.11–15, there is a refutation of Jewish slander which is contained in none of the other Gospels. In Matt. 5.17–19 the positive attitude of Jesus toward the Mosaic law is especially emphasized. These indications might be supplemented by a number of others.

MATTHEW IS NOT JUDAISTIC

Of course, however, the Jewish character of Matthew must not be misunderstood. In exhibiting Jesus especially as the Jewish Messiah, Matthew did not mean at all to deny that he was also Saviour of the Gentiles. Passages like Matt. 10.5, 6; 15.24, where the commission of the apostles in their preaching tour and of Jesus himself is limited to work among the Jews, are balanced by the great universalistic commission of Matt. 28.19, 20, in which the Gospel reaches its climax. Evidently the evangelist has merely recorded the facts. In the first place, Jesus' own ministry, with that of his disciples during his earthly life, was in the divine economy confined for the most part to Israel. In the second place, Jesus intended his work ultimately to be for the benefit of all nations. Matthew has recorded both sides of Jesus' teaching.

Certainly the Judaism of Matthew is as far removed as possible from being Judaistic. It was a strange vagary of criticism—now fortunately abandoned—by which the Gospel of Matthew was represented as being a party document written in support of men like the Judaizers of Galatians, who were opposed to Pauline Christianity. Evidently the one central purpose of Matthew, dominating all others, was to tell the truth about Jesus. If, in view of the Jewish nationality of his first readers he exhibited with especial clearness the work of Jesus for Israel, he was fully justified in so doing. He also with equal clearness represented Jesus as the founder of a Christian community separate from Judaism. He did full justice to the universalism of Jesus' message. The Jesus of the First Gospel is not only the Jewish Messiah, but also the Saviour of the world, and the Jesus, not of fiction, but of history.

Jesus as Teacher and Saviour

The Gospel of Matthew presents Jesus especially as a teacher. In modern times this side of the Gospel has sometimes been given an exclusive prominence which is quite foreign to the intention of the evangelist. To Matthew, as to every other New Testament writer, Jesus was first and foremost, not a teacher, but a Saviour. According to the whole of the New Testament, sound instruction of itself is quite insufficient for human needs. It is insufficient because of sin. Not only repentance is required, but also expiation of the terrible guilt of sin; not only instruction, but a new power.

Nevertheless, the power of God in salvation deals with men not as though they were sticks and stones, incapable of understanding the Father's love, but as beings who can receive the Spirit consciously and with gladness. Thus in the New Testament, and particularly in the Gospel of Matthew, the exercise of sovereign power appears hand in hand with instruction. Jesus is a Saviour; but as a Saviour he is also a teacher. If we have received his healing power, then we shall also obey his commands, and obey them, not blindly, as of compulsion, but with the free joy of gratitude and love.

'The Book of the Generation of Jesus Christ'

The first verse of the Gospel is evidently based upon the formula, occurring for the first time at Gen. 5.1, which marks off the divisions of the book of Genesis. It is most naturally regarded as a heading for the genealogy that follows in Matt. 1.2–17. There is only one objection to that view. In Genesis 'the book of the generations of Adam', or 'the generations of Shem' or the like, introduces an account, not of ancestors of the persons in question, but of their descendants. In Matt. 1.2–17, on the contrary, we have an account not of descendants of Jesus, but of ancestors. This objection has led some scholars to regard Matt. 1.1 as the title not of the genealogy but of the whole Gospel. The title would then represent Jesus as the beginning of a new race, or of a new period in the history of humanity.

This interpretation is unnecessarily subtle. It should rather be admitted that there is a difference between the phrase in Genesis and that in Matthew. The difference is very natural. In the case of Abraham the descendants were in view; in the case of the Messiah, the ancestors. Adam and Noah and Abraham were bearers of a promise; Christ was the culmination. Genesis looks forward; Matthew looks back. The difference in the use of the phrase is natural and significant.

The title, with the whole genealogy, is significant of what is to follow. At the very start, the ruling thought of Matthew's Gospel finds expression. Jesus is son of David, and son of Abraham; he is the culmination of the divine promise.

The Sermon on the Mount

In the Gospel of Matthew, more than in the other Synoptic Gospels, the teaching of Jesus is presented not merely in isolated sayings, but in extended discourses. Of these discourses, the 'Sermon on the Mount', chs. 5 to 7, is typical. Part of the material which it contains appears also in the Gospel of Luke, but in somewhat different form. It is altogether probable that Jesus frequently treated the same subjects on different occasions.

The Sermon on the Mount describes some characteristics of those who have been made citizens of the kingdom of God. It is not intended to be a compendium of all that man needs to know. To regard it as such is to do grave injustice to the other teaching of Jesus and to the teaching of his Spirit through the apostles. The Sermon on the Mount can really be understood only when it is taken in connection with the rest of the New Testament. One-sided emphasis upon even the most precious things is sure to result in impoverishment of the Church.

In the Sermon on the Mount Jesus is contrasting the laws of the kingdom especially with the laws promulgated by the Pharisees. The contrast has often been misinterpreted. Men have represented Jesus as a mild philanthropist who mitigated the severities of Moses. There could be no more complete reversal of the facts. Such misinterpretation is guarded against by Jesus himself. 'Except your righteousness shall exceed the righteousness of the scribes and Pharisees, ye shall in no wise enter into the kingdom of heaven.' Matt. 5.20. With all their insistence upon minute details, the Pharisees were really advocating, not too strict an interpretation of the law of Moses, but an interpretation not nearly strict enough. The Pharisees were satisfied with obedience to a set of external rules; Jesus demanded purity of heart. Jesus came not to make things easier, but to make things harder.

How then, if Jesus brought no relief from the inexorable demands of the law, if in remitting the petty, annoying externalities of Pharisaic legality, he imposed a law more searching and more unattainable than anything the Pharisees conceived—how could such a Jesus be represented as one whose yoke is easy and whose burden is light? Matt. 11.30. The answer is perfectly plain—Jesus was not only a teacher, but a Saviour; not only a lawgiver, but a helper. Without the cross, the Sermon on the Mount would be an intolerable burden; with the cross, it becomes the guide to a way of life. In the Sermon on the Mount, Jesus has held up an un-attainable ideal, he has revealed the depths of human guilt, he has made demands far too lofty for human strength. But, thank God, he has revealed guilt only to wash it away, and with his demands he has given strength to fulfil them. It is a sadly superficial view of the Sermon on the Mount which substitutes it for the story of the cross; a deeper understanding of it leads straight to Calvary. If God's demands were lower, then we might stand before him in our strength; but if his will is truly described in the Sermon on the Mount, then we are all of us guilty sinners, helpless and hope-less in the presence of his wrath.

The Sermon on the Mount has a strange fascination. It has laid deep hold upon the consciences of men. But it will remain for ever a dead letter, it will be thrust aside as the impracticable ideal of a fanatical dreamer, unless once for all human pride be aban-doned and men look for salvation not from their own goodness but from the divine sacrifice for sin. Sin is very terrible, but Christ has paid the penalty of it; the will of God is unattainable, but with God all things are possible. There is the whole gospel. It is being despised today. But anything short of it means the death of the Church. The modern theologians are right in emphasizing the ethical teaching of Jesus. Hear the Sermon on the Mount, and do as well as hear, and your life will be founded on the rock. But hear it, not from a mere teacher, but from the Saviour who died; not from a dead prophet, but ever anew from the living Lord.

TOPICS FOR STUDY

1. Collect the citations from the Old Testament which occur in the Gospel of Matthew. Which of them are peculiar to this Gospel?

2. Collect the discourses and incidents which are contained only in Matthew.

3. Construct a general outline of the Gospel.

4. Construct a detailed outline of Matt. chs. 5 to 7.

5. Collect information about the life of Matthew, noting peculiarities of his own references to himself as compared with those in the other Gospels.

6. Point out indications of the special interest felt by Matthew in the teaching of Jesus about the Church.

28: A GRAPHIC SKETCH OF THE LIFE OF JESUS

Study material: The Gospel according to Mark

The Tradition

AUTHORSHIP

Like the Gospel of Matthew, the Gospel of Mark does not itself mention the name of its author. The tradition as to authorship, however, is if anything even stronger than in the case of the First Gospel; and the origin of the tradition is even more difficult to understand unless it was founded upon fact. Mark was not even one of the apostles; at first he had acted in a purely subordinate capacity, Acts 13.5; and on one occasion his conduct had not been altogether beyond reproach, v. 13; ch. 15.38. If the intention was to enhance the authority of the Second Gospel by attributing it, falsely, to some great man of the apostolic age, Mark would certainly never have been chosen.

As in the case of Matthew, so in that of Mark it is Papias of Hierapolis who provides the earliest information about the production of the Gospel. Again also the words of Papias are quoted by Eusebius (Church History, iii, 39). The passage from Papias is as follows:

'This also the presbyter said: "Mark, on the one hand, being an interpreter of Peter, wrote accurately as many things as he remembered, yet not in order, the things which were either said or done by the Lord." For neither did he hear the Lord nor did he follow him, but afterwards, as I said, he followed Peter, who carried on his teaching as need required, but not as though he were making an ordered account of the oracles of the Lord; so that Mark committed no fault when he wrote some things as he had remembered them. For he had one care—that he should not leave out anything of the things that he had heard, or represent anything among them falsely.'

It will be observed that Papias is here represented as quoting from 'the presbyter'. Probably, however, it is only the first sentence that is quoted; the rest seems to be an explanation by Papias himself. By 'presbyter', or 'elder', Papias means not an officer in the Church, but a man of an older generation. The tradition is therefore very ancient. Papias himself lived in the former half of the second century; a man of a still older generation would probably have acquired his information about Mark well before A.D. 100. Such information is not to be lightly rejected.

DEPENDENCE UPON PETER

According to the presbyter, Mark was an 'interpreter' of Peter. If the word be taken strictly it means that Mark translated the words of Peter from one language into another—probably from Aramaic into Greek. On the whole, however, it is not probable, in view of linguistic conditions in Palestine and in the Church, that Peter would be unable to speak Greek. Perhaps, then, the sentence means that Mark was merely the mediator, in a general sense, of Peter's preaching. He presented the teaching of Peter to those who had not had the opportunity of hearing it themselves. Perhaps the meaning is that he had done so formerly by word of mouth. Perhaps, however, it is rather the Gospel itself that is referred to. By writing the Gospel Mark became an interpreter or mediator of the preaching of Peter.

But whatever meaning be given to the word 'interpreter', the general sense of the sentence—especially when taken in connection with the following explanation by Papias—is fairly clear. Mark derived the information for his Gospel not from personal acquaintance with the earthly Jesus, but from association with Peter.

This latter assertion is no doubt correct. It is supported by the character of the Gospel itself. There are passages in the Gospel which seem to be written from Peter's point of view, and the references to Peter are just what might be expected of an account based on Peter's own testimony.

APOSTOLIC AUTHORITY

The connection of Mark's Gospel with Peter serves to supplement what was said in chapter 1 about the apostolic authority of the New Testament. Those of the New Testament books that were not actually written by apostles were written by 'apostolic men'—by men who stood so close to the apostles as to be executors of part of their commission.

TIME, PLACE AND DESTINATION

The date of the Gospel of Mark is put by Christian tradition sometimes before and sometimes after the death of Peter. But it is
generally admitted that the Gospel was written before the destruction of Jerusalem in A.D. 70. With regard to the place of writing,
that form of tradition is to be preferred which points to Rome;
for it is supported by certain indications in the Gospel itself.
Unlike Matthew, Mark was evidently intended primarily, not for
Jewish, but for Gentile readers.

The Life of Mark

Although Matthew was an apostle, and Mark was only a helper of
the apostles, far more information has been preserved about the
latter than about the former.

A NATIVE OF JERUSALEM

John Mark was originally a resident of Jerusalem, Acts 12.12.
His mother's home was a meeting place for the Christians of that
city. To it Peter had immediate resort upon his release from prison.
Very possibly it was the house where the Last Supper was held,
Mark 14.12–25, where the disciples were accustomed to assemble
after the resurrection, and where the Spirit came upon them on
the day of Pentecost, Acts 1.13; 2.2. Possibly the young man who
followed Jesus to Gethsemane, Mark 14.51, 52, was none other
than the author of the Gospel. Of itself the incident seems trivial;
its insertion in the Gospel is best explained if it had some special
personal interest for the author. Apparently the young man had
followed Jesus from a distance without being a member of the
apostolic company, v. 51. It is therefore not altogether unnatural
to suppose that he had seen Jesus and the apostles depart after the
Supper, and had then followed them in the utmost haste. This
hypothesis would make him an inmate of the house where the
Last Supper was held.

Of course, however, these are mere combinations which may be
wrong. What seems to be fairly certain is that as a native of
Jerusalem Mark had in his youth seen Jesus without having become a regular follower of him.

A COMPANION OF PAUL

With regard to the subsequent life of Mark, a number of facts have been established in the study of The Acts and the Pauline epistles. Mark accompanied Paul and Barnabas from Jerusalem to Antioch after the 'famine visit', Acts 12.25. Then he was taken by them as a helper on the first missionary journey, ch. 13.5, but returned from Perga to Jerusalem, v. 13. At the beginning of Paul's second journey, Mark, along with Barnabas, separated from Paul, and went to Cyprus, ch. 15.36–39. Years afterwards, however, he appears in the company of Paul in Rome during Paul's first imprisonment, Col. 4.10; Philem. 24. After that time he probably visited the east, Col. 4.10; and during the second imprisonment Paul summoned him from the east to Rome, II Tim. 4.11. Despite the temporary trouble on the first journey the subsequent relations between Paul and Mark were most cordial.

A COMPANION OF PETER

If the New Testament emphasizes the connection of Mark with Paul, tradition lays stress upon his connection with Peter. Even in the very earliest form of the tradition Mark is represented as a constant hearer of Peter, and as having followed him upon his journeys. This tradition is supported by Peter's own words in I Peter 5.13. There Mark appears in the company of Peter and is represented as his 'son'—that is, his spiritual son or disciple.

IMPORTANCE OF THE DOUBLE RELATIONSHIP

The connection of Mark, during the same period of his life, both with Paul and with Peter is highly significant. In the first place it demonstrates clearly—what ought never to have been doubted—that Peter and Paul were in fundamental agreement. The same man could not have been so intimately associated with both apostles as their disciple and helper, if they had been preaching different gospels. Furthermore the connection of Mark with the two greatest of the apostles enhanced immeasurably his fitness to write a Gospel. As his early years in Jerusalem made him familiar with the conditions of the Palestinian life in which Jesus' ministry was carried on, and put him in possession of a wealth of primitive information, so his experience as a helper of Paul and of Peter acquainted him with every phase of the Christian mission. He knew not only the facts about Jesus, but also which of the facts the Gentiles most needed to know.

Peculiarities of the Gospel of Mark

BREVITY

The most obvious peculiarity of the Gospel of Mark is its brevity. It is by far the shortest of the Gospels, being only about five-eighths as long as Matthew.

DEEDS RATHER THAN DISCOURSES

The greater length of Matthew is due chiefly to the inclusion of discourses of Jesus. Matthew contains almost all of the material of Mark and adds to it long discourses like the Sermon on the Mount. The words of Jesus that are reported in Mark, with the exception of the parable discourse in ch. 4.2–32, the discourse about cleanness and uncleanness in ch. 7.6–23, and the 'eschatological' discourse in ch. 13—which themselves are not long—are confined almost exclusively to brief sayings. For the most part the Gospel of Mark is a collection of anecdotes. As in Matthew Jesus appears as a teacher, so in Mark he is presented as a worker. In the Second Gospel it is the power of Jesus, manifested in wonderful deeds of mercy, which is in the foreground. Of course the difference between Matthew and Mark must not be exaggerated. Both sides of the ministry of Jesus appear clearly in both Gospels; the difference is at most a difference of emphasis.

CHRONOLOGICAL ARRANGEMENTS

Probably the temporal sequence of events is better preserved in Mark than in either of the other two Synoptic Gospels. In Matthew, especially, logical arrangement often takes precedence of temporal; similar events and sayings are grouped together even though they were widely separated in time. Even Mark, it must be noticed, does not offer anything like a connected account of Jesus' life, but narrates only a few scattered incidents. In particular, he has omitted all mention of the early Judean ministry, which is to be placed before Mark 1.14, and of the successive visits to Jerusalem with which the work in Galilee was interspersed. With regard to these things the Synoptists generally must be supplemented by John. Nevertheless, in the Gospel of Mark it is perhaps somewhat easier than in Matthew or in Luke to distinguish successive stages in the public ministry of Jesus.

ROUGH AND VIVID STYLE

The style of Mark is very much rougher than that of Luke or even of Matthew. The influence of the Semitic languages is not avoided, colloquial words are freely used, no attempt is made to round off the sentences into a characteristic Greek form. The constant use of the word 'straightway' is typical both of the stylistic roughness and of the drastic vigour of the narrative. Vividness of description is obtained by many minute touches that are lacking in Matthew and in Luke. Mark alone tells us that the paralytic was 'borne of four', ch. 2.3, and that before the storm on the lake Jesus was in the stern of the boat on a pillow, ch. 4.38; Mark alone mentions the age of Jairus' daughter, ch. 5.42, and gives the original Aramaic form of the words by which Jesus raised her up, v. 41; Mark alone speaks of the 'green' grass upon which the five thousand were made to sit down, ch. 6.39; Mark describes the healing of the epileptic boy after the transfiguration with a wealth of detail that is absent from the other Gospels, ch. 9.14–29. These especially vivid touches which run through the Gospel of Mark confirm the tradition that the evangelist was directly dependent upon an eye-witness. Mark has enabled us to see with Peter's eyes.

The Heading

Like the Gospel of Matthew, the Gospel of Mark opens not with a sentence, but with a heading. As in the former case, however, the exact reference of the heading is uncertain. 'The beginning of the gospel of Jesus Christ' may, in the first place, mean merely, 'Here begins the gospel of Jesus Christ.' 'The gospel of Jesus Christ' would then be simply the story about Christ that is narrated in the book that follows.

In the second place, the phrase may be taken as a description of the contents of the book. The whole of Jesus' life would then be described as the beginning of that proclamation of the gospel which was afterwards continued by the apostles and by the Church.

In the third place, the phrase may be merely a heading for the section that immediately follows, for Mark 1.2–8, or for vs. 2–13. In this case the preaching of John the Baptist, with or without the baptism of Jesus, the descent of the Spirit, and the temptation, would be described as the beginning of, as preliminary to, the proclamation of the gospel, which is mentioned in vs. 14,15.

Perhaps the first interpretation is to be preferred as being the simplest, though it must be admitted that the phrase is a little puzzling.

Mark is the Missionary Gospel

It is significant that the Gospel of Mark begins not with the birth and infancy of Jesus, but with the ministry of John the Baptist and the subsequent preaching of Jesus in Galilee. Mark seems to be following with great exactness the scheme of early apostolic preaching as it is laid down in Acts 10.37–43. Apparently Mark is preeminently the missionary Gospel; it contains only those things which had a place in the first preaching to unbelievers. That does not mean that the things which Mark omits are necessarily less important than the things which it contains. Mark gives a summary, not exactly of the most important things about Jesus, but rather of the things which unbelievers or recent converts could most easily understand. Hence the omission of the mystery of the birth, of the profound teaching of the early Judean ministry, of the intimate instructions to the disciples. These things are of fundamental importance. But they can best be understood only after one has first acquired a thorough grasp of the public ministry, and of the death and resurrection of the Lord.

TOPICS FOR STUDY

1. Which sections of the material in Mark are contained (a) only in Mark, (b) in Mark and Matthew, (c) in Mark and Luke, (d) in Mark, Matthew and Luke, (e) in all four Gospels? (Four or five topics.)

2. Construct a full outline of the Gospel of Mark.

3. Point out indications that this Gospel was intended primarily for Gentiles rather than for Jews.

4. Supplement what is said in the chapter about the vivid and detailed character of the Marcan narrative.

29: A GREEK HISTORIAN'S ACCOUNT OF JESUS

Study material: The Gospel according to Luke

Authorship

The overpowering evidence for the Lucan authorship of The Acts was set forth in chapter 7. But without the slightest doubt the man who wrote The Acts also wrote the Third Gospel, to which he refers in Acts 1.1, 2.

Trustworthiness

Establishment of Lucan authorship at once ensures an essentially trustworthy character for the Gospel. As a companion of Paul on the missionary journeys, Luke not only came into contact with many Jerusalem Christians like Silas, but actually went to Palestine himself about A.D. 58, and probably spent two whole years in that country. During that period, in pursuance of his historical investigations, Luke 1.3, he must have listened to what apostles, relatives and original disciples of Jesus had to tell. An account of the life of Christ written by such a man must be of the very highest historical value.

Date

With regard to the date of the Gospel of Luke nothing very definite can be said. Though Christian tradition generally seems to place Luke after Matthew and Mark, Clement of Alexandria, who lived at the close of the second century, says that the Gospels containing the genealogies were written first. The date of the Third Gospel of course depends upon the date of The Acts. If The Acts was written at the very conclusion of the history which it narrates, as there is some reason for believing, then the Gospel, since it was written earlier still, Acts 1.1, cannot be dated later than A.D. 62.

If this view of the date of The Acts be rejected, then we must fall back upon two general considerations. In the first place, the double work of Luke must have been written at some time within the lifetime of a companion of Paul. In the second place, since The Acts displays absolutely no acquaintance with the Pauline Epistles, the Gospel of Luke and The Acts must have been written before those epistles came into universal use throughout the Church. These considerations would make a date after about A.D. 80 highly improbable.

Theophilus

Theophilus, to whom both the Gospel and The Acts are dedicated, was a man of high rank, as the title 'most excellent' shows, and no doubt was a Gentile. Whether he was already a Christian or had merely received information about Christianity, has been questioned. Perhaps the former view is the more probable. Theophilus seems to have been either a recent convert or else possibly a young man for whom the simple teaching of childhood needed to be replaced by more mature instruction.

The Prologue

From the prologue to the Gospel, Luke 1.1–4, it appears that Luke was not an eyewitness of the events that he narrates—or rather that he was not an eyewitness from the beginning. Both Luke himself and the predecessors whom he mentions were dependent upon what the eyewitnesses had to tell. If, however, Luke did not have the advantage of being an eyewitness, he lays claim to a true historical method in the composition of his work. This claim is amply substantiated by the character of the Gospel itself. The historical method of the author appears not only in the completeness and accuracy and orderly arrangement of the work, but also in the success with which Luke has brought the events that he narrates into connection with secular history. In the elaborate dating of the beginning of John the Baptist's ministry, Luke 3.1, 2, and in the numerous other references to imperial officials which are peculiar to the Third Gospel and The Acts, Luke has revealed himself as a citizen of the world and as a genuine Greek historian. It is well, in the interests of a complete picture, that one of the four Gospels was written not by a Jew but by a Greek.

Characteristics

The hints about the general characteristics of the Gospel of Luke which have already been derived from what the author has told us in the prologue must be supplemented by an examination of the book itself.

LITERARY QUALITY

In the first place, the author of the Third Gospel was evidently capable of a more elevated literary style than is to be observed in either of the other two Synoptists. The prologue itself is perhaps the most clearly typical Greek sentence in the New Testament. In the rest of the Gospel, the same literary tendency appears in the avoidance of colloquial words and of such irregularities of sentence structure as are to be observed especially in Mark.

SEMITIC INFLUENCE

This observation, however, is to be supplemented by one that seems to be exactly opposite. The literary tastes of the author of the Third Gospel have by no means obscured the Semitic and Palestinian basis of the narrative. Indeed some Hebraisms—usages modelled closely upon Hebrew—are more frequent in Luke than in any other part of the New Testament. This Semitic element in the style of the Third Gospel is to be explained first by the Palestinian sources, whether oral or written, that the author used, and secondly by Luke's own appreciation of the Bible style. Luke was thoroughly at home in the Septuagint translation of the Old Testament. That translation preserved the spirit and form of the original. It is not surprising, therefore, that for the narration of sacred events in Palestine, Luke was able to preserve the native beauty of his Palestinian sources and even to draw independently upon the rich store of Scripture phrase.

BEAUTY OF STYLE

To the power which Luke had of appreciating the beauty of his Palestinian sources, and to his own literary tact and skill, the Church owes an inestimable debt. Spiritual truth is not, indeed, dependent upon the literary form of its presentation; and the words of Jesus, even in the rugged narrative of Mark, are of exquisite beauty. Nevertheless, we could ill afford to lose the inspired poetry of Mary and Zacharias and Simeon, or the Old Testament glory of the infancy narrative, or the unrivalled dramatic simplicity of the walk to Emmaus.

GROUPING OF PECULIAR MATTER

Unlike Matthew, Luke has not scattered his peculiar material all through the Gospel, but has grouped a very considerable proportion of it, though by no means all, in the section that extends from Luke 9.51 to 19.27. Within these limits, for example, are included those priceless parables of Jesus—the parables of the Good Samaritan, of the Prodigal Son, of the Rich Man and Lazarus, of the Pharisee and the Publican, and others—which Luke alone has preserved.

EMPHASIS UPON LOVE AND COMPASSION

If Matthew emphasizes especially the teaching of Jesus, and Mark his power, Luke lays stress upon his compassionate love. For the author of the Third Gospel, Jesus was primarily a Saviour. The humanitarian interest of the evangelist appears in many little touches, and also in the choice of material. As a physician Luke was interested in the relief of suffering; as a philanthropist he had a special sympathy for poverty and all kinds of distress. The parables of the Good Samaritan and of the Prodigal Son, as has just been observed, are reported only by Luke.

Again, however, as in the case of the other evangelists, onesidedness should be avoided. The Jesus of the Third Gospel was no means merely a philanthropist. Luke does not conceal the startling radicalness of Jesus' demands, or the severity of his denunciations, or the depth of his hatred of evil. After all, according to Luke, as according to the other evangelists, Jesus was a Healer not merely of physical ills, but also, and primarily, of sin. The seeking love of God, as it appears so richly in the Third Gospel, is not the good-natured complacence that is being mistaken for it today, but a wonderful, paradoxical, saving will, that led the Son of God finally to the cross.

Typical Passages

The characteristics of the Gospel of Luke may perhaps be presented more vividly by an examination of a few typical passages. Two such passages, which we shall choose somewhat at random, are the narrative of the birth and infancy in Luke 1.5 to 2.52, and the parable of the Prodigal Son, ch. 15.11–32. Both of these are without any parallel in the other Gospels. Matthew provides an infancy narrative, but it is concerned for the most part with events different from those that appear in Luke.

THE NARRATIVE OF THE BIRTH AND INFANCY

It has often been observed that the characteristic Greek sentence of the prologue, Luke 1.1–4, is immediately followed by the most strongly Hebraistic passage in the New Testament. The Semitic style of Luke 1.5 to 2.52 becomes explicable only if Luke was here making use of Palestinian sources, either oral or written. This conclusion is confirmed by the whole spirit and substance of the narrative. In this narrative as clearly as anywhere else in the New Testament we find ourselves transplanted to Palestinian soil.

The early date of the narrative is as evident as its Jewish, Christian and Palestinian character. There is here no reference to concrete events in the later history of the Church. Messianic prophecy appears in its Old Testament form uncoloured by the details of the fulfilment. Evidently this narrative is no product of the Church's fancy, but genuine history told in the very forms of speech which were natural to those who participated in it.

The first two chapters of Luke are in spirit really a bit of the Old Testament continued to the very threshold of the New. These chapters contain the poetry of the New Testament, which has taken deep hold of the heart and fancy of the Church.

In this section of his Gospel, Luke shows himself to be a genuine historian. A biographer is not satisfied with narrating the public life of his hero, but prefaces to his work some account of the family, and of the birth and childhood. So our understanding of the ministry of Jesus becomes far deeper when we know that he grew up among the simple, devout folk who are described in the first two chapters of Luke. The picture of Mary in these chapters, painted with an exquisite delicacy of touch, throws a flood of light upon the earthly life of the Son of Man.

Beauty of detail, however, must not be allowed to obscure the central fact. The culmination of the narrative, undoubtedly, is to be found in the stupendous mystery of Luke 1.34, 35. Far from being an excrescence in the narrative, as it has sometimes been represented in an age of rampant naturalism, the supernatural conception of Jesus is the very keystone of the arch. In this central fact, Matthew and Luke, totally independent as they are, are perfectly agreed. By this fact Jesus is represented, more clearly perhaps than by anything else, as not a product of the world but a Saviour come from without.

THE PRODIGAL SON

The parable of the Prodigal Son, simple though it is, has often been sadly misinterpreted. It has been thought to mean, for example, that God pardons sin on the basis simply of human repentance without the necessity of the divine sacrifice. All such interpretations are wide of the mark. The parable is not meant to teach how God pardons sin, but only the fact that he does pardon it with joy, and that we ought to share in his joy.

Misinterpretation of the parable has come from the ignoring of its occasion. The key to the interpretation is given in Luke 15.1, 2. Jesus was receiving publicans and sinners. Instead of rejoicing at the salvation of these poor, degraded sons of Abraham, the Pharisees murmured. In rebuke, Jesus spoke three parables. One of them, the parable of the Lost Sheep, is reported also by Matthew, ch. 18.12–14; but the last two, the parables of the Lost Coin and of the Prodigal Son, appear only in Luke.

The teaching of all three of these parables is exactly the same. The imagery varies, but the application is constant. That application may be expressed very simply: 'God rejoices at the salvation of a sinner; if, therefore, you are really sons of God, you will rejoice too.' In the parable of the Prodigal Son, however, the application is forced home more poignantly than in either of the other two. In that parable alone among the three, the Pharisees could see—in the elder brother—a direct representation of themselves.

The incident of the elder brother, sometimes regarded as a mere detail, really introduces the main point of the parable. Everything else leads up to it. The wonderful description of the joy of the father at the prodigal's home-coming is all intended as a contrast to the churlish jealousy of the brother. The elder brother was as far as possible from sharing in the father's joy. That showed that he was no true son. Though he lived under the father's roof, he had no real inward share in the father's life. So it was with the Pharisees. They lived in the Father's house; they were, as we should say, members of the Church. But when salvation, in the person of Jesus, had at last come to the poor, sinful outcasts of the people, the Pharisees drew aside. God rejoiced when the publicans crowded in to Jesus; but the Pharisees held back. That showed that, after all, they were not, as they thought, true sons of God. If they had been, they would have shared God's feeling.

It should be noticed that the parable ends with an invitation. The elder brother is not harshly rebuked by the father, but tenderly urged to come in still. Will the invitation be accepted? The question is not answered; and there lies the crowning beauty of the parable. The Pharisees are still given the opportunity. Will they still share the joy of God at the return of his lost children? They must answer the question for themselves.

And we, too, have the same question to answer. If we are really children of God, then we shall not despise the outcasts and the sinners, but shall rejoice with him at their salvation. The parable is characteristic of the Gospel of Luke. Of course, Luke did not compose it. Nothing in the Gospel bears more indisputably the marks of Jesus' teaching. But from the rich store of Palestinian tradition Luke sought out those things which displayed sympathy for the downtrodden and the sick and the sinful. It was an inestimable service to the Church. Shall we heed the message? God rejoices at the salvation of a sinner. Shall we be sharers in his holy joy?

The Synoptic Problem

One of the most interesting and difficult of the problems that confront the student of the New Testament must here be dismissed with little more than a word. What is the literary relation between the first three Gospels? How did they come to be so much alike?

CONNECTION NOT MERELY IN THE EVENTS RELATED

Our first impulse, perhaps, is to say that the Synoptic Gospels are similar because they are concerned with the same things. This explanation, however, is quickly seen to be insufficient. It would explain the agreement in matters of fact. But the similarity between the Gospels extends also to the minutest coincidences of expression. Two trustworthy narrators of the same events, although they will agree in the facts, will, if they are independent of each other, differ widely in expression.

THEORIES OF LITERARY DEPENDENCE

A second explanation, therefore, suggests itself. Perhaps one of the Gospels was dependent upon one or both of the others. This explanation might serve to explain the similarity between Mark and Matthew and between Mark and Luke. But it utterly fails to explain the similarity between Matthew and Luke in those portions where both of these Gospels have no parallel in Mark. For if one thing is clear, it is that Matthew and Luke are quite independent of each other. That is demonstrated, if by nothing else, by a comparison of the infancy narratives at the beginning of these two Gospels.

In order, therefore, to supplement the theory of dependence of one Gospel upon another, it has been suggested that Matthew and Luke used in addition to Mark another common source which has now been lost. This so-called 'two-document theory' has won exceedingly wide acceptance among modern scholars. It is held in many modifications, but the essence of it is that Matthew and Luke had two written sources in common: (a) Mark, and (b) a source containing chiefly discourses of Jesus.

INFLUENCE OF ORAL TRADITION

The detailed evidence for and against the 'two-document theory' cannot here be discussed. At least this much, however, must be said: This theory, even if correct—which is by no means certain—is insufficient. It fails to explain the differences between the Gospels which run along with the similarities. If, for example, in the passages where Mark and Matthew are parallel, Matthew was dependent upon Mark and only upon Mark, then it is difficult to explain why he made just the changes that he did in the Marcan text. Some of the changes no doubt can be explained—as due to a desire for brevity or smoothness or the like—but many, if they be merely changes of what Mark wrote, seem to lack both rhyme and reason. What needs to be emphasized, therefore, against the modern one-sided acceptance of the two-document theory is that all of the evangelists stood in the full current of the oral tradition. When Luke or Matthew differ from Mark the differences should not be dismissed as mere unauthorized editorial changes, but should be regarded as preserving valuable independent information.

ORIGIN OF THE GOSPEL LITERATURE

In the earliest period, information about the life of Jesus seems to have been handed down by word of mouth. This supposition is supported by the absence of any reference to written Gospels in the epistles of Paul, and by what our Gospels themselves imply as to their antecedents. To us it seems strange that the words and deeds of Jesus were not at once committed to writing. But that is because we live in a day of notebooks and memoranda, when memory has fallen into decay. The disciples of Jesus lived among a people where the verbal memory was trained to a degree which to us seems phenomenal. It must always be borne in mind that the early Christians were not modern men, but Jews of the first century. The very sum and substance of ancient Jewish education was the memorizing of the Old Testament; and the words of Jewish teachers were preserved for centuries without being committed to writing. In such a country and at such a time the absence of written records did not necessarily involve any lack of tenacious faithfulness in the preservation of knowledge about Jesus. Stamped upon the tablets of Jewish minds, the story of Jesus' words and deeds was for a time at least as safe as though inscribed on stone or bronze.

In accordance with the habits of the time, the uniformity of oral tradition about Jesus no doubt extended to the very words as well as to the substance of the narrative. Handed down from one Jewish Christian preacher to another, anecdotes about Jesus and reports of his sayings would soon be spread in more or less fixed form throughout Palestine. One thing only would naturally be lacking in such a tradition. Oral tradition, though preserving individual anecdotes and individual discourses of Jesus intact, could hardly be expected to group any great mass of these incidents in a strictly chronological narrative. The lack of chronological arrangement in the Gospels is therefore only what was to be expected. The writers of the earliest extended records of Jesus' life had as their material detached incidents rather than systematic biographies.

Possibly even the detached anecdotes of Jesus' life, which at the very beginning were preserved by word of mouth, were very soon committed here and there to writing. Then larger or smaller collections of them would naturally be made. And finally, when imperative need arose, Matthew and Mark and Luke, familiar with differing forms of the oral tradition, familiar, too, in some cases with the written work of predecessors, produced the extended Gospels which are now in our hands.

Much of what has just been said is surmise. What should be insisted upon—what seems to be written plain upon the pages of the Gospels—is that Matthew and Mark and Luke were no mere compilers of the post-apostolic age, dependent solely upon written records, but genuine evangelists, living when the knowledge of the life of Christ was still flowing fresh and pure.

TOPICS FOR STUDY

1. Construct an outline of the Gospel of Luke (several topics).

2. Collect the material which is peculiar to Luke.

3. Explain fully the teaching of the parables (a) of the Prodigal Son, Luke 15.11–32, (b) of the Unrighteous Steward, ch. 16.1–13, (c) of the Rich Man and Lazarus, vs. 19–31 (three topics).

4. Collect the references in the Gospel of Luke to officials of the Roman Empire and to events in secular history.

5. Explain the prologue to the Gospel, Luke 1.1–4.

30: THE TESTIMONY OF THE BELOVED DISCIPLE

Study material: The Gospel according to John

Authorship

The Fourth Gospel does not mention the name of its author, but according to a very strong tradition it was written by one of the twelve apostles, John the son of Zebedee. The testimony of Irenæus, who wrote in the latter part of the second century, is particularly important, for in his youth Irenæus had listened to Polycarp, bishop of Smyrna, who in turn had been a hearer of John.

The tradition which attributes the Fourth Gospel to John the son of Zebedee is confirmed by the testimony of the Gospel itself. Although the book does not mention the name of its author it clearly implies who he was.

INDIRECTNESS OF THE TESTIMONY

This testimony of the Gospel itself is all the more valuable because it is indirect. If the name John had been mentioned at the beginning, then it might conceivably be supposed that an unknown author had desired to gain a hearing for his work by putting it falsely under the name of a great apostle. As it is, the inference that the author claims to be John the son of Zebedee, though certain, does not force itself upon the careless reader. A forger would not thus, by the indirectness of his claim, have deprived himself of the benefits of his forgery.

The testimony of the Gospel to its author must now be considered.

THE AUTHOR AN EYEWITNESS

In the first place, almost at the very beginning, we observe that the author claims to be an eyewitness of the life of Jesus. 'We beheld his glory,' he says in John 1.14. By beholding the glory of Christ he evidently does not mean merely that experience of Christ's power which is possessed by every Christian. On the contrary, the glory of Christ, as it is intended by the evangelist, is fully explained by such passages as ch. 2.11. The miracles of Jesus—palpable, visible events in the external world—are clearly included in what is meant. It will be observed that in ch. 1.14 it is very specifically the incarnate Christ that is spoken of. The evangelist is describing the condition of things after 'the Word became flesh'. Evidently, therefore, it was the earthly life of Jesus which the evangelist claims to have 'beheld'.

This conclusion is confirmed by I John 1.1–4. Scarcely anyone doubts that the First Epistle of John was written by the man who wrote the Gospel. When, therefore, the author of the Epistle speaks of 'that which we have heard, that which we have seen with our eyes, that which we beheld, and our hands handled, concerning the Word of life', evidently these words have significance for the Gospel also. The author fairly heaps up expressions to show, beyond all possibility of misunderstanding, that he had come into actual physical contact with the earthly Jesus.

THE UNNAMED DISCIPLE OF JOHN 1.35–42

The author of the Fourth Gospel, then, clearly claims to be an eye-witness of the earthly life of Christ. Further indications identify him with a particular one among the eyewitnesses. In John 1.35–42, an unnamed disciple of Jesus is mentioned. 'One of the two,' it is said in v. 40, 'that heard John speak, and followed him, was Andrew, Simon Peter's brother.' Who was the other? There is some reason for thinking that he was one of the two sons of Zebedee. But the matter will become clearer as we proceed.

Another question is why this disciple is not mentioned by name. The Fourth Gospel is not chary of names. Why, then, is the disciple who appears so prominently along with Andrew and Simon not mentioned by name? Only one plausible explanation suggests itself—the explanation that the unnamed disciple was the author of the Gospel, who, through a feeling common in the literature of antiquity, as well as of our own time, did not like to mention his own name in the course of the narrative. We have already observed that the author claims to be an eyewitness of the life of Christ, John 1.14. When, therefore, near the beginning of the narrative, a disciple of Jesus is introduced, rather mysteriously, without a name, when, furthermore, events in which this disciple was immediately concerned are narrated with unusual vividness and wealth of detail, vs. 35–42, the conclusion becomes very natural that this unnamed disciple is none other than the author himself.

THE BELOVED DISCIPLE

This conclusion, it must be admitted, so far as this first passage is concerned, is nothing more than a likely guess. But by other passages it is rendered almost certain.

In John 13.21–25, a disciple is mentioned as leaning on Jesus' breast and as being one whom Jesus loved. This disciple is not named. But who was he? Evidently he was one of the twelve apostles, for only the apostles were present at the Supper which is described in chs. 13 to 17. The disciple 'whom Jesus loved', however, was not only among the Twelve; he was evidently among the innermost circle of the Twelve. Such an innermost circle appears clearly in the Synoptic Gospels. It was composed of Peter and James and John. The beloved disciple was probably one of these three; and since he is clearly distinguished from Peter, ch. 13.24, he was either James or John.

The introduction of an unnamed disciple, which seemed significant even in John 1.35–42, becomes yet far more significant in the present passage. In the account of the Last Supper, a considerable number of the disciples are named—Peter, Judas Iscariot, Thomas, Philip, Judas not Iscariot—yet the disciple who is introduced with especial emphasis, whose very position at table is described with a wealth of detail far greater than is displayed in the case of any of the others, is designated merely as 'one of his disciples, whom Jesus loved'. The strange omission of this disciple's name can be explained only if he was the author of the book. Clearly the painter has here introduced a modest portrait of himself in the midst of his great picture.

Passing by John 18.15, 16, where 'the other disciple' is probably the author, and ch. 19.26, 27, where the repetition of the strange designation, 'the disciple . . . whom he [Jesus] loved', confirms the impressions derived from ch. 13.21–25, we discover another important indication in ch. 19.35. 'And he that hath seen hath borne witness, and his witness is true: and he knoweth that he saith true, that ye also may believe.' 'He that hath seen' can scarcely refer to anyone other than the beloved disciple who was mentioned just before as standing by the cross. In the present verse, this beloved disciple is represented as the one who is now speaking.

The identification of the beloved disciple with the author of the Gospel, which was implied before, here becomes explicit.

In John 20.1–10, 'the other disciple whom Jesus loved' is of course the same as the one who appears in ch. 13.21–25; 19.26, 27, 35.

TESTIMONY OF THE APPENDIX

In John 21.7, 20–23, the beloved disciple appears again, and in v. 24 he is identified, in so many words, with the writer of the Gospel. In this verse the first person plural is used; other persons seem to be associated with the author in commending the Gospel to the attention of the Church. This phenomenon is explained if the twenty-first chapter be regarded as a sort of appendix, perhaps added at the request of a circle of friends. It will be observed that ch. 20.30, 31 forms a fit ending to the book; what follows therefore appears the more like an appendix, though it was certainly written by the author's own hand and published before his death along with the rest of the book.

WHY ARE JOHN AND JAMES NOT MENTIONED BY NAME?

The conclusion of our investigation is that the author of the Fourth Gospel indicates clearly that he was either one or the other of the two sons of Zebedee. This conclusion is confirmed by the curious circumstance that neither one of these men is mentioned in the Gospel by name. How did they come to be omitted? They were in the very innermost circle of Jesus' disciples; many apostles far less prominent than they are named frequently on the pages of the Gospel. There can be only one solution of the problem: one at least of these men is, as a matter of fact, introduced in the Gospel as the beloved disciple, and the reason why he is introduced in such a curiously anonymous way and why his brother also is not named, is that the author felt a natural delicacy about introducing his own and his brother's name into a narrative of the Lord's life.

One statement that has just been made requires qualification: it is not quite true that the sons of Zebedee are not designated by name in the Gospel. They are not indeed called by their individual names, but in ch. 21.2, they are designated by the name of their father. Possibly this slight difference of usage between chapter 21 and the rest of the Gospel has something to do with the fact that chapter 21 seems to be an appendix.

THE AUTHOR WAS NOT JAMES, BUT JOHN

The author of the Fourth Gospel, then, identifies himself with one or the other of the sons of Zebedee. As to which one of the two is meant there cannot be the slightest doubt. James the son of Zebedee was martyred in A.D. 44, Acts 12.2. There is abundant evidence that the Fourth Gospel was not written so early as that; and John 21.20–23 apparently implies that the author lived to a considerable age. Evidently, therefore, it is John and not James with whom the author identifies himself.

IS THE GOSPEL'S OWN· TESTIMONY TRUE?

Thus the singularly strong tradition which attributes the Fourth Gospel to John the son of Zebedee is supported by the independent testimony of the book itself. Conceivably, of course, that testimony might be false. But it is very hard to believe that it is. It is very hard to believe that the author of this wonderful book who, despite all the profundity of his ideas, exalts in a very special manner the importance of simple testimony based upon the senses, John 19.35; I John 1.1–4, has in a manner far subtler and more heinous than if he had simply put a false name at the beginning palmed himself off as an eyewitness of the Saviour's life. Many learned men have found it possible to accept such a view; but the simple reader of the Gospel will always be inclined to dissent. The author of this book has narrated many things hard to be believed. But there are still found those who accept his solemn testimony; there are still found those in whom the purpose of the book is achieved, who through this Gospel believe that Jesus is the Christ, the Son of God, and believing have life in his name, John 20.31.

Relation to the Synoptic Gospels

THE FOURTH GOSPEL SUPPLEMENTARY

According to tradition, the Fourth Gospel was written during the later life of the author, while he was residing at Ephesus. For many years, almost until the close of the first century, John was the great leader of the church in Asia Minor. Tradition informs us also that the Gospel of John was not only written later than the Synoptic Gospels, but was intended to supplement them. This explains admirably many features of the book. It explains, for example, why such important events as the baptism of Jesus and the institution of the Lord's Supper, and also the greater part of the Galilean ministry, are omitted. Knowledge of these things is presupposed. The Fourth Gospel was written for those who already knew the Synoptic account of Jesus' life.

STYLE

In many respects the Gospel of John stands in sharp contrast with the other three. There is a contrast, in the first place, in style. Though the Synoptic Gospels differ characteristically from one another in style, yet there is a certain family resemblance among them, whereas the Fourth Gospel goes its own way. The Gospel of John is remarkable for the very small vocabulary that it uses, and for the extreme simplicity and monotony of its sentence structure. Yet these peculiarities, which in an ordinary writer might be repulsive, become in this book, on account of the sublimity of the thought, conducive to a certain inimitable grandeur and dignity. The absence of human art, of nicely turned sentences, serves only to reveal with the greater clearness the glory of the incarnate Word.

CHOICE OF MATERIAL

In the second place, there is a striking difference in the material of the narrative. One chief reason for this difference has already been noticed—it is to be sought in the desire of the evangelist to supplement the work of his predecessors.

Chronology. The Fourth Gospel helps to complete something like a chronological outline of the ministry of Jesus. Thus from John 2.13 to 3.36 we learn that there was an early Judean ministry before that public appearance in Galilee which is narrated in Mark 1.14, 15. From John also it appears that the ministry of Jesus extended over several years—a circumstance which is only implied in the Synoptic Gospels. John mentions at least three passovers within the public ministry, and either mentions or implies a fourth, John 2.13, 23; (5.1); 6.4; 13.1. Probably therefore the public ministry of Jesus lasted at least three years.

Visits to Jerusalem. Most of what is narrated in the Gospel of John took place in or near Jerusalem, to which Jesus made repeated visits that are only hinted at in the other Gospels. The Synoptists confine themselves almost exclusively to the Galilean ministry.

Private Instruction. Finally, whereas the Synoptists lay special emphasis upon the public preaching of Jesus, the Gospel of John has preserved certain more intimate discourses like those which Jesus held with his apostles at the Last Supper, John, chs. 13 to 17. Apparently the Synoptic Gospels had their rise in the missionary activity of the Church—they have preserved those things which beginners in the faith or unbelievers need to know first; whereas the Gospel of John reveals certain profounder elements of Jesus' teaching.

THE JESUS OF THE GOSPELS

It should be observed, however, that the Synoptists and John present substantially the same conception of Jesus' person. What is taught more explicitly by John is clearly implied by the other three. To all of the evangelists Jesus was no mere man but the Son of God come in the flesh for the salvation of the world.

Contents

THE PROLOGUE

The Gospel of John begins with a remarkable prologue, ch. 1.1-18; and this prologue begins with what is for us a difficult problem. What is the meaning of 'the Word'? (v. 1.) The simplest answer is that the term merely designates Jesus as the revealer of God. 'The word of God' is a common phrase, referring to the divine message which comes either through the Scriptures or through the lips of a prophet or apostle. But God has not only spoken in written or oral language; he has also spoken through a person. That person was Jesus Christ. There is a written Word, and there is also an incarnate Word. So the simple Christian usually understands the first verse of John. As the grand sentence of the Authorized Version of Hebrews 1.1, 2 puts it: 'God, who at sundry times and in divers manners spake in time past unto the fathers by the prophets, hath in these last days spoken unto us by his Son.' The Son is God's final 'Word' to men.

This simple explanation of the term 'Word' in John 1.1, though undoubtedly it contains a large measure of truth, must perhaps be supplemented by other considerations. During the period in which the Fourth Gospel was written, the term 'Word' had passed through a considerable history. On Palestinian ground the 'word' of God had been personified so boldly as almost to seem like a real person separate from God, who acted as the agent of his will. By Philo, the great representative of Alexandrian Judaism, the term 'Logos', which in Greek means either 'word' or 'reason', had been used in a very special philosophical sense, to designate a sort of function or manifestation of God by which the world was formed. It is possible that one or the other or both of these uses of the term 'Word' or 'Logos' had contributed to John's usage. In any case, however, the conception which John gives of the Logos is quite different from that which appears in Philo. The same phraseology, to a quite remarkable extent, is used; but the ideas conveyed are totally different. It is doubtful whether the Logos of Philo is even conceived of as a person; in John of course the conception is intensely personal. Especially the idea of the incarnation of the Logos, v. 14, has absolutely no parallel in the current philosophy.

In general, it must be concluded that the connection of the term 'Word' in John with the usage of Philo, even if it exists at all, does not go to the root of the matter. At the most, John can only mean to say to his Greek readers: 'You have heard of the *Logos* in contemporary philosophy; but now you must substitute a truer conception. The true "Word" of God was Jesus Christ. Learn about him and you will have no further need for fruitless speculations like those of Philo.' Even this much, however, is doubtful. The simpler interpretation may be right. John may mean nothing more than that Jesus was God's supreme revelation to men. It is noteworthy that the term 'Word' is not applied to Jesus in the report of Jesus' own discourses. John was able to distinguish what Jesus while on earth actually said about himself from the description of him which an evangelist might formulate.

The prologue provides at the very start the heavenly point of view from which the whole of the Gospel history must be contemplated. Verse 14, especially, strikes the key note of the book. The Fourth Gospel is intended to exhibit the glory of the incarnate Son of God. It exhibits it not merely by the adulation of a disciple, not merely by the rehearsing of Christian experience, but by simple testimony to what actually occurred on earth. The testimony of an eyewitness to the glory of the incarnate Word—that forms the content of this book.

JOHN THE BAPTIST

The first section of the Gospel, together with a number of subsequent passages, lays special stress upon the testimony of John the Baptist to Jesus. This circumstance has been explained by the hypothesis that there were in Asia Minor certain disciples of John the Baptist who had not become Christians. The existence of such a sect, however, is doubtful. More probably the emphasis upon John the Baptist's confessed inferiority to Christ is directed against non-Christian Jews, who reverenced John as a prophet. Even this hypothesis, however, is perhaps not necessary. The prominence of John the Baptist in the Fourth Gospel may be due simply to the historical importance of his witness, and to the fact that the evangelist himself—if he be identified with the unnamed man of John 1.35-42—had been one of his disciples.

Although the baptism of Jesus, with accompanying events, is not narrated in the Fourth Gospel, the event of Mark 1.10, 11 is referred to, John 1.32-34. The Synoptic narrative is here apparently presupposed as already known to the readers.

THE FIRST MIRACLE

Chapter 2.1-11 narrates the first of Jesus' miracles. The miracles of Jesus, according to the evangelist, were manifestations of his glory, v. 11; compare ch. 1.14.

THE CLEANSING OF THE TEMPLE

At the time of the first passover after his baptism, Jesus engaged in a ministry of teaching in Jerusalem. At the beginning of this ministry he expelled those who carried on business in the temple area, ch. 2.13-22. The Synoptic Gospels—for example Mark 11.15-17—narrate a cleansing of the temple in connection with Jesus' last visit to Jerusalem. Many scholars regard the two accounts as accounts of the same event; but even if we remember the lack of chronological arrangement in the Synoptic Gospels, it is more probable that the temple was cleansed twice. It cannot be supposed that the covetous traders heeded permanently the first rebuke of Jesus; and if they returned, would Jesus tolerate their presence the last time any more than the first?

NICODEMUS

The discourse with Nicodemus, John 3.1-21, is one of the most familiar passages in the Bible. But although knowledge of it is almost universal, inward acceptance is far less common. Christianity today is often regarded merely as the introduction of a new motive into men's lives, as one of the means for the betterment of humanity, as an improvement of the old rather than the creation of something new. In other words it is regarded as anything rather

223

H

than a new birth. The Church is in sad need of the heavenly message. After relying long upon her own power, she needs now to wait for the mysterious power of the Spirit of God. That power will not come by human effort. But God's mercy is wonderful. 'The wind bloweth where it listeth.'

THE WOMAN AT THE WELL

After the testimony of John the Baptist to Christ in John 3.22–30, with what is perhaps a comment of the evangelist, vs. 31–36, John narrates what happened as Jesus was passing through Samaria on his way to Galilee. Again we have one of the passages that has entered into the very depths of the Church's life. Everything else might be lost—organization, methods of work, accumulated resources—but without the living water that Christ can give the Church is dead.

THE NOBLEMAN'S SON

The healing of the nobleman's son, John 4.46–54, is not narrated in the Synoptic Gospels. The event of Matt. 8.5–13; Luke 7.2–10 is only somewhat similar. The nobleman's son was apparently healed during a preliminary sojourn of Jesus in Galilee before the beginning of the Galilean ministry that the Synoptists describe.

OPPOSITION OF THE JEWS

At the feast which is mentioned in John 5.1, the opposition between Jesus and the religious leaders at Jerusalem became acute. This opposition runs through the rest of the narrative. The opponents in the Fourth Gospel are often called 'the Jews'. Of course the evangelist himself was a Jew, and many of the Jews believed; but the nation as a whole, especially as represented by its leaders, before the Gospel was written had definitely rejected the message of Christ.

A HARD SAYING

The sixth chapter introduces us to the very height of the main Galilean ministry. The feeding of the five thousand is one of the few events which appear in all four Gospels. At the time when it occurred Jesus' popularity had reached its highest point. The people were ready to take him by force and make him a king, John 6.15. But soon after there was a change. Jesus was not the kind of Messiah that the people wanted. Discouraged by the 'hard saying',

v. 60, many even of the disciples turned away. The apostles, however, remained. 'Lord,' said Peter, 'to whom shall we go? thou hast the words of eternal life.' These words may be applied to the modern Church. In our day also, many are going back and walking no more with Jesus. One by one they are swept away by the mighty current of an unbelieving culture. Shall we also go away? Or shall we say with Peter, 'Lord, to whom shall we go? thou hast the words of eternal life'?

THE REST OF THE GOSPEL

The rest of the Gospel cannot be treated here even in barest outline. The purpose of the whole is given in John 20.31. 'These are written, that ye may believe that Jesus is the Christ, the Son of God; and that believing ye may have life in his name.' In a mighty army of men and women of all ages, the purpose of the book has been gloriously achieved. How shall it be with us?

TOPICS FOR STUDY

1. Where does the author of the Fourth Gospel present himself in general as an eyewitness of the life of Jesus?
2. Where does he indicate that he was John the son of Zebedee?
3. Outline the life of John.
4. Construct an outline of the Gospel of John.
5. What events are narrated both in John and in one or more of the Synoptic Gospels?
6. What does John add to our knowledge of events connected with the crucifixion and resurrection of Jesus?

31: THE JESUS OF THE GOSPELS

Study material: The Four Gospels

After having studied the four Gospels in their character as books, it may now be well to sum up in bare outline the information which they contain. The subject of all four Gospels is Jesus Christ—his life, his death and his resurrection.

No Complete Biography in the Gospels

At the very beginning it should be observed that the Gospels do not contain sufficient material for a complete biography. Long years in the life of Jesus are left entirely blank; the Synoptic Gospels, in particular, narrate for the most part only isolated incidents from a very limited portion of Jesus' ministry. Nevertheless, we should be thankful for the information that we possess rather than indulge in complaints for what God has not thought good to give us. Fragmentary as they are, the Gospels succeed wonderfully in showing what manner of person Jesus was when he was on earth—and what manner of person he still is in heaven. Enough is told in the Gospels to enable us to believe in the Lord, and, believing, to have life in his name.

Outline of the Gospel Account of Jesus

BIRTH AND INFANCY

The birth of Jesus was a holy mystery. It occurred at Bethlehem, the original home of David's family. In accordance with ancient promise, God had at last bestowed the righteous King.

The circle of people in which Jesus was born seems to have been largely unaffected by Pharisaic formalism or by the worldliness of the Sadducees. Mary, the mother of Jesus, and Elisabeth her relative, and Joseph and Zacharias, were truly and humbly waiting for the consolation of Israel. In them the piety of the prophets was still alive.

226

YOUTH

After the birth of Jesus and the subsequent flight into Egypt, Joseph and Mary returned with the Child to Nazareth in Galilee, their original home. Here Jesus was brought up in humble subjection to his human parents, with a normal human development of body and mind. The puerilities of the apocryphal Gospels, where the child Jesus is represented as working useless and even malevolent miracles, stand in marked contrast to the noble simplicity of the New Testament narrative. Only one incident is narrated from the long 'silent years' at Nazareth; but that incident is of profound significance. The scene of Jesus with the rabbis at Jerusalem has often been sadly misinterpreted. Jesus was not trying to display his wisdom or put the learned men to shame; he was a true learner from the Scriptures. The word which he spoke when his parents found him in the temple is worth pages of narrative. It throws a vivid flood of light upon the mystery of Jesus' consciousness. The youthful Jesus, with his humble subjection to parents and teachers, was like no other man that ever lived; he had been entrusted with a Son's commission.

JESUS AND JOHN

At about thirty years of age, Jesus followed the multitudes who went to the Jordan to hear John the Baptist, the strange new prophet of righteousness. John himself was conscious of being but a forerunner; and by a divine revelation recognized the son of his relative, Mary, as the greater One whose shoe's latchet he was not worthy to unloose. After Jesus had been baptized, not to wash away his own sins—for he had none—but as part of his identification with the life of his people, and after the ensuing temptation, where the newly proclaimed Messiah rejected all earthly, temporal conceptions of his office, Jesus returned to the Jordan and was sought out by a number of the disciples of John, who recognized him as the Messiah and afterwards became his constant companions.

BEFORE THE IMPRISONMENT OF JOHN

Then followed a visit to Galilee, where Jesus attended the marriage feast at Cana, and then a ministry in Judea, when the temple was cleansed, the opposition of the leaders aroused, and a wonderful conversation held with one of the rabbis who sought out Jesus by night. In Judea, the disciples of Jesus, like John, engaged in baptizing; but soon Jesus withdrew through Samaria into Galilee. All of these events after the temptation are narrated only by the Fourth Gospel. They happened before the imprisonment of the Baptist, and before the opening of that Galilean ministry which the Synoptists describe, Mark 1.14.

POPULARITY IN GALILEE

That ministry itself, moreover, was interrupted by visits to Jerusalem which the Synoptists do not relate. At the beginning of the main Galilean ministry, Jesus seems to have adopted a new method of teaching. His Messiahship was for a time kept in the background. The reason is plain. The Jewish people were so thoroughly imbued with an external, political notion of the Messiah, that if Jesus had encouraged them they would have tried to degrade him to the rôle of a military leader. Before proclaiming his Messiahship, it was necessary for him to show that his kingdom was something far higher and more spiritual than an earthly realm.

In the Galilean ministry Jesus appears as teacher and as healer. Throughout he was in the midst of the people. He was a guest at their feasts, he entered both into their joys and into their sorrows. There was nothing ascetic about him. His denunciations were of unparalleled sternness; but they were always denunciations of evil.

THE TRANSITION*

At first he attained a high degree of popularity. The people were attracted by his beneficent works of power, and awed by the strange authority of his teaching. Finally, however, after the feeding of the five thousand, there came a change. The profound teaching about the bread of life was not understood. Jesus was a disappointment. Many began to leave him. The apostles, however, remained. 'Lord,' said Peter, 'to whom shall we go? thou hast the words of eternal life.' In the midst of conflicting opinions, the apostles held firm to their initial belief that Jesus was the Messiah, Matt. 16.13–16.

THE TRAINING OF THE TWELVE

Popularity did not depart all at once. But toward the close of the Galilean ministry Jesus devoted himself more and more to the instruction of his intimate disciples. Though they had remained steadfast, there was much for them to learn. Above all they needed to learn that discipleship of Jesus is a path of suffering. Jesus predicted his death and also the subsequent glory of the resurrection. But the disciples did not understand.

DEATH AND RESURRECTION

At last the hour had come. Jesus entered Jerusalem for the last time. It was a triumphal entry. Even in its outward form, it was an entry of the Messiah. The real Messiah, however, was different from what had been expected. The Pharisees in particular could not accept him. A Messiah who rebuked their hypocrisy, a Messiah who said nothing about revenge on their enemies—away with such a Messiah as that!

As he had foreseen, Jesus was delivered over to the Gentiles to be put to death. The cup of his suffering was full. But it was no useless suffering. Through the cross came victory—victory over guilt and sin and death. Such was the Father's gracious will. The death of Jesus was a triumphant sacrifice for the sins of the world.

The life of Jesus did not end with the crucifixion. He rose from the dead. The tomb was empty on that morning of the first day of the week. In Jerusalem and in Galilee the Lord appeared to his disciples, and still he is the leader of his Church.

God and Man

Jesus is not simply an interesting character of history. The Gospels, indeed, portray him clearly as a man. He lived a genuine human life. But they also portray him as something far more than a man. The prologue of the Fourth Gospel might be a prologue of all the four. Jesus was God come in the flesh.

HUMANITY IN THE SYNOPTISTS

The former feature is perhaps especially clear in the Synoptists. According to the first three Gospels, Jesus led a genuine human life from birth to death. As a child he grew not only in stature, but also in wisdom. He was subject to human parents and to the requirements of the Jewish law. Even after the inauguration of his ministry the human conditions of his life were not superseded. He was even tempted like other men. He grew weary and slept. He suffered hunger and thirst. He could rejoice and he could suffer sorrow. He prayed, as did other men, and worshipped God. He needed strengthening both for body and for mind. No mere semblance of a human life is here presented, but a genuine man of flesh and blood.

HUMANITY IN JOHN

But if the Jesus of the Synoptists is a true man, how is it with the Jesus of John? Does the Fourth Gospel present merely a heavenly being who walked through the world untouched and unruffled by the sin and misery and weakness that surrounded him? Only a very superficial reading can produce such an impression. The Fourth Gospel indeed lays a supreme emphasis upon the majesty of Jesus, upon his 'glory' as it was manifested in works of power and attested by God himself. But side by side with these features of the narrative, as though to prevent a possible misunderstanding, the author presents the humanity of Jesus with drastic touches that can scarcely be paralleled in the Synoptists themselves. It is John who speaks of the weariness of Jesus at the well of Samaria, ch. 4.6; of the human affection which he felt for Lazarus and Martha and Mary, ch. 11.3, 5, 36; and for an individual among the disciples, ch. 13.23; of his weeping, ch. 11.35; and indignant groaning, v. 38; and of his deadly thirst, ch. 19.28. As clearly as the other evangelists John presents Jesus as a man.

DIVINITY IN JOHN

In the second place, all four Gospels, if they present Jesus as a man, also present him as something far more than a man. With regard to the Gospel of John, of course the matter is unmistakable. The very first verse reads: 'In the beginning was the Word, and the Word was with God, and the Word was God.' Jesus according to John was plainly no product of the world, but God come in the flesh, John 1.14. The teaching of Jesus himself, as it is reported in the Fourth Gospel, is concerned with the relation of perfect unity that exists between the Father and the Son.

DIVINITY IN THE SYNOPTISTS

In the Synoptists the supernatural character of Jesus is somewhat less on the surface. His teaching, as the Synoptists report it, is largely concerned not directly with his own person, but with the kingdom that he came to found. Even his Messiahship is often kept in the background; the demons are often commanded not to reveal it.

A closer examination, however, reveals the essential unity between the Synoptists and John. If the supernatural character of Jesus appears in the Synoptists less plainly on the surface, it is really no less pervasive at the centre. It does not so often form the subject of direct exposition, but it is everywhere presupposed. The doing by Jesus of what only God can do, Mark 2.5, 7; the sovereign way in which he legislates for the kingdom of God, Matt. 5.17–48; his unearthly holiness and complete lack of any consciousness of sin; the boundlessness of his demand for obedience, Luke 9.57–62; his expected freedom from limitations of time and place, Matt. 28.20; the absolutely central place which he claims for himself as ruler and judge; the substantiation of all his lofty claims by wonderful power over the forces of nature—these are only indications chosen almost at random of what is really plain upon every page of the Synoptic Gospels, that the Jesus who is there described is no mere human figure but the divine Saviour of the world. The invitation of Matt. 11.28–30, which is typical of the Synoptic teaching, would have been absurd on the lips of anyone but the Son of God.

Moreover, the divine nature of Jesus is not merely implied in the Synoptic Gospels; there are times when it even becomes explicit. The relation of perfect mutual knowledge that exists between Jesus and the Father, Matt. 11.27, reveals a perfect unity of nature. The Jesus of the Synoptists, as well as the Jesus of John, might say, 'I and the Father are one'.

There are boundless mysteries in the life of Jesus. But if we keep close to the Gospel picture those mysteries will be for us instinct with reality and life. Departure from the Gospel conception has often brought disaster. Some, for example, have held fast to the divinity of Christ, and denied his humanity. They have either regarded his human life as a mere semblance, or else denied that his human body had a human soul. Such errors deprive us of our Saviour. If Jesus be not true man, God has not come close to us. Others have accepted the humanity of Jesus, and denied his divinity. But it is an incomprehensible humanity that they portray. Jesus as a mere man is full of contradictions. How could a calm, good, great man think that he was divine? Still others have regarded Jesus as neither man nor God, but something in between the two. That conception is pagan mythology, not Christian faith.

From all such errors, the Church must turn ever anew to the Gospels. 'The only Redeemer of God's elect is the Lord Jesus Christ, who, being the eternal Son of God, became man, and so was, and continueth to be, God and man in two distinct natures, and one person, for ever.' (Westminster Shorter Catechism, 21.) Such, in brief, is the Gospel account of Jesus. Every clause of that definition was wrought out, originally, in bitter controversy; every clause contains an essential element of Gospel teaching; and every clause has been tested and approved in the long centuries of the Church's life.

TOPICS FOR STUDY

1. Supply Biblical references for the outline of the life of Jesus which is given in the chapter.

2. Construct a full outline of the events between the baptism of Jesus and the imprisonment of John the Baptist.

3. What do the Gospels tell about the emotions which Jesus felt or expressed (several topics)?

4. What is the meaning of the title 'Son of Man' as applied to Jesus?

5. What is the meaning of 'the kingdom of God'?

6. When did Jesus predict his death and resurrection, either in literal or in figurative terms?

7. Enumerate the miracles which were wrought by Jesus. How many were not miracles of healing?

32 : A DOCUMENT OF THE JERUSALEM CHURCH

Study material: The Epistle of James

The Author

WELL KNOWN IN THE CHURCH

The writer of the Epistle of James is designated in the Epistle itself as 'James, a servant of God and of the Lord Jesus Christ'. Of itself the designation might apply to any Christian. But the character of the Epistle narrows the possibilities. The Epistle is addressed in a tone of authority either to the whole Church or else to the Jewish Christian part of it. Evidently, therefore, the writer was not some obscure Christian who happened to bear the common name, James, but a man who had a right to make his voice heard, and a man, indeed, who was so well known that he did not need to name his special office or title in order to be identified by his readers. Upon second thought, the very modesty of the title, 'servant of God and of the Lord Jesus Christ', is seen to enhance rather than obscure the prominence of the author. A lesser man would have needed to establish his identity more closely.

Who then was this James who held a position of unique authority in the Church? After the close of the apostolic age there never was anyone called James who could have spoken in this authoritative way. We must therefore search in the apostolic age itself.

Three men in the New Testament—excluding one who is altogether obscure—bear the name of James. They are James the son of Zebedee, James the son of Alphæus, and James the brother of the Lord.

NOT JAMES THE SON OF ZEBEDEE

The first of these, James the son of Zebedee, has been seriously considered as the author of the Epistle. It must be remembered, however, that he died in A.D. 44, Acts 12.2, and there are some indications that the Epistle was hardly written quite so early as that. Moreover, it is exceedingly unlikely that James the son of Zebedee ever possessed that kind of unique position in the Church which would have rendered some special designation in James 1.1 unnecessary. He was always overshadowed either by Peter or by James the Lord's brother. Finally, there is no tradition worth considering in favour of regarding the Epistle as the work of this James.

NOT JAMES THE SON OF ALPHÆUS

These objections, with the exception of the first, apply even more strongly to James the son of Alphæus. Though one of the twelve apostles, this James seems to have been quite obscure. No reader would ever guess that he was meant, unless he were carefully distinguished from the more prominent men of the same name.

JAMES THE BROTHER OF THE LORD

There remains only James the brother of the Lord; and he satisfies all the conditions of the problem. He was not, indeed, one of the twelve apostles, and during the earthly life of Jesus was not even a believer at all, John 7.5. But having been granted a special appearance of the risen Lord, I Cor. 15.7, and having united himself with the little company of apostles and faithful women who were waiting for the coming of the Spirit, Acts 1.14, he became afterwards the leader of the Jerusalem church, Acts 12.17; 15.4–29; Gal. 2.9; Acts 21.18.

Of course, the headship of the Jerusalem church did not exalt James above the twelve apostles, who had been given their authority by Jesus himself. The Twelve seem to have devoted themselves after a short time especially to the work of preaching the gospel outside of Jerusalem, whereas James continued in permanent charge of the local congregation. Nevertheless, although the position of James was not absolutely supreme, it was at least unique. As leader of the Jerusalem church, James could designate himself without fear of confusion simply as 'James, a servant of God and of the Lord Jesus Christ'. Evidently it is James the brother of the Lord who appears in James 1.1 as the writer of the Epistle.

The Readers

THE ADDRESS

The Epistle is addressed 'to the twelve tribes which are of the Dispersion'. Literally understood these words refer simply to the Jews who lived outside of Palestine. A limitation, however, becomes necessary when we reflect that the readers were evidently Christians. If James addresses the letter simply to Jews, he means, of course, those Jews whom he could reach, namely Jewish Christians. Perhaps he means to imply that they, and not their non-Christian countrymen, constituted the true Israel.

Possibly, however, the address is to be taken in a purely figurative sense. 'The twelve tribes of the Dispersion' may refer to the Christian Church in its entirety without distinction of race. In some books of the New Testament the Church is regarded as the true Israel. The name occurs in this sense in Gal. 6.16, and the idea runs through all that Paul says about the Christians as the true sons of Abraham and true heirs of the promise. It is possible that James also had adopted this manner of speaking.

THE READERS WERE JEWS

But no matter which interpretation be adopted, the Epistle was evidently addressed to Jewish Christians. If the whole Church is intended by the phrase in the first verse, then the whole Church at the time when the Epistle was written was composed chiefly of men of Jewish race. The Jewish nationality of the readers appears not only in details, like the parallels with Jewish literature and the use of the untranslated Hebrew word 'Sabaoth', James 5.4, but also in the general character of the conditions that are presupposed. The faults against which the Epistle is directed—faith without works, words without deeds, censoriousness, ambition, inordinate love of teaching, toadying to wealth and position, contemptuous treatment of the poor, covetousness under the cloak of religion—are typically Pharisaic; and peculiarly Gentile faults like idolatry and impurity, which are so prominent in such an Epistle as First Corinthians, are conspicuous by their absence. In this Epistle James is helping his Jewish readers to transcend formalistic Judaism in practice as they had already transcended it in belief. They had already accepted Jesus as Messiah—let them now act like true disciples of his, and not like disciples of the Pharisees!

235

The Date

According to Josephus, the Jewish historian, James 'the brother of Jesus, who is called Christ' was condemned and stoned at the instance of Ananus the high priest, after the death of the procurator Festus and before the arrival of his successor. This would put the death of James in A.D. 62. Apparently Hegesippus, a Jewish Christian writer of the second century, whom some scholars are here inclined to follow, puts it a little later, just before the outbreak of the Jewish war in A.D. 66. If therefore the Epistle was written by James, it could not have been written after A.D. 66 at the very latest.

Probably, indeed, it was written a considerable time before that date. The question depends upon the relation of the Epistle to the teaching of Paul. In ch. 2.14–26 James discusses the connection between faith and works in a way that is entirely incomprehensible if the teaching of Paul was already in view. Evidently there is no contradiction of Paul—indeed, as we shall see, there is profound agreement with him—and yet the words of Paul are strangely reversed. If Paul himself or even some perversion of Paul's teaching were the object of attack, surely the exact relation to Paul would have been made plain. Furthermore, James ignores altogether the question of the validity of the Jewish law and the position of Gentiles in the Church. Such questions could not have been ignored after the conflict between Paul and the Judaizers. Evidently, therefore, the Epistle of James was written before the Apostolic Council of Acts, ch. 15; Gal. ch. 2. This Epistle is a document of the primitive period of the Jerusalem church before the rise of any prominent Gentile Christianity. As such it is evidently of unique historical importance.

The Christianity of James

The Epistle of James has been called the least Christian book in the New Testament. Superficially this judgment is true. The name of Jesus occurs only twice in the epistle, James 1.1; 2.1, and there is no specific reference to his life and death and resurrection. A close examination, however, reverses the first impression.

JAMES AND THE SYNOPTIC DISCOURSES

In the first place, the ethical teaching of James is permeated by the spirit of Jesus. Even the form of the Epistle displays a marked affinity for the discourses of the Synoptic Gospels, and the affinity in content is even more apparent. Many striking parallels could be cited; but what is more convincing than such details is the indefinable spirit of the whole. The way in which James treats the covetousness, the pride, the heartlessness, the formalism, the pettiness and the meanness of his readers, is strikingly similar to the way in which his Master dealt with the Pharisees. James does not indeed actually cite the words of Jesus; but the absence of citations makes the underlying similarity all the more significant. The writer of this Epistle did not live at a time when the knowledge of the words of Jesus was derived from books; rather he had himself listened to the Master—even though he was not at first a disciple—and was living in a community where the impression of Jesus' teaching and Jesus' person was still fresh in the memory of those who had known him on earth.

JAMES AND CHRISTIAN DOCTRINE

In the second place, moreover, the Christianity of James is religious as well as ethical. Of course it could not be like the teaching of Jesus if it were merely ethical; for everything that Jesus taught even about the simplest matters of human conduct was determined by the thought of the heavenly Father and by the significance of his own person. But by the religious character of the Epistle of James even more than this is meant. Like all the writers of the New Testament James was well aware of the saving significance of Jesus' death and resurrection. For him as well as for the others, Jesus was Lord, ch. 1.1, and a Lord who was possessed of a heavenly glory, ch. 2.1. James, as well as the others, was waiting for the second coming of Christ, ch. 5.8. He does not directly refer to the saving events that form the substance of Christian faith; but he takes them everywhere for granted. The word of truth through which the disciples have been formed by God, ch. 1.18, the implanted word, v. 21, that needs ever to be received anew, can hardly be anything else than the apostolic gospel as it was proclaimed in the earliest speeches of Peter which are recorded in The Acts, and as it found its rich unfolding in the teaching of Paul. Just because that gospel in our Epistle is presupposed, it does not need to be expounded in detail. The men to whom James was writing were not lacking in orthodoxy. If they had been, he would have set them right, and we should have had another exposition of the gospel. As a matter of fact their fault was in practice, not in theory; and it is in the sphere of practice that they are met by James. The Epistle would be valueless if it stood alone. It does not lay the foundation of Christian faith. But it shows how, upon that foundation, may be built not the wood, hay and stubble of a wordy orthodoxy, but the gold and silver and precious stones of an honest Christian life.

This Epistle, then, might be misleading if taken by itself; but it becomes salutary if it is understood in its historical connections. Far from disparaging Christian doctrine—as the modern Church is tempted to suppose—it builds upon doctrine. In that it agrees with the whole of the Bible. Christianity, as has been finely said, is a life only because it is a doctrine. Only the great saving events of the gospel have rendered possible a life like that which is described in the Epistle of James. And where the gospel is really accepted with heart as well as mind, that life of love will always follow.

The practical value of the Epistle may perhaps best be realized through an examination of the very passage which has given the greatest difficulty.

Faith and Works

APPARENT CONTRADICTION OF PAUL

In James 2.14–26 the writer is apparently in direct conflict with Paul. According to Paul, justification is by faith alone and not by the works of the law—see for example, Gal. 2.14–21; according to James, a man is justified by works and not only by faith, James 2.24. Upon closer examination, however, the contradiction is seen to be one of form and not of substance; and like other apparent contradictions in the Bible it serves only to reveal the Scripture combination of rich variety with perfect unity.

WHAT IS MEANT BY FAITH?

According to James, faith without works is dead; according to Paul, faith is all-sufficient for salvation. But what does James mean by faith? The answer is perfectly plain. The faith which James is condemning is a mere intellectual assent which has no effect upon conduct. The demons also, he says, have that sort of faith, and yet evidently they are not saved, James 2.19. What Paul means by faith is something entirely different; it is not a mere intellectual assent to certain propositions, but an attitude of the entire man by which the whole life is entrusted to Christ. In other words, the faith that James is condemning is not the faith that Paul is commending.

The solution of the whole problem is provided by Paul himself in a single phrase. In Gal. 5.6, he says, 'For in Christ Jesus neither circumcision availeth anything, nor uncircumcision; but faith working through love'. 'Faith working through love' is the key to an understanding both of Paul and of James. The faith about which Paul has been speaking is not the idle faith which James condemns, but a faith that works. It works itself out through love. And what love is Paul explains in the whole last division of Galatians. It is no mere emotion, but the actual fulfilling of the whole moral law. 'For the whole law is fulfilled in one word, even in this: Thou shalt love thy neighbour as thyself.' (Gal. 5.14.) Paul is fully as severe as James against a faith that permits men to continue in sin. The faith about which he is speaking is a faith that receives the Spirit who gives men power to lead a holy life.

WHAT IS MEANT BY WORKS?

Moreover, as the faith which James condemns is different from the faith which Paul commends, so also the works which James commends are different from the works which Paul condemns. Paul is speaking about 'works of the law'—that is, works which are intended to earn salvation by fulfilling the law through human effort. James says nothing in ch. 2.14–26 about works of the law. The works of which he is speaking are works that spring from faith and are the expression of faith. Abraham offered Isaac as a sacrifice only because he believed God. His works were merely an evidence that his faith was real. Such works as that are insisted upon by Paul in every epistle. Without them no man can inherit the kingdom of God, Gal. 5.21. Only—and here again James and Paul are in perfect agreement—such works as that can spring only from faith. They can be accomplished not by human effort, but only by the reception of the power of God.

THE VALUE OF JAMES

If James had had the epistles of Paul before him he would no doubt have expressed himself differently. He might have said, not that faith without works is dead, but that faith without works is not true faith at all. This is what he clearly means. But the expression of his thought is all the more poignant because it is independent. His stern, terse insistence upon moral reality in religion, of which the passage just considered is only a typical example, provides a valuable supplement to the rest of the New Testament. Of itself it would be insufficient; but taken in connection with the Gospels and with Paul it contributes a necessary fibre to the woven cord of Christian character.

Contents of the Epistle

The opening of the Epistle, like that of the letters contained in Acts 15.23–29; 23.26–30, is constructed according to the regular Greek form.

After the opening, James speaks first of trials or temptations. Rightly used they will lead to perfection. If, however, there is still imperfection, it can be removed by prayer to God. The imperfection which is here especially in view is an imperfection in wisdom. Apparently the readers, like the Pharisees, had laid an excessive stress upon knowledge. The true wisdom, says James, can be obtained, not by human pride, as the readers seem to think, but only by prayer. Prayer, however, must be in faith—there must be no wavering in it. Pride, indeed, is altogether blameworthy. If there is to be boasting, it should certainly be not in earthly wealth but in those spiritual blessings which often reverse earthly distinctions. Returning to the subject of temptations, James insists that in their evil they do not come from God, but from the depths of man's own desires. From God comes no evil thing, but every perfect gift; and in the gospel God has bestowed upon us his richest blessing.

That gospel must be received with all diligence. It will exclude wrath and insincerity. True religion consists not merely in hearing but in doing; good examples of the exercise of it are the visitation of the fatherless and widows and the preservation of one's own personal purity of life.

Faith in Christ, James continues in similar vein, excludes all undue respect of persons. Indeed God in his choice of those who should be saved has especially favoured the poor. The rich as a class are rather the oppressors of the Christians. Surely then the Christians should not favour rich men for selfish reasons. The law of love will exclude all such unworthy conduct.

That law of love requires an active life. Faith, if it be true faith, leads to works. Away with a miserable faith that is expressed only in words!

Words, indeed, are dangerous. The tongue is a prolific source of harm. Evil speech reveals the deep-seated corruption of the heart. The readers must be careful, therefore, about seeking the work of a teacher. The true wisdom, which fits a man to teach, is not of man's acquiring, but comes from God.

Quarrelling—which was produced especially by the inordinate ambition among the readers to pose as teachers—must be counteracted by submission to God.

The constant thought of God excludes all pride in human planning. Especially the rich must reflect upon the transitoriness of earthly possessions, and above all must be sure that their wealth is honestly gained.

Finally, patient waiting for the Lord, the example of the Old Testament saints, and the earnest practice of prayer will make effective all the exhortations of the Epistle.

TOPICS FOR STUDY

1. Point out parallels between the Epistle of James and the teaching of Jesus as it is recorded in the Synoptic Gospels (about two topics).

2. Tell all that is known (a) about James the brother of the Lord, (b) about the other men of the same name who are mentioned in the New Testament (two topics).

3. Summarize and explain the teaching of the Epistle (a) about prayer, (b) about wealth and poverty, (c) about good and evil speaking (three topics).

33: JESUS THE FULFILMENT OF THE OLD TESTAMENT

Study material: The Epistle to the Hebrews

The Author

HEBREWS NOT WRITTEN BY PAUL

The Epistle to the Hebrews is the only one of the New Testament books whose author is neither named in the book itself nor made known through any trustworthy tradition. Many of us are accustomed to think of the Epistle as the work of Paul, but this view did not win general acceptance in the Church until the fourth century. In the early period, although some regarded Paul as the author, others held different views.

THE TRADITION

At Alexandria in the latter part of the second century Paul was thought to be the author of the Epistle to the Hebrews; but in North Africa a little later Tertullian attributed the Epistle to Barnabas, and in other portions of the Church the Pauline authorship was certainly not accepted. In the west, the Pauline authorship was long denied and the inclusion of the Epistle in the New Testament resisted. At last the Alexandrian view won universal acceptance. The Epistle to the Hebrews became an accepted part of the New Testament, and was attributed to Paul.

Clement of Alexandria, who had apparently received the tradition of Pauline authorship from Pantænus, his predecessor, himself declares that Hebrews was written by Paul in the 'Hebrew' (Aramaic) language, and was translated by Luke into Greek. The notion of a translation by Luke was based upon no genuine historical tradition—Hebrews is certainly an original Greek work—but was simply an hypothesis constructed to explain the peculiarities of the Epistle on the supposition that it was a work of Paul.

THE VALUE OF THE TRADITION

The tradition of Pauline authorship is clearly very weak. If Paul had been the author, it is hard to see why the memory of the fact should have been lost so generally in the Church. No one in the early period had any objection to the Epistle; on the contrary it was very highly regarded. If, then, it had really been written by Paul, the Pauline authorship would have been accepted everywhere with avidity. The negative testimony of the Roman church is particularly significant. The Epistle was quoted by Clement of Rome at about A.D. 95; yet at Rome as elsewhere in the west the Epistle seems never in the early period to have been regarded as Pauline. In other words, just where acquaintance with the Epistle can be traced farthest back, the denial of Pauline authorship seems to have been most insistent. If Clement of Rome had regarded Paul as the author, the history of Roman opinion about the Epistle would have been very different.

On the other hand, on the supposition that there was originally no tradition of Pauline authorship, the subsequent prevalence of such a tradition is easily explained. It was due simply to the evident apostolic authority of the Epistle itself. From the start, Hebrews was felt to be an authoritative work. Being authoritative, it would be collected along with other authoritative works. Since it was an Epistle, and exhibited a certain Pauline quality of spirit and subject, it would naturally be associated with the other works of the greatest letter writer of the apostolic age. Being thus included in a collection of the Pauline Epistles, and being regarded as of apostolic authority, what was more natural than to attribute it to the apostle Paul? Such, very possibly, was the origin of the Alexandrian tradition.

This tradition did not win immediate acceptance, because the rest of the Church was still aware that the Epistle was not written by Paul. What led to the final conquest of the Pauline tradition was simply the character of the book iteslf. The question of Pauline authorship, in the case of this book, became connected with the question of apostolic authority. The Church had to choose between rejecting the book altogether, and accepting it as Pauline. When she finally adopted the latter alternative, undoubtedly she chose the lesser error. It was an error to regard the Epistle as the work of Paul; but it would have been a far greater error to exclude it from the New Testament. As a matter of fact, though the book was not written by Paul, it was written, if not by one of the other apostles, at least by an 'apostolic man' like Mark or Luke. Scarcely any book of the New Testament bears clearer marks of true apostolicity.

INTERNAL EVIDENCE

The argument against Pauline authorship which is derived from tradition is strongly supported by the contents of the Epistle itself. In the first place, it is exceedingly doubtful whether Paul could have spoken of himself as having had the Christian salvation confirmed to him by those who had heard the Lord, Heb. 2.3. Knowledge of the earthly life of Jesus was indeed conveyed to Paul by ordinary word of mouth from the eyewitnesses; but the gospel itself, as he insists with vehemence in Galatians, was revealed to him directly by Christ. In the second place, the style of the Epistle is very different from that of Paul, being, as we shall see, far more carefully wrought. In the third place, the thoughts developed in Hebrews, though undoubtedly they are in perfect harmony with the Pauline epistles, are by no means characteristically Pauline. It is a little hard to understand, for example, how Paul could have written at such length about the law without speaking of justification by faith or the reception of Gentiles into the Church. This last argument, however, must not be exaggerated. Undoubtedly Paul would have agreed heartily to everything that Hebrews contains. Paul and the author of this Epistle have developed merely somewhat different sides of the same great truth.

The Destination

THE READERS PROBABLY JEWS

The earliest title of the Epistle, 'To the Hebrews', though it is not part of the Epistle itself, may preserve a genuine tradition about the original readers. On the whole the Epistle looks as though it were intended primarily for Jews. To them the elaborate demonstration of the superiority which Christ possesses over the ceremonies of the old dispensation would be of special value, particularly if the temple in Jerusalem was still standing.

THE READERS A DEFINITE GROUP

At first sight, the Epistle to the Hebrews looks more like a treatise than an epistle. Instead of prefixing an address, like those which are to be found in the letters of Paul and even in the Epistle of

James, the author plunges at once into the very heart of his great subject. We might suppose, therefore, that if the work was especially destined for any particular circle of readers its destination was at any rate very broad. Perhaps, for example, it was addressed, if not to the whole Church, at least to all Jewish Christians throughout the Church. Closer examination, however, creates a different impression. The opening is quite general; but further on we discover definite reference to the circumstances of the readers. Evidently they lived in a narrowly circumscribed locality and had a common life. The author hopes to be restored to them, Heb. 13.23; and Timothy, too, may be expected to visit them. One does not write in this way to persons scattered throughout the world.

RELIGIOUS CONDITION OF THE READERS

From the Epistle, indeed, some rather definite information can be gathered with regard to the religious condition of the readers. At the beginning of their Christian life, they had passed through a severe persecution, Heb. 10.32–34, in which apparently their leaders had suffered martyrdom, ch. 13.7. The first persecution had been endured bravely, and the Christian community had also approved itself by liberality to the saints, ch. 6.10. The latter grace was still being practised when the Epistle was written; but otherwise the condition of the readers gave cause for alarm. Although a considerable time had elapsed since the introduction of the gospel, spiritual perception had become so dull that the readers, instead of being teachers, must still be learners of the very rudiments—they must still be fed with milk like babes, ch. 5.11–14. The tendency to laxness in the religious life had manifested itself, for example, in the neglect of Christian meetings, ch. 10.25. Indeed, the writer is apprehensive lest the readers should actually fall away from the faith altogether. Against such apostasy the most solemn warnings are directed—especially chs. 6.4–8; 10.26–31; 12.25. Apparently another time of grievous persecution has come, ch. 12.3–13. All through the Epistle there runs a note of encouragement as well as of warning. By the memory of their former bravery and of the heroic death of their former leaders, by diligent use of the means of grace, by a becoming submission to their present leaders, ch. 13.17, by the example of the heroes of the faith, ch. 11, and particularly of Jesus himself, ch. 12.2, 3, above all by a fearful and thankful realization of the overwhelming majesty of the divine High

Priest, the readers are exhorted to be steadfast in the present fiery trial.

The Date

The Epistle to the Hebrews was certainly written before A.D. 95, for at about that time it was quoted by Clement of Rome. The mention of Timothy in ch. 13.23 perhaps does not carry us much farther, for Timothy, who was a grown man at about A.D. 50, Acts 16.1–3, may have lived till the end of the first century. The Epistle, however, does not bear any of the marks of late origin. The question of date is closely connected with the question whether in the Epistle the temple at Jerusalem is regarded as still standing. This question cannot be settled with certainty. But on the whole the continuance of the Levitical ceremonies seems to be assumed in the Epistle, and there is no clear reference to their cessation. Probably therefore the Epistle to the Hebrews was written before the destruction of Jerusalem in A.D. 70.

The Theme

The purpose of the Epistle to the Hebrews is intensely practical. The practical purpose, however, as in the other New Testament books, is not attained by mere exhortation, but by an appeal to solid fact. In this case it is attained by the orderly development of a great theme. In the Epistle to the Hebrews, Christian devotion is stirred by the representation of Jesus as the culmination of the old dispensation.

THE PROBLEM OF LAW AND GOSPEL

The question of the relation between the old dispensation and the new was a serious problem in the early Church. On the one hand, Paul had represented the Mosaic law as in one sense abrogated by the coming of Christ. Christians are not obliged to unite themselves with the chosen people in order to be saved; works of the law can never earn the favour of God. For Gentiles to observe Jewish ceremonies is to make void the grace of God. On the other hand, Paul himself, as well as the other apostles, insisted upon the continued authority of the Old Testament. But the Old Testament contains the law. How then could the law be abrogated if the Old Testament was still in force?

FALSE SOLUTIONS OF THE PROBLEM

The problem was solved in a number of ways. Some of these ways were false. Marcion, for example, about the middle of the second century, simply cut the knot. The Old Testament, he said, as well as the law, is invalid. Indeed the Old Testament and the law never were valid; they were the work not of the good God, that Christians worship, but of another power. This solution was unhesitatingly rejected by the Church. It was contrary not only to the whole of the apostolic teaching, but also to the example of Jesus himself.

Another false solution of the problem was advocated in an epistle probably of the early second century, which was falsely attributed to Barnabas. This so-called Epistle of Barnabas rejected not indeed the Old Testament itself, but the entire Jewish interpretation of it. The ceremonies of the Mosaic law, according to the author, were intended to be merely symbolic of Christian truth; the literal interpretation of them on the part of the Jews was a colossal error. This solution also was rejected by the Church; in it violence was evidently done to the plain meaning of the Old Testament. The Old Testament does clearly demand a separation of Israel from other nations and the observance by Israel of sacrifices and feasts and fasts. So, indeed, the Old Testament was interpreted by Jesus himself.

THE TRUE SOLUTION

Before either of these false solutions had been proposed, the true solution of the problem had already been provided by the Epistle to the Hebrews. In this Epistle the authority of the Old Testament is recognized to the full, and full justice is also done to its plain literal meaning. The ceremonies of the Mosaic law were really intended to be observed by the chosen people. But according to the Epistle to the Hebrews these ceremonies were never valuable merely for their own sake; they were valuable because of the spiritual truth which they conveyed in sensible form, and in particular because of their prophetic witness to Christ. The key to the Epistle is given at the very beginning: 'God, who at sundry times and in divers manners spake in time past unto the fathers by the prophets, hath in these last days spoken unto us by his Son.' (Heb. 1.1, 2, A.V.) It is the same God who spoke in the old dispensation and in the new; but the manner of his speaking has changed. In the Old Testament law he spoke by means of symbols; in the gospel he speaks plainly and fully through his Son.

The progressiveness of the divine revelation, then, is the master thought of the Epistle. Christ is the culmination of the long succession of lawgiver and prophets. They existed for his sake; they were a preparation for him. In particular, the high priest of the Mosaic law was a type of Christ. He performed in imperfect, external manner that spiritual service which Christ performs by his death and by his continued intercession for his followers. The author of the Epistle was wise in developing his theme so fully. The Old Testament law has still a message even after the fulfilment has come. Through sign and symbol, through forerunner and prophet, the Christian can still be led to a new appreciation of the great High Priest.

TOPICS FOR STUDY

1. Construct an outline of Hebrews.
2. Was the temple at Jerusalem still standing when Hebrews was written?
3. Explain the comparison between Jesus and Melchizedek, Heb. 6.20 to 7.28.
4. Outline the conception of Christ as High Priest.
5. Collect the exhortations of the Epistle, as distinguished from the didactic passages.
6. Collect and explain the designations of Christ in this Epistle. Which is the most frequent designation?

34: CHRISTIAN FORTITUDE

Study material: The First Epistle of Peter

The Author
The First Epistle of Peter, unlike the last Epistle that we have studied, contains the name of the author in the first verse. In the further course of the Epistle, also, the author represents himself as an eyewitness of the earthly life of Jesus, I Peter 5.1. If the author was 'a witness of the sufferings of Christ,' he must have been one of the small group of disciples who were with Jesus at the end. The address and the Epistle itself, therefore, agree in attesting the apostolic authorship. That Peter was the author of the Epistle is also attested by a strong tradition.

The Readers

IN ASIA MINOR
The Epistle is addressed 'to the elect who are sojourners of the Dispersion in Pontus, Galatia, Cappadocia, Asia, and Bithynia'. The five provinces named embrace all of Asia Minor with the exception of the southern coast. The order is rather peculiar; it is perhaps due to the order of the route which the bearer of the Epistle was to follow.

GENTILE CHRISTIANS
But what is the meaning of 'sojourners of the Dispersion'? Since 'the Dispersion' was a fixed term for Jews living outside of Palestine, it seems natural at first sight to take the phrase as designating the Jewish Christians of the provinces in question. This interpretation is clearly excluded by the Epistle itself. Passages like ch. 1.18; 4.3 make it perfectly clear that the readers of the Epistle were predominantly at least of Gentile extraction. The phrase 'sojourners of the Dispersion', then, must be intrepreted figuratively to

refer to the Christian Church. The Christians are like the 'Dispersion' of the Jews in being strangers in an alien world.

Place of Writing

NOT BABYLON

The place where the Epistle was written might seem to be fixed by ch. 5.13, 'She that is in Babylon, elect together with you, saluteth you.' But what is meant by 'Babylon'? Undoubtedly the first impulse of the modern reader is to think of Babylon on the Euphrates. Many suppose that the Epistle was written from there. This view, however, is beset with serious difficulties. Undoubtedly it is possible. In the first century after Christ, the ancient Babylon, though decayed, was still in existence. But there is no good evidence whatever that Peter ever went to Babylonia, and the presence of Silvanus, v. 12, and Mark, v. 13, so far in the east is even more surprising.

ROME

On the other hand, a figurative interpretation of the word 'Babylon' removes all difficulties. In the book of Revelation, 'Babylon' is clearly a designation of Rome. Rome, the capital of the Roman Empire was, in its power and in its worldliness, the Babylon of the first century after Christ. If the writing of the Epistle in Babylon on the Euphrates would be surprising, the writing of it in Rome is exactly what might have been expected. The presence of Peter in Rome in his later life is attested by an exceedingly strong Christian tradition, and the presence of Mark—compare Col. 4.10; Philem. 24—and Silvanus in that city is also natural.

This figurative interpretation of 'Babylon' is supported by the figurative language of the verse itself and of the whole Epistle. Evidently 'she that is in Babylon, elect together with you' does not refer to a woman—it would certainly be a strange designation of an individual—but designates a church. If 'Babylon' be taken figuratively, then the figurative language which certainly prevails in part of the verse would merely extend over the whole. Moreover, the designation of Rome as 'Babylon' is in accord with the imagery which runs all through the Epistle. Throughout the Epistle, as we have observed, the Church is represented as a people separated like the Jews of the Dispersion from its natural home. This exile of the people of God on earth is, if Rome be meant in our verse, represented more particularly as a Babylonian exile. As the exile of the Jews was at first an exile to Babylon, so the exile of the early Christian Church was an exile in the Roman Empire, of which the capital was the Babylon of that time. The First Epistle of Peter was written from the centre of earthly power to the holy race which has on earth no permanent home. From the metropolis of the world empire came the exhortation to be separate from the world!

Date

If First Peter was written from Rome, then within certain limits its date is fixed. Peter could scarcely have arrived in Rome before the first Roman imprisonment of the apostle Paul; for if he had done so, Paul would probably have alluded to the fact in the Epistle to the Romans, or in Colossians, Philemon, Ephesians or Philippians. Very possibly he arrived while Paul was in Spain or in the east, during the time between the two imprisonments. In that case, since Second Timothy, which was written from Rome during the second imprisonment, contains no allusion to Peter's presence, it is probable that Peter had either left the city or had died before Paul's second arrival. Many scholars suppose that he was martyred in the persecution which Nero instituted in A.D. 64. The form of Peter's martyrdom, according to John 21.18, 19, as well as according to tradition, was crucifixion. Paul, the Roman citizen, was beheaded; Peter, like his Master, suffered the more shameful death. Such shame was the truest glory—and glory not of Peter, but of God, v. 19.

Peter and Paul

The churches that are addressed in First Peter had been founded by Paul and his emissaries. The apostle to the Jews, Gal. 2.8, here engages in Gentile work. The division of labour between Paul and the pillars of the Jerusalem church, v. 9, was never intended in an exclusive sense. From the beginning Peter laboured here and there for Gentiles and Paul for Jews. Such activity was welcomed in every case by both parties. But the development of the Church brought changes. The original apostles were scattered farther and farther from Jerusalem; Jewish Christianity occupied less and less of the Church's thought. Hence it happened that Peter, in his travels, came at length to the centre of the Gentile world and addressed a letter to specifically Pauline churches.

It has even been suggested that the letter may have been written by request of Paul himself. When Paul went to Spain he may have felt the need of leaving a brother apostle in charge of his work. A letter from the leader among the original apostles would bring the Christians of Asia Minor to the best possible realization of the unity of the Church.

Certainly, at any rate, the First Epistle of Peter attests a full agreement with the Christianity of Paul. Peter had probably read the Epistles of Paul to the Ephesians and to the Romans; and even where he does not show direct dependence upon Paul he is in fundamental harmony with the Pauline gospel. It is by no means necessary to suppose that the similarity of Peter to Paul must have been due altogether to dependence of one upon the other. The truth is that First Peter only makes somewhat clearer a fact which should never have been doubted—that the apostolic gospel was everywhere fundamentally the same. To all of the apostles Jesus was a divine Lord; by all his death was regarded as a sacrifice for the sins of the world; by all his resurrection was declared to be the beginning of an entirely new life, into which every Christian enters through faith.

Exhortation and Fact

At the time when First Peter was written, the readers were undergoing persecution. The letter was intended to make them steadfast. Steadfastness, according to Peter, is to be attained not by mere exhortation, but by exhortation based upon the facts of the gospel. If the Christian salvation is what it is declared to be at the beginning of the Epistle, ch. 1.3–12, then there can be no such thing as wavering or discouragement. The 'wherefore' of v. 13 is the hinge upon which the Epistle turns.

Separateness from the World

Throughout the Epistle the separateness of Christians from the world is represented under a great variety of figures. Christians have been begotten anew, chs. 1.3, 23; 2.2; they have been called into a holy fellowship, ch. 1.15; ransomed out of slavery by the precious sacrifice of Christ, vs. 18–21; they are stones in a building of which Christ is the chief stone of the corner, ch. 2.4, 5; like Israel of old they are an elect race, a royal priesthood, a holy nation, ch. 2.9, 10, now scattered as strangers in a hostile world, chs. 1.1, 17; 2.11, 12; 5.13, but with a sure inheritance in heaven, ch. 1.3–5.

The modern Church is in grave danger of forgetting the distinctiveness of her gospel and the glorious isolation of her position. She is content to be merely one factor in civilization, a means of improving the world instead of the creator of a new world.

The first readers of the Epistle were subject to a similar danger, though it arose from a somewhat different cause. Today we are no longer subject to persecution; but the danger is fundamentally the same. The world's friendship may be even more disastrous than the world's hatred. The readers of First Peter were tempted to relinquish what was distinctive in their faith in order to avoid the hostility of their heathen neighbours; we are tempted to do the same thing because the superficial respectability of modern life has put a gloss of polite convention over the profound differences that divide the inner lives of men. We, as well as the first readers of the Epistle, need to be told that this world is lost in sin, that the blood of Christ has ransomed an elect race from the city of destruction, that the high privileges of the Christian calling demand spotless purity and unswerving courage.

THE CHARACTER OF THE PERSECUTION

The character of the persecution to which the readers of the Epistle were subjected cannot be determined with perfect clearness. It is not even certain that the Christian profession in itself was regarded officially as a crime. Apparently charges of positive misconduct were needed to give countenance to the persecutors, I Peter 2.12. The Christians needed to be warned that there is no heroism in suffering if the suffering is the just punishment of misdeeds, chs. 2.20; 4.15. What particular charges were brought against the Christians it is of course difficult to determine. Perhaps they were sometimes charged with gross crimes such as murder or theft. But a more frequent accusation was probably 'hatred of the human race,' or the like. The Christians were thought to be busybodies. In setting the world to rights they seemed to meddle in other people's affairs. In claiming to be citizens of a heavenly kingdom, they seemed indifferent or hostile to earthly relationships. As subjects of the emperor and of his representatives, the Christians were thought to be disloyal; as slaves, they seemed disobedient.

DUTIES OF EARTHLY LIFE

In view of these accusations, Peter urges his readers to avoid all improper employment of their Christian freedom. Christian freedom does not mean licence; Christian independence does not mean indifference. There is no reason why a good Christian should be a bad citizen, even of a heathen state, ch. 2.13–17, or an unprofitable servant, even of a harsh master, vs. 18–25, or a quarrelsome wife, even of an unconverted husband, ch. 3.1–6. On the contrary, Christians must approve themselves not only in the spiritual realm, but also in the ordinary relationships of this life.

APPLICATION TO MODERN CONDITIONS

Here again these truths are important for the present day. Now as always fervent realization of the transcendent glory of Christianity tends sometimes to result in depreciation of ordinary duties. Men of exceptional piety sometimes seem to feel that civilization is unworthy of their attention, even if it is not actually a work of Satan. Of all such vagaries the First Epistle of Peter is the best corrective. Truth is here admirably guarded against the error that lurks at its root. The very Epistle that emphasizes the separateness of the Church from the world, that teaches Christian people to look down upon earthly affairs from the vantage ground of heaven, is just the Epistle that inculcates sober and diligent conduct in the various relationships of earthly life. In the effort at a higher morality, the simple, humble virtues that even the world appreciates should not be neglected; piety should involve no loss of common sense. Now as always the Christian should be ready to give a reason for the faith that is in him; now as always he should be able to refute the slanders of the world; now as always he should commend his Christianity by his good citizenship. Only so will the example of Christ be fully followed. Jesus was in possession of a transcendent message; but he lived the life of a normal man. The Christian, too, is a man with a divine mission; but like his Master he must exercise his mission in the turmoil of life. He must not be a spoilsport at feasts; his is no desert rôle like John the Baptist's. Christianity has a mission from without; but its mission is fulfilled in loving contact with the world of men.

THE CHRISTIAN'S DEFENCE

The Christians who suffered persecution should first of all, according to Peter, defend themselves to the very best of their ability. They should do their best to remove dishonour from the name of Christ. They should show the baselessness of the accusations which are brought against them. Then, if they still suffer, it will be clearly suffering for Christ's sake. Such suffering is glorious.

It is a test from which faith emerges strong and sure, ch. 1.7; it is true conformity to the example of Christ, chs. 2.21–24; 3.18; 4.1, 13.

Purity and Courage

From the separateness of the Church two results, according to Peter, should follow—in the first place purity, and in the second place courage. Members of a holy race, purchased by the precious blood of Christ, elect from before the foundation of the world, cannot engage in those evil practices which were natural to them in their former state. And citizens of a heavenly commonwealth, members of a holy family, with Christ as their supreme example of courage and self-denial, can never fear anything that men can do.

TOPICS FOR STUDY

1. Construct an outline of the Epistle.
2. Compare the Epistle (a) with the epistles of Paul, (b) with the Epistle of James, (c) with the speeches of Peter reported in The Acts, (d) with the teaching of Jesus (three or four topics).
3. Outline the history of Silvanus. What did Silvanus do in connection with the Epistle?
4. Where was each of the provinces which are named in the address?

I

35: THE CHRISTIAN'S ATTITUDE TOWARD ERROR AND IMMORALITY

Study material: The Second Epistle of Peter and the Epistle of Jude

The Author of Second Peter

The author of the Second Epistle of Peter is clearly designated at the beginning as 'Simon [or, as some manuscripts have it, "Symeon," according to the original Hebrew form of the name] Peter, a servant and apostle of Jesus Christ'. In II Peter 1.14, moreover, the author appears as the disciple to whom the risen Christ spoke the words that are recorded in John 21.18; in vs. 16–18 he designates himself clearly as an eyewitness of the earthly life of Jesus and in particular of the transfiguration, Matt. 17.1–13; and in ch. 3.15 he puts himself on a parity with the apostle Paul. Throughout the whole Epistle the author writes as one of the twelve apostles would naturally write

The Readers

THE ADDRESS

In the address of the Epistle the readers are designated only in the most general terms. Of itself, 'them that have obtained a like precious faith with us in the righteousness of our God and the Saviour Jesus Christ,' refers to all Christians; but the actual destination of the letter might be narrowed by special instructions to the bearer. The general terms used in the address, therefore, do not exclude the view that the letter was addressed to some special church or group of churches.

'THE SECOND EPISTLE'

The destination of the letter would be fixed if the interpretation of II Peter 3.1, 'This is now, beloved, the second epistle that I write unto you,' were certain. If these words refer to our First Epistle of Peter, then the readers of Second Peter were the same as the readers of First Peter—they were the Christians of Asia Minor. If, however, the former Epistle to which allusion is here made was not First Peter but some letter which has now been lost, then the passage affords no information about the readers.

THE LETTER OF PAUL

The uncertainty is not removed by the reference in ch. 3.15; for the letter which Paul wrote to the readers of Second Peter is here designated in such general terms that it might be identified with any one of a number of the extant epistles. The most that can be said with certainty is that the author of Second Peter probably has in view some group of readers more limited than the whole Church. Probably, however, the group was of rather wide extent: the personal element in the relation between author and readers is almost entirely lacking in this Epistle; individuals are not mentioned either among the persons addressed or in the company of the author.

The Occasion

EXHORTATION TO HOLINESS

In the first chapter, the occasion of the Epistle is described in general terms. The author desires to lay emphasis upon the necessity of a sound moral life. Christian faith should work itself out in a comprehensive chain of virtues, vs. 5–7. The conquest of sin has not in this life reached its conclusion. By diligent moral effort the Christian must make his 'calling and election sure'. Abundance in goodness will mean an abundant entrance into the kingdom of Christ, vs. 3–11.

APPEAL TO AUTHORITY

In vs. 12–21 this exhortation is buttressed by an appeal to the authority of the apostles and of the Scriptures. As an eyewitness of the majesty of Christ, Peter is fully competent to put his readers in remembrance of everything that is necessary to the right development of their faith and life; but his authority, far from superseding, only confirms the authority of Old Testament prophecy.

THE FALSE TEACHERS

The special reason for this strong emphasis upon a sound moral life and upon the authority that buttresses it becomes clear in the last two chapters of the Epistle. Holy living had been neglected, and apostolic and scriptural authority despised, by certain false teachers. The activity of these teachers is described partly in the future tense and partly in the present. Their coming is sometimes predicted as a thing about which the readers are to be warned, and sometimes represented as already in the past. Perhaps the explanation is that the false teachers had already been active in the churches from which Peter was writing or in others with which he was acquainted, but had not yet made their way to the readers of the Epistle.

Characteristics of the False Teachers

LAXITY IN MORALS

The most characteristic thing about the false teachers was their laxity in morals. Impurity, II Peter 2.2, 10–16, 18, 19; 3.3; covetousness, ch. 2.3, 14, 15; impatience of authority, irreverence and pride, vs. 1, 10–12, 18, 19; ch. 3.3, were rife among them. These moral faults, moreover, were in their case not due merely to the weakness of human nature, but were actually defended by an appeal to principle. Here, as so often, immorality was excused by argument, sin was based upon error.

MISUSE OF PAULINE EPISTLES

Apparently the false teachers appealed to the Pauline epistles in support of their manner of life, ch. 3.16. Paul had laid great stress upon Christian liberty; the false teachers misused his words, ch. 2.19. It was an error which Paul himself had foreseen and combated—for example in the sixth chapter of Romans and the fifth chapter of Galatians. The liberty about which Paul wrote was not liberty to sin, but liberty to stop sinning; it was liberty from the enslaving despotism of the flesh; it was liberty that involved service, Gal. 5.13. Paul himself had provided the best corrective for this misunderstanding of his letters. The misunderstanding was due only to evil desire. The most powerful agency for the conquest of the flesh was being perverted to an opposite purpose, II Peter 3.15, 16.

DENIAL OF CHRIST'S COMING

Another element in the theory of the false teachers was a denial of the Christian hope of Christ's coming, ch. 3.3, 4. The reason for the denial is not perfectly clear. Perhaps the long delay, the dampening of early hopes, had gradually produced a sceptical attitude; perhaps scepticism was rooted rather in some philosophical theory. At any rate, the mockers emphasized the permanence of the world. There never has been change, they said, and there never will be. This error also was subservient to sin. If there is to be no end of the world, if the expectation of judgment becomes dim, then men think they can do as they please. The thought of Christ's appearing has always been a mighty stimulus to moral effort in the Church.

Other principles of the false teachers are obscure. Their denial of the Master that bought them, ch. 2.1, was perhaps practical rather than theoretical. Apparently they laid claim to a deeper knowledge than that which was possessed by the general run of Christians and perhaps even by the apostles, v. 12. They were not afraid of spiritual powers, whether good or bad, vs. 10, 11, 18. Some of these things become clearer in the Epistle of Jude, where the same or similar false teachers are described.

Against this false teaching Peter emphasizes the authority of Christ and his apostles, and of the Scriptures. God has not left the Church at the mercy of every wind of doctrine. For the immorality of the offenders Peter has stern and salutary denunciation.

The Epistle of Jude

AUTHOR

The writer of the Epistle of Jude is designated as 'Jude, a servant of Jesus Christ, and brother of James'. (Jude 1.1.) The name 'Jude' is in Greek the same as 'Judas'. A number of persons of this name are mentioned in the New Testament, but there can be no serious doubt as to the one who is meant here. Evidently James, who was the brother of Jude, is mentioned as one who needed no special designation. Not James the son of Zebedee or James the son of Alphæus, therefore, but the great James, the brother of the Lord, and leader of the Jerusalem church, is intended. The writer of the Epistle, then, was a brother of the brother of Jesus. Of course he could have been called a brother of Jesus himself, but because of his reverence for the Lord, he prefers the title of servant. Jude, like every other believer, was 'a servant of Jesus Christ'.

Jude actually appears in the Gospels among the brothers of

Jesus. Curiously enough there was also a Judas among the Twelve, in addition to Judas Iscariot, as there were also among the Twelve two men of the name of James; and what is more, this apostle Judas had some relation, perhaps as son or perhaps as brother, to a man named James, Luke 6.16; Acts 1.13. However, the similarity of names is to be regarded as merely a coincidence.

JUDE AND SECOND PETER

The Epistle of Jude is concerned almost exclusively with the denunciation of certain immoral persons who had crept into the Church. Evidently these persons stood in the closest relation to the false teachers of Second Peter, and they are combated in largely the same terms. The verbal resemblances between the two Epistles make it perfectly evident that the author of one made use of the other. It is not so clear, however, whether Peter made use of Jude, or Jude made use of Second Peter. Something may be said for either view.

DATE AND DESTINATION

Probably Second Peter was written in the closing years of Peter's life, and Jude may perhaps be put some years later still. The address of Jude is quite broad, Jude 1.1. It does not appear where the Epistle was first intended to be read. The little Epistle is full of a fine moral vigour; and although it is so much like Second Peter it has striking characteristics of its own.

Value of Second Peter and Jude

Although Second Peter and Jude are not so familiar as most of the New Testament, yet even these two brief Epistles have entered deep into the mind and heart of the Church.

EXPRESSIVE PHRASES

Even the inimitably expressive phrases and sentences that have been derived from the Epistles have produced no small enrichment of Christian life. The 'exceeding great and precious promises', and the 'partakers of the divine nature' of II Peter 1.4, the chain of virtues in vs. 5–7, the 'make your calling and election sure' of v. 10, the 'sure word of prophecy' of v. 19, the description of inspired prophecy in vs. 20, 21—'no prophecy of the scripture is of any private interpretation. For the prophecy came not in old time by the will of man: but holy men of God spake as they were moved by the Holy Ghost'—the 'vexed his righteous soul' of ch. 2.8, the 'railing accusation' of v. 11 (cf. Jude 9), the 'stir up your pure minds by way of remembrance' of II Peter 3.1, the 'not willing that any should perish, but that all should come to repentance' of v. 9, the 'faith which was once delivered unto the saints' of Jude 3, the magnificent doxology of vs. 24, 25—a review of these passages as they appear in the Authorized Version will bring some realization of the profound influence which even the most obscure books of the New Testament have exerted both upon the English language and upon the character of Christian men.

The influence of Second Peter and Jude, however, is not merely the influence of isolated phrases. The Epistles as a whole have a distinctive message for the Church. That message is twofold. It embraces in the first place an emphasis upon authority, and in the second place an insistence upon holiness.

THE EMPHASIS UPON AUTHORITY

The adversaries who are combated in Second Peter and Jude were impatient of restraint. Apparently they distinguished themselves, as possessing the Spirit, from the ordinary Christians, as being merely 'natural', Jude 4, 19; II Peter 2.12. They appealed to their own deeper insight, instead of listening to what apostles and prophets had to say. In reply, Peter and Jude insisted upon the authority of the Old Testament prophets, and upon the authority of the apostles, which was ultimately the authority of Christ. See especially II Peter 3.2.

A similar insistence upon authority is greatly needed today. Again men are inclined to appeal to an inward light as justifying freedom from ancient restraints; the Christian consciousness is being exalted above the Bible. At such a time, renewed attention to Second Peter and Jude would be salutary. False notions are rife today with regard to apostolic authority. They can be corrected by our Epistles. Peter as well as Paul exerts his authority not in an official or coldly ecclesiastical way, but with an inimitable brotherliness. The authority of the apostles is the authority of good news. Subjection to such authority is perfect freedom.

The authority which Peter and Jude urge upon their readers is a double authority—in the first place the authority of the Old Testament, and in the second place the authority of Christ exerted through the apostles. For us, however, the two become one. The apostles, like the Old Testament prophets, speak to us only through the Bible. We need to learn the lesson. A return to the Bible is the deepest need of the modern Church. It would mean a return to God.

INSISTENCE UPON HOLINESS

The second characteristic of Second Peter and Jude is the insistence upon holiness. Religion is by no means always connected with goodness. In the Greco-Roman world, the two were often entirely separate. Many pagan cults contained no ethical element whatever. The danger was therefore very great that Christianity might be treated in the same way. The early Christians needed to be admonished ever and again that their God was a God of righteousness, that no unclean thing could stand in his presence.

Insistence upon holiness is in itself no peculiarity of Second Peter and Jude. It runs all through the New Testament. But in these Epistles it is directed more definitely perhaps than anywhere else against the opposite error. The opponents of Peter and Jude did not merely drift into immorality; they defended it on theoretical grounds. They were making a deliberate effort to reduce Christianity to the level of a non-ethical religion. Such theoretical defence of immorality appears, indeed, in a number of places in the apostolic Church. A certain party in Corinth, for example, made a wrong use of Christian freedom. But what is more or less incidental in First Corinthians forms the main subject of Second Peter and Jude. Christianity is here insisting upon its thoroughly ethical character.

At first sight the message might seem obsolete today. We always associate religion with morality; we can hardly understand how the two ever could have been separated. It is to be feared, however, that the danger is not altogether past. In our thoughts we preserve the ethical character of Christianity. But how is it with our lives? How is it with our religious observances? Are we not constantly in danger of making religion a mere cult, a mere emotional excitement, a mere means of gaining earthly or heavenly advantages, a mere effort to bribe God by our worship? The danger is always with us. We need always to remind ourselves that Christian faith must work itself out in holy living.

Peter in his second Epistle has provided us with one important means to that end. It is the thought of Christ's coming. There can be no laxity in moral effort if we remember the judgment seat of Christ.

TOPICS FOR STUDY

1. Construct outlines of both Epistles.

2. Compare Second Peter (a) with First Peter, and (b) with Jude (two topics).

3. Present the teaching of the Epistles about apostolic authority and the authority of the Old Testament.

4. Distinguish the different persons mentioned in the New Testament who bore the name of Jude or Judas.

5. Outline the history of the relations between Peter and Paul.

36 : THE LIFE OF THE CHILDREN OF GOD

Study material: The Epistles of John

Authorship, Destination and Date of the First Epistle

That the First Epistle of John was written by the apostle John is indicated first by Christian tradition and second by the remarkable similarity of the Epistle, both in form and in content, to the Fourth Gospel. The Epistle was probably addressed generally to the Christians of Asia Minor, or of the province of Asia, and was no doubt written during the latter part of the apostle's life.

As in the Gospel, so also in the Epistle the author presents himself clearly as an eyewitness of the life of Jesus, I John 1.1–3; 4.14; as in the Gospel he lays stress upon simple testimony. Even those things which have been noticed as characteristic of his style are connected ultimately with the teaching of Jesus. In both Gospel and Epistle, the beloved disciple has reproduced what he heard in Galilee and in Judea, though in both he has made the memory a living, spiritual fact.

Occasion

Although the Epistle is so indefinite in its destination, it was produced under special circumstances and with a special purpose. In First John, as in many others of the New Testament books, truth appears in conflict with error. The occasion of writing was the prevalence of certain false opinions and a certain false manner of life. The author desires to maintain his spiritual children in their allegiance to the truth. Polemic does not indeed here dominate the whole Epistle, as in the case of the Epistle of Paul to the Galatians. The author uses error merely as a starting point for a free exposition of Christian truth. Nevertheless, the polemic element is very important; it cannot be neglected if the Epistle is to be understood.

The Incarnation

In some way or other the opponents had denied the reality of the incarnation—that is, they had denied the truth that 'the Word became flesh'. They had denied that the Son of God really assumed a complete human nature and led a complete human life. Such denials were regarded by John as destroying the very essence of the gospel. Against them the apostle emphasizes his own testimony. What he himself had seen and heard in Galilee and in Judea was sufficient to show that in the person of Jesus Christ, God actually 'walked among men'.

A Life of Love

The error about the person of Christ which John combats in the Epistle was apparently connected with certain other errors both of thought and of conduct. The speculations of the adversaries might naturally lead to the intellectual pride which is rebuked in I John 2.4, and to the claim of sinlessness which is perhaps presupposed in ch. 1.8. At any rate, whether these errors were derived from the central error of the antichrists, ch. 2.18–26; 4.1–6, or not, the writer of the Epistle lays supreme emphasis upon the connection between faith and practice. There must be no mistake about it, says John. 'He that saith, I know him, and keepeth not his commandments, is a liar, and the truth is not in him.'

The keeping of the commandments of God, however, is not represented in the Epistle simply as obedience to a mass of disconnected rules. Like Jesus and like Paul, John sums up the law in the one great commandment of love. Christian love, according to the First Epistle of John, is not a mere sentiment; it is not the indiscriminate good-humour which is sometimes being mistaken for it today. It is compatible with the profoundest hatred of error, and the most zealous contending for the truth. There is nothing weak or sickly or effeminate about it. On the contrary, it requires an heroic mastery of selfishness and pride and passion.

Christian love, according to John, cannot be acquired by human effort. 'Herein is love, not that we loved God, but that he loved us, and sent his Son to be the propitiation for our sins.' Only the children of God are capable of love—only those who have been begotten again, who have been started in a new life by a mysterious act of God's gracious power. Without Christ we were leading the life of the world; Christ alone has enabled us to love. 'For whatsoever is begotten of God overcometh the world: and this is the victory that hath overcome the world, even our faith.' (I John 5.4.)

The Second and Third Epistles

'THE ELDER'

The writer of the Second and Third Epistles of John is designated, without any name, as 'the elder'. The term 'elder' could be used in two senses. It could refer either simply to age, or to an office in the Church. In II John 1; III John 1, it is not clear which meaning is intended. Perhaps both meanings are in view. Perhaps the writer was on the one hand a man of venerable years, and on the other hand possessed of authority at least analogous to that of the 'elders' or 'presbyters' of the individual churches.

The designation is especially appropriate if it is to be applied to the apostle John. During a long period of his life John was the head of the whole group of churches in the province of Asia. He was revered as a man of an older generation, and as one of the immediate disciples of Jesus. He alone among the apostles was spared to guide the Church. Such a man could well be designated simply as 'the elder'. In his case there was no fear of misunderstanding. There were many 'elders' in the individual churches, but this was 'the elder,' the man who bore the title in a unique sense. It was not unnatural that John should designate himself in the Epistles as 'elder' rather than 'apostle'. Peter also calls himself the 'fellow-elder' of the Church officers among his readers, I Peter 5.1. In the case of John, the title is especially suited to the fatherly tone which is adopted in the Epistles.

There is, therefore, in the term 'elder' nothing inconsistent with the tradition which makes the apostle John the author of the Second and Third Epistles. This tradition is plainly supported by the character of the Epistles. Despite their brevity the Johannine style appears in them in quite unmistakable fashion. The peculiarities are fully explained by the striking peculiarities in purpose and occasion. The Gospel and the First Epistle are great general works intended evidently for the whole Church or for a large part of the Church; while the Third Epistle is primarily a private letter, and the Second, if not addressed to individuals, is addressed at any rate to a single church.

THE THIRD EPISTLE

Since the Third Epistle is clearer in certain respects than the Second, it may conveniently be treated first. It is addressed to an individual Christian named Gaius. The occasion of the letter is perfectly plain. Gaius had shown himself hospitable to strangers; and the letter is written to encourage him in this grace, and to bespeak a welcome for certain brethren who are evidently bearers of the letter. These same men had been entertained by Gaius before, they had borne testimony to his hospitality in the presence of the church where John was residing, and now the apostle commends them to him again. Apparently Demetrius, v. 12, was one of the company of travellers.

These travellers were missionaries, who had left their homes for the sake of Christ, vs. 7, 8. Since they could naturally receive nothing from outsiders, their brethren should give them loyal support, and thus become fellow workers for the gospel which the missionaries proclaimed. The encouragement to Gaius was the more necessary because his hospitality was by no means imitated by all. Indeed, the church of which Gaius was a member could not successfully be appealed to, because it was under the influence of a certain Diotrephes, who not only refused to receive the missionaries but even ventured to expel those who did so. The apostle does not despair of his authority over the church. He hopes to bring Diotrephes to account. But meanwhile the letter is written that the travelling brethren may not be in want, vs. 9, 10.

THE SECOND EPISTLE

The Second Epistle of John is addressed to 'the elect lady and her children'. The first impulse of the reader is to take these words literally. According to the literal interpretation, the letter would be addressed simply to a Christian family. A number of indications, however, favour the figurative interpretation by which 'the elect lady and her children' designates a church. The writer could hardly write to an individual Christian lady as he does in v. 4, 'I rejoice greatly that I have found certain of thy children walking in truth'. 'Certain of thy children' would be a very unnatural form of expression if all the 'children' referred to formed a group no more numerous than a single family. The way in which 'the children of thine elect sister' are mentioned in v. 13 points in the same direction. Probably both 'the elect lady' and the 'elect sister' are figurative designations of churches. Such a figure of speech is not unprecedented—we found a similar usage in I Peter 5.13.

At any rate, whether the readers formed only a single family or a church, the chief purpose of the letter was to warn them against the same error as that which is combated in First John. The truth was in danger. Men were denying the coming of Jesus Christ in the flesh. If advocates of such teaching should seek hospitality, they should be ruthlessly rejected. Just as hospitality to men like Demetrius and his companions is a furtherance of the truth, so hospitality to these men is a furtherance of deadly error. Above all things the readers must be loyal to the truth; and loyalty to the truth leads to a life of love.

Value of the Shorter Epistles

These last two Epistles of John do not deserve the neglect which they have sometimes suffered. Despite their brevity—they are the shortest books of the New Testament—they are instructive in a number of ways.

HISTORICAL

It is exceedingly interesting, for example, to compare them with the private letters of the same period which have been discovered in Egypt since the last decade of the nineteenth century. In form, the opening of the Third Epistle is very much in the manner of the papyrus letters. Compare, for example, with III John 1–4 the following opening of a letter of the second century after Christ: 'Apion to Epimachus his father and lord, heartiest greetings. First of all I pray that you are in health and continually prosper and fare well with my sister and her daughter and my brother. I thank the lord Serapis. . . .' (The translation is that of Professor Milligan.) The differences, however, are even more instructive than the resemblances. What was said in chapter 1 about the epistles of Paul applies in full measure to the epistles of John. Even the epistolary forms are here modified so as to be the vehicle of a new message and a new spirit.

Furthermore, the two Epistles, especially Third John, cast a flood of light upon the internal development of the Church. In one respect indeed the historical significance of the Third Epistle has sometimes been exaggerated. It is not true that we have here the emergence of the monarchical episcopate—that is, the pre-eminence of one presbyter, called a 'bishop', over his brother presbyters. Diotrephes does not appear clearly as a bishop. At about A.D. 110 in the Epistles of Ignatius the episcopate is very prominent; but Third John belongs to an earlier period.

Nevertheless, this concrete picture of the internal affairs of a late first-century church is absolutely unique. The period is very obscure; these few brief lines illumine it more than pages of narrative. The travelling preachers of Third John are particularly interesting. Similar missionaries appear also in the 'Didache', a sort of church manual which may probably be dated in the early part of the second century. In that later period, however, care had to be taken lest the hospitality of the churches should be abused 'But let every apostle,' says the writer—the word 'apostle' is used in a very broad sense to designate wandering preachers—'who comes to you be received as the Lord. He shall remain, however, no more than one day, or if necessary two. If he remains three days he is a false prophet.' Such precautions, we may be sure, were not needed in the case of Demetrius and his companions.

PRACTICAL

Despite its individual address and private character, the Third Epistle of John is not an ordinary private letter. Like all the books of the New Testament, it has a message for the entire Church. The devout reader rises from the perusal of it with a more steadfast devotion to the truth and a warmer glow of Christian love.

TOPICS FOR STUDY

1. Construct outlines of the Epistles of John.
2. Compare the Gospel of John with the First Epistle.
3. Point out similarities and differences between the Second and Third Epistles on the one hand and the First Epistle on the other.
4. Compare the Second with the Third Epistle.
5. Describe in detail the error combated in the First and Second Epistles, and show how it was harmful to Christian faith.
6. What is the teaching of the Epistles about sin and forgiveness?

37: THE MESSAGES OF THE LIVING CHRIST

Study material: Revelation chs. 1 to 3

Authorship

Unlike the Gospel and Epistles of John, the book of Revelation itself mentions the name of its author, Rev. 1.1, 4, 9; 22.8. The name, John, however, was so common in the early Church that of itself it is insufficient to establish the identity of the man who bore it; and no special title of the author appears anywhere in the book, although ch. 22.9 classes the author with the prophets. The very use of the bare name without further designation, however, shows that the John who wrote the book was well-known among the readers. The readers especially in view were the Christians of the province of Asia, of which Ephesus was the capital. Probably, therefore, the author was none other than the famous John of Ephesus, namely, John the apostle, the son of Zebedee.

This conclusion is confirmed by direct testimony on the part of ancient writers. The testimony of Justin Martyr, of the middle of the second century, is particularly clear. He attributes the Apocalypse definitely to the apostle John. The very tradition, moreover, which establishes the Ephesian residence of the apostle John also makes that same John the author of our book.

Banishment to Patmos

At the time of the revelation upon which the book was based, and probably also at the time when the book itself was written, John was on the island of Patmos, off the coast of Asia Minor, not far from Ephesus, Rev. 1.9. He was on the island 'for the word of God and the testimony of Jesus'. Probably these words mean that John was banished by the authorities of the province because of his Christian activity. This interpretation is supported by Christian tradition; early writers mention the banishment of John to Patmos.

Date

This tradition fixes the date of the Apocalypse in the latter part of the reign of the emperor Domitian, and declares that upon the accession of Nerva John returned to Ephesus. Domitian was succeeded by Nerva in A.D. 96. According to tradition, therefore, the Apocalypse was written a short time before that date. Many scholars have dated the book about twenty-five years earlier, shortly after the death of Nero in A.D. 68, but on the whole the traditional dating is the more probable.

Readers

After a brief introduction, Rev. 1.1–3, the author inserts what looks considerably like one of the addresses of a Pauline epistle, vs. 4, 5. In it the book is directed to 'the seven churches that are in Asia'. According to v. 11, this destination was determined by command of Christ. In the same verse the identity of the seven churches is fixed.

Formally, therefore, the book is addressed to seven definite churches in the province of Asia; it might almost be called an epistle. A closer examination, however, shows that a wider circle of readers is in view. More explicitly than most of the other New Testament books, the Apocalypse is intended for the Church universal. The universal destination of the book is perhaps indicated even by the choice of the narrower address. One reason why seven churches and only seven were singled out for special messages is probably that seven is a symbolic number. The seven churches of Asia represent the totality of the Church of Christ.

The Author a Prophet

The book of Revelation is designated in ch. 1.3 as a prophecy; the author regarded himself clearly as a prophet. There were many prophets in the early Church; several of them, such as Agabus, will occur to every reader of The Acts. In I Cor. 12.28 the gift of prophecy appears in the second place—immediately after the apostleship—in a list of spiritual endowments. That an apostle should also be a prophet is not surprising; the gifts of the Spirit were by no means mutually exclusive.

The Meaning of 'Apocalypse'

With perfect propriety, therefore, the last book of the Bible might

271

have been called 'the Prophecy of John'. As a matter of fact, however, another term, 'Revelation', has been used. That term has been derived directly from the very first word of the book itself. In its Greek form the word is 'Apocalypse'; 'Revelation' is an exactly corresponding word of Latin derivation. Both 'Apocalypse' and 'Revelation' designate first of all the divine act by which mysteries, formerly hidden, have been disclosed, and secondly, by a natural transition, the book in which these disclosures are handed on to later generations.

It will be observed that an apocalypse is simply one particular kind of prophecy. Every apocalypse is a prophecy, but not every prophecy is an apocalypse. A prophet is one who speaks as the mouthpiece of God for the instruction or encouragement or warning of the Church. The substance of his speaking may be of various kinds; it may consist of prediction or of exhortation. A recipient of 'revelations', however, in that narrower sense of the word with which we are now concerned, is one who has actually seen visions of heavenly things.

Nevertheless, although the Apocalypse is a record of visions, and was written consciously under the impulsion of the Spirit, it is by no means uninfluenced by previous works. To a degree that is perhaps not paralleled by any other New Testament book, the Apocalypse is suffused with the language and with the imagery of the Old Testament. Though there is not a single formal quotation, the Old Testament Scriptures have influenced almost every sentence of the book. Particularly the books of Ezekiel and Daniel, which, like the Apocalypse, are composed largely of the records of visions, have supplied much of the imagery of the New Testament work.

This wide-spread influence of the Old Testament upon the Apocalypse is by no means surprising. The Apocalypse is based upon direct revelation, but direct revelation is not necessarily out of relation to everything else. On the contrary, it uses the language which its recipients can understand; and part of the language of the apostle John was the phraseology and imagery of the Old Testament.

The Interpretations of the Apocalypse

The interpretations of the Apocalypse may be divided into four classes.

UNFULFILLED PROPHECIES

According to one method of interpretation, the prophecies of the book are all unfulfilled. In the last days there will be a mighty revival of evil like that which is symbolized by the dragon and the beast and the false prophet, there will be plagues and woes like those which are described in connection with the seals and the trumpets and the bowls, and there will be a triumph of God's people and an eternal blessedness of the new Jerusalem. This interpretation would place the Apocalypse out of analogy with the other prophecies of the Bible. Prophecy is seldom out of all connection with the immediate present. Even where the prophetic vision reaches to the very end of time, the fulfilment or the preparation for the fulfilment is to begin at once. In the Apocalypse, as in other prophecy, there is evident reference to the circumstances of the original readers.

CONTEMPORARY EVENTS

A second method of interpretation goes to an opposite extreme. By this method the prophecies of the book are thought to be concerned merely with events of the writer's own age. 'The beast' is the Roman Empire; 'Babylon' is the city of Rome; the author expected the destruction of both to take place within a few years' time. In its thoroughgoing form this interpretation also is to be rejected. It degrades the Apocalypse to the level of a mistaken prediction, and reduces the self-evidencing glories of the book to trivialities. Evidently the outlook of the seer was far broader and far more spiritual than it is represented by the advocates of this interpretation.

THE WHOLE HISTORY OF THE CHURCH

By a third method of interpretation, the first two methods are combined. The book is written distinctly in view of conditions of the first century, its predictions concern partly the immediate future; but there is also an outlook upon remoter ages. By this interpretation the prophecies are held to provide an epitome of the whole of history from the first coming of Christ to his second coming.

MIXTURE OF DISCORDANT TRADITIONS

A fourth method of interpretation, which has become influential in very recent years, abandons all hope of discovering a unitary message in the book, and proceeds to divide it into its component parts. The analysis was carried on first by literary criticism. An older work of the time of Nero was supposed to have been revised at a later period; or non-Christian Jewish works were supposed to have been incorporated in the present work by a Christian compiler. This sort of literary criticism has in the last few years given place sometimes to a subtler method. Investigation is now directed to the materials of which the book is composed, whether those materials were embodied in previous literary works or only in previous traditions. The ultimate source of much of the material is found in Babylonia or other eastern countries; this material is thought to be not always in accord with the context into which in our Apocalypse it has been introduced.

This method must emphatically be rejected. It contains, indeed, an element of truth. Undoubtedly the Apocalypse makes use of already-existing materials. But these materials are, for the most part at least, of genuinely Hebrew origin; and they have been thoroughly assimilated for the purposes of the present prophecy. The Apocalypse is not a compilation full of contradictions, but a unitary work, with one great message for the Church.

WRONG USE OF THE THIRD METHOD

Of these four methods of interpretation the third has been here adopted. The prophecies of the Apocalypse concern the entire history of the Church. Undoubtedly this interpretation is subject to abuse. It has been employed in the interests of special controversy, as when the Protestants saw in the scarlet woman a representation of papal Rome.

PRINCIPLES, NOT INDIVIDUAL FACTS

All such abuses may be avoided, however, if the interpreter will remember that the book deals with great principles, rather than with individual facts. The beast is neither the Roman Catholic Church, nor the religion of Mohammed, nor the Turkish Empire. Undoubtedly it expressed itself in some phases of each of those institutions. But no one of them can be identified with it outright. The beast of the Apocalypse is nothing less than the blatant, godless power of worldly empire, however that power may be manifested. At the time of John it was manifested especially in the empire of Rome. Even Rome, however, cannot be identified with

the beast entirely without qualification. Even Rome had its beneficent side. John as well as Paul, even in the fire of persecution,
might have expressed the thought of Rom. 13.1–7. Peter also wrote
in the midst of persecution; yet Peter could say, 'Be subject to
every ordinance of man for the Lord's sake: whether to the king,
as supreme; or unto governors, as sent by him for vengeance on
evil-doers and for praise to them that do well.' I Peter 2.13, 14.

The other side of Rome's power, it is true, was prominent at the
close of the century. More systematically than before, Rome had
begun to persecute the Church of God. By the demand of emperor-
worship she had tried to put her stamp upon the followers of Jesus.
Through her priesthood she had endeavoured to lead men astray.
In these things she was a manifestation of the beast. As such she
was execrated and resisted to the death by every loyal Christian.
There could be no hope of compromise. Hope lay rather in the
power of God. God would give the just reward; God would give
the final victory. Such was the message of the Apocalypse.

The message is of perennial value. The beast is not yet dead.
His methods are different, but still he oppresses the Church.
Wherever his power is felt—whether in ruthless oppression or
impious warfare or degrading superstition—there the prophecy of
John is a comfort and an inspiration to the people of God.

Undoubtedly this method of interpretation, which detects in the
book principles rather than individual facts, involves a reduction
in the amount of direct information which the Apocalypse may be
thought to give. A detailed account, whether of the progress of the
Church, or of the final catastrophe, is by this interpretation no
longer found in the book.

The Opening Vision

The first vision which was seen by the writer of the Apocalypse
was a vision of Christ, Rev. 1.12–20. The details of that vision, as
they are reproduced in the book, are of symbolic significance. They
were intended not to produce an artistic picture, but to teach
spiritual truth; by them all, the majesty of the risen Christ is
revealed. This first vision is the key to all the rest. The Apocalypse
is concerned throughout with the glory of the risen Christ.

The Messages to the Seven Churches

The first vision is followed by a most surprising passage, the
messages or 'letters' to the seven churches, Rev. chs. 2, 3. After

having been introduced to the presence of the risen Christ in all his heavenly glory, the reader is suddenly brought down again to earth; after being prepared for heavenly mysteries, he finds himself in the midst of ecclesiastical pettiness. It is a startling transition.

CHRIST AND HIS SERVANTS

The very abruptness of the transition, however, is essential to an understanding of the book. By the messages to the seven churches, we learn that Christ is never remote from his servants. The terrible Christ of the first vision is acquainted with every detail of congregational life, and with every nook and corner of the individual soul. There is the central lesson of the seven messages. They are messages, not of John, but of Christ. The same Christ whose dreadful majesty has just been revealed takes stern account of the lovelessness of Ephesus, of the guilty tolerance of Pergamum and Thyatira, of the spiritual deadness of Sardis, of the insipid lukewarmness of Laodicea—and takes account also of the faithful witnessing of Smyrna and Philadelphia. Christ is no less watchful now than then. From him we can never hope to hide. To the seven messages of the Apocalypse must be added, as we read, a solemn message to ourselves.

THE SEVEN CITIES

The churches that are addressed in the seven messages were all situated in the Roman province of Asia. A glance at a good map will show that the order of the messages represents the route that would naturally be taken by a messenger making a circuit of the eastern central portion of the province; and geographers have pointed out that the seven cities are so situated as to be centres from which the book could be circulated through a very wide expanse of country. Perhaps a number of the seven churches were founded by Paul himself; probably all of the others, like Laodicea, were founded during his lifetime and under his influence. Since the death of Paul, however, important changes had occurred in Asia, and another leader, formerly one of the pillars of the original Jerusalem church, had taken the place of the great apostle to the Gentiles.

PERSECUTION

Though the messages are very brief, each is sufficient to produce a wonderfully vivid impression of the church that is addressed.

None of the churches is like any one of the others. On the other hand, however, certain features appear in all or nearly all of the seven. Evidently, for example, at the time when the book was written, the Christians of Asia Minor were enduring a wide-spread persecution. Persecution came partly at the instigation of the Jews, but the pagan authorities were also hostile. Steadfastness, at such a time, was required of every Christian. Martyrdoms had actually occurred—one of the martyrs is mentioned by name—and others might be expected in the near future. The true Christian must display no trace of cowardice; he must bravely witness to his Lord.

WORLDLINESS

Yielding to persecution, however, was by no means the only danger that threatened the Church; worldliness was also an insistent peril. The churches of Asia were situated for the most part in magnificent cities, full of the splendour of the ancient world. Wealth and power were everywhere exalted above moral purity. Religion, in particular, was largely concerned with magnificent display. In pagan Asia Minor during the first century, piety and goodness were often entirely separate; religion was often merely one expression of overweening pride.

The Church was being affected by her environment. The first enthusiasm was long past. Christians were becoming satisfied with life in this world; they were in danger of losing their citizenship in heaven. Persecutions served to hasten the process. Must the disciple of Christ really refuse to worship the emperor? Might he not accommodate himself to the conditions of the world as it was? What harm would he suffer by outward conformity to the customs of the age?

Laxity in morals, moreover, seems to have been excused by false theorizing. As previously among the readers of Second Peter and Jude, so in Asia Minor at the close of the first century, sin was being buttressed by error. A sect called the Nicolaitans, boasting of a knowledge that transcended the simplicity of holy living, and of a freedom that permitted compromise with impurity and heathenism, was tolerated in a number of the churches.

At the first mention of the Nicolaitans, in the letter to Ephesus, Rev. 2.6, nothing whatever is said about their tenets. Their error, however, was not merely theoretical, but practical, for it was their 'works' that the Lord is represented as hating. In the letter to Pergamum, the Nicolaitans are probably meant in v. 14. Like

Balaam, they enticed the people of God to idolatry and impurity. The form which their idolatry took was the eating of meats offered to idols. The question of meats offered to idols was no simple matter. In the First Epistle to the Corinthians Paul had permitted the eating of such meats under certain circumstances, but had sternly forbidden it wherever it involved real or supposed participation in idolatrous worship. The form in which it was favoured by the Nicolaitans evidently fell under the latter category. In a time of persecution, the temptation to guilty compromise with heathenism must have been insidious; and also the low morality of the Asian cities threatened ever and again to drag Christian people back into the impure life of the world.

In the letter to Thyatira, also, 'the woman Jezebel' is apparently to be connected with the same sect, for the practical faults in Thyatira and in Pergamum were identical. Jezebel, the Phœnician wife of Ahab, was, like Balaam, a striking Old Testament example of one who led Israel into sin. It is significant that the woman Jezebel in Thyatira called herself a prophetess, Rev. 2.20. This circumstance seems to indicate that the Nicolaitans had excused their moral laxity by an appeal to special revelations. The impression is confirmed by v. 24. Apparently the Nicolaitans had boasted of their knowledge of the 'deep things', and had despised the simple Christians who contented themselves with a holy life. At any rate, whatever particular justification the Nicolaitans advanced for their immoral life, they could not deceive the all-searching eye of Christ. Their 'deep things' were deep things, not of God, but of Satan!

Who is meant by 'the woman Jezebel'? Some interpreters, who suppose that the 'angel' of the church was the bishop, regard Jezebel as a designation of the bishop's wife. This whole interpretation is, however, beset with serious difficulty. Perhaps 'the woman Jezebel' does not refer to an individual at all, but is simply a figurative designation of the Nicolaitan sect. The description of the coming retribution in vs. 21–23 seems to be highly figurative.

It will be observed that the sin of the churches at Pergamum and Thyatira was not limited to those who actually accepted the Nicolaitan teaching. Even to endure the presence of the guilty sect was the object of the Lord's rebuke. Toward the works of the Nicolaitans only hatred was in place, Rev. 2.6. That is a solemn lesson for modern indifferentism. Tolerance is good; but there are times when it is a deadly sin.

The Purpose of the Apocalypse

At such a time, the Apocalypse was written. In it the eye of Christ is turned upon degenerate congregations; in it the piercing sword of his word cuts down the sophistries of sin. If, however, Christ appears in the Apocalypse as a terrible avenger, he also appears— and yet more clearly—as a strong captain and deliverer. In this book the veil of sense is lifted. Christ is revealed to all who will read. To the faithless and the cowardly and the impure, he is revealed as an avenger. To all true disciples, dismayed by fiery trials, exhausted by weary waiting, he is revealed as a living Saviour. In the midst of persecution and mocking, ever subject to the shadow of death, they are given a vision of an almighty Captain. For them there is no room for discouragement. For them Christ is ever at the door.

TOPICS FOR STUDY

1. Give some account of each of the seven cities mentioned in Rev. chs. 1 to 3.

2. Construct a complete outline of Rev. chs. 1 to 3.

3. Characterize each of the seven churches in your own words. Classify the letters according as they contain praise or blame (several topics).

4. Describe the Nicolaitans.

5. What is meant by the 'angels' of the several churches?

6. What is meant by Satan's throne, Rev. 2.13?

7. What is the teaching of Rev. chs. 1 to 3 about the saving work of Christ?

38: A VISION OF THE FINAL TRIUMPH

Study material: Revelation chs. 4 to 22

The second and third chapters of the Apocalypse deal with plain, concrete conditions in the churches of Asia Minor. The rest of the book, from the fourth chapter on, is concerned with a series of mysterious visions. Yet the two parts stand in intimate relation. The visions were given in view of the circumstances described in the seven letters. In that time of persecution and of worldliness, the Church was warned and strengthened by a revelation of the true meaning of history. A new vision was granted, like that which came to the servant of the Old Testament prophet at Dothan. In this wonderful book the persecuted churches of Asia, hemmed in by the might of the Roman Empire, had their eyes opened to behold the fiery horses and chariots of God's protecting care.

Symbolism

The revelations of the book are couched in symbolic terms. Not the heavenly realities themselves—for they are invisible and unspeakable—but symbols of the realities are revealed. This symbolism appears plainly in the very first vision of the book. It is not to be supposed that the risen Christ has hair as white as wool, or feet like burnished brass, or a voice like the voice of many waters, Rev. 1.14, 15. Clearly these details are merely expressive of the many-sided majesty of Christ; to take them literally would be almost absurd.

Yet despite this clear indication at the very beginning, many Christians have fallen into the mistake of an over-literal interpretation of this book. Such literalism is not really true to the meaning of the divine author, and it has been productive of much harm to the Church. The analogy of Old Testament prophecy is here in point. There were prophecies in the Old Testament about a coming king of David's line. To some extent these prophecies were even literally fulfilled. Jesus was actually born of the seed of David. But when literal interpretation became bald and unspiritual it was false. It led to the attempt of the multitude to take Jesus by force and make him a king; it led to the quarrelling of the disciples about great places in the coming kingdom. Faithfulness to the prophecies was not always in proportion to the literalness with which they were understood. Men needed to learn that Jesus' kingdom is not of this world.

So it is with the Apocalypse. By a mistaken pressing of the letter of this book, the true spiritual teaching of it has sometimes been lost. More, perhaps, than any other book of the New Testament the Apocalypse requires in the interpreter a sane spiritual-mindedness. The book yields its true comfort only to those who have ears to hear.

The Scene in Heaven

After the messages to the seven churches, the seer is introduced to a heavenly scene, Rev. chs. 4, 5. God the Father and Christ and the Holy Spirit and adoring nature and the Church are here represented by strange and majestic symbols. The seven Spirits of God are probably the Holy Spirit in his manifold manifestations; the four living creatures represent nature with its ceaseless activity and its ceaseless praise; the four and twenty elders represent the Church. In this vision Christ is represented by a symbolism very different from that which is used in ch. 1.12–16. There he appeared as a mighty warrior or ruler; here he appears as a Lamb. No one symbol is sufficient to express the many aspects of Christ's person. Certainly the symbol of the Lamb is fundamental in the whole book. The majestic Son of God, to whom all power was given in heaven and on earth, was the same as he who had died for the sins of the world. The death of Christ in behalf of his Church is the very basis of this book as of the whole New Testament. In plain, unsymbolic language it appears at the beginning, in the glorious doxology of ch. 1.5–7.

The book which Christ alone can open, ch. 5, is the book of destiny. Christ alone can unlock the secrets of history. The Lamb who was slain is the beginning and end of the Church's life.

The Seals and Trumpets and Bowls

The opening of the seven seals, Rev. 6.1 to 8.1, is paralleled by the blowing of the seven trumpets, chs. 8.2 to 11.19, and the pouring out of the seven bowls, chs. 15, 16. It must not be supposed that the events symbolized by these three series are intended to be subsequent one to another. Rather is each series a symbol for the whole course of Christian history. Each series apparently begins at the beginning and continues to the end. There is indeed progress, but it is a progress not of time, but of the plainness of the revelation. The great facts of divine wrath and mercy are revealed in ever bolder symbols.

These three series are all of them expressive of wrath and tribulation. But the first two of them, at least, contain episodes which indicate the protection of the Church amid the surrounding woe. Those who belong to Christ need have no fear.

Conflict of Evil and Good

In the section which begins with the twelfth chapter, the conflict of the powers of evil against the powers of good, which is implied in the whole book, becomes more explicit. At the head of the evil forces stands the great dragon, who represents Satan. His emissaries upon earth are the two beasts, the beast from the sea, and the beast from the land. The latter is apparently identical with 'the false prophet'. (Rev. 16.13; 19.20; 20.10.) The seat of Satan's earthly power is 'Babylon', which is symbolized as a woman. These symbols have been interpreted in many different ways. Furthest from the mark, perhaps, were those interpretations which detected references to definite events or definite institutions in later Church history. Thus the first beast was regarded by many Protestants as representing the Church of Rome. Such interpretations are now for the most part abandoned.

The Beast

By most modern expositors the first beast is thought to symbolize the Roman Empire, and the scarlet woman, or Babylon, the city of Rome itself. This interpretation certainly contains at least a measure of truth. The reference to the seven hills of Rome in Rev. 17.9 is unmistakable; and the commerce of the Roman Empire is vividly described in ch. 18.11–19. Rome has clearly supplied at least the imagery for a large part of the book.

It does not follow, however, that the reference to Rome exhausts the meaning of the imagery. Indeed there are indications to the contrary. The beast is the Roman Empire, but not the Roman Empire in its entirety and not the Roman Empire alone. The symbols of the book are representative not directly of individual events or definite institutions, but of great principles. So the beast represents primarily the pride of worldly power; and Babylon the pride of worldly wealth. The Roman Empire, with its capital, was a signal embodiment of these principles. At the time when the Apocalypse was written, Rome was engaging in an impious persecution of the Church and was enticing the followers of Christ by the allurements of a godless civilization. It is no wonder that the prophet in his vision saw the forces of evil arrayed in the trappings of Rome.

The Blessedness of the Church

As the darker side of the prophecy has not a special but a progressive fulfilment, so it is also with the prophecy of the blessedness of the Church. Not the manner of the Church's victory, and not the time of it, is in view, but the great fact itself. Of what is the new Jerusalem a symbol, as it is described in Rev. 21.9 to 22.5? The casual reader will probably answer that it is a symbol of the future blessedness of the people of God. But the matter is not quite so certain as at first appears. Is not the new Jerusalem, after all, but a picture of the Church of all ages—considered, however, not as the world considers it, but as God considers it, not as it actually is on earth, with all its sufferings and divisions and sins, but as it is in principle and in the plan of God? Might we not possess the blessedness of this scene here and now if we would but yield ourselves fully to the influence of the Holy Spirit?

Each of the two interpretations has something to be said in its favour. The question between them cannot be determined with perfect certainty. Fortunately the question is not so important as it might seem. Whether the new Jerusalem represents the final condition of the blessed, or is an ideal picture of the present Church, in either case the general teaching of the book is plain. If the future blessedness is intended, then clearly that blessedness is to be anticipated here and now; if the present age is meant, then clearly that age is described only as it is a foretaste of heaven. The message of the Apocalypse is a message of hope. As the world sees it, the Church is in misery; but God will give the victory, and already, in principle, the victory is won.

The Apocalypse, according to any right interpretation, is a vision of final triumph. That triumph is a triumph of Christ. Behind all the lurid imagery of the book, behind the battles and the woes, and behind the glories of God's people, stands the figure of the Saviour. With him the book began, and with him, too, it ends. He is the same who lived the life of mercy and of glory on earth, the same who died for our sins on the cross. To the Lamb all power is given—all power in heaven and on earth. By him all enemies are conquered; by him the whole earth will be judged. To those who bear the mark of the beast he is an Avenger; to his Church he is an ever-living Saviour.

TOPICS FOR STUDY

1. Construct an outline of Rev. chs. 5 to 22 (several topics).
2. Compare the accounts of the seals and trumpets and bowls.
3. What is meant by the second beast, or the false prophet? (Rev. 13.11; 16.13; 19.20; 20.10.)
4. What is meant by the new Jerusalem? Where else in the New Testament is there a similar conception?
5. What is meant by 'a time, and times, and half a time' (Rev. 12.14)? What is the origin of this expression? Where else in the Apocalypse is a corresponding period of time mentioned?
6. What is meant by the 'thousand years' of Rev. ch. 20? Mention some of the other symbolic numbers in the Apocalypse and point out the meaning of the symbolism.
7. What is the teaching of the study material about the person and work of Christ? In what particulars is this teaching similar to that in the Gospel of John?

39 : REVIEW

So far in this book we have provided something like an outline of apostolic history. In what follows the method will be different; the arrangement will be no longer chronological, but topical. First, however, the previous outline must be reviewed. Before passing on to topical study, the reader should make sure that he can at least tell the bare story of the apostolic Church.

In order to assist in the labour of review, a brief summary of the first part of the book chapters 1–26 will here be provided. This summary should be supplemented by an exercise of memory, and by reference not only to the earlier chapters, but also to The Acts.

The Preparation for the Gospel

Though the apostolic Church was not a product of the world, it did not stand altogether out of relation to previous history. For it, on the contrary, there was in the providence of God a manifold preparation. The Roman Empire provided universal peace and facilities for intercourse (chapter 2); Hellenism provided a common language (chapter 3); Judaism, through the precious deposit of Old Testament revelation, was a forerunner of the gospel itself. The Judaism of Palestine nurtured the lives of Jesus and his first apostles (chapter 4); the Judaism of the Dispersion, through its synagogues, provided everywhere a picked audience and an important educational preparation (chapter 5). In Messianic prophecy, the gospel was proclaimed afore (chapter 6). The world was ready for the truth. God's time at last had come.

The Founding of the Church

Apostolic history begins with the resurrection of Jesus and closes with the death of the last apostle. The earlier and more important part of this history is narrated by a companion of the apostle Paul in The Acts (chapter 7). The beginning was the resurrection of Christ. That event was the foundation of the Christian Church, and that event, together with the death on the cross, formed from the first the substance of the gospel proclamation (chapter 8).

The Church in Palestine

The apostolic Church, founded by means of the resurrection, was endued with power by the coming of the Holy Spirit at Pentecost, and at once began a glorious mission. Preaching at Jerusalem was attended with remarkable success; opposition from the Sadducee rulers was checked by popular favour; Pharisaic persecution, which arose when the true radicalness of the new sect became more fully known (chapter 9) resulted only in the spread of the gospel to Samaria and beyond (chapter 10). At first, only Jews had been won; but gradually, under the impulse of the Spirit, the gospel was extended also to Gentiles. Samaria, the Ethiopian, Cornelius, were the first steps in the process (chapter 11). By the conversion of Paul a leader was provided (chapter 12); and by the work of certain Jews of Cyprus and Cyrene, a Gentile missionary church (chapter 13).

The Work of Paul

The first systematic mission to Gentiles, which embraced Cyprus and the southern part of the province of Galatia (chapter 14), aroused the opposition of certain legalists; but the unity of the Church was preserved by the wise attitude of the original apostles (chapter 15). The Gentile mission could therefore proceed without hindrance. A second missionary journey took Paul through Asia Minor to Troas, then through Macedonia to Greece, and finally back to Syrian Antioch (chapter 16). During a long stay at Corinth, on this journey, Paul wrote two short letters of encouragement and instruction to the recently formed Thessalonian church (chapter 17).

The third missionary journey extended through Asia Minor to Ephesus, where missionary activity was maintained for three years, then to Corinth and to Jerusalem. Probably on this journey, at Ephesus, the Epistle to the Galatians was written to certain churches in Galatia proper in the northern part of the Roman province of that name, in order to check a recrudescence of legalistic error (chapter 18). From Ephesus, also, Paul wrote the letter called First Corinthians to the church at Corinth, in order to regulate a number of problems connected with congregational life (chapter 19); and on his way through Macedonia he wrote Second Corinthians, to bring to a conclusion the trouble caused by opposition to his apostolic authority (chapter 20). Finally, at Corinth, he wrote the Epistle to the Romans, as a summary of the gospel that he had been championing, and as a preparation for his approaching visit to the imperial capital (chapter 21).

The arrest of Paul at Jerusalem did not hinder the plan of God. Though a prisoner, Paul arrived at length at Rome and continued the proclamation of the gospel (chapter 22). At Rome, during his imprisonment, he wrote at least four letters; a letter to the church at Colossæ, correcting speculation and practical error by an appeal to the all-sufficiency of Christ; a private letter to an individual in the Colossian Church, bespeaking mercy for a runaway slave (chapter 23); a circular letter to certain churches of Asia Minor (chapter 24); and a letter of thanks and encouragement and exhortation to the devoted church at Philippi (chapter 25).

After being released from Rome, Paul visited probably Spain and certainly the east. While in the east he wrote the First Epistle to Timothy and the Epistle to Titus, in order to provide instruction about teaching and organization. Imprisoned again at Rome, under the shadow of approaching death, he wrote the Second Epistle to Timothy (chapter 26).

Important Extra–Biblical History

The Roman historian Tacitus tells of a persecution of the Christians at Rome at the time of the burning of the city in A.D. 64. The emperor Nero, suspected of starting the fire, sought to remove suspicion from himself by accusing the Christians. The latter had already become unpopular because of their peculiar ways, and were thought to be guilty of abominable crimes; but the cruelty of Nero almost exceeded the wishes of the populace. The Christians were put to death under horrible tortures. Many were burned, and their burning bodies served as torches to illumine the emperor's gardens.

The beheading of Paul has often been brought into connection with this persecution, but more probably it occurred a few years later. Paul had been released from his first imprisonment, and his second imprisonment, at the time of the Neronian outbreak, had not yet begun.

The extent of the Neronian persecution cannot be determined

K

with certainty. Probably, however, although there was no systematic persecution throughout the empire, the provinces would not be altogether unaffected by what was happening at Rome. The causes of popular and official disfavour were always present; it required only a slight occasion to bring them actively into play.

THE DESTRUCTION OF JERUSALEM

Even more important than the Roman persecution of A.D. 64 was the destruction of Jerusalem in A.D. 70. At the outbreak of the war which culminated in that catastrophe, the Jerusalem Christians took refuge in Pella, east of the Jordan; Jerusalem ceased to be the centre of the Christian Church. After the war, the Jerusalem church never regained its old position of leadership; and specifically Jewish Christianity, suffering by the destruction of the national Jewish life, ceased to be influential in Christian history.

THE PROGRESS OF THE GOSPEL

From the years between the destruction of Jerusalem and the closing years of the century, scarcely any definite incidents can be enumerated. Undoubtedly the missionary activity of the Church was continuing; the gospel was making rapid progress in its conquest of the empire. In this missionary activity probably most of the twelve apostles were engaged; but details of their work are narrated for the most part only in late tradition.

JOHN AT EPHESUS

At some time—whether before or after A.D. 70 is uncertain—the apostle John went to Ephesus, and there became the leader of the Asian church. Detailed information about his position and the churches under his care is provided not only in trustworthy tradition—especially that which comes through Irenæus from Polycarp, the hearer of John—but also in the writings of John himself. The two shorter Epistles of John, though each embraces only a small page, are extraordinarily rich in information about congregational matters, and even more instructive are the seven messages of the Apocalypse. By means of the latter the moral condition of the church in Asia Minor is characterized with a vividness that is scarcely to be paralleled for any other period of the apostolic age.

THE PERSECUTION UNDER DOMITIAN

During the latter part of the residence of John in Asia Minor there was an important event in the history of the Church. This was the outbreak of the persecution under Domitian—a persecution which apparently exceeded in extent, if not in severity, every persecution that had preceded it. Under Domitian the Roman authorities became definitely hostile; apostasy from Christ was apparently demanded systematically of the Christians—apostasy from Christ and adhesion to the imperial cult. The latter, in the Apocalypse, is represented as an example of the mark of 'the beast'; the Roman Empire, as would have been unnatural in the days of Paul, appears in that book as an incorporation of Satanic power. The long conflict between the Church and the empire had at last begun. Which side would be victorious? In the Apocalypse the answer is plain. The Lord himself was fighting for his Church!

The gospel is no aspiration in the hearts of dreamers; it is a real entrance of divine power into the troubled battle-field of human history!

The Apostolic Church and the
Church of Today

40: THE CHURCH AND THE WORLD

Study material: Matt. 16: 13–20; John chs. 15 to 17;
Acts 2: 43–47; 4: 23 to 5: 16; 11: 19–30;
The Epistle to the Ephesians

Distinctiveness of the Apostolic Church

The Church in the apostolic age, which will form the subject of our study in the remainder of this book, stood in the midst of a hostile environment. She did not shrink from the conflict; she never entered into any compromise with a religion of works, or with heathenism; she was never content to make common cause with the non-Christian world; she was never content with a divided allegiance. There were noble men in pagan antiquity—noble according to the world's standard—but the Church did not think of receiving them into her fold. By lowering her exclusive claim, she could easily have escaped persecution. By allowing the law as well as faith in Christ to be regarded as a means of salvation, she could have conciliated the Jews, 'the stumbling-block of the cross' would have been done away, Gal. 5.11; by permitting the worship of the emperor along with the worship of Jehovah, she could have avoided a clash with the Roman authorities; earnest pagans would probably have been glad to honour Jesus along with Seneca. If the early Christians had been imbued with the same spirit as that of some modern easy-going Church members, they would have entered gladly into some such compromise. As a matter of fact, they preferred to be triumphantly intolerant. 'In none other is there salvation: for neither is there any other name under heaven, that is given among men, wherein we must be saved.' (Acts 4.12.)

The All-sufficiency of Christ

Such intolerance is unpopular today. Its unpopularity, however, is due partly to misconception. The intolerance of earnest believers does not involve a harsh and repellent attitude toward the non-Christian world. On the contrary, it is compatible with the broadest sympathies. Just because the Christian is conscious of a great possession which is lacking to the world, he desires to share it with all men. The intolerance of the early Church was an intolerance that resulted in blessing. Christ, to the early Christians, was the only Saviour—no other could be tolerated beside him—but though he was the only Saviour, he was a Saviour sufficient for all.

The all-sufficiency of Christ is today being lost from view. It may be rediscovered by a study of the apostolic Church. That is the purpose of the present chapter. What was there in apostolic Christianity that was peculiar? Wherein did the early Church differ from the surrounding world? What was the justification of its exclusive claim?

Distinctiveness of Jewish Christianity

Before studying thus the distinctiveness of the early Church, we must notice a striking difference between Jewish Christianity and Gentile Christianity. The latter was far more sharply and obviously distinguished from its environment than was the former. The church at Corinth, for example, was evidently something entirely new; entrance into it meant a sharp break in the lives of the converts; even in externals the Corinthian Christians were different from their neighbours. In Jerusalem, on the other hand, Christians and non-Christians would have seemed to a superficial observer very much alike. They were united, for example, in a common worship; the Christians, like the rest of their countrymen, attended the temple service, and observed the Jewish fasts and feasts. This conformity of the Jerusalem Christians to Jewish customs, how- ever, provides no justification for conformity of the Christian Church to non-Christian custom today. Judaism, it must be remembered, was a revealed religion; the Jews were God's chosen people. Conformity to the Mosaic law did not obscure, but rather emphasized, the distinctness of God's Church from the surround- ing world; for under the Old Testament dispensation the Jewish nation was itself the Church. The example of the Jerusalem church, therefore, does not justify secularism. The conformity of the early Christians was at the most conformity to a superseded dispensation of God; it was not conformity to the world.

As a matter of fact, however, the boundary between the Jeru- salem church and the surrounding Judaism was by no means indistinct. The Christians were widely different from the other Jews.

JOY

In the first place, there was a striking difference of spirit. Contemporary Judaism, as represented by the Pharisees, was a religion of gloom. God's people lay groaning under foreign oppression; the kingdom had departed from Israel. There was indeed a hope of vengeance; the ancient prophecies would be fulfilled; Israel would again be free. But deliverance was delayed. 'How long,' was the cry, 'how long, O Lord, how long?' In the little company of Jesus' disciples, a very different spirit prevailed; joy reigned there instead of sorrow. The promised King had at last appeared; by his resurrection he had triumphed over sin and death. Though hidden for a time from the eye of sense, he was present through his Spirit, and would surely come again in like manner as he had gone. The night of mourning was past; the day had already dawned; the servants of Christ had entered upon a joyous conquest. In the desert of Pharisaic Judaism, the band of Jesus' disciples was an oasis of peace and joy.

LOVE

The joyousness of the Jerusalem Christians, however, was not the only characteristic that distinguished them from their non-Christian countrymen. Even more distinctive than joy was love. The disciples had learned from Jesus a fresh interpretation of the law. They had learned to sum it up in the one great commandment of love. This interpretation was not indeed altogether new; it was anticipated in the Old Testament. But it had become sadly obscured, and Jesus made it shine afresh with an unprecedented lustre. In the early Church, there was a tremendous shifting of emphasis. Ceremonies were still observed—and observed with the deepest reverence—but they were subordinated to the commandment of love.

NEW CUSTOMS AND A NEW POWER

Even in externals, moreover, the Christians were different from other Jews. They observed, indeed, the common Jewish customs, but they added to them certain customs of their own. Baptism, practised already by John the Baptist, was in the Church given a new meaning. The common meals were a sign of fellowship. The Lord's Supper was a distinctively Christian passover. Common meetings for instruction and prayer separated the disciples from

their unconverted countrymen. Finally, the Church was in possession of a miraculous power. The healing of the lame man at the
Beautiful Gate of the temple was only an example. Evidently God
was in the midst of the disciples of Jesus.

THE LORDSHIP OF JESUS

Such were some of the most obviously distinctive features of the
early Jerusalem church. Various though they were, however, they
had a common cause. That common cause was simply Jesus Christ
himself. The disciples of Jesus, no matter how much they might
have in common with the devout Jews of their time, could not be
anything but a peculiar people. Bring a man into really vital connection with Jesus Christ, no matter what the circumstances or
what the time, and you have made of him a new creature. The really
distinguishing mark of the early Christians was that among them
Jesus was Lord.

The lordship of Jesus was expressed in various ways. It was
expressed, in the first place, in teaching. The disciples had learned
from Jesus a way of life. The lordship of Jesus was also expressed—
what is far more—in salvation. Jesus had died, and by his death he
had brought forgiveness of sin. Forgiveness was not something
that could be earned, through man's own effort, by minute
observance of a host of commandments. It was a free gift. In other
words, it was to be attained by faith. Faith, not works, was the
fundamental principle of the disciples' life. A momentous difference from Pharisaism!

Salvation, moreover, was more than forgiveness. By his death
Jesus brought forgiveness; by his resurrection he brought power.
The power of sin was broken at last. Men were enabled at last to
walk in the way of life. The lordship of Jesus expressed itself, then,
not only in teaching and in forgiveness, but also in power. Jesus
himself was present among the little company of his disciples. He
was present not in bodily form, but in a yet more glorious way; he
was present through his Spirit. The Spirit manifested himself in
works of healing, in the mysterious gift of tongues and in one
dreadful act of vengeance. But he also appeared in holy lives. Joy
and love and purity were the fruit of the Spirit.

Distinctiveness of Gentile Christianity

In the Gentile world, the Christian communities were even more
sharply distinguished from their environment than they were

among the Jews. The moral standards of the age were startlingly low. Magnificent temples were devoted to the most disgraceful practices; wealth and power were servants of luxurious vice. The preaching of philosophers and the ridicule of satirists were powerless to check the current of the time; religion, to a large extent, was either divorced from any ethical appeal, or else positively devoted to the encouragement of sin. The great cities particularly —those cities whose scant remains are the wonder of the civilized world—were strongholds of iniquity.

In such an age, a strange new sect began to appear in various places throughout the empire. The phenomenon in itself was by no means peculiar; the age was pre-eminently an age of religious propaganda. But this particular sect was unique.

SIMPLICITY

It was unique, for example, in the extreme simplicity of its rites. Instead of the gorgeous ceremonial of the religions of the east— then spreading over the whole of the civilized world—the Christians practised merely two simple sacraments. Their new converts were baptized with water, as a sign of cleansing; their fellowship with one another and with their Founder was symbolized by a meal of bread and wine. There seemed to be but little that could hold the sect together, but little that could make it attractive to the world.

HOLINESS

Yet, strangely enough, the new sect continued to grow; it made converts in all of the great cities. The converts, moreover, were affected in a most remarkable way. Practices formerly regarded as indifferent or even praiseworthy suddenly came to be loathed; new customs suddenly came to be substituted for the social usages of the day.

Such might have been the impression of a pagan observer of that time. To us, of course, the matter presents itself in a very different light; to us the customs of the Christian sect seem natural and praiseworthy; it is the lax morals of the surrounding paganism that fill us with disgust. The reason is that we have been nurtured, together with the early Christians, in the same school; we as well as they have learned from the apostles of Christ. But what is natural to us was in the first century surpassingly strange. In the midst of the ancient world, truly evangelical communities were found—communities where essentially the same type of virtue prevailed as that which forms the glory of truly evangelical Christian homes. The fact has become so familiar that we cease to wonder at it. But in reality there is hardly a greater wonder in all history.

The ideal, it is true, was by no means fully realized; a study of the Pauline Epistles will show how hard was the fight against heathenism. But the ideal was there in its purity, in individuals it was realized from the start, and the history of the first few Christian generations is a history of progressive victory. A comparison of the early Gentile churches with the surrounding civilization is a comparison of light with darkness, of pure and healthy life with loathsome disease.

IN THE WORLD, BUT NOT OF IT

The distinctiveness of the early Church is the more remarkable because it was maintained altogether without artificial aid. Instead of withdrawing into remote districts, where purity might have been more easily maintained, the Christians fought their battle in the very strongholds of Satan's realm. Corinth, for example, a city which was a synonym for loathsome impurity, was the seat of one of the most flourishing churches. That unwholesome mixture of east and west which had its seat on the isthmus of Greece formed the materials for an apostolic church. The address of Paul's First Epistle to the Corinthians, 'Unto the church of God which is at Corinth,' is, as Bengel remarked, 'a joyful and mighty paradox'. 'The church of God at Corinth'—that phrase is a paradox indeed, almost a contradiction in terms. What could God have to do with Corinth?

Yet the miracle, by divine grace, became glorious reality. There was really a true church on the isthmus of Corinth. It was composed, moreover, of no strangers from a better country, who had lost their way in the great city, but of the ordinary inhabitants of Corinth itself. Slaves and humble tradesmen, with a few men of better position, formed the rank and file of the congregation. Truly these were but sorry materials with which to build a holy church.

The Cross and the Spirit

How was the marvel accomplished? There is the practical question, if we are to profit by the example of history.

It was not accomplished by exhortation or by the influence of a noble example. Such a method would have been employed by some modern Christian workers; but it was not employed by Paul, and Paul, it must be remembered, was the instrument in founding the Corinthian church. About the first preaching in Corinth we are not left at all in the dark; the First Epistle to the Corinthians provides the clearest information. 'I determined,' says Paul, 'not to know anything among you, save Jesus Christ, and him crucified', ch. 2.2. Christ crucified was the foundation of the Corinthian church.

The story of the cross, moreover, was not, on the lips of Paul, a mere story of a noble martyrdom, the mere climax of an inspiring biography. So the story is treated by many modern preachers; but to Paul such treatment would have seemed absurd. The death of Christ, to Paul, was a death on our behalf, by which the dreadful punishment of our sins was laid once for all upon the Saviour. Such a view alone could work the miracles of the Pauline mission. The cross of Christ, conceived not merely as an example of heroic self-denial, but as a divine sacrifice for sin, by which we sinners become sure of the divine favour and start fresh upon a new life with sin forever wiped away—that and that alone was the message that transformed Corinthians into a church of God.

The results of that message in Corinth were manifest. Acceptance of the message was accompanied by the gift of the Holy Spirit; and the fruit of the Spirit—everywhere essentially the same —was 'love, joy, peace, longsuffering, kindness, goodness, faithfulness, meekness, self-control'. The modern Church endeavours sometimes to produce these things by artificial means, but the effort results in dismal failure. The fruit of the Spirit is no laboratory product. It cannot be produced by any mere improvement of social conditions, or by any multiplication of new motives. It appears only in God's good time, by the mysterious working of God's power, when the seed of the Spirit's presence brings forth the abundant harvest of a holy life. Christ crucified—a divine Sacrifice received by simple faith—alone produced the Church of God at Corinth and alone will transform our lives today.

Terms Descriptive of Discipleship
The lordship of Christ may profitably be studied by an examination of some of the various names which in the New Testament are applied to the Church and its individual members. The individual titles should be studied first. After all, the Church exists for the individual believer rather than the individual believer for the

Church. The primary relation is the relation between Christ and the individual soul. Brotherhood comes only through the union of individuals with a common Lord.

'CHRISTIANS'

Probably the first title that occurs to us today to designate the individual members of the Church is the title 'Christian'; yet as a matter of fact that title appears only three times in the New Testament, and then only as it was taken from the lips of unbelievers. In accordance with the explicit testimony of Acts 11.26, the name was given for the first time at Antioch; it had no place, therefore, in the early Jerusalem church. A moment's thought will reveal the reason. The name 'Christians' would have meant to a Jew adherents of the 'Christ', or the 'Messiah'. Obviously no Jew would have applied such a name specifically to the disciples of Jesus; for all the Jews, in one sense or another, were adherents of the Messiah. The Jews were adherents of him by way of anticipation; the disciples thought he had already appeared; but all earnest Jews alike would have rejoiced to be called by his name.

Evidently the name was applied in Antioch by the pagan population. The Church had become so clearly separate from Judaism that a separate name for it was required. The name 'Christian' suggested itself very naturally. 'Jesus Christ' was for ever on the lips of these strange enthusiasts! 'The Christ' was indeed also spoken of by the Jews, but only careful observers would necessarily be aware of the fact. The Messianic hope was an internal concern of the synagogues, with which outsiders would usually have little to do. The new sect, on the other hand, brought the title 'Christ' out from its seclusion; 'Christ' to these enthusiasts was something more than a title, it was becoming almost a proper name; like 'Jesus', it was a designation of the Founder of the sect, and accordingly a name so easily modelled upon it could be used to designate the sect itself.

In Acts 26.28, the name appears as used by Agrippa; in I Peter 4.16, also, it is evidently taken from the lips of the opponents of the faith. The Christians, however, Peter implies, need not be ashamed of the name which has been fastened upon them. Rather let them strive to be worthy of it! It is the highest honour to be called by the name of Christ; and if they are true 'Christians', their confession will redound to the glory of God.

In modern times, the name is often misapplied; the use of it is broadened and weakened. Nations are declared to be Christian although only a very small percentage of their citizens really deserve the name; teaching is called Christian though it is only similar in some respects to the teaching of Christ. Such a use of terms should be avoided wherever possible; the original poignancy of the designation should be restored. Properly speaking, 'Christian' means not 'like Christ' but 'subject to Christ'. A Christian is not one who admires Christ or is impressed with Christ's teaching or tries to imitate Christ, but one to whom Christ is Saviour and Lord.

Are we willing to be known as 'Christians' in that sense? At the time of First Peter, it would have been a serious question; an affirmative answer would have meant persecution and perhaps death. But it is also a serious question today. Confession of Christ involves solemn responsibilities; dishonour to the 'Christian' means dishonour to Christ; the unworthy servant is a dishonour to his Master. But let us not fear; Christ is Helper as well as Lord.

'DISCIPLES'

The earliest designation of the followers of Jesus was 'disciples' or 'learners'; during the earthly ministry perhaps scarcely any other designation was commonly used. Jesus appeared at first as a teacher; the form of his work was somewhat like that of other teachers of the Jews. Nevertheless, although he was a teacher from the beginning, he was also from the beginning something more. He had not only authority, but also power; he was not only Teacher, but also Saviour. His followers were not merely instructed, but were received into fellowship; and that fellowship made of them new men. 'Disciples' in the Gospels is more than 'learners' or 'students'; it is a fine, warm, rich word; the Teacher was also Friend and Lord.

The same term was continued in the early Palestinian Church, and the resurrection had brought an incalculable enrichment of its meaning. The 'disciples' were not merely those who remembered the words of Jesus, but those who had been redeemed by his blood and were living now in the power of his Holy Spirit. If we use the term, let it be in the same lofty sense. Let us be learners, indeed; let us hear the words of Jesus, as they are recorded in the Gospels; but let us hear them not as from a dead teacher, but ever anew from the living Lord.

'SAINTS'

A third designation is 'saints'. This term is used as a title of the Christians in Acts 9.13, 32, 41; 26.10, and frequently in the epistles of Paul and in the Apocalypse. Its use in the New Testament is very different from some uses of it that appeared at a later time. The Roman Catholics, for example, employ the term as a title of honour for a number of persons carefully limited by the Church; Protestants often designate by it persons of exceptional purity or goodness. In the New Testament, on the contrary, the title 'saints' is clearly applied to all Christians.

In the original Greek the word is exactly the same as a word meaning 'holy'; it is simply the adjective 'holy' used as a noun. 'Saints', therefore, really means 'holy persons'. Unfortunately, however, the word 'holy', as well as the word 'saint' has undergone modifications of usage. 'Holy,' in the Bible, is not simply another word for 'good' or 'righteous', but expresses a somewhat different idea. It has the idea of 'sacred' or 'separate'—separate from the world. God is holy not merely because he is good, but because he is separate. Undoubtedly his goodness is one attribute—perhaps the chief attribute—that constitutes the separateness; but other attributes also have their place. His omnipotence and his infinitude, as well as his goodness, make him 'holy'.

The word 'holy' or 'saint' as applied to Christians has fundamentally the same meaning. Believers are 'holy' because they are in communion with the holy God and therefore separate from the world. Undoubtedly the most obvious element in their separateness is their goodness; the moral implications of the term 'holy' are sometimes so prominent that the specific meaning of the word seems obscured. But that specific meaning is probably never altogether lost. Christians are called 'saints' because they are citizens, not of the present evil world, but of a heavenly kingdom.

The familiar word, thus interpreted, has a startling lesson for the modern Church. Can modern Christians be called 'saints', in the New Testament sense? Are we really separate from the world? Are we really 'a chosen generation, a royal priesthood, an holy nation, a peculiar people'? I Peter 2.9, A.V. Do we really feel ourselves to be strangers and pilgrims in the earth? Or are we rather salt that has lost its savour? Have we become merged in the life of the world?

'BRETHREN'

A fourth designation is concerned, not with the relation of the believer to Christ or to the world, but with the relation of believers among themselves. That designation is 'brethren'. It is a very simple word; it requires little explanation; the rich meaning of it will be unfolded in the whole of the remainder of this book.

'CHURCH'

After studying the New Testament terms that denote the disciples of Jesus individually, it will now be well to turn for a moment to the chief designation of the body of disciples considered as a unit. That designation is 'church', or in the Greek form, *ecclesia*.

The word *ecclesia* is in itself a very simple term indeed. It is derived from the verb 'call' and the preposition 'out'. An *ecclesia* is a body of persons called out from their houses to a common meeting place, in short it is simply an 'assembly', and an assembly of any kind. This simple use of the word is found in Acts 19.32, 39, 41; the Greek word which is there translated 'assembly' is exactly the same word as that which is elsewhere translated 'church'.

Even before New Testament times, however, the word had begun to be used in a special, religious sense. Here, as so often, the Septuagint translation of the Old Testament prepared the way for New Testament usage. In the Septuagint the word *ecclesia* was used to denote the solemn assembly of the people of Israel. That assembly was of course religious as well as political, for Israel was a theocratic nation. Hence it was no abrupt transition from previous usage when the New Testament writers selected the word *ecclesia* to denote the Christian congregation.

In the New Testament, the word is used in various ways. In the first place, it designates the body of Christians who lived in any particular locality. So, for example, the epistles of Paul are addressed to individual 'churches'. In the second place, however, the word designates the whole body of Christians throughout the world. This usage is prominent in the Epistle to the Ephesians, but it also appears even in the Gospels, in the memorable words of Jesus at Cæsarea Philippi, Matt. 16.18. It is a wonderfully grand conception which is thus disclosed by the familiar word. 'The Church' is a chosen people, ruled by the Lord himself, a mighty army, engaged, not in earthly warfare, but in a spiritual campaign of salvation and love.

'THE KINGDOM OF GOD'

One further conception requires at least a word. What is meant by 'the kingdom of God'? This conception is evidently related to the conception of 'the Church', but the two are not identical. The kingdom of God is simply that place or that condition where God rules. As the kingdom of Cæsar was the territory over which Cæsar held sway, so the kingdom of God is the realm where God's will is done. In one sense, of course, the kingdom of God embraces the whole universe, for nothing is beyond the reach of God's power. But in the New Testament the term is used in a far deeper sense; it is used to denote the realm where God's will is done, not of necessity, but by willing submission. Wherever human hearts and wills are in true accord with the will of God, there the 'kingdom' has come.

In one sense the kingdom of God belongs to the future age. It is never realized fully upon earth; there is here always some lurking trace of sinful resistance. Nevertheless, in the New Testament the kingdom is by no means always represented as future. Though it has not yet been fully realized, it is already present in principle; it is present especially in the Church. The Church gives clear, though imperfect, expression to the idea of the kingdom; the Church is a people whose ruler is God.

Entrance into the Church is not to be obtained by human effort; it is the free gift of God through the Lord Jesus Christ. No other gift is so glorious. If we are members of that chosen people, we need fear nothing in heaven or on earth.

TOPICS FOR STUDY

(Note: A concordance should be used constantly in the study of this and the subsequent chapters.)

1. Elaborate in your own words the exact meaning of the following designations of the followers of Jesus: (a) 'Christians,' (b) 'disciples,' (c) 'saints,' (d) 'brethren.' Give as full an account as possible of the New Testament use of these terms (four topics).

2. Explain the New Testament use of the word 'church'. Where does this word occur in the Gospels?

3. Enumerate and explain some of the figures of speech which the New Testament uses to designate the Church.

4. Mention some of the ways in which the Church was distinguished from the people about it (a) in Palestine, (b) in the Gentile world (two topics).

41 : THE CHRISTIAN MESSAGE

Study material: Acts 2 : 14–42; 3 : 11 to 4 : 4; 10 : 34–43; 13 : 14–43; 14 : 14–18; 16 : 22–34; 28 : 17–31; I Thess. ch. 1; I Cor. 2 : 1–5; Gal. 3 : 1; I Cor. 15 : 1–8

The Christian Church, which was studied in an introductory way in the last lesson, came forward from the beginning with a gift for the world. That gift was not silver or gold, not the mere improvement of conditions upon the earth, but a message. The duty of the Church was primarily to give men news of something that had happened in the past and had a glorious effect in the present.

The Witness-Bearing of the Apostles

COMMANDED BY JESUS

This duty of telling a story, of bearing a witness, was imposed upon the apostles by the Lord himself before his ascension. 'Ye shall receive power,' said Jesus, 'when the Holy Spirit is come upon you: and ye shall be my witnesses both in Jerusalem, and in all Judæa and Samaria, and unto the uttermost part of the earth.' Acts 1.8. The apostles were not disobedient to the command; they became witness-bearers for Jesus, and no suffering or persecution could close their mouths.

ACCOMPLISHED THROUGH THE HOLY SPIRIT

Their witness-bearing, however, was carried on, not by their own strength, but by the Holy Spirit whom Jesus had promised. During the earthly ministry of Jesus, the apostles had been possessed of little power, they had even deserted their Master, in cowardly flight or positive denial, at the hour of his deepest need; but now, on the day of Pentecost, immediately after the Spirit came, we find Peter saying: 'Ye men of Israel, hear these words: Jesus of Nazareth, a man approved of God unto you by mighty works and wonders and signs which God did by him in the midst of you, even as ye yourselves know; him, being delivered up by the determinate counsel and foreknowledge of God, ye by the hand of lawless men did crucify and slay: whom God raised up, having loosed the pangs of death: because it was not possible that he should be holden of it. . . . Let all the house of Israel therefore know assuredly, that God hath made him both Lord and Christ, this Jesus whom ye crucified.' (Acts 2.22, 23, 36.) That was uncompromising testimony indeed. In the very presence of the murderers of Jesus, Jesus was proclaimed as Lord. The strange boldness of that testimony manifested the power of the Holy Spirit even more plainly, perhaps, than it was manifested by the tongues of fire.

Jesus was proclaimed, moreover, not merely as Lord, but also as Saviour. 'Repent ye,' said Peter, 'and be baptized every one of you in the name of Jesus Christ unto the remission of your sins; and ye shall receive the gift of the Holy Spirit.' (Acts 2.38). The offer of salvation never came at a more surprising time. To the people who had made themselves guilty of the death of Jesus, Jesus was offered as a Saviour from death; to those who had cried, 'His blood be on us, and on our children', Matt. 27.25, that same blood became the means of forgiveness. Denunciation of sin went hand in hand with the gift of salvation. So it has always been with the Christian message.

The boldness of the apostles on the day of Pentecost was due to no mere temporary exaltation of feeling; it was continued in the days and years that followed. The rulers supposed that an official rebuke would put a stop to the message; they charged Peter and John 'not to speak at all nor teach in the name of Jesus'. Acts 4.18. They might as well have charged the wind not to blow; 'Peter and John answered and said unto them, Whether it is right in the sight of God to hearken unto you rather than unto God, judge ye: for we cannot but speak the things which we saw and heard.' (vs. 19, 20.) That is the spirit of the Christian message throughout the centuries. The commission of the humblest Christian, as well as of the greatest apostle, comes from God. The form of the testimony differs: the apostles told what they saw and heard, we repeat their testimony by the promulgation of their writings. But we as well as the apostles have made of the testimony a present fact; we as well as they can point to the blessed effects of the testimony upon life.

The Contents of the Message

THE EARTHLY LIFE OF JESUS

The contents of the apostolic message cannot be determined fully by the speeches in the first few chapters of The Acts; for in the early days in Jerusalem many things could be taken for granted and therefore did not need to be set forth in detail. The main facts in the earthly life of Jesus, for example, were known to friend and foe alike; the enemies had accepted even the miracles, though they had attributed them to the power of Beelzebub, Matt. 12.24. Peter on the day of Pentecost could say, with regard to these things, 'even as ye yourselves know'. Acts 2.22. No doubt even such 'God-fearing' Gentiles as Cornelius had heard something of the story of Jesus, which is reviewed before Cornelius by Peter, ch. 10.36–38. In Palestine, in the early days, missionary preaching could presuppose considerable knowledge of Jesus' earthly ministry.

Nevertheless, the detailed story of that earthly ministry formed from the beginning an integral part of the Christian message; it was told in detail wherever it was unknown, and intimate acquaintance with it was furthered in every possible way. The Synoptic Gospels, if not in completed form, at least in the incidents that they contain, were a product of the Palestinian Church. If men were to believe in Jesus, they needed to know what manner of person he was.

THE CROSS

In the second place, the Christian message contained a narrative, and an explanation, of the death of Jesus. The story of the cross never formed a mere part of a biography; it was always regarded as having a meaning of its own. At first, no doubt, before unconverted Jews, that meaning could not be explained with any fulness. As long as the cross was a stumblingblock, it was useless to try to explain its deeper significance. What Peter did, therefore, very naturally, was to show that the cross was no disproof of the claims of Jesus, first because it was in accordance with prophecy, and second because it was followed by the resurrection. It fitted the prophetic picture of the Messiah, and the shame which it involved was wiped out by the Easter victory.

THE MEANING OF THE CROSS

'Jesus was delivered up,' Peter said, 'by the determinate counsel and foreknowledge of God.' (Acts 2.23; compare ch. 3.18.) What happened by the determinate counsel of God was no mere meaningless chance. Its meaning is explained to us fully in the epistles of Paul, but was not discovered by Paul. To Paul the significance of the cross was absolutely fundamental, and evidently he regarded himself as holding essentially the same view about it as was held by the other apostles. Against the Judaizers it had to be defended, at least in some of its implications, but not against Peter, Gal. 2.14–21. The disagreement between Paul and Peter at Antioch, vs. 11–13, was a disagreement of practice, not of principle.

What then was this significance of the cross? Why did Paul lay such supreme emphasis upon the death of Christ? Why, at Corinth, did he determine to know nothing 'save Jesus Christ, and him crucified'? The answer is very simple: Jesus, according to Paul, died 'for our sins'; when he died, he took our place. We were under the curse of the law; Christ, by his death, became a curse for us, Gal. 3.13. When Christ died, we all died, II Cor. 5.14. Sin is terrible guilt; it demands a just punishment; nothing that we can do can wipe it out; 'the soul that sinneth, it shall die'. But Christ died for us; and we therefore go free. What Christ offers men by his death is, in simple language, a fresh start. The offer is perfectly free. All that we have to do is accept it; 'accepting it' is another way of saying 'faith'.

THE POWER OF THE CROSS

This preaching of the cross of Christ had a wonderful power in the days of Paul; and it also has a wonderful power today. People say that they do not understand it; they said exactly the same thing in ancient Corinth; now as then 'the word of the cross is to them that perish foolishness'. I Cor. 1.18. Yet now as then the same word, unto those who are saved, is 'the power of God'. It is perfectly true that the cross of Christ cannot be fully understood. How can one person take upon himself the punishment of another's sins? We cannot fully answer the question; we cannot fully explain how Christ bore our sins. But we know at least that he did so; God can do many things that man cannot explain. The simple fact is that the word of the cross, in Corinth, through all the Christian centuries, and in the world today, has proved itself to be 'the power of God'. It is the supreme wonder of God's love.

THE RESURRECTION

In the third place, the apostolic message proclaimed the resurrection of Christ from the dead; indeed, without that proclamation all the rest of the message would have been valueless. 'If Christ hath not been raised,' said Paul, 'your faith is vain; ye are yet in your sins.' The resurrection was the plain, irremovable fact that showed Christ to be Lord and Saviour. So it was presented by Peter and his companions in Jerusalem: 'This Jesus did God raise up, whereof we all are witnesses.' Acts 2.32. The apostles were not philosophers; they were not men who could discourse eloquently about the eternal problems of God and the world; they were just witnesses. They told what they 'saw and heard', ch. 4.20. Paul could be an apostle only because he, too, had seen the risen Lord, I Cor. 9.1.

The witness of the apostles to the resurrection was believed by the three thousand persons on the day of Pentecost; it has been believed by the Church throughout the ages. There is good reason for believing it; the resurrection of Christ is a fact of history.

Moreover, though the resurrection is a fact of past history, it has effects in the present, wherever the testimony to it is believed. If Jesus rose from the dead, he is now alive; and, what is more, he is now active. Acceptance of the testimony to the resurrection, if it be true acceptance, means not merely recognition of a cold fact; it means faith in a living person. Those who accept the Christian message aright, accept the Lord Jesus Christ as Saviour and Lord.

The effects of such acceptance were gloriously manifested on the day of Pentecost. They were manifested first of all in the disciples themselves. The risen Christ, Peter said, 'hath poured forth this, which ye see and hear'. Acts 2.33. What Peter meant by 'this' was the miraculous gift of tongues. That gift was a particularly plain, palpable manifestation of the power of the risen Christ. Another similar manifestation was the healing of the lame man, ch. 3.16. Such miracles, however, were not the only way in which the living Christ proclaimed his presence. He showed himself also in the ennobled lives of men.

These things were done by the risen Christ through his Spirit. The Spirit of God, or the Holy Spirit, is also called in the New Testament the Spirit of Christ. The Holy Spirit confirmed the testimony of the apostles. The apostles told men that they had seen the risen Lord; the Spirit crowned that testimony with manifestations of the Lord's power. As it was in the apostolic age, so it is today. There are still many occasions when the Christian preacher can declare in triumph: 'Christ "hath poured forth this, which ye see and hear".' The fruits of the Spirit, though no longer miraculous, are plain.

The Effects of the Message

The Christian message in the apostolic Church was a message of power. The story of its progress is full of dramatic vigour; it appeals even to the non-Christian historian. The story of the apostolic age is full of surprises—the sudden transformation of bitter Jewish enemies into humble disciples; the triumphant spread of the faith when everything seemed opposed; the establishment of Christian churches in the very centres of pagan vice; the astonishingly rapid preparation for the conquest of the empire; and all this accomplished, not by worldly wisdom, but by simple men who only had a bit of news—a bit of news, and God!

The triumphs of the gospel, however, were not confined to the age of the apostles. The apostolic age was prophetic of the Christian centuries. There were many days of darkness; but the Church always emerged again triumphant. So it will be today. God has not deserted his people; he will attest his truth with the power of his Spirit; there is no room for discouragement. One thing, however, should be remembered; the victories of the Church are victories, not of brilliant preachers, not of human wisdom or human goodness, but of the cross of Christ. Under that banner all true conquests move.

TOPICS FOR STUDY

1. Collect the missionary speeches that are reported in The Acts. Point out and explain the peculiarities of each (three or four topics).

2. What information do the Pauline Epistles afford about Paul's missionary preaching (several topics)?

3. Explain in your own words how the death of Jesus was a death 'for our sins'.

4. What is the meaning for us of the resurrection of Jesus?

5. Give a brief, plain summary of what is meant by 'the gospel'.

42 : THE WORD AND THE
SACRAMENTS

Study material: II Tim. 3: 14–17; II Peter 1: 12–21;
Matt. 28: 18–20; Rom. ch. 6; I Cor. 10: 16, 17; 11: 17–34

The last two chapters were in a certain sense introductory to all
those which follow. Before studying the apostolic Church in detail,
we asked in the first place what the apostolic Church was, what
distinguished it from the surrounding world; and in the second
place, what its fundamental business was, what it was there for,
what God intended it to do. In chapter 40, in answer to the former
of these two questions, we discovered that the apostolic Church
was simply the company of those to whom Jesus Christ was
Saviour; and in chapter 41, in answer to the second question, we
learned that the primary business of the Church was to tell a piece
of good news.

The reception of that good news, about the life and death and
resurrection of Jesus Christ, brought men into communion with
God. In the present chapter, and in the two that follow, we shall
ask how that communion was maintained. Communion with God,
in the apostolic age, as well as today, was different from communion with one's fellow men, in that men are seen while God is
unseen. It is quite impossible to ignore the presence of human
friends; they touch our lives in a thousand unmistakable ways. But
many men succeed in ignoring God; he does not force himself
upon our attention; we do not see his form with the bodily eye or
hear his voice with the bodily ear. How then may we maintain
ourselves consciously in his presence?

It will be our object to discover how the apostolic Church solved
the problem, and then to apply the example to our own lives. We
shall see that God has provided certain very simple means by
which we can be maintained in his presence. Those that we shall
particularly study are, first, the Word and the sacraments; second,
prayer; third, the congregation. In this chapter we shall study the
Word and the sacraments.

Bible-reading in the Apostolic Church

It is not hard to show that the apostolic Church was a Bible-reading Church. References to the Old Testament appear everywhere in the apostolic writings, and evidently the writers knew that these references would be generally understood.

THE MISSIONARY USE OF THE BIBLE

In the Palestinian Church, indeed, and among Jewish Christians throughout the Empire, the Old Testament was familiar to the converts even before they became Christians at all; they had been devout Jews, and the Bible formed the very sum and substance of Jewish education. This familiarity of non-Christian Jews with the Old Testament was of course an incalculable assistance to the Christian mission. The Old Testament Scriptures testified of Christ, and the first preachers made full use of the Scripture testimony. Peter's first speech, on the day of Pentecost, is full of the appeal to Old Testament prophecy. Almost half the speech is taken up with continuous quotations, to say nothing of frequent references interspersed through the rest.

This missionary use of the Bible, moreover, could be extended even to Gentiles. It must be remembered that Judaism in the first century was an active missionary religion (chapter 5). Many Gentiles, although they had not definitely united themselves with the Jewish people, had accepted the Jewish conception of God and many ideas of Jewish morality. Furthermore, they attended the Jewish synagogues and in the synagogues, or in private reading, they became familiar with the Old Testament Scriptures. These Gentile 'God-fearers' were found both in Palestine itself—Cornelius is a good example—and also in all the great cities of the Greco-Roman world.

THE EXAMPLE OF THE ETHIOPIAN

A fine instance of the way the Old Testament could be used to bring men to Christ is given in the story of the Ethiopian treasurer, Acts 8.26–40. The Ethiopian was reading the fifty-third chapter of Isaiah; it had aroused his interest. 'I pray thee,' he said, 'of whom speaketh the prophet this? of himself, or of some other?' v. 34. Philip did not miss his opportunity; in preaching the gospel of Jesus he began 'from this scripture', the very passage that the Ethiopian had been reading. It was certainly a fine place to begin.

The fifty-third chapter of Isaiah leads straight to the very heart of the gospel; it treats of the atoning death of Christ. The Scripture had served its purpose well; the Ethiopian was baptized, and went on his way rejoicing.

The missionary use of the Bible needs to be practised today. The surest way of winning men is to start them in Bible-reading. The Bible itself is the best missionary.

THE USE OF THE BIBLE BY CHRISTIANS

The Bible, however, is of course not only a missionary book; it is also a means of maintaining Christian people in the presence of God. As it would be impossible to maintain a human friendship if the human friend had absolutely no power of speech, so it is impossible to maintain communion with God unless we listen to what God has to say—and God speaks to us in the Bible.

(1) *Bible-reading everywhere presupposed.* For this use of the Bible we have the unmistakable example of the apostolic Church. Bible-reading, it is true, in the New Testament, is not very frequently inculcated in so many words, and there is not very frequent mention of it in the narrative portions. But this very silence is even more impressive than words could possibly be. It shows that the reading of the Bible was not only practised, but that it was practised as a matter of course. The New Testament is simply suffused with the Jewish Scriptures; knowledge of the Old Testament is not only displayed by the apostolic writers themselves but also presupposed in the readers; the absence of definite inculcation of Bible-reading can therefore only mean, not that such inculcation was repudiated, but simply that it was thought unnecessary. The early Church for the most part did not need to be urged to read the Bible; it stood far above all that; it was founded upon the Bible and was unquestionably loyal to the Bible. In the use of the Scriptures it was following the example of Jesus himself; the Scriptures entered into the very depths of Jesus' life; it would have been inconceivable if Jesus' disciples had at this point deserted their Master's example.

(2) *Bible-reading Among Gentile Christians.* Evidently the use of the Old Testament was not confined to the Jewish–Christian part of the Church. When Gentiles were converted, one of the first things that the missionaries did was to make them familiar with the Bible. Some of the Gentile converts, even outside of Palestine, had studied the Bible before their conversion; former 'God-fearers'

were no doubt numerous in many of the churches. The other Gentiles were speedily made acquainted with the Scriptures. Paul evidently presupposes a knowledge of the Old Testament even in writing to churches where most of the readers were clearly converts from an unmixed paganism.

(3) *Definite Commendations of Bible-reading.* The definite commendations of Bible-reading in the apostolic Church, therefore, are only supplementary to what is everywhere presupposed. These commendations, however, are abundantly explicit. Paul meant what he said when he declared that the sacred writings were able to make Timothy wise unto salvation and that 'every scripture inspired of God, is also profitable for teaching, for reproof, for correction, for instruction which is in righteousness'. II Tim. 3.15, 16. Peter was also in earnest when he said that 'no prophecy of scripture is of private interpretation. For no prophecy ever came by the will of man: but men spake from God, being moved by the Holy Spirit'. II Peter 1.20, 21.

The New Testament added to the Old

At the time when the Church was founded, the only Bible of course was the Old Testament. No New Testament books had yet been written. Something closely corresponding to the New Testament, however, was to be found at the very beginning. The early Jerusalem church had information about the sayings of Jesus, and these sayings were undoubtedly regarded as equal in authority to the Old Testament Scriptures. Whatever Jesus affirmed was true; whatever he commanded must be done. Moreover the Jerusalem church 'continued steadfastly in the apostles' teaching'. Acts 2.42. The apostles' teaching no doubt included the report of what Jesus had said, but it was hardly confined to that—it must have concerned itself also with the interpretation, as well as with the bare report, of Jesus' life and death and resurrection. The reverent attention of the Church to the teaching of the apostles was certainly in accord with Jesus' intention; he had endued the Twelve with an ample authority: see for example John 16.12, 13.

At a somewhat later time within the apostolic Church, these two things—the words of Jesus and the teachings of the apostles—were incorporated in the inspired books which make up the New Testament. The New Testament was present from the beginning in germ; the addition of its books to the Old Testament Scriptures was accepted very naturally. There is definite information that epistles of Paul were read in the churches, I Thess. 5.27; Col. 4.16; compare Rev. 1.3, 11; 22.18, 19.

The Sacraments

A second means of maintaining the life of communion with God was afforded to the apostolic Church by the sacraments. A sacrament is an action by which spiritual truth is set forth in visible form. According to the New Testament there are two Christian sacraments, both of them instituted by Christ himself. They are baptism and the Lord's Supper. Baptism was instituted by the great commission, Matt. 28.19; the Lord's Supper by the command, 'This do in remembrance of me.' I Cor. 11.24. Undoubtedly both sacraments were observed by the Church from the beginning.

BAPTISM

In baptism, the washing with water signifies primarily cleansing from sin. Provided that significance is maintained, the mode of administration of the sacrament may be varied. Water may be applied by immersion, or, as is done in most churches today, by sprinkling. The sacrament may be applied, moreover, either to grown persons or to the children of believing parents. Baptism in the New Testament is a sign of membership in the Church; but children who are dedicated by Christian parents to the Lord belong to the Church even before they make their own confession. The warrant for infant baptism is to be sought not so much in individual passages as in more general considerations of what the sacrament means. The family, according to the New Testament, is the unit of Christian life, Acts 16.31, 33; children have a share in the covenant relationships of their parents.

Baptism and Circumcision. The sacrament of baptism had its truest predecessor in circumcision, the Old Testament sign of union with the covenant people. Baptism as well as circumcision is a sign of the covenant, though the varied symbolism marks the advance of the new covenant over the old.

Christian Baptism and the Baptism of John. In form, moreover, and to a considerable extent also in meaning, Christian baptism in the early Church was prepared for by the baptism of John the Baptist, which had even been continued by the disciples of Jesus during Jesus' earthly ministry, John 4.1, 2. Both the baptism of John and Christian baptism symbolized cleansing from sin; compare Acts 2.38 with Matt. 3.6, 11.

Christian baptism, however, differed from every rite that had preceded it by its definite reference to Christ, and by its definite connection with a new manifestation of the Holy Spirit.

Baptism 'into Christ'. In the apostolic writings, baptism is sometimes spoken of as a baptism 'into Christ'. Gal. 3.27; Rom. 6.3. The meaning of this phrase has often been obscured both in translation and in interpretation. The phrase 'into Christ' in this connection means something more than 'with reference to Christ'; it means rather 'into a position within Christ'. The Christian, according to a common Pauline expression, is 'in Christ'; he is in such close union with Christ that the life of Christ might almost be described as the atmosphere which he breathes. To be baptized 'into Christ' means to come by baptism into this state of blessed union with the Saviour.

Baptism and Faith. At this point, however, a serious question arises. How can baptism be described as the means by which the Christian comes into union with Christ, when at other times salvation is declared to be by faith? One solution of the difficulty would be simply to say that baptism and faith are both necessary—a man must believe if he is to be saved, but he must also be baptized. Clearly, however, this view does not represent the meaning of the New Testament. The passages where faith alone is represented as the condition of salvation are too strong; especially the vigorous contrast which Paul sets up between faith and works prevents any inclusion of such a work as baptism along with faith as an additional condition of acceptance of God. The true solution is that baptism is related to faith, or rather to the regenerative work of the Holy Spirit, as the sign is related to the thing signified. Baptism represents the work of the Spirit; it is a means which the Spirit uses. If it stood alone, it would be a meaningless form, but when it is representative of spiritual facts it becomes a channel of divine grace.

THE LORD'S SUPPER

The Lord's Supper, as well as baptism, is the continuation of an Old Testament sacrament; it is the successor of the Jewish passover. On the evening when the Lord's Supper was instituted, Jesus was eating the passover with his disciples; and although he changed the symbolism he left the fundamental significance of the sacrament essentially the same. The killing of the passover lamb was regarded as a sacrifice for sin; it foreshadowed the one true sacrifice on the cross. That sacrifice was at last to be made; as it was fore-shadowed by the Jewish rite, so it was to be commemorated by the Christian sacrament. 'As often as ye eat this bread, and drink the cup, ye proclaim the Lord's death till he come.' I Cor. 11.26. The breaking of the bread and the pouring out of the wine signify the death of the Lord. In this sacrament, as elsewhere in the New Testament, the death of Christ is put in the very centre of the Christian faith. The reason is plain. The death of Christ was not merely the end of a blessed life; it was the gracious saving act by which we receive the favour of God.

The Lord's Supper is primarily a proclamation of the death of Christ. If the Son of God had merely lived a life of love, had merely carried on a ministry of teaching and of healing in Galilee, without ever dying for our sins, then the sacrament would be meaningless. Nevertheless, the Lord's Supper is something more than a mere proclamation of a blessed event of long ago; it is not merely a commemoration of the death of Christ, but also an application of it. The divine sacrifice for sin is in the Lord's Supper applied in a plain, visible way to all the disciples. The Lord himself breaks the bread that represents his body; the Lord himself pours out the cup. Christ is the Host at this blessed Supper; by his broken body and shed blood he offers us communion with himself, like that which the disciples enjoyed on the last evening in the upper room. We feed upon the body and blood of Christ in the high spiritual sense that by faith we obtain from Christ's death pardon for our sins and a fresh start in the full favour of God. These benefits we obtain not by our own efforts, but by a free gift.

THE CONTINUITY OF THE SACRAMENTS

The observance of the sacraments makes us feel the continuity of the Church's life; the sacraments bind us to the past. The simple act of baptism has been repeated without interruption from the days when the disciples on the day of Pentecost, obeying the command of Christ, baptized three thousand persons unto the remission of their sins; subsequent additions to the membership of the Church have been marked by the same act. The Lord's Supper, the simple breaking of the bread and pouring out of the cup, has been repeated from the evening when Jesus sat with his disciples; the long history of the sacrament has been a history of blessing. Shall we too have a share? Shall we too sit with the Lord at his table?

TOPICS FOR STUDY

1. Show the exact meaning of the express commendations of Bible-reading which are to be found in the New Testament.

2. Supplement what is said in the chapter about the use of the Bible in the early Church. Collect the quotations from the Old Testament that are to be found in the early speeches of Peter or in one of the Pauline epistles.

3. Compare the four accounts of the institution of the Lord's Supper.

4. Are any other references to the Lord's Supper to be found in the New Testament? What evidence is there that the Supper was celebrated throughout the early Church?

5. Summarize the teaching of Paul about baptism.

6. What is meant by baptism 'into Christ'?

7. On what occasions described in the New Testament is it improbable that immersion was the mode used in baptism?

43: PRAYER

Study material: Acts 1: 12–14; 2: 41, 42; 4: 23–31;
Rom. 1: 8–10; 8: 12–27; Phil. 1: 3–11; James 5: 13–18

The Bible and the sacraments, which were studied in the last chapter, are primarily means by which God speaks to us; in this chapter we shall study the means by which we speak to God. That means is prayer. Without prayer, communion with God would be impossible; prayer is the very atmosphere of the Christian life.

The Answerer of Prayer

The prayers of the apostolic age reveal with startling clearness the apostolic conception of God; and one chief reason why our prayers fall short of the apostolic standard is that our idea of God is different.

GOD IS A PERSON

In the first place, true prayer always conceives of God as a person; whereas much of modern religious thinking conceives of him as only another name for the world. Human life, it is said, is a part of the life of God; every man, to some degree, is divine. Such a philosophy makes prayer logically impossible. It is impossible for us to speak to an impersonal world-force of which we ourselves are merely an expression; the personal distinction between man and God is absolutely essential to prayer.

The transcendence of God as over against the world is grandly expressed in the prayer of the Jerusalem church, recorded in Acts 4.24; the Jerusalem Christians addressed God as the Lord who made 'the heaven and the earth and the sea, and all that in them is'. God, in other words, is not another name for the world, but creator of the world. He is indeed present in the world; not a single thing that happens is independent of him; the world would not continue for a moment without God's sustaining hand. But that means, not that God is identical with the world, but that he is Master of it

L

God pervades all things; he is present everywhere; but he is also free.

That conception pervades all the prayers of the apostolic Church; in all of them man comes to God as one person to another. God is free; God can do what he will; through Christ he is our Father. He is not bound by his own works; he is independent of nature; he will overrule all things for the good of his children. Such is the God that can answer prayer.

GOD IS AN INFINITE AND HOLY PERSON

If, however, the prayers of the apostolic age conceive of God as a person, they also conceive of him as very different from men. Here, also, they provide a salutary example for the modern Church. Many devout Christians of today, in avoiding the error which has just been described, in thinking of God plainly as a person, are inclined to fall into the opposite mistake. In their clear realization of God as a person they think of him as a person exactly like ourselves. They regard the difference between God and man as a difference of degree rather than a difference of kind; they think of God as merely a greater man in the sky. The result of such thinking is disastrous for prayer. Prayer, to be sure, is here not absolutely destroyed; communion with God remains possible; but such communion is degraded. Communion loses that sense of mystery and awe which properly belongs to it. Man becomes too familiar with God; God takes merely the leading place in a circle of friends; religion descends to the plane of other relationships. Prayer to such a God is apt to become irreverent. If our prayers are to lift us fully into the presence of God they must never lie on the same plane with the communion that we enjoy with our fellow men, but must be filled with a profound sense of God's majesty and power.

The danger of permitting prayer, on account of its very privilege, to become a commonplace thing is one that threatens us all. It may be overcome, however, in the first place, by the contemplation of nature. 'The heavens declare the glory of God; and the firmament showeth his handiwork'—and it is a terrible, mysterious God that they reveal. The stupendous vastness of the universe and the baffling mystery of the surrounding infinity oppress the thoughtful mind with a profound sense of insignificance. And God is the Maker and Ruler of it all, the One in whom all the mystery finds its explanation! Such is the employment of nature in the prayer of the Jerusalem church, Acts 4.24.

All the prayers of the apostolic Church illustrate the principle which is now being emphasized. There is never anything trite or vulgar about the prayers that are contained in the New Testament; they are all characterized by a wonderful dignity and reverence.

If the infinity and omnipotence of God should prevent any irreverence in our prayers, the thought of his holiness is perhaps even more overwhelming. We are full of impurity. Who can stand before the white light of God's awful judgment throne?

GOD IS A GRACIOUS PERSON

Nevertheless, despite the majesty and holiness of God, he invites us into his presence. It is a stupendous wonder. No reasoning could have shown it to be probable; only ignorance can regard it as a matter of course. If God were only a somewhat greater man, there would have been comparatively little mystery in prayer; but communion with the infinite and eternal and holy One, the unfathomed cause of all things, is the wonder of wonders. It is a wonder of God's grace. It is too wonderful to be true; yet it has become true in Christ. True prayer brings us not before some God of our own devising, before whom we could stand in our own merit without fear, but into the dread presence of Jehovah. Let us not hesitate to go; God has called us; he loves us as a Father, far more than we can ever love him. Prayer is full of joy; the joy is so great that it is akin to fear.

The Influence of Jesus' Teaching upon the Prayers of the Apostolic Church

In studying the prayers of the apostolic age, it must always be remembered that they stood upon the foundation of Jesus' example and precept.

THE EXAMPLE OF JESUS

With all his power and holiness Jesus was not above asking for strength to perform his gracious work; after that long, wearying day in Capernaum he 'departed into a desert place, and there prayed'. Mark 1.35. In the hour of agony in Gethsemane, he prayed a truly human, though holy, prayer: 'Abba, Father, all things are possible unto thee; remove this cup from me: howbeit not what I will, but what thou wilt.' Mark 14.36. Prayer, moreover, was not something which Jesus reserved for himself; clearly it was a privilege which he extended to all his disciples. In the prayer that he taught his disciples, he summed up all that our prayer should be, Matt. 6.9–13.

GOD AS FATHER

One thing in particular was derived by the apostolic Church from Jesus—the conception of God as Father. This conception appears in the epistles of Paul as a matter of course; evidently it was firmly established among the readers; it no longer required defence or explanation. Yet it had not lost, through long repetition, one whit of its freshness; in Paul it is never a mere phrase, but always a profound spiritual fact.

Obviously this idea of the fatherhood of God was of particular importance for prayer. It taught the disciples 'to draw near to God with all holy reverence and confidence, as children to a father, able and ready to help' them. (Westminster Shorter Catechism, 100.) The characteristic way of addressing God even in the Gentile churches of Paul was 'Abba, Father'. Gal. 4.6; Rom. 8.15. The Aramaic word 'Abba' is sufficient to show that this hallowed usage was based ultimately upon the teaching and example of Jesus; the word was the very one that Jesus had used both in his own prayers, for example, in Gethsemane, Mark 14.36, and in the 'Lord's Prayer' which he taught to his disciples.

THE RIGHT OF SONSHIP

What needs to be observed especially, however, is that the right of addressing God as 'our Father' was not in the apostolic Church extended to all men. Certainly no justification for such an extension could have been found in the teaching of Jesus; it was not the unbelieving multitude, but his own disciples, to whom Jesus taught the Lord's Prayer, Matt. 5.1; 6.9; Luke 11.1, 2. Paul is even more explicit; the cry 'Abba, Father' was to him a proof that a great change had taken place, that those who had been formerly under bondage to the world had now become sons of God. This change Paul represents especially under the figure of adoption, Gal. 4.5; men have to be adopted by God before they can call God Father; and adoption is accomplished only by the work of Christ, vs. 4, 5.

THE INTERCESSION OF THE SPIRIT

The cry, 'Abba, Father' can never be uttered by sinful man alone, but only by the power of Christ's Spirit. The prayers even of the redeemed are faulty. But the Holy Spirit takes up their cry. 'And in like manner the Spirit also helpeth our infirmity: for we know not how to pray as we ought: but the Spirit himself maketh intercession for us with groanings which cannot be uttered; and he that searcheth the hearts knoweth what is the mind of the Spirit, because he maketh intercession for the saints according to the will of God.' Rom. 8.26, 27.

There lies the true ground of confidence in prayer. Prayer does not derive its efficacy from any merit of its own, but only from the goodness of God. Let us not worry too much as to whether our prayers are good or bad; let them only be simple and sincere; God knows our weakness; his Spirit will make intercession for us far better than we can intercede for ourselves.

The Church began with Prayer

The apostolic Church had its roots in prayer; it began with a company of praying disciples. After Jesus had ascended into heaven, the apostles returned to Jerusalem and there engaged in prayer, Acts 1.14. With them were united the women who had been disciples of Jesus, and the mother and brethren of Jesus. These, it is said, 'continued steadfastly in prayer'.

The Steadfastness of the First Christian Prayers

THE REASON FOR STEADFASTNESS

The steadfastness of their prayer is deserving of special attention; we should take the example to heart. One great trouble with our prayers is simply that we do not take enough pains with them. It is a great mistake to suppose that prayer is always so spontaneous as to require no labour. On the contrary, if prayer is crowded in hurriedly only here and there amid what we secretly regard as the really important concerns of life, then no wonder it is unattended with blessing. God is not mocked; he will never be satisfied with the loose odds and ends of our time.

Furthermore, in seeking a blessing from prayer, we must not be easily discouraged. It may be said without irreverence that prayer, like other Christian activities, must be learned by practice. The practice of course does not concern itself with the form of prayer; God cares little for nicely turned sentences. What is really needed is practice in the essentials of prayer, the persistent effort, renewed every day of our lives, to make God sharer in all our joys and all our sorrows. There is such a thing as a habit of prayer. The habit

323

cannot be formed without conscious effort; the results of it cannot always be observed at every point; but the final issue is a life of power.

THE STEADFASTNESS CAN BE IMITATED BY US

The steadfastness, then, of the little company of waiting disciples is worthy of special imitation. It is not, indeed, so easy for us as it was for them. They had just passed through a wonderful experience; they had become witnesses of the risen Christ; they had received a glorious promise. No wonder they 'continued steadfastly in prayer'. But the same attitude is not unattainable for us. Our lives seem to the world to be commonplace, but they do not seem so to us, if we have the eye of faith. To us also a wonderful promise has been given; upon us also a mighty task has been imposed. If we continue 'steadfastly in prayer', like the first disciples, we too, as well as they, shall be endued with the power of the Holy Spirit.

THE STEADFASTNESS WAS PERMANENT

Steadfastness in prayer, moreover, was continued even after the Spirit had come; it was continued by the new converts as well as by the original company, Acts 2.42. Evidently prayer was not a temporary thing, it was not something to be resorted to now and then in order to accomplish special purposes, but was a regular part of the normal Christian life. Even in that time of an exuberant spiritual experience, simple means were necessary to maintain the disciples consciously in the presence of God and give them strength for their allotted tasks. Certainly they are necessary today; without them we should sink back inevitably into the religious deadness of the world.

A Prayer of the Early Church

In Acts 4.24–30, we find one of the few prayers which are actually recorded at any length in the New Testament.

THE OCCASION

The occasion was a notable one. Peter and John had been arrested because of their proclamation of Jesus and the healing of the lame man which they had accomplished in Jesus' name. When questioned regarding their authority, they had boldly confessed that the miracle had been wrought solely by the power of him whom the rulers had put to death. Threats and warnings had had no effect upon them; they intimated very plainly that they would obey God rather than men. The rulers for the present could do no more than threaten, for the disciples enjoyed the favour of the people.

Peter and John were restored, therefore, to their own company. To their account of their triumphant escape the disciples responded with the glorious prayer that has just been mentioned.

RECOGNITION OF THE MAJESTY OF GOD

It is a prayer, primarily, of petition, in view of the threatened dangers of the Church. It begins, however, with recognition of the majesty of God, Acts 4.24. This fact is highly instructive; it reveals one chief reason why the prayers of the apostolic Church were often so much more powerful than ours. Too often we are inclined to regard prayer as a mere mechanical device for obtaining what we desire. There could be no greater mistake; it should never be forgotten that prayers are addressed to God, and that God is a mighty person. The efficacy of prayer depends upon the mysterious will of the creator; prayer is not a mere lever for starting a machine; true prayer should always begin, like the prayer of the Jerusalem Christians, with reverent, wondering adoration of the living God.

RECOGNITION OF THE GOODNESS OF GOD

It should be observed, however, that the prayer pleads not only the majesty of God, but also his goodness; it pleads the divine promise. The apparent victory of Herod and Pontius Pilate over Jesus need cause no discouragement; it had been foreseen. The victory also had been foreseen; the enemies of Jesus had accomplished only what God's counsel had foreordained; the present threatenings would also be overruled; the prayer for boldness in the work and for the blessing of God upon it was sure to be answered. The whole prayer is suffused with the triumphant feeling that God was on the side of the Church. If God was for them, who could be against them?

That confidence, however, was attained by the Christians, not on the ground of any merit of their own, but simply on the ground of Christ. God was for the Church only because he was for Christ; the Church took refuge in the Lord's Anointed. That is what we mean when we offer our prayers 'in the name of Christ'; these words are implied, though not expressed, in all the prayers of the apostolic age. Of ourselves we could never hope to be heard; we are sinners deserving of God's wrath and curse. But God has had pity on us; by Christ and his atoning death he has opened up to us a new and living way of approach to the throne of grace.

THE ANSWER

The prayer of the Jerusalem Christians was gloriously answered. 'When they had prayed, the place was shaken wherein they were gathered together; and they were all filled with the Holy Spirit, and they spake the word of God with boldness.' Acts 4.31. That fulfilment was prophetic of the whole history of the Church. Boldness of speech has always been the result of genuine prayer; the great advances of the Christian mission have always been the result of prayerful preparation.

Prayer in the Narrative of The Acts

In the apostolic Church, indeed, prayer accompanied every important step; indeed if the narrative were only more complete we should no doubt discover that nothing whatever, great or small, was done without prayer. The apostles prayed before they laid their hands on the men who had been chosen to administer charity, Acts 6.6; Paul was praying—and praying no doubt in deepest anguish of soul—when the vision came to Ananias, ch. 9.11, and he was also praying, in the temple, when Christ gave him the command to depart to the Gentiles, ch. 22.17, 18; Peter raised up Dorcas from the dead by the power of prayer, ch. 9.40; Cornelius, with such light as he had under the old dispensation, was leading a life of prayer even before he became a Christian, ch. 10.2, 4, 30; Peter was praying on the housetop when he received his momentous revelation about the acceptance of the Gentiles, v. 9; the glorious deliverance of Peter in A.D. 44 was preceded by the earnest prayer of the Church for him, ch. 12.5; the company in the house of Mary was praying when the answer was at the door, v. 12; Barnabas and Paul were sent out upon the first Gentile mission with the prayers of the Antioch church, ch. 13.3; 14.26; when they left the newly formed churches they committed them with prayer to the Lord, ch. 14.23; Paul and Silas were praying in the inner prison at Philippi just before they were triumphantly delivered, ch. 16.25; Paul and the elders of Ephesus kneeled down and prayed before their parting at Miletus, ch. 20.36; the similar parting on the beach at Tyre was also accompanied with a common prayer, ch. 21.5; Paul offered a prayer of thanksgiving in the time of most desperate danger on the sea, ch. 27.35, and with prayer healed the father of Publius, ch. 28.8.

Thanksgiving in the Pauline Epistles

These instances of prayer are contained even in the book of The Acts, which is chiefly interested in the external progress of the Church. In the epistles, where the depths of Christian experience are revealed, prayer is perhaps even more prominent.

Nearly all the Pauline Epistles, for example, begin with a prayer of thanksgiving. This very fact is itself instructive; we are entirely too much inclined to limit our prayers to mere petition; we are too much inclined to resort to prayer only in times of great stress when all other means have failed. Such conduct is madness; God is not our servant, at our beck and call, who might be willing to keep out of our way till we think we need him; if we neglect him in prosperity we may call in vain when adversity comes. Without thanksgiving, joy is far-more dangerous to the Christian life than sorrow; when we are satisfied with worldly blessings, we think we have no need of God. Thanksgiving wards off the danger. By making God a sharer in the blessings that he has given, these blessings do not separate us from him, but keep us all the more fully in his presence.

Prayer in Adversity

In II Cor. 12.8, 9, we have information about the most intimate, the most personal of the prayers of Paul. The apostle had been afflicted with a persistent illness; it had apparently hampered him in his work, and caused him acute distress. In his trouble he called upon the Lord; and by that prayer Paul's affliction has been made to redound to the lasting instruction and encouragement of the Church. In the first place, the prayer concerns not spiritual matters, or the needs of the Church at large, but a simple affair of the physical life. As life is constituted here on earth, we are intimately connected with the physical world; the body is necessary to the soul. But God is Master of earth as well as of heaven; even the simplest needs of life may be laid before him in prayer. To teach us that, we have here the example of Paul, as well as the precept of the Saviour himself. In the second place, the prayer was answered, and answered in a very instructive way. The illness was not removed; but it was made an instrument of blessing. The purpose of it was revealed: 'My power,' said Christ, 'is made perfect in weakness.' Physical suffering is worth while if it leads to heroism and faith. Such is often the Lord's will. He himself trod the path of suffering before us, and in his case as in ours, the path led to glory. In the third place, this prayer was addressed, not to God the Father, but to Christ. Compare Acts 7.59, 60. Without doubt 'the Lord' in II Cor. 12.8, as practically always in the Pauline Epistles, refers to Christ. Usually, in the New Testament, prayer is addressed, through Christ, to God the Father; but there is no reason why it should not be addressed to the Son. The Son as well as the Father is a living Person; and the Son as well as the Father is God. It is well that we have apostolic examples for prayer addressed directly to the Saviour. Christ, to Paul, was no mere instrument in salvation, that had served its purpose and was then removed; he was alive and sovereign, and the relation to him was a relation of love. In a time of acute physical distress, Paul turned to the Saviour. Three times he called, and then the answer came. The answer will always come in the Lord's way, not in ours; but the Lord's way is always best.

Confession in the First Epistle of John

Confession, also, in the apostolic Church was an integral part of prayer; it is emphasized especially in the First Epistle of John, ch. 1.9, 10. It means simply that we desire not to hide anything from God, that there is no dark lurking-place of our soul where we are unwilling to let the light of God shine. God knows, our openness is not due to freedom from sin; of itself it would be a terrible thought—this thought of God's all-seeing eye. But through Christ it becomes, though still solemn, a thought that brings comfort and help. For the sake of Christ, God searches out our sin, not in order to condemn us, but in order to save us; he searches sin out in order to cleanse us from it.

In true prayer, moreover, the whole of the life is opened unreservedly before God, not only sin, but also perplexity. In time of trouble we often crave of a friend, not advice, or help, but first of all understanding and sympathy. It is a relief merely to give expression to our perplexity before a sympathetic friend. A similar solace is what we obtain, in tenfold measure, by prayer. God understands us better than we understand ourselves. If we will really open our lives freely to him, concealing none of our sin or sorrow or uncertainty or weakness, God will surely understand and sympathize. Troubles become light, if God bears them with us.

Such blessed favour and openness and sympathy we enjoy only

through the Saviour. True, God loved us even when we were yet sinners; but love, in God, is not miserable, characterless good humour; God's love is always joined with a holy hatred of sin. Love, however, was stronger than sin; it celebrated its triumph in the cross. By the gift of his own Son, God brought us near. It was God's doing, not our own. We can only accept, and wonder. Through Christ, we are made sons of God; through Christ, we can come to God in prayer, 'as children to a Father, able and ready to help us'.

'If It Be Thy Will'

Prayer in the apostolic Church was always accompanied by submission to the will of God, I John 5.14. For that submission the early Christians had the highest of examples, the example of the Master himself. In the agony of his human soul in Gethsemane, he prayed for a definite thing; but he also said, 'Nevertheless not my will, but thine, be done.' Luke 22.42. We too, as well as the apostolic Church, should surely follow the example of our Saviour; if he, in his greatness and goodness, could submit to the will of the Father, surely we should not be less submissive. The limitation, 'if it be thy will', does not deprive prayer of its meaning; it means simply that God knows best. He will do for us, not less, but more, than we can ask or think.

TOPICS FOR STUDY

1. Summarize the example of the apostolic Church with regard to (a) petition, (b) confession, (c) thanksgiving (three topics).

2. Why do we say 'in the name of Christ' in our prayers, and what do we mean by it?

3. Why do we say 'if it be thy will', and what do we mean by it?

4. How did the apostolic Church come to address God in prayer as 'Father'? What is meant by that form of address?

5. Collect the cases where Paul says he prayed for his converts, and where he asks for their prayers for himself.

44 : THE CONGREGATION

Study material: Acts 4: 23–31; 11: 1–18; 15: 6–29; 19: 8–10;
20: 7–13; James 2: 1–13; I Cor. 1: 10–17; 11: 2 to 14: 40;
I Tim. ch. 2; Heb. 10: 19–25

The reading of the Bible and prayer may be practised either in public or in private, and the Lord's Supper is distinctly a matter of the congregation. This chapter, therefore, includes much of the material that has just been studied, though looked at from a somewhat different point of view.

Congregational Meetings in the Apostolic Church

The need of congregational meetings was clearly recognized in the apostolic Church. The author of the Epistle to the Hebrews warns his readers not to forsake the assembling of themselves together, Heb. 10.25, and what is there taught by precept is taught elsewhere, just as clearly, by example.

CONGREGATIONAL MEETINGS IN PALESTINE

In studying the congregational meetings of the apostolic churches it must be remembered that the Christian community in Jerusalem continued for many years its participation in the worship of temple and synagogue. Specially Christian meetings, therefore, were at first not the sole expression of the collective worship of the Jerusalem Christians. Nevertheless, such meetings were undoubtedly held, even from the beginning. From the days when the one hundred and twenty brethren were gathered together before Pentecost, the Church was not without some outward expression of its distinctive life.

As Indicated in The Acts. The circumstances of such early meetings of the congregation are, however, obscure. The very considerable numbers of the converts, Acts 2.41, 47; 4.4; 5.14, would perhaps sometimes make it difficult to gather the whole congregation together in one place; if, however, that were done, it would perhaps be usually in some part of the temple area. There seem to have been general meetings—for example, Acts 15.1–29—but it is perhaps not necessary to suppose that they included every individual member of the Jerusalem church.

Certainly, however, no members of that first Christian community neglected the assembling of themselves together. Evidently the sense of brotherhood was strongly developed, and evidently it expressed itself not only in the regular relief of the needy, Acts 6.1, but also in meetings for instruction and worship and prayer, ch. 2.42; 4.23–31. These meetings were only outward indications of a wonderful unity of mind and heart, ch. 4.32. The cause of that unity was the common possession of the Spirit of God.

As might have been expected in a book which is interested chiefly in the outward extension of the kingdom, the book of The Acts gives us little detailed information about the conduct of these earliest Christian meetings. Probably, however, the example of the Jewish synagogue made itself strongly felt. There was no violent break with Judaism; a new spirit was infused into ancient forms. The resemblance between the synagogue service and even the fully developed Christian meetings of today was noted in connection with chapter 4.

As Indicated in the Epistle of James. The Epistle of James perhaps helps somewhat to supply the need of detailed information. That epistle, as was observed in chapter 32, was written by the head of the Jerusalem Church, and probably to Jewish Christians before A.D. 49. Apparently, therefore, we have in James 2.1–6 some welcome information about Christian assemblies, if not in Jerusalem, at least in other Jewish Christian churches. In v. 2, the word 'synagogue' is applied to the meeting which is described, but that word in Greek means simply 'gathering together'—almost the same word is used in Heb. 10.25. The use of the word by James shows simply that at that early time 'synagogue' had not become purely a technical designation of a non-Christian Jewish assembly.

So interpreted, the passage in James indicates—what might indeed have been expected—that the early Christian meetings were not always perfect. A Pharisaical habit of respect of persons and desire for the chief seats had crept even into the Church. If similar faults appear in modern times, we should not despair, but should fight against them in the spirit of James.

CONGREGATIONAL MEETINGS IN THE PAULINE CHURCHES

With regard to the Pauline churches information about the conduct of religious services is far more abundant than it is with regard to the churches of Palestine; for we have here the inestimable assistance of the Pauline epistles.

The Place of Meeting. From The Acts it appears that Paul regularly began his work in any city by preaching in the Jewish synagogue, but that the opposition of the Jews soon made it necessary to find another meeting place. Often, a private house, belonging to one of the converts, served the purpose, Rom. 16.23; I Cor. 16.19; Col. 4.15; Philem. 2. Sometimes there seem to have been a number of such house-churches in the same city; yet common meetings of all the Christians of the city seem also to be presupposed. In Ephesus Paul used for his evangelistic work a building or a room belonging to a certain Tyrannus, who was probably a rhetorician. The erection of buildings especially for Christian use belongs of course to a considerably later time.

The Time of Meeting. The frequency of the meetings does not appear, and may well have varied according to circumstances. There is some indication, however, that the first day of the week, the present Sunday, was especially singled out for religious services, I Cor. 16.2; Acts 20.7. The same day is apparently called 'the Lord's day' in Rev. 1.10.

Temporary Gifts of the Spirit. In the actual conduct of the meetings, some features appear which are not to be observed in the modern Church. A number of the gifts discussed in I Cor. chs. 12 to 14—for example, miracles, speaking with tongues, the interpretation of tongues, and prophecy in the strict sense—have become extinct. The cessation of them need cause no wonder; the apostolic age was a time of beginnings, when the Church was being established by the immediate exercise of the power of God; it is no wonder that at such a time the Spirit manifested himself as he did not in later generations. There is a fundamental difference between the apostolic age and all subsequent periods in the history of the Church.

Nevertheless, all the essential features of our modern church services were present from the earliest time about which we have detailed information. The example of the apostles is here very explicit.

Scripture-reading. In the first place, the Pauline churches certainly practised the reading of the Bible. That would be proved sufficiently by the evident familiarity of the Christians with the Old Testament Scriptures; for in those days such familiarity would undoubtedly be received in large measure by having the Bible read aloud. The example of the synagogue would also have its influence. It must be remembered that some even of the Gentile converts were familiar with the synagogue service before they became Christians. But there is also the explicit testimony of I Thess. 5.27, Col. 4.16. There the reading of Pauline epistles is specifically enjoined. The Apocalypse also was clearly intended to be read aloud, Rev. 1.3; 22.18.

Preaching. In the second place, there was preaching. No doubt this part of the service often took a somewhat different form from that which it assumes today. Prophecy, for example, was a kind of preaching which has been discontinued. The exercise of the gift of 'teaching' perhaps corresponded more closely to the sermons of the present day; certainly an exposition of the Scripture passages read would have been according to the analogy of the Jewish synagogue. At any rate, in some form or other, there was certainly instruction in the Scriptures and in the gospel, and exhortation based upon that instruction.

Prayer. In the third place, there was prayer; directions for public prayer are given at some length in I Tim. ch. 2; and there are indications that prayer was practised also in the meetings of the Corinthian church. See for example, I Cor. 11.4, 5.

Singing. In the fourth place, there was probably singing, though the direct information about this part of the service is slight. See, for example, I Cor. 14.26; Eph. 5.19. Certainly no elaborate argument is necessary in order to exhibit the Scripture warrant for singing in the worship of God. Psalms were sung in Old Testament times to an instrumental accompaniment, and there is no evidence that the customs of the Church were changed in this respect under the new dispensation. Indeed, if singing is an expression of joy, it would seem to be especially in place after the fulfilment of the promises has come.

THE PART OF INDIVIDUALS IN CORINTH AND TODAY

The First Epistle to the Corinthians, in particular, especially in chs. 12 to 14, gives a vivid picture of the congregational meetings of the Corinthian church. Those meetings were manifestly under the control of the Holy Spirit. Although faults had appeared, they were not the faults of coldness and formalism which are so common today. The principles, however, which Paul lays down for the guidance of the Corinthians are of permanent value. They are of value, moreover, not merely to the leaders in the Church, but to every individual Christian. Every Christian, even in the most carefully regulated services of our modern churches, may take a real part in the prayer and in the praise; the usefulness of the service is by no means dependent merely upon minister and choir; that service is truly useful in which the individual members of the congregation are sincerely offering up prayers and praises in their hearts as the Spirit gives them utterance.

Neglect of the Apostolic Example

There is a widespread tendency today to desert the example of the apostolic Church in the matter of congregational meetings. The decline in church attendance and in attendance upon congregational prayer meetings is one of the lamentable signs of the times. For the neglect of public worship, various excuses are offered; but all of them disappear in the light of the apostolic example.

Some people, for example, think they can worship God better as he is revealed in nature; others think that a good book, read at home, will edify them more than the sermon of their own minister.

THE WORSHIP OF GOD IN NATURE

It should be observed, in the first place, that in the vast majority of cases such excuses are the merest pretence. Those who stay away from church in order to take a walk in the country very seldom use their outing in order to worship God. They may pretend to themselves as well as to others that they are worshipping God, but what they are really doing is usually just taking a holiday. God is not just another name for nature; a man can enjoy nature without thinking of God at all. To the truly devout man, of course, the wonders of the earth and sky reveal the God who made them; but the revelation seldom comes to the man who stays away from church. Paul recognized the revelation of God in nature in the first chapter of Romans, but the first chapter of Romans would be of little value without the eighth.

PRIVATE DEVOTIONAL READING INSTEAD OF CHURCH

Similarly, the man who stays away from church in order to read a better sermon at home seldom carries out his plan. What he actually reads when the time comes is usually the Sunday paper or a magazine. Of course, if the choice really had to be made between private devotional reading and attendance upon church, the decision might be doubtful. But as a matter of fact the choice never has to be made; it is always possible to engage both in private devotions and also in public worship. The former can be scattered all through Sunday and even through the week; the latter demands only an hour or two at stated times.

The Need of Fellowship

The Christian life is complex; it has various needs. One of the most important needs is satisfied by the public services of the congregation; it is the need of Christian fellowship. It would be extremely hard for a man to retain any living faith in Christ if he were the only believer in the world. No Christian is so strong that he does not need help from others. Even the apostle Paul felt the need of fellowship with those who were weaker than himself. He longed to be with the Roman Christians, not merely that he might impart unto them some spiritual gift, but also that he with them might be comforted in them, he by their faith and they by his, Rom. 1.11, 12. The wonderful unity of the apostolic Church never could have been maintained without the congregational meetings which the New Testament mentions.

The Motive of Duty

The profit of church attendance may not appear on every occasion. Without doubt it often requires an effort to be in one's accustomed place in the sanctuary; it is often far easier and more comfortable to remain quietly at home. Sermons no doubt are often far from interesting, public prayers may lack fervour, hymns may be out of tune. In the matter of church attendance, as in every other exercise of the Christian life, an appeal must often be made to the sense of duty. The reward appears, however, in the long run. If one attends church only when one feels like it, of course little benefit will be obtained; but attendance from a sense of duty, with which nothing is allowed to interfere, will help to build up old-fashioned, stalwart Christian lives. What began, moreover, by being a duty, becomes gradually a cherished privilege; there is a wonderful efficacy in the family pew.

The Motive of Love

So far, however, we have not even touched upon the highest motive of all. We have defended the regular attendance upon public worship merely as a means of strengthening one's own life. Merely from the point of view of personal profit it is well not to neglect going to church.

BENEFIT TO FELLOW CHRISTIANS

As a matter of fact, however, that is a very one-sided way of considering the question. A man should go to church not merely to receive, but also to give. This principle is clearly brought out in I Cor., chs. 12 to 14. Those gifts of the Spirit are to be given the preference which lead to the edification of the church. Suppose, for the sake of the argument, that a man is convinced of his own independence—is convinced that he can profit more from mere rest or from private devotions than from attending a church service. Even then he has not excused himself. For the question arises: what of his duty to others? Surely it must be admitted at least that there are some persons in the Church who cannot do without public worship; in order to prove that, it is merely necessary to imagine what the Church would be like if all public services were abolished. But the services would surely be very dismal if all of the stronger or more independent Christians should stay away. The duty of church attendance, therefore, cannot be avoided. Even if it were not a need of one's own individual life, it would be a duty to the brethren.

BENEFIT TO THE UNCONVERTED

It is a duty, furthermore, even to those who are unconverted. In I Cor. 14.24, 25, Paul gives a vivid account of the effect made on an unbeliever by attendance upon a church service. Although the particular reference in this passage is to the effect of prophecy as compared with speaking with tongues, evidently the salutary impression is regarded as coming from the presence of the Spirit in the whole congregation. That impression may be made by a modern service. The form of the Spirit's activity differs; but if the public service of the Church be supported with real faithfulness, the unbeliever who comes in will still 'fall down on his face and worship God, declaring that God is among you indeed'. The witness-bearing of the Church by which the gospel shall be spread throughout the whole world, Acts 1.8, is not only individual, but collective, and the collective witnessing is carried on chiefly by means of public services.

TOPICS FOR STUDY

1. What information can be derived from the Epistle of James about the congregational meetings of Palestinian churches?

2. Where were the meetings of Pauline churches held? What evidence is there as to the day of the week on which they were held?

3. Enumerate the parts of the service as they can be learned from the First Epistle to the Corinthians.

4. Describe the gifts of tongues in detail.

5. What is meant by each of the gifts mentioned in I Cor. 12.8–10? How was the unity of the Church preserved in the midst of this variety?

6. What principles does Paul bring to bear upon the regulation of the Corinthian meetings?

7. What are the essential parts of a modern church service? Show how each of these parts was practised in the apostolic age.

45: THE RELIEF OF THE NEEDY

Study material: Acts 2: 43–47; 4: 32–37; 5: 1–11; 6: 1–6; 11: 27–30;
24: 17; I Cor. 16: 1–4; II Cor. chs. 8, 9; 12: 16–18;
Rom. 15: 22–33; I Thess. 4: 9–12; II Thess. 3: 6–16; I Tim. 5: 3–16

The last three chapters have dealt with those practices of the Christian life which serve to keep a man consciously in the presence of God. The duty which will be studied in this chapter also serves the same purpose, though more indirectly. Indeed, every common duty, rightly performed, every good thing that is done as unto God and not unto men, adds to the depths of religious experience.

The Community of Goods in Jerusalem

During the first days in Jerusalem, in the very first burst of enthusiasm, time was found for the exercise of the homely grace of giving. 'And all that believed were together, and had all things common; and they sold their possessions and goods, and parted them to all, according as any man had need.' Acts 2.44, 45.

THE COMMUNITY OF GOODS WAS NOT SOCIALISM

At first sight, as was observed in connection with chapter 9, this community of goods looks almost as though it were a communistic plan; it looks almost as though the early Christians relinquished their private property altogether and lived wholly by means of a common treasury. If such had been the plan, the Jerusalem church would have been like one of the later monastic orders, in which the relinquishment of private property was one of the conditions of membership. A similar rule prevailed in the first century among the Essenes, a curious Jewish sect.

VOLUNTARY CONTRIBUTING

As a matter of fact, however, the Church avoided admirably the dangers of such a plan. The sale of possessions and goods was voluntary. It did not mean that the relinquishment of private property was required of every man who became a Christian.

Ananias and Sapphira were condemned, not for keeping back a part of the price of their land, but solely for pretending to have given all, Acts 5.4.

LIBERAL CONTRIBUTING

Nevertheless, the sale of lands and houses by the wealthier members of the congregation seems to have been quite general; the language used in Acts 4.34, 35 is very strong. Among those who performed this service of love was Barnabas, who served the Church at a later time in still more important ways, vs. 36, 37. Christianity, to these early disciples, was a very serious matter. It involved the dedication of absolutely everything that a man had—money and land and homes, as well as spiritual possessions. The relinquishment of all private property was not demanded by the Church as a formal condition of membership; it was perhaps seldom carried out with absolute thoroughness; but a true Christian must at least be perfectly willing to resort to it if the need arose. The same ideal is valid today. Many Christians suppose that they have done their full duty if they devote a definite part of their income to the service of God. As a matter of fact God demands nothing less than the whole. If he permits a part to be used for the possessor's own comfort—and he usually does—it is a matter not of right, but of grace.

THE UNITY OF THE CHURCH

Evidently Luke regards the voluntary community of goods among the Jerusalem Christians as valuable because it gave expression to the unity of the Church. Unity is very imperfect if it is concerned only with economic conditions, but it is also imperfect if it shrinks from the sacrifice of physical ease. The relief of the needy in the early Church was a plain evidence of sincerity.

THE ADMINISTRATION OF THE GIFTS

At first the administration of the gifts of the Church was carried on by the apostles. Those who sold lands or houses 'brought the prices of the things that were sold, and laid them at the apostles' feet'. Acts 4.34, 35. In time, however, the need arose for a somewhat more elaborate organization; the nature of that organization will be noticed in the next chapter. Here we are concerned rather with the manner in which the gifts were distributed.

To some extent at any rate, the distribution was carried on in a very unpretentious way—simply by the providing of a daily ration, possibly of money, but more probably, perhaps, of food. This daily distribution was for the benefit of the widows, Acts 6.1. At a later time, when the Pastoral Epistles were written, the 'widows' seem to have formed a rather closely defined class—the term seems to have acquired a semi-technical significance. Here, however, the word is probably used in its ordinary sense. Widows would be especially dependent upon the bounty of the Church.

Difficulty, however, had arisen; there seemed to be danger that the distribution of relief, which at first had been a joyful expression of Christian unity, might actually split the Church into two parties. The Greek-speaking Christians thought that their widows were not being so well treated as those who belonged to the native Palestinian, Aramaic-speaking part of the congregation. Fortunately the difficulty was triumphantly surmounted. The apostles simply observed that the distribution of charity demanded more time than they were able to give; special assistants were secured, and all went well.

THE DIGNITY OF THE CHURCH'S BUSINESS

The example may well be heeded. It merely shows that the business affairs of the Church should be conducted on sound business principles. It that was true in the first simple days in Jerusalem, it is even more clearly true in our complex modern life. Moreover, it should be observed that the seven men who were to take charge of the distribution were carefully chosen, and that they were 'full of the Spirit and of wisdom'. Even the worldly side of the Church's work is a holy thing; if we engage in it, even in the humblest capacity, we are performing a service of genuine dignity.

The Contribution of Antioch

The expression of Christian unity which was found in the relief of the needy within the Jerusalem church soon extended itself over a wider area. Acting on the prophecy of Agabus, the church at Antioch sent aid to the distressed brethren at Jerusalem by the hand of Barnabas and Saul, Acts 11.27–30; 12.25. This action was highly significant. There were two great centres of Christian influence; Jerusalem was the centre of Jewish Christianity, Antioch was becoming the centre of a Gentile mission. The generous response of the Christians of Antioch to the need of their Jerusalem brethren placed the two branches of the Church in close union; there was no rivalry between them; they were visibly united in the bonds of Christian love.

The Contribution of the Pauline Churches

The same unifying influence which was exerted by the Antioch collection was continued also by a great collection throughout the Pauline churches. The inception of the matter is apparently to be placed at the time of the Jerusalem Council of Acts 15.1–29; Gal. 2.1–10. At that time the original apostles recognized to the full the apostolic independence of Paul; Paul, they said, had evidently already been chosen by God to be apostle to the Gentiles, as Peter to be apostle to the Jews. They were in full sympathy with the Gentile mission, which had been placed in the hands of Paul. Only, they said, in one respect at least they would like Paul to be also an apostle to the Jews—they begged, namely, that he would remember the poor of the Jerusalem church, Gal. 2.10. Paul undertook the fulfilling of this request with the utmost willingness and zeal. He had already engaged in a similar service by commission of the church at Antioch, Acts 11.30; 12.25, and now he extended the work throughout all his churches. The matter of the collection occupies considerable space in the epistles, I Cor. 16.1–4; II Cor. chs. 8, 9; Rom. 15.22–29, and evidently was regarded by the apostle as of the utmost importance. The exposition will serve to illustrate the apostolic principles of Christian giving.

The Pauline Collection According to First Corinthians

THE BEGINNING IN GALATIA AND IN CORINTH

Writing from Ephesus during his long stay in that city, Acts 19.1 to 20.1, Paul tells the Corinthians that he had already given directions about the collection to the churches of Galatia, I Cor. 16.1; he had probably done so either during the second visit to Galatia, Acts 18.23, or by letter after his arrival at Ephesus. Now he asks the Corinthians—very simply and briefly, and evidently presupposing previous information on the part of his readers—to prosecute the collection during his absence in order that when he should arrive at Corinth everything might be ready.

LAYING IN STORE ON THE FIRST DAY OF THE WEEK

The manner in which the collection was to be managed is exceedingly interesting. 'Upon the first day of the week,' Paul says, 'let each one of you lay by him in store, as he may prosper'. (I Cor. 16.2.) Apparently there was no permanent church treasury for the reception of the gifts, every man was to save his own money at home, very much as private collection boxes may be used today. The laying up of the money, however, was to take place on the first day of the week; we have here probably an early trace of the Christian Sabbath. Perhaps we may conclude that the act of giving was regarded as a part of religious worship. Such a conclusion is in thorough harmony with all that Paul says about the collection. Some people seem to feel that the taking of an offering rather mars the dignity of a church service. In reality it has that effect only if it is executed in the wrong spirit. Christian giving is treated by Paul as a legitimate part of the worship of God.

THE DELEGATES OF THE CORINTHIAN CHURCH

When Paul should arrive at Corinth, he was to receive the collection and either send or take it to Jerusalem by the help of delegates whom the Corinthians themselves should choose. The purpose of choosing these delegates appears more plainly in Second Corinthians.

The Pauline Collection According to Second Corinthians

THE SITUATION

After the writing of the First Epistle to the Corinthians, there had followed a period of serious estrangement between Paul and the Corinthian church. Naturally enough the collection suffered during this period, as did other Christian activities. At the time of Second Corinthians, perhaps about a year after the first letter had been written, Paul was obliged to remind his readers that although they had begun the work the year before, much remained still to be done, II Cor. 8.10; 9.2. Nevertheless, Titus, during his recent visit to Corinth, when the repentance of the church had become manifest, had apparently been able to take the matter again in hand. Such seems to be the most probable interpretation of ch. 8.6; 12.18. If Titus did take up the matter on the very visit when the rebellion against Paul had been only with difficulty quelled, that is a striking indication of the importance which Paul and his associates attributed to the collection. It was not a matter that could wait until some convenient season; it had to be taken in hand vigorously, even perhaps at the risk of misunderstanding and suspicion, the very moment when Paul's relation to the church became again tolerably good.

COURTESY OF PAUL

Paul's treatment of the collection is characterized by admirable delicacy and tact, as is invariably the case when he handles money matters. Instead of berating the Corinthians roundly for their delinquency, as so many modern organizers would have done, he seeks to win them over by worthier methods. He points, indeed, to the example of the Macedonian Christians, in order to fire the zeal of the Corinthians. The poverty of the Macedonian churches had not stood in the way of their liberality; they had given up to their power and indeed beyond their power; they had given, not of compulsion, but willingly, dedicating themselves as well as their goods to the Lord, II Cor. 8.1-5. But the Corinthians are allowed to draw their own conclusion; Paul does not force it upon them. He does not press the matter home brutally; he does not put the Corinthians to shame by expressly pointing out how much more generously the poorer Macedonian Christians had contributed than they. Indeed he gives his readers full credit; he courteously calls their attention to the fact that it was they who had made the beginning, v. 10, and that he had been able to boast of them to the Macedonians, so that their zeal had stirred up their Macedonian brethren, ch. 9.1, 2. He appeals especially to the pride that they ought to feel in the boasting which Paul had ventured upon in their behalf; Paul had boasted to the Macedonians that Achaia had been prepared for a year; how sad an end it would be to such boasting if Macedonians should go to Corinth with Paul and should find that the collection was not ready after all! Paul urges the Corinthians not to leave any part of the work until after his arrival; if they do, they will put both him and themselves to shame, vs. 1-5.

With equal delicacy Paul hints that the achievements of the Corinthians in other directions ought to be supplemented by this grace of giving. The Corinthians, according to the first Epistle, had been very proud of their power of 'utterance' and their 'knowledge'; to these Paul can now add—after the loyalty of the church has finally been established—earnestness and love, II Cor. 8.6-8; but all these excellences will be incomplete unless there is also liberality. The Christian life must express itself in the simpler graces, if the more conspicuous activities are to be of genuine value.

NO UNFAIR BURDENS TO BE BORNE

The delicacy of Paul's treatment of the matter is observed also in II Cor. 8.10–15; he is careful to explain that the Corinthians are not asked to lay unfair burdens upon themselves. There should be an equality among Christians; it is now time for the Corinthians to give rather than to receive, but if circumstances should change they might count on the aid of their brethren. Furthermore, no one should be discouraged if he can give only a little; 'if the readiness is there, it is acceptable according as a man hath, not according as he hath not'.

CHEERFUL GIVING

Paul urges his readers, indeed, to be bountiful. 'He that soweth sparingly shall reap also sparingly; and he that soweth bountifully shall reap also bountifully.' II Cor. 9.6. But this bountifulness was to be secured, not by pressing out the last penny, but by promoting real cheerfulness in giving. 'Let each man do according as he hath purposed in his heart: not grudgingly, or of necessity: for God loveth a cheerful giver.' The Pauline method is wisest in the end. Men can seldom be bullied into liberality; they will give liberally only when giving becomes, not a mere duty, but a joy. Cheerfulness in giving, moreover, possesses a value of its own, quite aside from the amount of the gift; it is a true expression of Christian communion.

THE UNITY OF THE CHURCH

Evidently Paul desired to accomplish by the collection something even more important than the relief of the Jerusalem poor. Many Palestinian Christians—not only extreme Judaizers, but also apparently considerable numbers among the rank and file—had been suspicious of the Gentile mission, Acts 21.20, 21. Such suspicions would be allayed by deeds more effectively than by words; a generous offering for the poor of the Jerusalem church would show that Jews and Gentiles were really united in the bonds of Christian love, II Cor. 9.12–14.

THE GLORY OF GOD

Ultimately, however, the purpose of the collection, as of all other

Christian activities, is to be found, according to Paul, in God. 'For the ministration of this service not only filleth up the measure of the wants of the saints, but aboundeth also through many thanksgivings unto God.' The unity of the Church, inspiring though it is, is desired, not for its own sake, but for the sake of the glory of God. By the simple means of the collection, Paul hopes to present a united Church—united in thanksgiving and in love—as some poor, human return to him who has granted us all the 'unspeakable gift' of salvation through his Son.

SOUND BUSINESS METHODS

The arrangements which Paul made for the administration of the gifts are as instructive in their way as are the lofty principles that he applied. In order to avoid base suspicions, II Cor. 8.20; 12.16–18, he determined that delegates approved by the Corinthians themselves should carry the gifts to Jerusalem, I Cor. 16.3, 4, and secured for the prosecution of the work in Corinth men who had the full endorsement of the churches, II Cor. 8.16–24. The lesson is worth learning. It will not do to be careless about the money matters of the Church; it will not do to say that the Church is above suspicion. Like Paul, 'we take thought for things honourable, not only in the sight of the Lord, but also in the sight of men'. In other words, we must be not only honourable in managing the money affairs of the Church, but also demonstrably honourable. To that end sound business methods should always be used. The accounts of the Church should be audited, not with less care, but if anything with more care, than those of ordinary business enterprises.

The Pauline Collection According to Romans

In the Epistle to the Romans, written from Corinth a little after the time of Second Corinthians, Paul speaks of the collection again, Rom. 15.22–29, 31. He is on the point of going with the gifts to Jerusalem, and asks the Roman Christians to pray that the ministration of the Gentiles may be 'acceptable to the saints'. There is no reason to suppose that such prayers were unanswered; Paul was cordially received by the Jerusalem Christians, Acts 21.17–26; the trouble which caused his arrest came from non-Christian Jews.

The Temporal and the Eternal

In the matter of helping the poor, the Church has never forgotten

345

her duty; and she is coming to a new realization of it today. It is an encouraging sign of the times; it is in accord with the true spirit of apostolic Christianity. It is useless to give a man a sermon when he needs bread; poverty, at its worst, sometimes prevents the gospel even from being heard. One fact, however, should be remembered —material benefits were never valued in the apostolic age for their own sake, they were never regarded as substitutes for spiritual things. That lesson needs to be learned. Social betterment, though important, is insufficient; it must always be supplemented by God's unspeakable gift. 'The things which are seen are temporal; but the things which are not seen are eternal.' II Cor. 4.18.

TOPICS FOR STUDY

1. Why was the relief of the needy in the apostolic Church directed especially to Christians rather than to outsiders? In what respects are conditions different today?

2. Show (1) how the apostolic Church guarded itself against idleness and pauperism, and (2) how it promoted respect for those who were in real need.

3. What did Paul hope to accomplish by the collection for the saints at Jerusalem?

4. Narrate the progress of the collection in detail.

5. Give a full summary of II Cor. chs. 8, 9, pointing out the motives which Paul brought to bear in favour of the collection and the ways and means which he adopted in the execution of his plan (several topics).

46: ORGANIZING FOR SERVICE

Study material: Acts 1: 15–26; 6: 1–6; 11: 27–30; 14: 23; 15: 1–35;
20: 17–38; 21: 17–26; I Thess. 5: 12–22; II Thess. 3: 6–15:
I Cor. 5: 1 to 6: 11; ch. 12; 16: 15, 16; Rom. 12: 3–8; Eph. 4: 11, 12;
Phil. 1: 1, 2; I Peter 5: 1–4; I Tim. 3: 1–13; 5: 17–22; Titus 1: 5–9

The Apostles

The earliest leaders of the Church were unquestionably the apostles. They had received from Jesus a commission to continue his work; they were witnesses of the resurrection. The apostles, therefore, naturally formed the nucleus of the little band of disciples who waited for the Spirit in the upper room, and of the larger community which was quickly formed after Pentecost. In addition to the Eleven, and to Matthias, who was chosen to fill the traitor's place, James the brother of the Lord soon came to occupy a position of leadership. Apparently he was head of the local Jerusalem church, in distinction from the Twelve, whose work was more general.

The Seven

The simple rule of the apostles soon became insufficient; the increasing complexity of the Church's business demanded a division of labour. The apostles remained as before in supreme control; but in order that they might continue to devote themselves to preaching and teaching, seven assistants were chosen to deal with the distribution of relief to the poor. These seven men performed some of the functions of the officers who were afterwards called deacons; whether or not they were actually 'deacons' is uncertain. At any rate, by their appointment the need of a division of labour among the officers of the Church was clearly recognized.

The Elders

EARLIEST MENTION OF THE OFFICE

In Acts 11.30 other officers of the Palestinian church are mentioned in an incidental way. It is simply said that when the church at

Antioch relieved the distress of the Judean Christians the gifts were sent to the 'elders'. The elders are here introduced entirely without explanation; the narrative gives absolutely no information about the time and manner of their appointment or about their duties.

ORIGIN OF THE OFFICE

Nevertheless the origin of the office of 'elder' is by no means altogether obscure; for the office was certainly derived from Judaism. Jewish elders are mentioned frequently in the Gospels and in The Acts; together with chief priests and scribes they had representatives in the Sanhedrin. 'Elders' appear indeed frequently in the Old Testament; their authority seems to have been both local and general.

THE ELDERS IN PALESTINE

The elders appear a second time in connection with the Jerusalem council; at that time they stood alongside the apostles at the head of the church, Acts 15.2, 4, 6, 22, 23. The rank and file of the congregation, however, were present at the deliberations, v. 12, and united in the decision, v. 22. On the occasion of Paul's last visit to Jerusalem, the elders of the church appear again, Acts 21.18. The Epistle of James, which reflects Palestinian conditions before the Jerusalem council, also speaks of 'elders of the church'. James 5.14.

THE ELDERS IN GENTILE CHURCHES

Even before the time of the council, 'elders' were appointed by Paul and Barnabas for the predominantly Gentile churches of southern Galatia, Acts 14.23. The action of Paul and Barnabas in appointing elders was highly significant. The churches of Lycaonia and Phrygia had only recently been rescued from heathenism; their continued existence seemed exceedingly precarious; they could no longer be protected by the presence of the missionaries. Under such circumstances, the elders were appointed to safeguard them against apostasy and error; it was a necessary precaution. What was still more necessary, however, was the watchful care of the great unseen Leader of the Church. Paul and Barnabas commended the churches, not merely to human pastors, but 'to the Lord, on whom they had believed'.

How Were the Elders to be Chosen?

With regard to the government of the apostolic Church a number of interesting questions can never be definitely answered. For example, how were the elders to be chosen?

SOMETIMES APPOINTED BY THE APOSTLES

Such passages as Acts 14.23; Titus 1.5, do not settle the question. According to the former passage, elders were appointed in the churches of southern Galatia by Paul and Barnabas. But it must be remembered that the authority of the apostles was peculiar and temporary. Because the apostles had power to appoint elders it does not follow that any individuals at a later time would possess a similar power. The situation, at the time of the first Christian mission, was peculiar; small bodies of Christians had just been rescued from heathenism; at first they would need a kind of guidance which could afterwards safely be withdrawn. According to Titus 1.5, Titus was to appoint elders in the churches of Crete. But clearly Titus, like Timothy, was merely a special and temporary representative of the apostle Paul; for Titus to appoint elders, under the definite direction of Paul, was no more significant than for Paul to appoint them himself.

THE RIGHT OF CONGREGATIONAL ELECTION

On the whole, it may be confidently maintained that the Presbyterian method of choosing elders—namely the method of election by the whole congregation—is more in accordance with the spirit of apostolic precedent than any other method that has been proposed. Throughout the apostolic Church, the congregation was evidently given a very large place in all departments of the Christian life. The Jerusalem congregation, for example, had a decisive voice in choosing the very first Church officers who are known to have been added to the apostles, Acts 6.2–6. In Thessalonica and in Corinth the whole congregation was active in the matter of church discipline, II Thess. 3.14, 15; I Cor. 5.3–5; II Cor. 2.6. The whole congregation was also invited to choose delegates for carrying the gifts of the Corinthian church to Jerusalem, I Cor. 16.3. These are merely examples. It must be remembered, moreover, that the authority of the congregation in the apostolic age was limited by the authority of the apostles, which was special and temporary; when the apostles should be removed, the congregational functions would be increased. Yet even the apostles were exceedingly careful not to destroy the liberties of the rank and file. Nowhere in the apostolic Church were the ordinary church members treated as though they were without rights and without responsibilities. Indeed, even when the apostles appointed elders, they may have previously ascertained the preferences of the people.

Organization According to the Epistles of Paul

SIMPLICITY AND INFORMALITY

The Pauline Epistles tell us surprisingly little about the organization of the churches, but they show at least that the organization was very simple and informal. In I Thess. 5.12, 13, the Thessalonian Christians are exhorted to esteem those that labour among them and are over them in the Lord. Whether the persons here referred to were 'elders' is not said; apparently their possession of authority was connected with their willingness to labour for the good of the congregation.

FREEDOM OF THE CORINTHIAN CHURCH

In the First Epistle to the Corinthians, particularly, where congregational affairs are treated with unusual fulness, the absence of any stress upon definite church offices is exceedingly striking. Evidently great freedom prevailed; the congregational meetings, in particular, were not regulated by any strong central authority; everything was left to the guidance of the Spirit. Paul does not try to check this freedom by any elaborate rules; he merely demands that the freedom of the individual shall always be subordinated to the edification of the church. The Corinthian Christians are urged to 'be in subjection' unto such persons as the household of Stephanas, and unto 'every one that helpeth in the work and laboureth'. I Cor. 16.15, 16. Here, as in Thessalonica, willingness to serve the church seems to have had an important part in conferring authority. What the exact place of 'governments', ch. 12.28, was in the organization of the church, it would be difficult to say. 'Teachers' appear in the third place in the list of those who possess gifts of the Spirit; apparently, therefore, individuals who had the power of instruction had begun to be singled out from the rest, but it is perhaps unlikely that they formed a very definite class.

'BISHOPS'

In Phil. 1.1 'bishops and deacons' are mentioned, but the term 'bishop' is not to be regarded as the designation of a distinct office. The word here means simply 'overseer'; it is not a technical term.

In Acts 20.28 the elders of the church at Ephesus are said to have been made 'bishops' or 'overseers' in the flock. In Titus 1.5–7, also, elders and bishops are clearly identified. It is perhaps safe to draw the conclusion that the 'bishops' of Phil. 1.1 were merely the elders of the church; the elders are here designated by one of their functions, the function of oversight over the congregation.

THE PASTORAL EPISTLES

In the Pastoral Epistles, more clearly than elsewhere in the New Testament, the 'elders' and 'deacons' appear as incumbents of definite offices; the need of definiteness of organization had become more and more apparent. Careful directions are given to Timothy and to Titus about the qualifications of the officers. Their duties are not described in any detail, but it appears that some of the elders laboured not only as rulers but also as teachers, I Tim. 5.17.

The Example of the Apostolic Church

The name of the 'Presbyterian' Church is derived from the Greek word for 'elder', which occurs frequently in the New Testament. This use of an apostolic term is supported, it may fairly be maintained, by a real faithfulness to the apostolic example. Even a cursory examination will reveal striking points of similarity between the organization which was established by the apostles and that which prevails in the Presbyterian Churches.

In the first place, the 'elders' of any individual congregation in the apostolic age were equal to one another in authority; no one man was exalted as 'bishop' above the rest. There is no apostolic warrant, therefore, for an 'episcopal' form of government. The government of a congregation was vested, not in one person, but in a body of persons, just as is the case in the Presbyterian Church today.

In the second place, there is no evidence whatever that the 'elders' or any other permanent officers were regarded as successors of the apostles, in possession of apostolic authority; there is no New Testament warrant, therefore, for the doctrine of 'apostolic succession', according to which ecclesiastical authority is for ever vested in a self-perpetuating 'clergy'. In the New Testament, the elders appear pretty clearly as representatives of the congregation.

In the third place, the officers of the apostolic Church were not regarded as 'priests'; they were not regarded as mediators between

God and man. The term 'priest' in its highest sense was reserved for Christ; in a broader sense it was applied to every Christian, I Peter 2.5, 9; Rev. 1.6; 5.10; 20.6.

The main outlines of the Presbyterian form of government, therefore, as it is distinguished from all episcopal and sacerdotal usage, are to be found in the apostolic age; the completed system has been derived, by legitimate development, from the apostolic precedent.

Relation of the Congregations to One Another

So far, the organization of the apostolic Church has been considered only in so far as it concerned the individual congregation; a word must now be said about the relation of the congregations to one another.

That relation, in the apostolic age, was undoubtedly very close. The Pauline epistles, in particular, give an impression of active intercourse among the churches. The Thessalonian Christians 'became an ensample to all that believe in Macedonia and in Achaia'; the story of their conversion became known 'in every place'. I Thess. 1.7-10. In the matter of the collection, Macedonia stirred up Achaia, and Achaia Macedonia, II Cor. 8.1-6; 9.1-4. The faith of the Roman Christians was 'proclaimed throughout the whole world'. Rom. 1.8. Judea heard of the missionary labours of Paul, Gal. 1.21-24; fellowship between Jews and Gentiles was maintained by the collection for the Jerusalem saints. Evidently the apostolic Church was animated by a strong sense of unity.

This feeling of unity was maintained especially by the instrumentality of the apostles, who, with their helpers, travelled from one congregation to another, and exerted a unifying authority over all. Certainly there was nothing like a universal Church council; Christian fellowship was maintained in a thoroughly informal way. In order that such fellowship should be permanent, however, there would obviously be an increasing need for some sort of official union among the congregations. When the apostles passed away, their place would have to be taken by representative assemblies; increasing complexity of life brought increasing need of organization. The representative assemblies of the Presbyterian Churches, therefore, meet an obvious need; and both in their free, representative character and in their unifying purpose it may fairly be claimed that they are true to the spirit of the apostolic age.

Principles

The apostolic precedent with regard to organization should always be followed in spirit as well as in form. Three principles, especially, are to be observed in the Church organization of the apostolic age. In the first place, there was considerable freedom in details. No Christian who had gifts of any kind was ordinarily prevented from exercising them. In the second place, there was respect for the constituted authority, whatever it might be. Such respect, moreover, was not blind devotion to a ruling class, but the respect which is ennobled by love. Finally, in Church organization, as in all the affairs of life, what was regarded as really essential was the presence of the Holy Spirit. When Timothy laid his hands upon a new elder, the act signified the bestowal of, or the prayer for, divine favour. This last lesson, especially, needs to be learned today. Without the grace of God, the best of Church organizations is mere machinery without power.

TOPICS FOR STUDY

1. How were the elders chosen in the apostolic Church? How are they chosen in the various modern Churches?

2. Describe the duties of the elders in the apostolic Church and in modern Churches.

3. What does the New Testament say about deacons? What are their duties in modern Churches?

4. What was meant by the laying on of hands in the apostolic Church? Collect the passages where this act is mentioned.

5. Point out the difference between the apostolic Church on the one hand and the Roman Catholic and Protestant Episcopal Churches on the other in the meaning attached to the term 'bishop'.

6. What is the origin and meaning of the term 'clergy'?

7. How were relations between the several congregations maintained in the apostolic age, and how are they maintained today?

8. Describe some of the purposes which are subserved by Church organization.

9. What is Church discipline, and why is it needed?

47: A MISSION FOR THE WORLD

Study material: Matt. 28: 18–20; Acts 1: 8; 8: 1 to 11: 26;
13: 1 to 15: 35; Rom. chs. 9 to 11; Eph. 2: 11 to 3: 21

At the beginning of the apostolic age, the Christian Church would have appeared to a superficial observer to be an insignificant Jewish sect; at the close of the period, it was a world religion. The transformation is one of the most remarkable phenomena of history. The underlying causes of it, and the steps in its production, will form the subject of our study in this chapter.

The Command of Christ

The idea of a mission for the world was no afterthought; it was implanted in the Church at the very beginning, by direct command of Christ. 'Go ye therefore,' said the risen Christ on the mountain in Galilee, 'and make disciples of all the nations.' Matt. 28.19. 'Ye shall receive power,' said Jesus just before his ascension, 'when the Holy Spirit is come upon you: and ye shall be my witnesses both in Jerusalem, and in all Judæa and Samaria, and unto the uttermost part of the earth.' Acts 1.8. These two commands form the very charter of the Church, and the programme of her work.

When was the Gentile Mission to be Begun?

Many steps needed to be taken before the commands could be fulfilled; the fulfilment was not sudden, but progressive. Despite the explicitness of Jesus' words, much was left to the future guidance of the Holy Spirit.

In the first place, there was the question of time. Because the Christian mission was to extend to the uttermost part of the earth, it did not follow that the extension was to take place at any definite time. At first the disciples were fully occupied in Jerusalem; how soon should they begin to widen the circle?

Upon What Conditions were Gentiles to be Received?

There was also, however, a far more important question. The gospel was to be carried to all nations—so much was perfectly clear in the command of Jesus. But upon what conditions was it to be offered? About this question there was room for serious difference of opinion.

MISSIONARY ACTIVITY OF JUDAISM

It must be remembered that the ideal of a mission for the world was not in itself at all new. It had been foreshadowed in magnificent prophecies of the Old Testament; the nations were to resort to Jerusalem, righteousness and peace and the knowledge of Jehovah were to cover the whole earth. The ideal, moreover, was actually being realized to some extent by contemporary Judaism. Judaism in the first century was an active missionary religion; it had not yet sunk into its age-long seclusion. It was carrying on an active propaganda through the synagogues and through missionary literature. Converts were being made in all the great cities of the Greco-Roman world; all the synagogues were frequented by proselytes and 'God-fearers'.

NATIONAL LIMITATIONS OF JUDAISM

Despite this missionary activity, however, Judaism remained a distinctly national religion; every convert who was to share its full privileges must relinquish his old nationality as well as his old religion. Those who refused to take this decisive step were at best converts of the second rank; they formed a fringe about the chosen people, but were not admitted into the inner circle.

THE UNIVERSALISM OF CHRISTIANITY

At first it looked as though Christianity were to adopt a similar policy. The earliest Christians continued to be pious Jews; they probably rejoiced in their descent from Abraham; they attended the temple services and fulfilled all the requirements of the Mosaic law. Of course they regarded this external connection with Israel as insufficient; Jesus was the only Saviour; without him connection with the covenant people would not save from the wrath of God. But because connection with Israel was insufficient, it did not follow that it was unnecessary. Jesus was the Jewish Messiah; must not all his disciples be Jews?

The question was by no means settled by the letter of Jesus' parting command. The gospel was to be preached to the whole world, but would not acceptance of the gospel necessarily involve union with the chosen race? Judaism had already been a missionary religion; perhaps Christianity was merely an enrichment of the Jewish mission—an enrichment due to the presence of the promised King.

Such limitations, under the guidance of the Spirit, were gradually overcome. It came to be seen that faith in Christ is all-sufficient —where faith is found, observance of the Jewish law is no longer necessary. The ceremonies of the law were merely prophetic of the priesthood of Christ—when the reality had come, the shadows were no longer necessary. Christ marked the beginning of a new dispensation; the middle wall of partition was done away; separation of Israel from the world had served merely a temporary purpose; God's time at last had come; the mystery was at last revealed; Jew and Gentile had access in one faith unto the Father. In Christ there cannot be Greek and Jew; Christ is all, and in all.

The Widening Circle

JUDAIC CHRISTIANITY

The steps by which this great truth was revealed to the Church were traced in some detail in the first part of this book. At first the disciples of Jesus appeared as pious Jews; even the Pharisees could have little objection to them. Soon, however, especially through the preaching of Stephen, it became evident that faith in Christ really involved the ultimate transcending of the law and the consequent breaking down of the middle wall of partition between Israel and the world. The recognition of this fact led to the first persecution; but that persecution could not hinder the march of the army of God.

THE BEGINNINGS OF GENTILE CHRISTIANITY

Those who were scattered abroad preached the gospel far more widely than before, and in an ever freer and more plainly radical form. Samaritans accepted the gospel with as manifest results as had been seen in the most orthodox of the Jews; an Ethiopian treasurer was led, by the Old Testament Scriptures and by the word of a true evangelist, to Christ; Peter, under divine guidance, received the Gentile Cornelius and his friends.

THE MISSIONARY LEADER AND THE MISSIONARY CENTRE

These steps took place in close connection with Jerusalem; they prepared for the final acceptance of the Gentile mission by the mother church. Other preparations, however, were no less important. A great leader was provided by the conversion of Paul; a centre of Gentile influence was founded at Antioch through the instrumentality of certain unnamed Jews of Cyprus and Cyrene; a systematic Gentile mission was undertaken by the Antioch church. Finally, at the Jerusalem Council, the principles of Gentile freedom were approved in no uncertain terms by the original apostles; Gentiles were to be received without being required to become Jews; Christianity was declared to be not for any one nation, but for the world.

THE HAND OF GOD

All these manifold preparations revealed the hand of God. God used many instruments, but the result to be attained was one. By many paths, under many leaders, the Christian Church was being led onward, in the execution of its mission, to the uttermost part of the earth.

Many obstacles, it is true, remained to be overcome. Extreme Judaizers had to be refuted; Gentile freedom had to be defended and explained. But the victory was sure; God was fighting for his Church.

THE APOSTOLIC AGE

The first mission in Cyprus and southern Galatia was followed by astonishing conquests in Macedonia and Greece. Philippi, Thessalonica, Corinth, became the seats of flourishing congregations. A third missionary journey established an influential work at Ephesus; all of proconsular Asia heard the gospel message. Finally, the leading missionary, though a prisoner, continued his preaching at Rome. On his release he probably carried out even his bold project of preaching in Spain. The gospel had been extended to the bounds of the known world.

THE CHRISTIAN CENTURIES

The following centuries brought a continuation of the missionary programme. At first ignored or despised, Christianity soon made itself feared and hated; then gradually, by the power of the divine

Spirit, the Roman Empire was conquered by the cross; then, in the wreck of ancient civilization, the barbarian conquerors forsook their ancient gods for the God and Father of Jesus Christ; and the light of the gospel was kept alive through all the darkness of the Middle Ages. At last, in the Reformation of the sixteenth century, the veil was removed from men's eyes, Paul was rediscovered, the gospel burst forth once more with power.

THE PRESENT OPPORTUNITY

Finally, in our own day, another great advance has been made. The missionary movement has at last been undertaken again with a wider scope than ever before. The call has come in no uncertain way; it has come through the awakening of the nations. Artificial barriers have been removed; distance has been annihilated; a highway has been established to the ends of the earth. Truly God has set before us an open door. Shall we pass through with the message of peace?

TOPICS FOR STUDY

1. What was settled by the case of Cornelius? What was left to be settled?

2. What was the importance of the founding of the Church at Antioch?

3. By what means were the original apostles led to approve of the Gentile mission?

4. Who objected to the Gentile mission? Why did they object?

5. Point out the essential difference between the Gentile mission of Judaism and the Gentile mission of Christianity.

6. How did (a) Paul and (b) the author of Hebrews show that Judaism was superseded?

48: THE CHRISTIAN IDEAL OF PERSONAL MORALITY

Study material: Matt. chs. 5 to 7; I Thess. ch. 5; Gal. 5: 13 to 6: 10;
I Cor. 6: 12–20; II Cor. 6: 11 to 7: 1; Rom. chs. 6 to 8, 12 to 15;
Col. 2: 6 to 3: 17; Eph. 4: 17 to 5: 21; 6: 10–20;
I Peter 1: 13 to 2: 12; 3: 13 to 4: 11

Asceticism not the Apostolic Ideal

Standards of personal morality in the Greco-Roman world were exceedingly low. Practices which we regard as disgraceful were then thought to be matters of indifference. The world was sunk in luxury and vice.

At such a time, Christianity came forward with an ideal of purity. In doing so, however, it avoided the excesses of 'asceticism'. The danger was serious; disgust with current vices might well have led to the desire of complete withdrawal from the world. Such a desire was cherished by various sects of that day. The material world was sometimes thought to be evil in itself; by some 'Gnostic' sects of the second century, for example, it was supposed to have been created by an evil being hostile to the good God. A somewhat similar philosophical tendency seems to have been present even in the apostolic age, and it led logically to an ascetic manner of life, which sought to suppress altogether the bodily appetites. 'Handle not, nor taste, nor touch,' Col. 2.21, was the sum and substance of ascetic morality.

The apostles were careful to avoid such an extreme. They pointed out that 'the earth is the Lord's, and the fulness thereof', I Cor. 10.26; that God created meats 'to be received with thanksgiving by them that believe and know the truth' (I Tim. 4.3); that 'every creature of God is good, and nothing is to be rejected, if it be received with thanksgiving: for it is sanctified through the word of God and prayer'. (vs. 4, 5.)

The Ideal of Consecration

How, then, was purity maintained in the apostolic Church? The answer is clear. Purity was maintained, not by avoidance of the good things that God has given, but by consecration of them to his

N

359

service. 'I beseech you therefore, brethren, by the mercies of God, to present your bodies a living sacrifice, holy, acceptable to God, which is your spiritual service.' Rom. 12.1.

REDEMPTION AND CONSECRATION

The consecration described in Rom. 12.1 follows logically from the Christian salvation. The Christian does not belong to himself; he has been 'bought with a price'. I Cor. 6.20; 7.23. 'Ye were redeemed,' says Peter, 'not with corruptible things, with silver or gold, from your vain manner of life handed down from your fathers; but with precious blood, as of a lamb without blemish and without spot, even the blood of Christ.' I Peter 1.18, 19. What God has purchased for himself by so precious a sacrifice is holy; the bodies of Christian people are temples of the Holy Spirit, I Cor. 6.19, and members of Christ, v. 15. There can be no higher motive for holy living. If our bodies were our own, we might use them as we please, for our own selfish enjoyment; but as it is, they belong to God; to dishonour them is to dishonour him. 'Let not sin therefore reign in your mortal body, that ye should obey the lusts thereof: neither present your members unto sin as instruments of unrighteousness; but present yourselves unto God, as alive from the dead, and your members as instruments of righteousness unto God.' Rom. 6.12, 13.

CONSECRATION AND SERVICE

Consecration to God means also devotion to the service of one's fellow men. We are sometimes accustomed to distinguish our duty to ourselves or to God sharply from our duty to our fellow men; we are accustomed to condone self-indulgence if it is coupled with benevolence. As a matter of fact, all self-indulgence is really selfish; our powers were not given us to be wasted. There is so much dreadful misery in the world, so much need for honest service. If, in the face of human need, a man wastes his strength in destructive indulgence of passions and appetites, he is guilty of the most sordid selfishness. Idleness is the handmaid of vice; a great task requires purity and strength. In the Christian, idleness is without excuse; in fighting Christ's battle a man is delivered from an aimless life; every blow that he strikes has value, not only for time, but also for eternity.

The Realization of the Ideal

The apostolic Church, then, presented as the motive to a holy life the thought of the holiness of him to whom we belong and in whose service we stand. It did not present this motive, however, as in itself sufficient; on the contrary it recognized the hopeless insufficiency of any motive whatever. The apostles proclaimed not merely a new ideal, but a new power. How was the consecrated life to be achieved? That was the great question; the answer to that question was the really characteristic feature of apostolic teaching.

THE POWER OF SIN

The insufficiency of mere motives is due to the weakness of sinful humanity. That weakness can be ignored only by a very superficial philosophy; it was certainly not ignored by the apostolic Church. Sin, according to Paul, is not a mere succession of wrong actions; it is not true that a man is able every time to choose either good or evil; he is able to do good if he chooses, but he does not choose; the will of man has become enslaved to a dreadful Satanic power.

The apostolic teaching is here strikingly confirmed by everyday experience. The thraldom of evil habit is a strange, unreasonable thing; it simply ought not to be; but it is a fact all the same, and until it is clearly faced there is little hope of any real moral improvement. The apostles faced the dreadful fact of sin with an openness and frankness which is startling to some easy-going people today. Sin, according to Paul, is a mighty power, in the presence of which man is helpless. 'It is no more I that do it, but sin which dwelleth in me.' Rom. 7.17. At first sight, such a doctrine might seem to take away a man's responsibility; if it is no more I that do it, how can I still feel guilt? As a matter of fact, however, the effect is exactly the opposite. The men who have actually felt most deeply the guilt of sin have been just the men who regarded it as a deadly power, lying far beneath the individual acts. The reason is plain. If every action stands by itself, then a wrong choice at any particular time is, comparatively speaking, a trifling thing; it may easily be rectified next time. But if sin is a mighty Satanic power, then acts of sin, perhaps comparatively trifling in themselves, show that we are under the dominion of such a power, that we are on the way to an abyss of evil that has no bottom.

THE NEW BIRTH

How shall we get free from this power of sin? That is the great
question, and it was gloriously answered in the apostolic Church.
We get rid of the power of sin, according to the apostles, by nothing
less than a new birth, the beginning of a new life. That new life
does not come by human effort, but by a wonderful act of the
divine Spirit. It is joined, however, with the simple act of faith,
which the Spirit works in our hearts. It is possible to tell whether
you have the new life; you are sure to have it if you have believed
sincerely in Christ and if the fruits of the Spirit are becoming
manifest in your conduct.

THE CHRISTIANS' BATTLE

In this new and blessed life, sin has no rightful place. Remnants of
it remain, but they should be rapidly diminishing remnants. A
Christian life that permits a man just to knock along in very much
the old way, making a poor, ineffectual battle against evil habit, is
no true Christian life at all. Many nominal Christians are far too
easily satisfied with the progress of their inner lives; their satisfaction will be sadly disturbed if they examine the precept and example
of the apostolic Church. The apostles took Christianity very
seriously. No words were too strong to express their view of the
complete break that takes place in a man's life when he becomes a
Christian. The Christian has died to sin; he has broken away, not
partially, but completely, not temporarily, but for ever, from his
old habits, Rom. ch. 6. 'They that are of Christ Jesus have crucified
the flesh with the passions and the lusts thereof.' Gal. 5.24. 'I have
been crucified with Christ; and it is no longer I that live, but Christ
liveth in me.' Gal. 2.20.

Christianity is not the gentle, easy-going thing that is sometimes
mistaken for it; it is not a mere sentimental means of comfort in
the troubles of life. It involves heroic self-denial; it means the uncompromising relinquishment of sin. There is no greater mistake
than that of supposing that the sacrifice of Christ enables a man to
go quietly along, tolerating what the world calls pardonable faults
in his life. On the contrary, there are no such things as pardonable
faults; there are faults even in the Christian, but, if he is a true
Christian, he is fighting, not only a battle against them, but a
winning battle. You must take your choice; you must choose either
sin, or Christ; you cannot have both. If you are a Christian the

results must very soon appear. They must appear in those hard things that lie nearest home—in personal honesty, in purity of thought as well as of life, in uncompromising self-control.

The Christian life, then, is a battle. But it is a battle in which we have a great Captain and a great Helper. It may seem hard to put sin away, but if we yield ourselves to the blessed power of the Holy Spirit, we shall surely win. 'The flesh lusteth against the Spirit, and the Spirit against the flesh'—but the Spirit, thank God, is stronger!

Contrasts

The sharp difference between the Christian life and the life of the world was set forth in the apostolic teaching by means of various contrasts.

DEATH AND LIFE

In the first place, there was the contrast between death and life. The man of the world, according to the apostles, is not merely ill; he is morally and spiritually dead, Col. 2.13; Eph. 2.1, 5. There is no hope for him in his old existence; that existence is merely a death in life. But God is One who can raise the dead; and as he raised Jesus from the tomb on the third day, so he raises those who belong to Jesus from the deadness of their sins; he implants in them a new life in which they can bring forth fruits unto God. A moral miracle, according to the New Testament, stands at the beginning of Christian experience. That miracle was called by Jesus himself, as well as by the apostles, a new birth or 'regeneration'. It is no work of man; only God can raise the dead. See John 1.13; 3.1–21; I John 2.29; I Peter 1.3, 23.

DARKNESS AND LIGHT

The contrast between darkness and light, also, was common to the teaching of Jesus and that of his apostles. It appears particularly in the Gospel of John, but there are also clear traces of it in the Synoptists, Matt. 5.14–16; the righteous are 'the sons of the light'. Luke 16.8. In the writings of the apostles the contrast appears in many forms. 'Ye are all sons of light,' said Paul, 'and sons of the day: we are not of the night, nor of darkness; so then let us not sleep, as do the rest, but let us watch and be sober.' I Thess. 5.5, 6. 'Ye were once darkness, but are now light in the Lord: walk as children of light.' Eph. 5.8. God has called us 'out of darkness into his marvellous light'. I Peter 2.9. The contrast serves admirably to represent the honesty and openness and cleanness of the true Christian life.

FLESH AND SPIRIT

An even more important contrast is the contrast of flesh and Spirit, which is expounded especially by Paul. 'Flesh' in this connection means something more than the bodily side of human nature; it means human nature as a whole, so far as it is not subjected to God. 'Spirit' also means something more than might be supposed on a superficial examination. It does not mean the spiritual, as distinguished from the material, side of human nature; but the Holy Spirit, the Spirit of God. The warfare, therefore, between the flesh and the Spirit, which is mentioned so often in the Pauline epistles, is a warfare between sin and God.

The flesh, according to Paul, is a mighty power, which is too strong for the human will. It is impossible for the natural man to keep the law of God. 'I know,' says Paul, 'that in me, that is, in my flesh, dwelleth no good thing: for to will is present with me, but to do that which is good is not. . . . I find then the law, that, to me who would do good, evil is present. For I delight in the law of God after the inward man: but I see a different law in my members, warring against the law of my mind, and bringing me into captivity under the law of sin which is in my members.' Rom. 7.18, 21–23. In this recognition of the power of sin in human life, Paul has laid his finger upon one of the deepest facts in human experience.

The way of escape, however, has been provided; sin has been conquered in two aspects. It has been conquered, in the first place, in its guilt. Without that conquest, everything else would be useless. The dreadful subjection to the power of sin, which becomes so abundantly plain in evil habit, was itself a punishment for sin; before the effect can be destroyed, the guilt which caused it must be removed. It has been removed by the sacrifice of Christ. Christ has died for us, the Just for the unjust; through his death we have a fresh start, in the favour of God, with the guilty past wiped out.

Sin has been conquered, in the second place, in its power. Together with the very implanting of faith in our hearts, the Holy Spirit has given us a new life, a new power, by which we can perform the works of God. A mighty warfare, indeed, is yet before us; but it is fought with the Spirit's help, and by the Spirit it will finally be won.

THE OLD MAN AND THE NEW

As the contrast between the flesh and the Spirit was concerned with the causes of the Christian's escape from sin, so the contrast now to be considered is concerned with the effects of that escape. The Christian, according to Paul, has become a new man in Christ; the old man has been destroyed. The Gentiles, he says, are darkened in their understanding, and alienated from God, Eph. 4.17–19. 'But ye did not so learn Christ; if so be that ye heard him, and were taught in him, even as truth is in Jesus: that ye put away, as concerning your former manner of life, the old man, that waxeth corrupt after the lusts of deceit; and that ye be renewed in the spirit of your mind, and put on the new man, that after God hath been created in righteousness and holiness of truth.' Vs. 20–24; compare Col. 3.5–11. This putting on of the new man is included in what Paul elsewhere calls putting on Christ, Gal. 3.27; Rom. 13.14. The true Christian has clothed himself with Christ; the lineaments of the old sinful nature have been transformed into the blessed features of the Master; look upon the Christian, and what you see is Christ! This change has been wrought by Christ himself; 'it is no longer I that live,' says Paul, 'but Christ liveth in me'; Christ finds expression in the life of the Christian. It is noteworthy, however, that the 'putting on' of Christ, which in Gal. 3.27 is represented as an accomplished fact, is in Rom. 13.14 inculcated as a duty. It has been accomplished already in principle—in his sacrificial death, Christ has already taken our place in the sight of God—but the practical realization of it in conduct is the lifelong task which every earnest disciple, aided by the Holy Spirit, must prosecute with might and main.

TOPICS FOR STUDY

1. Collect and summarize the teaching of the apostles with regard to (a) honesty, (b) purity and self-control, (c) bravery (three topics).

2. What are some of the motives which the apostles applied in favour of holy living? Show how these motives are superior to those suggested by worldly considerations.

3. Describe, in supplement to the chapter, the New Testament teaching about the way to conquer evil habit. What is the relation between 'doctrine' and practice?

49: CHRISTIANITY AND HUMAN RELATIONSHIPS

Study material: Luke 9: 57–62; 14: 25, 26; Matt. 5: 31, 32;
15: 1–9; 22: 15–22; James ch. 2; II Thess. 3: 6–16; I Cor. 7: 8–24;
Rom. 13: 1–7; Col. 3: 18 to 4: 1; The Epistle to Philemon;
Eph. 5: 22 to 6: 9; I Tim. 6: 9, 10; I Peter 2: 11 to 3: 12

The Ideal of Consecration

The apostolic Church offered men, not a mere improvement of
conditions in this world, but an escape from the world into a
heavenly kingdom. That escape was to be consummated when
Christ should come again, at the final establishment of the kingdom
in power; but in principle it was accomplished already. Though
outwardly remaining citizens of Jerusalem, or Antioch, or Tarsus,
or Corinth, the early Christians belonged already, in principle and
in spirit, to the new age, in which God's will is done.

This 'other-worldliness' of the apostolic Church might have led
to a contemptuous attitude toward earthly institutions. If the
citizenship of the Christian is in heaven, should he not avoid en-
tangling alliances with the things of this world? Such reasoning
was very influential in the later history of the Church; it led to
monasticism, to the celibacy of the clergy, and to a general discrediting of the ordinary relationships of life. In the apostolic age,
however, the danger was avoided. The secret of its avoidance was
consecration. The various relationships between man and man are
not ends in themselves; if regarded as of independent value they
become stumblingblocks. But when devoted to the service of God
they bring incalculable enrichment. Indeed they give to the
Christian man his opportunity of service. The Christian, therefore,
should not withdraw from the world into a sort of inward aloof-
ness; he should cultivate a real warmth of affection toward his
fellow men; he should enter with enthusiasm into the various
departments of human endeavour; but he should always consecrate
these things to the service of God. By so doing he will by no means
lose the enjoyment of earthly achievements or earthly blessings;
God will never spoil his own gifts; dedication of human powers to
God will not destroy, but only heighten them.

The Family

Undoubtedly the most fundamental of the human relationships which are to be used in the service of God is the bond that unites members of the same family. In the apostolic Church, certainly, the family was given the foremost place; it seems to have been regarded as the significant unit in the membership of the Church. See, for example, Acts 16.31.

THE TEACHING OF JESUS

Jesus himself taught that the relation between husband and wife rests ultimately upon no mere human law, but upon an ordinance of God, Matt. 19.3–6. There can be no higher warrant. Such a bond is inviolable and sacred, and in it the whole of family life is involved.

THE TEACHING OF THE APOSTLES

In the apostolic writings the teaching of Jesus about the family is extended; there are several passages where the duties of husbands and wives and parents and children and servants are expressly set forth: Col. 3.18 to 4.1; Eph. 5.22 to 6.9; I Peter 2.18 to 3.7. In I Tim. 3.4, 5, 11, also, the ideal of a well-ordered household is insisted upon. According to these passages, the duties of the different members of a household are various. Parents, for example, must rule, and children must obey. But all of the duties may be summed up in the one great duty of love. Love to God does not destroy the simple love of man toward man; where love is of the true Christian sort, there family life will be a blessing; and without love all else is useless. Christian love, fortunately, is not a mere matter of inclination; it is susceptible of cultivation; and by the help of the Holy Spirit, through prayer and patient effort, it may come even to those who have known it not.

Society

A second class of human relationships which was modified and ennobled by apostolic teaching was exceedingly complex—it may be summed up under the general term, 'society'. This term, used in a broad sense, includes such relationships as those between master and servant, employer and employee, buyer and seller, rich and poor.

APOSTOLIC CHRISTIANITY NOT A SOCIAL REFORM MOVEMENT

Social conditions in the apostolic age were exceedingly bad. There were favoured classes, living in vicious luxury, and great hordes of the poor and the down-trodden. There was especially the great institution of slavery, impairing the dignity of free labour, permeating all nations and all peoples, and producing a thousand miseries. Under such conditions the Church might have been expected to come forward with a social programme. Certainly there were great evils to be righted; many institutions of the ancient world were out of accord with the fundamental principles of the gospel. As a matter of fact, however, Christianity seemed to exhibit a remarkable patience in its attitude toward the evil institutions of the time. It made no loud demands for social equality; it indulged in no denunciations of slavery; it apparently assumed the continuance of the distinction between rich and poor.

THE EARLY CHRISTIANS HAD NO IMMEDIATE POWER OVER EXISTING INSTITUTIONS

The explanation is to be found partly, no doubt, in the circumstances of the early Christians. 'Not many wise after the flesh, not many mighty, not many noble' were called. Those humble men and women were excused from instituting a social revolution simply because they did not have the power. The acquiescence by the apostolic Church, therefore, in certain imperfect social institutions does not necessarily excuse similar acquiescence today. The Church has now, in the providence of God, become rich and powerful; and with additional power comes additional responsibility.

THE APOSTOLIC CHURCH HAD SOMETHING BETTER THAN SOCIAL REFORM

There is, however, a far deeper reason for the moderate attitude which the apostolic Church assumed toward existing institutions. The fundamental fact is that the Church refrained from a definite programme of social reform simply because she had something far better; she postponed the improvement of earthly conditions in order to offer eternal life. The improvement of conditions upon this earth is in the providence of God a long and painful process; while it was proceeding souls would have been lost; the first duty of the Church was obviously to offer to everyone, man or woman, rich or poor, bond or free, the inestimable gift of salvation. If a man has communion with the living God, all else can wait.

CHRISTIANITY INDEPENDENT OF EARTHLY CONDITIONS

Accordingly, the apostolic Church promised men not silver and gold, the improvement of earthly conditions, but an abundant entrance into heaven. It is this spiritual and heavenly character of Christianity which makes the Christian offer universal. A gospel which promises merely an improvement of the world is dependent upon worldly conditions. If Christianity is merely a happy and successful life in this world, then a man may be deprived of it by disease, or ill fortune, or unjust suspicion, or death. As a matter of fact, Christianity is a life in communion with God, and that can be maintained in poverty and in plenty, in slavery and in freedom, in life and in death. The Christian offer is extended to everyone, and every earthly condition, no matter how degrading or how painful, can be used in the service of God.

The State

A third institution, or group of institutions, with which the apostolic Church came into contact, was the state. Here also there was room for much bitterness. The government of the Roman world had its beneficent features, but we should have thought it, as a whole, a crushing despotism. The true interests of those who were governed often had the smallest possible place in the thoughts of the rulers; the Christians especially were often made to feel the oppressive hand of the civil magistrate. Yet even under such conditions, even when constantly liable to the most unjust persecutions, Paul could write that 'the powers that be are ordained of God', and that 'rulers are not a terror to the good work, but to the evil', and that the Christian should 'be in subjection, not only because of the wrath, but also for conscience sake', Rom. 13.1–7, and that supplications should be made 'for kings and all that are in high place', I Tim. 2.1, 2; and Peter could exhort his readers to 'be subject to every ordinance of man for the Lord's sake', and to 'honour the king'. I Peter 2.13–17. No matter how imperfect the special expression of legal authority might be at any particular time, the principle of it was to be recognized to the full. Christianity was not to be confused with lawlessness.

Christianity and Social Service

The consecration of human relationships to God does not involve any depreciation of what is known today as 'social service'. On the contrary it gives to social service its necessary basis and motive power. Only when God is remembered is there an eternal outlook in the betterment of human lives; the improvement of social conditions, which gives the souls of men a fair opportunity instead of keeping them stunted and balked by poverty and disease, is seen by him who believes in a future life and a final judgment and heaven and hell, to have value not only for time, but also for eternity, not only for man, but also for the infinite God.

SOCIETY OR THE INDIVIDUAL?

It is sometimes regarded as a reproach that old-fashioned, evangelical Christianity makes its first appeal to the individual. The success of certain evangelists has occasioned considerable surprise in some quarters. Everyone knows, it is said, that the 'social gospel' is the really effective modern agency; yet some evangelists with only the very crudest possible social programme are accomplishing important and beneficent results! The lesson may well be learned, and it should never be forgotten. Despite the importance of social reforms, the first purpose of true Christian evangelism is to bring the individual man clearly and consciously into the presence of his God. Without that, all else is of but temporary value; the human race is composed of individual souls; the best of social edifices will crumble if all the materials are faulty.

EVERY MAN SHOULD FIRST CORRECT HIS OWN FAULTS

The true attitude of the Christian toward social institutions can be learned clearly from the example of the apostolic Church. The first lesson that the early Christians learned when they faced the ordinary duties of life was to make the best of the institutions that were already existing. There was nothing directly revolutionary about the apostolic teaching. Sharp rebuke, indeed, was directed against the covetousness of the rich. But the significant fact is that such denunciations of wealthy men were addressed to the wealthy men themselves and not to the poor. In the apostolic Church, every man was made to know his own faults, not the faults of other people. The rich were rebuked for their covetousness and selfishness; but the poor were commanded, with just as much vehemence, to labour for their own support. 'If any will not work,' said Paul, 'neither let him eat.' II Thess. 3.10. In short, apostolic Christianity sought to remove the evils of an unequal distribution of wealth, not by a violent uprising of the poor against the rich, but by changing the hearts of the rich men themselves. Modern reform movements are often very different; but it cannot be said that the apostolic method is altogether antiquated.

THE ENNOBLING OF EXISTING INSTITUTIONS

Certainly the apostolic method has been extraordinarily successful; it has accomplished far more than could have been accomplished by a violent reform movement. A good example is afforded by the institution of slavery. Here, if anywhere, we might seem to have an institution which was contrary to the gospel. Yet Paul sent back a runaway slave to his master, and evidently without the slightest hesitation or compunction. That action was a consistent carrying out of the principle that a Christian man, instead of seeking an immediate change in his social position, was first of all to learn to make the best of whatever position was his already. 'Let each man abide in that calling wherein he was called. Wast thou called being a bondservant? care not for it: nay, even if thou canst become free, use it rather. For he that was called in the Lord being a bondservant, is the Lord's freedman: likewise he that was called being free, is Christ's bondservant. Ye were bought with a price; become not bondservants of men. Brethren, let each man, wherein he was called, therein abide with God.' I Cor. 7.20–24. The freedom of the Christian, in other words, is entirely independent of freedom in this world; a slave can be just as free in the higher, spiritual sense as his earthly master. In this way the position of the slave was ennobled; evidently the relation of Onesimus to Philemon was expected to afford both slave and master genuine opportunity for the development of Christian character and for the performance of Christian service.

THE SUBSTITUTION OF GOOD INSTITUTIONS FOR BAD

In the long run, however, such conceptions were bound to exert a pervasive influence even upon earthly institutions. If Philemon really adopted the Christian attitude toward one who was now 'more than a servant, a brother beloved' in Christ, then in the course of time he would naturally desire to make even the outward relationship conform more perfectly to the inward spiritual fact.

371

The final result would naturally be emancipation; and such was the actual process in the history of the Church. Slavery, moreover, is only an example; a host of other imperfect social institutions have similarly been modified or removed. What a world of progress, for example, is contained in Gal. 3.28: 'There can be neither Jew nor Greek, there can be neither bond nor free, there can be no male and female; for ye are all one man in Christ Jesus.' Not battles and revolutions, the taking of cities and the pulling down of empires, are the really great events of history, but rather the enunciation of great principles such as this. 'Ye are all one man in Christ Jesus'—these words with others like them have moved armies like puppets, and will finally transform the face of the world.

TOPICS FOR STUDY

1. Collect and summarize the teaching of the apostles with regard to (a) the family, (b) the state, (c) wealth and poverty (three topics).

2. Describe the social and economic condition (a) of the early churches of Palestine, (b) of the early Gentile churches.

3. Indicate points of resemblance and points of difference between the social responsibilities of the Church today on the one side, and those of the apostolic Church on the other.

4. Mention some of the social reforms which have been accomplished under the influence of Christianity. Contrast the social ideals of the Greco-Roman world with those of the apostolic Church.

5. What is the proper relation between 'social service' and personal evangelism?

50 : THE CHRISTIAN USE OF THE INTELLECT

Study material: Luke 1 : 1–4; Acts 2 : 14–40; 13 : 15–41; 15 : 1–29;
17 : 16–34; 18 : 24–28; The Epistle to the Galatians;
I Cor. 1 : 18 to 3 : 23; ch. 15; Rom. chs. 1 to 8

The Facts about Jesus

'THE APOSTLES' TEACHING'

The early Jerusalem church, at the very beginning of its life, is
declared to have 'continued steadfastly in the apostles' teaching'.
Acts 2.42. What that teaching was cannot be determined in detail;
certainly, however, it included an account of the words and deeds
of Jesus; the Synoptic Gospels beyond doubt grew immediately
out of the primitive teaching which was carried on by the eyewitnesses in Jerusalem. From the very beginning, then, the Church
was engaged, not only in prayer and worship and service, but also
in study. Evidently God had use for the intellect as well as for the
feelings and the will.

USEFULNESS OF THE TEACHING

The usefulness of studying the life of Jesus is at once apparent.
The characteristic thing about the Christians in Jerusalem, the
feature that separated them from the surrounding Judaism, was
their acceptance of Jesus as Lord and Saviour. But how could they
accept and worship him whom they did not know; and how could
they know him except by listening to accounts of what he had said
and done? Christian knowledge, it is true, was no mere collection
of bits of information; it was knowledge, not merely of isolated
facts, but of a Person. But knowledge of a person is inseparably
connected with knowledge of the facts about him; the way we come
to know one of our friends is by observing his acts and listening to
his words. Such knowledge does not come all at once; real, intimate, personal knowledge of the character of a man comes only
after years of observation. The case is not altogether different in
regard to the knowledge which the early Church had of Jesus. He

revealed himself, indeed, through his Spirit; but in enlarging and deepening the knowledge of him, the Spirit made use of an ever fuller acquaintance with the facts of his earthly life.

THE STUDY OF THE GOSPELS

In this respect the example of the early Church is particularly needed today. Many Christian people seem to have the notion that communion with the living Christ is somehow entirely independent of ordinary knowledge of the earthly Jesus. There could scarcely be a greater mistake. The teaching of the apostles in the Jerusalem church about the words and deeds of Jesus served a very definite purpose; and the same purpose is served today by the four Gospels. In order to live in close communion with Christ, one must know what sort of person Christ is, and the way to know what sort of person he is, is to study the record of his earthly life. God might have chosen other methods for us; but as a matter of fact he has chosen this method; even the Holy Spirit does not teach us independently of the Gospel narrative. The Church can never, therefore, dispense with old-fashioned, patient study. Such study is quite insufficient if it is not applied in daily life; but on the other hand the best of application is useless if there is nothing to apply.

The Explanation of the Facts

A CHRISTIAN THEOLOGY

Knowledge of the events in Jesus' earthly ministry was not all that was imparted in the early teaching of the apostles. There was also, no doubt, explanation of the blessed acts of God by which salvation had been wrought. Such explanation occupies a very large place in the New Testament; it appears especially in the epistles of Paul. In the greatest and most inspiring chapters of his epistles Paul explains why the death of Christ was necessary, what his death means, how he rose from the dead. These things, added to what had already been taught in the Old Testament, form a Christian 'theology'.

THE VALUE OF THEOLOGY

Many Christians today have a horror of theology; they suppose it must necessarily be a cold and lifeless thing. As a matter of fact, theology is merely thinking about God. Every Christian must think about God; every Christian to some degree must be a theologian.

The only question is whether he is to be a bad theologian or a good theologian. If he ·contents himself with his own preconceived notions, or gives free scope to his own natural feelings, he will be a bad theologian; he will soon find himself cherishing a miserable, imperfect, unworthy conception of God which makes God a mere creature of man's fancy. If, on the other hand, he makes himself acquainted, through patient study, first with the teaching of the Bible about God, then with the mighty acts of God that the Bible records, then with the Bible explanation of these acts, he will soon be in possession of a 'theology' which will give backbone to his whole religious life. There need be nothing technical about such a theology; it may not even be called 'theology' at all; it may be expressed in language that a child can understand; but whatever it is called and however it is expressed, it is absolutely necessary for a genuine Christianity. Christianity is based, not upon the shifting sands of human feeling, but upon solid facts; and the apprehension and understanding of facts inevitably requires the use of the intellect.

THEORY AND PRACTICE

Intellectual effort is indeed quite insufficient to make a man a Christian. The New Testament contains emphatic denunciations of a mere intellectual conviction that has no effect upon life. Of such a bare theoretical belief James declared that 'the demons also believe, and shudder'. James 2.19. But because intellectual apprehension is insufficient, it does not follow that it is unnecessary. The very best knowledge of Jesus will not help you unless you accept him as Saviour; but on the other hand it is hard to see how you can accept him as Saviour unless you know something about him.

The Refutation of Error

THE EXAMPLE OF PAUL

If the apostolic use of the intellect was concerned with the establishment of the truth, it was also concerned with the refutation of error. 'If any man,' said Paul, 'preacheth unto you any gospel other than that which ye received, let him be anathema,' Gal. 1.9, and after he had used that uncompromising language he proceeded to make it good, not merely by denunciation, but by painstaking argument. In the Epistle to the Galatians Paul was defending the gospel of free grace over against the Judaizers' exaltation of human merit. Many people nowadays would have dismissed the whole controversy as a mere theological subtlety; but Paul thought differently. He saw clearly that religion is based upon facts, and that facts must be established by the reason which God has given us. Accordingly, it is in a thoroughly reasonable and earnest way that Paul defends the doctrine of justification by faith.

THE NEED OF THE EXAMPLE

Emulation of Paul's example is always necessary. False ideas about the gospel are the greatest obstacles to a healthy Christian life; bad theology and good religion will not live together permanently in peace. If you want to live right, you must also take care to think right. Thinking right involves intellectual effort, which is distasteful to many people in this practical age; but the end to be attained is worth the trouble. Intellectual conquests are just as necessary for the progress of the gospel as are conquests in the external world; every thought, as well as every deed, must be brought 'into captivity to the obedience of Christ'. II Cor. 10.5.

The Wisdom of the World and the Wisdom of God

GOD SPEAKS TO BE UNDERSTOOD

Some Christians are inclined to misinterpret I Cor. 1.18–30, where the wisdom of the world is contrasted with the 'foolishness' of the Christian message; they draw from this passage the inference that all exercise of the human intellect in matters of religion is to be rejected. Such an inference is altogether unwarranted; indeed it is really a reversal of Paul's meaning. Paul is discrediting that use of the intellect which seeks to arrive at the way of salvation by human ingenuity; the modern Christians of whom we are speaking would reject that use of the intellect which seeks to understand what God has said. When God speaks, we must surely make our very best effort to understand; in that effort we must surely apply our minds as well as our hearts. God has given us our reason; surely we must use it in receiving what he has to say.

THE SPIRIT OF GOD REVEALS THE THINGS OF GOD

Indeed, Paul himself, immediately after the passage which has just been mentioned, goes on to speak of a wisdom of God that is to be received by full-grown Christian men; and of that wisdom he gives wonderful examples in the great theological passages of his epistles.

That wisdom, it is true, cannot be received by the intellect alone, it requires also a pure heart, and above all it requires the Spirit of God, I Cor. 2.11, 14–16.

THE SPIRIT OF GOD AND THE FACULTIES OF MAN

The Spirit of God does not destroy, but rather quickens and ennobles, the endowments of man. One of the most important of such endowments is the mind. There is such a thing, therefore, as a Christian use of the intellect, and it is of absolutely fundamental importance. Ignorant people are indeed sometimes used of God for the highest service, but not people who are wilfully ignorant. God does not require brilliant gifts, but he does require the diligent use of whatever gifts we have.

The Problem of Christianity and Culture

If physical health and strength and the companionship of human friends may be made useful in the Christian life, surely the same thing is true of intellectual gifts. The most powerful thing that a man possesses is the power of his mind. Brute force is comparatively useless; the really great achievements of modern times have been accomplished by the intellect. If the principle of consecration is true at all—if it is true that God desires, not the destruction of human powers, but the proper use of them—then surely the principle must be applied in the intellectual sphere.

The field should not be limited too narrowly; with the purely logical and acquisitive faculties of the mind should be included the imagination and the sense of beauty. In a word, we have to do with the relation between 'culture' and Christianity. For the modern Church there is no greater problem. A mighty civilization has been built up in recent years, which to a considerable extent is out of relation to the gospel. Great intellectual forces which are rampant in the world are grievously perplexing the Church. The situation calls for earnest intellectual effort on the part of Christians. Modern culture must either be refuted as evil, or else be made helpful to the gospel. So great a power cannot be safely ignored. Modern culture is a stumblingblock when it is regarded as an end in itself, but when it is used as a means to the service of God it becomes a blessing. Undoubtedly much of modern thinking is hostile to the gospel. Such hostile elements should be refuted and destroyed; the rest should be made subservient; but nothing should be neglected. Modern culture is a mighty force; it is either helpful to the gospel or else it is a deadly enemy of the gospel. For making it helpful neither wholesale denunciation nor wholesale acceptance is in place; careful discrimination is required, and such discrimination requires intellectual effort. Here lies a supreme duty of the modern Church. Patient study should not be abandoned to the men of the world; men who have really received the blessed experience of the love of God in Christ must seek to bring that experience to bear upon the culture of the modern world, in order that Christ may rule, not only in all nations, but also in every department of human life. The Church must seek to conquer not only every man, but also the whole of man. Such intellectual effort is really necessary even to the external advancement of the kingdom. Men cannot be convinced of the truth of Christianity so long as the whole of their thinking is dominated by ideas which make acceptance of the gospel logically impossible; false ideas are the greatest obstacles to the reception of the gospel. And false ideas cannot be destroyed without intellectual effort.

Such effort is indeed of itself insufficient. No man was ever argued into Christianity; the renewing of the Holy Spirit is the really decisive thing. But the Spirit works when and how he will, and he chooses to employ the intellectual activities of Christian people in order to prepare for his gracious coming.

TOPICS FOR STUDY

1. Outline some of the arguments which the apostles used in support of Christianity (a) before the Jews, (b) before Gentiles (two topics).

2. What does Luke 1.1–4 teach about the Christian use of the intellect?

3. Mention some distinctly argumentative passages in the epistles.

4. What is the special need of the Christian use of the intellect at the present day?

5. How may learning be combined with childlike faith and religious fervour? How do men come to fall into intellectual pride?

6. Why does the Church need creeds and confessions?

51: THE CHRISTIAN HOPE AND
THE PRESENT POSSESSION

Study material: Acts 1: 6–11; 2: 1–36; Rom. ch. 8; I Cor. ch. 2;
3: 16, 17; ch. 15; II Cor. chs. 3 to 5; Gal. 5: 16–26; Phil. ch. 1;
I Thess. 4: 13 to 5: 11; II Thess. ch. 2; II Peter 3: 1–13;
The Book of Revelation

A type of religious effort has become prevalent today which is directed chiefly to the present life; the improvement of worldly conditions is often regarded as the chief end of man. All such tendencies are strikingly at variance with apostolic Christianity. The apostolic Church was intensely other-worldly. The chief gift that the apostles offered was not a better and more comfortable life in this world, but an entrance into heaven.

The End of the World

Only the great outlines of the events connected with the end of the world are revealed in the New Testament. Minute details cannot be discovered except by an excessively literal method of interpretation, which is not really in accord with the meaning of the apostolic writers. Some have supposed, for example, that there are to be two resurrections, first a resurrection of the Christian dead and long afterwards a resurrection of other men; expectation of a thousand-year reign of Christ upon earth has been widely prevalent. Such beliefs are not to be lightly rejected, since they are based upon an interpretation of certain New Testament passages which is not altogether devoid of plausibility; but on the whole they are at least doubtful in view of other passages, and especially in view of the true nature of prophecy. God has revealed, not details to satisfy our curiosity, but certain basic facts which should determine our lives.

Those basic facts, connected with the end of the world, are a second coming of Christ, a resurrection of the dead, a final judgment, an eternity of punishment for the wicked and of blessing for those who have trusted in Christ. It is not maintained that these facts stand absolutely alone; certainly they are fully explained, at least in their spiritual significance; but the devout

Bible-reader should be cautious about his interpretation of details.

The Second Coming of Christ

While the apostles were looking sadly into heaven at the hour of the ascension, 'two men stood by them in white apparel; who also said, Ye men of Galilee, why stand ye looking into heaven? this Jesus, who was received up from you into heaven, shall so come in like manner as ye beheld him going into heaven'. Acts 1.10, 11. The Christian hope was thus implanted in the Church at the very beginning; Jesus would come again!

This hope runs all through the history of the apostolic age; Jesus was taken away only for a time; the present age is to be succeeded by a glorious time when God's people shall enter into their final inheritance. The conversion of the Thessalonian Christians is described by Paul as a turning 'unto God from idols, to serve a living and true God, and to wait for his Son from heaven, whom he raised from the dead, even Jesus, who delivereth us from the wrath to come'. I Thess. 1.9, 10. In this passage the expectation of Christ's return is placed beside the belief in the one true God and in the resurrection, as a cardinal element in the Christian faith.

The times and the seasons—I Thess. 5.1; compare Acts 1.7— indeed, were in God's hands; it was not known when Christ would come. But this uncertainty merely added to the intensity of the hope. Many of the early Christians seem to have thought that they themselves would live until the coming of Christ; the Thessalonian Christians were distressed because some of their number had died without witnessing the end. To overcome such discouragements Paul has to explain that it makes little difference whether a man be alive or dead at Christ's appearing; the dead shall rise from their tombs, and all together shall be caught up to meet the Lord, I Thess. 4.13–18.

The Resurrection of the Body

The consummation of the Christian hope involves far more than the immortality of the soul; the apostles clearly taught that there would be a resurrection of the body. In I Cor. ch. 15, Paul defends the doctrine of the resurrection at some length, apparently in opposition to the Greek doctrine of immortality. The final state of the blessed will be no mere shadowy existence of disembodied spirits; the soul will be clothed with a true body, II Cor. 5.1–10.

At the resurrection, however, the body will be changed from its earthly form; 'flesh and blood cannot inherit the kingdom of God', I Cor. 15.50; we shall all be changed, v. 51. This mention of a transformation is one thing that saves the apostolic teaching about the future age from any of those materialistic notions that worked harm in the later history of the Church. The future life, as Jesus himself had taught, Matt. 22.30, will be quite different from the life on earth. Earthly passions and appetites will be no more. The body of our humiliation will be fashioned anew that it may be conformed to the body of Christ's glory, Phil. 3.21. The chief element in the Christian life, transforming and ennobling every description of heavenly bliss, is the expectation of final holiness. There is nothing sordid or selfish about the apostolic description of heaven; the Christian hope is intensely moral; the Christian looks for something more than his own enjoyment; man's chief end is to glorify God as well as to enjoy him for ever.

The Judgment

The joy which the apostolic Church had in the Christian hope can be appreciated only when that hope is viewed against the dark background of fear. To the early Christians the thought of Christ's appearing was full of terror as well as full of joy; it is because we have lost the terror that we no longer appreciate the joy. The apostles, in accordance with the teaching of Jesus, were convinced that the end of the world is to be a time of judgment. 'We must all be made manifest before the judgment-seat of Christ; that each one may receive the things done in the body, according to what he hath done, whether it be good or bad.' II Cor. 5.10. Such an expectation, to an awakened conscience, is terrible. Every man without exception has sinned; every man is subject to the wrath of God. Wrath is now concealed by forbearance, but at the last day there will be no concealment and no excuse. Human righteousness will be tried and found wanting, an eternal destruction will be in store. Let us not deceive ourselves. The world's standards will seem sadly antiquated on the Judgment Day. There will be hope only in the grace of God, and in the Saviour whom he has given. But that hope, thank God, is sure!

The Intermediate State

One question of detail cannot altogether be ignored. What did the apostles teach about the condition of the believer between death and the final resurrection? Upon this subject, the New Testament says very little, but it becomes clear at least that the believer, even when absent from the body, is to be present with the Lord, II Cor. 5.8, and that to die is to be with Christ, Phil. 1.23. On the whole, no better statement of the apostolic teaching about the 'intermediate state' can be formulated than that which is contained in the Westminster Shorter Catechism, Q. 37: 'The souls of believers are at their death made perfect in holiness, and do immediately pass into glory; and their bodies, being still united to Christ, do rest in their graves, till the resurrection.' The hope of an immediate entrance into bliss at the time of death should not be allowed, however, to obscure the importance of the resurrection. The resurrection of the body will be necessary to 'the full enjoying of God to all eternity'. (Q. 38.)

Hope and Possession

The life of hope, which is now being led by the Church, is sharply contrasted by the apostles with the life of sight which is to follow, II Cor. 5.7; Rom. 8.24, 25; now we love Christ without having seen him, I Peter 1.8, but we shall one day see him as he is, I John 3.2. At first sight, therefore, it might seem as though the attitude of the early Christians were the same as that of the Jews, who thought of the world as groaning under the forces of evil, and relief as lying altogether in the future. Nothing could be farther from the fact; the Church from the very beginning was animated by an exuberant and triumphant joy.

The chief explanation is that the salvation of the Christians in one sense has already been achieved. The present world, it is true, is evil, but Christians are no longer citizens of the present evil world, Gal. 1.4. Christ has already delivered them out of the power of darkness, Col. 1.13; their citizenship already is in heaven, Phil. 3.20. They have already been pronounced righteous by the heavenly Judge; the sentence of acquittal has already gone forth; there can be no more condemnation; the issue of the final judgment for the true believer is sure. The Christian salvation, in other words, is not only an inspiring hope; it is also a present possession.

Two strains, therefore, run through apostolic Christianity, and the union of the two is one of the profoundest characteristics of the primitive Church. In the first place, there was a wonderful intensity of hope. It was as though the disciples could scarcely bear to wait for the appearing of their Lord. The whole creation, to the mind of Paul, was groaning and travailing in pain, until it should be delivered from the bondage of corruption into the liberty of the glory of the children of God, Rom. 8.21, 22. The present time was a time of suffering and of earnest expectation, vs. 18, 19. Yet, on the other hand, the apostolic Church was full of present joy; blessings which at one time are represented as already possessed. At one time, the Christians are declared to be waiting for their adoption, Rom. 8.23; at another time, with equal clearness, adoption is represented as already past, Gal. 4.1–7. At one time, the Christians are exhorted to put on Christ, as though that act were something still to be achieved, Rom. 13.14; at another time everyone who was baptized is declared to have put on Christ already, Gal. 3.27. These are only examples; they will suffice to show that the Christian salvation was represented by the apostles as both present and future.

The Holy Spirit

The contradiction is only apparent. It is explained especially by the presence of the Spirit of God. According to apostolic teaching, the Christians are still battling against suffering and against sin, but the battle has been transformed from defeat into victory. Jesus was taken away from his disciples on the day of the ascension, and the time of his promised return was not revealed. But another promise was more immediate in its fulfilment. 'Ye shall be baptized in the Holy Spirit,' said Jesus before his ascension, 'not many days hence. . . . Ye shall receive power, when the Holy Spirit is come upon you.' Acts 1.5, 8. A Church that has the Holy Spirit is not a Church that is merely awaiting salvation; it is a Church that has already been saved. The Spirit is the creator of that very faith by which a man turns to Christ, and that first gift leads inevitably to all the rest. The relation between the Christians' hope and his present possession is explained in one word in Eph. 1.14, where the Holy Spirit, as he is now manifested, is spoken of as 'an earnest of our inheritance', a first instalment of the final blessing. Much still remains to be hoped for, the present world is sunk in wickedness, evil lurks even in the Christian himself, it is a long way to the final glory. But though the final blessedness has not been given, we are not left to grope in the dark in order to discover what it is; a sample of it has already been granted. In the mysterious, loving power of God's Spirit, transforming us we scarcely know how, giving us an ever-increasing victory over sin, we are delivered from all fear;

God has begun a good work in us, and he will also perfect it until the day of Jesus Christ.

TOPICS FOR STUDY

1. Collect some passages where the apostles mention the final punishment of the unrepentant. Are these passages any more terrifying than the teaching of Jesus on the same subject?

2. Outline the teaching of the apostles about the second coming of Christ and the final state of those who are saved.

3. Collect passages to show how the thought of the second coming of Christ was made effective in the apostolic age for holy living.

4. What does the New Testament teach about the condition of believers between their death and the resurrection?

5. What does the New Testament teach about (a) the divinity and (b) the separate personality of the Holy Spirit?

6. Outline the New Testament teaching about (a) regeneration and (b) sanctification (two topics).

52: RETROSPECT: THE FIRST CHRISTIAN CENTURY

Throughout this book the wonderful richness of apostolic Christianity has been revealed. A similar richness should characterize our own service. Attention to the apostolic example will remove all one-sidedness from the life of the Church.

The Church and Her Message

The apostolic Church was clearly separated from the surrounding world. Her separateness was particularly palpable in the corrupt Gentile cities, but even in Jewish circles it was plain; the exclusive lordship of Christ made of the early Christians a peculiar people (chapter 40). Yet this peculiar people had a gift for the world. That gift was a piece of information, centring in the cross and resurrection of Jesus Christ. The cross brought forgiveness of sins; the resurrection made men sharers in a new life; acceptance of the message meant vital communion with the living God (chapter 41).

The Means of Grace

That communion was maintained by certain simple means. The reading of the Bible and the hearing of the apostles' teaching revealed the nature of God and the character of the salvation which he had provided. The sacraments taught by symbols what the Bible taught in words, and placed the seal upon the benefits of the gospel (chapter 42). Prayer, with its opportunity of personal communion with God, was a never-failing source of strength (chapter 43), and congregational meetings gave expression to the brotherhood of believers (chapter 44).

Service

The temporal needs of the brethren were not neglected; love found expression in the relief of physical distress as well as in spiritual service (chapter 45). Service of all kinds, as well as the life of the Church in general, was furthered by a simple organization under 'elders' (chapter 46). Under the special leadership of the apostles, and the immediate guidance of the Holy Spirit, the gospel soon spread far and wide in the Gentile world (chapter 47).

Life in the Spirit

Inward progress kept pace with outward conquests; the power of the Spirit brought victory over sinful desires (chapter 48), and transfigured human relationships (chapter 49); consecration of intellectual powers furthered the development and defence of a Christian theology (chapter 50). Much, indeed, was reserved for the final consummation in heaven, when Christ should once more be apprehended by sight as well as by faith, but the Holy Spirit was a present pledge of full salvation (chapter 51).

The Lesson of History

Such, in briefest outline, were some of the outstanding features of the apostolic Church. That Church is still alive; an unbroken spiritual descent connects us with those whom Jesus commissioned. Times have changed in many respects, new problems must be faced and new difficulties overcome, but the same message must still be proclaimed to a lost world. Today we have need of all our faith; unbelief and error have perplexed us sore; strife and hatred have set the world aflame. There is only one hope, but that hope is sure. God has never deserted his Church; his promise never fails.

SOME OTHER BANNER OF TRUTH TRUST TITLES

THE FOUR GOSPELS, David Brown

A COMMENTARY ON THE NEW TESTAMENT, Matthew Poole

New Testament Commentary by William Hendriksen

MATTHEW

MARK

LUKE

JOHN

ROMANS   Volume I

GALATIANS

EPHESIANS

PHILIPPIANS/COLOSSIANS & PHILEMON

I & 2 THESSALONIANS

I & 2 TIMOTHY & TITUS

Romans by Dr. D. M. Lloyd-Jones

ATONEMENT & JUSTIFICATION

ASSURANCE

THE NEW MAN

THE LAW

THE SONS OF GOD

THE FINAL PERSEVERANCE OF THE SAINTS